Beyond Greek

Beyond Greek

THE BEGINNINGS
of LATIN LITERATURE

Denis Feeney

Harvard University Press

CAMBRIDGE, MASSACHUSETTS
LONDON, ENGLAND

Harvard University Press paperback edition, 2019
First printing

Library of Congress Cataloging-in-Publication Data

Feeney, D. C., author.
Beyond Greek : the beginnings of Latin Literature /
Denis Feeney.
pages cm
Includes bibliographical references and indexes.
ISBN 978-0-674-05523-0 (cloth : alk. paper)
ISBN 978-0-674-98658-9 (pbk.)
1. Latin literature—Greek influences.   2. Greek
language—Influence on Latin.   3. Comparative
literature—Greek and Latin.   4. Comparative
literature—Latin and Greek.   I. Title.
PA3010.F55 2016
870.9'001—dc23
2015005784

For the team—Clare, Michael, Susan,
James, Margaret, and Peter

Contents

Preface

I have been interested for many years in the problems involved in this book, and I could not have written it without the generous help of many people, especially those who have answered my questions on topics beyond my competence. I have found it illuminating for myself to try to take account of comparative evidence, particularly from the ancient Near East, in order to put the Roman case in perspective, and I have made this comparative material part of the argument in the hope that others will also find it illuminating. Yet I am very much aware that I am technically incompetent in this comparative zone. The only script I command is the alphabet, and the only languages I know are ones that are encoded in that script. I am, then, especially grateful to the great generosity of a number of scholars who have responded with kind patience to my ignorant enquiries: Stephanie Dalley, John Dillery, Andrew George, Tom Hare, Simon Hornblower, Marwan Kilani, Barry Powell, Josephine Crawley Quinn, Tessa Rajak, Christopher Tuplin, and Michael Wachtel. I thank Stephanie Dalley in particular for inviting me to her stimulating Workshop on Translation and Bilingualism in Ancient Near Eastern Texts (Wolfson College, Oxford, March, 14–15, 2013); it was a privilege to try to learn from her and her colleagues.

I have tried to be scrupulous in acknowledging my debts, yet I am aware that I may have lost track of the origin of certain points. I was startled to go back to my copy of Toynbee's *Hannibal's Legacy* and discover that his brilliant chapter on "The creation of a literature in Latin on the pattern of the literature in Greek" had copious marginal annotations in my handwriting from when I first bought it as a graduate student; in the interim before I came back to these problems I had completely forgotten this important piece of writing and had internalized many of Toynbee's arguments. I hope that this is a unique case, but I fear it may not be.

I have given talks on various of the topics covered here at a number of venues: Auckland University, Baylor University, Boston College, Cambridge University, Columbia University, Fordham University, Institute for Classical Studies (London), Oxford University, Rutgers University, Stanford University, Swarthmore College, University College London, University of Geneva, and the University of Texas–Austin. I must in particular acknowledge Hermione Lee's invitation to deliver the Syme Lecture at Wolfson College, Oxford, in November 2011. I have learned a great deal from the responses of the people who heard these talks, and I have been rescued from many errors and misconceptions by their feedback; no doubt many errors and misconceptions remain, for which I alone am responsible. For these responses, and for other help, I am grateful in particular to Emma Dench, Renaud Gagné, Peter Garnsey, Sander Goldberg, Leon Grek, John Henderson, Lucy Jackson, Bob Kaster, Barbara Kowalzig, David Langslow, Dawn Lavalle, Brigitte Le Guen, Fiachra Mac Góráin, Gesine Manuwald, Terry McKiernan, Jonathan Prag, Nicholas Purcell, Peter Rhodes, John Scheid, Ronnie Shi, Christopher Smith, Vance Smith, Nic Terrenato, Tim Whitmarsh, Peter Wilson and his Sydney colleagues, Peter Wiseman, Greg Woolf, and the students in my Fall 2010 graduate seminar on "The beginnings of Latin literature." Wiebke Denecke, John Dillery, and Johanna Hanink, with great kindness and generosity, made it possible for me to read the final versions of their important books before they were published, while Sandy Hardie, Josephine Crawley Quinn, and Greg Woolf also shared portions of work in progress to my great benefit. The Press readers read the draft with remarkable care and insight, and gave me invaluable comments, to which I have tried to do justice; Sharmila Sen, my editor, has helped and encouraged me from the start, and has made a real difference to how I think of the issues. Finally, I owe particular debts to Barry Powell, from whom I learned that script is not language, and who read drafts of the chapters on translation; to David Bellos, a great translator in his own right, who also read those chapters and whose inspirational scholarship and leadership of Princeton's Program in Translation and Intercultural Communication have made such a difference to his friends, colleagues and students at Princeton; to Harriet Flower, who read Chapters 4 and 5 with an acute eye and made it possible for me to test drive those chapters at Princeton with her Spring 2014 seminar on the middle Republic; Joshua Katz, who read a penultimate draft and not only gave me very valuable comments but rescued me from a number of errors; Stephen Hinds, who has once again shouldered the burden of reading complete drafts, who gave me my main title (one of the Press readers suggested the subtitle), and whose insight and support have, as always, made such a difference at every stage; and to Marco Fantuzzi, who likewise read the whole draft, and helped me in innumerable ways.

I began systematic work on the book in Lent Term 2010 when I was on sabbatical leave as a Visiting Fellow Commoner at Trinity College, Cambridge, and I finished it in Hilary Term 2014 when I was on sabbatical leave as a Visiting Fellow at Corpus Christi College, Oxford; I owe thanks to the Guggenheim Foundation and the American Council of Learned Societies for the support which made the first leave possible, to Princeton University for their support for both leaves, and to Trinity and Corpus Christi Colleges for their kind hospitality, which helped make both visits so memorable. As I wrote up the last chapters, the holdings of the Corpus Christi College library proved a life-saver, and I am grateful to the College and the library staff for this resource. The classicists at Corpus kept up the dialogue throughout the year; they also heard a paper on bilingual education and gave me a great deal to think about in their responses. In particular, I thank Tim Whitmarsh for allowing me to share his teaching set during 2013–14, and for sharing his books and his ideas too. Finally, thanks to Joseph Solodow for his list of corrections for the paperback edition.

Citations of works and collections follow the system of *The Oxford Classical Dictionary,* 3rd ed., with the new collection of the fragments of the Roman historians (Cornell (2013)) cited as *FRHist;* fragments of the tragic authors are cited with the numbering of Ribbeck (1897), apart from Ennius, who is cited from Jocelyn (1969); fragments of nondramatic and non-Ennian early Latin poetry are cited from Blänsdorf (2011), or else (as indicated) from Courtney (1993); Ennius' *Annales* are cited from Skutsch (1985). Inevitably, important work was appearing even as I finalized the MS for the Press. I have not been able to consult, for example, E. Csapo et al., *Greek Theatre in the Fourth Century* BC (Berlin: De Gruyter, 2014), or J. Fisher, *The* Annals *of Quintus Ennius and the Italic Tradition* (Baltimore: Johns Hopkins, 2014).

All translations are mine unless stated otherwise, and all dates are BCE unless stated otherwise.

Beyond Greek

Introduction

S OME TIME probably between the years 20 and 15, the poet Ovid, then still in his twenties, published the following poem to crown his first book, a slim volume of fifteen elegiac love poems:[1]

Why, gnawing Envy, impute an idler's existence to me?
    Why dismiss your poet as a drone?
What's your complaint? That I've failed (though young and healthy) to follow
    Tradition, or chase the dusty rewards
Of a soldier's career? That I haven't mugged up dull lawsuits,   5
    Or sold my eloquence like a whore
In the courts and Forum? Such labours are soon forgotten.
    What *I* seek is perennial fame,
Undying world-wide remembrance. While Ida and Tenedos
    Still stand, while Simois still runs swift to the sea,   10
Old Homer will live. While clustering grapes still ripen
    And wheat still falls to the scythe
Hesiod's works will be studied. The verse of Callimachus—
    Weak in imagination, strong on technique—
Has a worldwide readership. Sophoclean tragedy   15
    Is safe from Time's ravages. While sun and moon

Survive, so will Aratus. While the world holds one devious servant,
    Stern father, blandishing whore, or ponce on the make
Menander's immortal. Rough Ennius, spirited Accius
    Have names time will never destroy. What age   20
Will not cherish great Varro's epic of Argo's voyage,
    Jason's quest for the Golden Fleece?
The work of sublime Lucretius will prove immortal
    While the world itself endures;
And so long as Rome's empire holds sway over the nations,   25
    Virgil's country poems, his *Aeneid,* will be read.
While Cupid's armoury still consists of bow and arrows
    Tibullus' elegant verse
Will always be quoted. From lands of sunset to sunrise, Gallus,
    Gallus and his Lycoris, will be renowned.   30
Though Time, in time, can consume the enduring ploughshare,
    Though flint itself will perish, poetry lives—
Deathless, unfading, triumphant over kings and their triumphs,
    Richer than Spanish river-gold. Let the crowd
Gape after baubles. To me may golden Apollo proffer   35
    A cup, brimming over, from the Castalian spring
And a wreath of sun-loving myrtle. May my audience always
    Consist of star-crossed lovers. Never forget
It's the living that Envy feeds on. After death the pressure
    Is taken off. All men get their due in the end.   40
So when the final flames have devoured my body, I shall
    Survive, and my better part live on.

The poet begins by defending his career choice, bragging that he will achieve far more fame as a poet than he could have achieved through more conventional career paths. He proves his point by listing great poets of the past whose fame will live on, starting—audaciously—with the first and greatest Greek poet, Homer, at the top (9–10). Next come Hesiod and Callimachus, Sophocles and Aratus, and Menander. At this point a new list begins, of poets writing in Latin. As the Greek list had begun with the primal epic poet Homer, so the Latin list begins with Ennius (19), the first Roman poet to write epic in the hexameter of Homer, born in 239, some 220 years before Ovid is writing. After him comes the tragedian Accius, born around 170, followed by the epic poet Varro of Atax (born in 82), the philosopher-poet Lucretius (born around 95), Virgil (born in 70), the master of three genres (bucolic, didactic, epic), and then two predecessors in love elegy, Tibullus and Gallus, who had both died while Ovid was a young man.[2] Like all of them, the argument runs, Ovid too will live through his poetry. And so it has proved to be.

Modern readers are so used to Romans writing in this way that it requires a conscious effort to apprehend what an extraordinary phenomenon is actually at issue here. According to Ovid's presentation, Roman literary tradition is a continuation of Greek literary tradition, and a development of it too, with new genres such as the love elegy of Gallus, Tibullus, and Ovid himself coming into being in Latin. We need to take stock of the fact that no one other than a Latin-speaker could have made such a statement in the year 15. Ovid's bold assertion of a kind of continuity between a body of literature in Greek and a body of literature in Latin had in fact already been explicitly made just over a hundred years earlier, around 130 or so, and it had been made by one of the Latin authors named by Ovid (line 19), the tragedian Accius. This man not only composed dramas for performance, but also wrote a kind of literary history, a work called *Didascalica* which was able to represent Roman literature as a continuation of Greek literature, part of the same phenomenon—a claim that could not possibly have been made by any other contemporary culture.[3] When Lamberton, then, says that "our concept of a corpus of European literature with its origins in archaic Greece is a modern construct," one could substitute "Roman" as the penultimate word.[4]

If we go back just over a hundred years before Accius wrote his *Didascalica,* to around 240 or so, there are no texts whatsoever to put in the Latin list as a counterpart for anything in the Greek one. In fact, apart from the Greeks themselves, no other culture known to the Romans in Ovid's time had a canonically organized and widely disseminated body of generically diverse literary texts of the kind that Ovid is pointing to in his elegy, and no other people apart from the Romans could conceivably lay out a historical account according to which they were adopting Greek literary forms *en masse* and taking them over into their own vernacular. Ovid himself is not thinking of the issues in these terms, of course: for him, the fact that there is a literature in the Latin language on Greek models is part of the way the world is, and he is not positioning these traditions within a framework of comparison with other cultures. But if we look at Ovid's poem from this comparative perspective, then we can recover a sense of astonishment at the fact that there *is* a Roman literature—a Grecizing literature in the Latin language—in the first place: his poem can startle us into being reminded of just how extraordinary it was that the Romans should equip themselves with a literature in Latin based on the literature of the Greeks.[5]

How did this happen? How did Ovid come to be able to write his poem? This book is about the process that made it possible for Ovid to produce what we call "*Amores* 1. 15." It is about the fact that there is a literature in Latin when there should really not have been one.

The Contingency of Latin Literature

The entire process was contingent and unpredictable to the highest degree. The creation of a Roman literature on Greek models was not just a matter of time, something that was bound to happen sooner or later, but instead one of the strangest and most unlikely events in Mediterranean history. Scholars regularly wonder why a literature in the Latin language did not emerge sooner: "Roman literature begins some five centuries later than Greek. The fact is more surprising than one might think. . . . Why a Roman literature did *not* develop before the third century B.C. is a real puzzle."[6] Yet it should probably not have developed at all, and there are other societies, ones which did not develop a Hellenizing vernacular literature, where one might have more easily imagined such a development taking place.[7] We have no evidence that anyone else did what the Romans did, taking over systematically the Greek forms of tragedy, comedy, epic, or historiography into their own vernacular languages. In fact, as we shall see in Chapter 8, depending on how one defines "literature"—and that large question is one of the main issues to be addressed in this book—we have no evidence that any other culture known to the Romans in the middle of the third century had an equivalent to the institution of literature that we recognize in the Hellenistic world. It looks as if we should be more startled by the existence of a literature in *Greek:* "We take the Greeks as our model, forgetting that the Greeks did everything differently from everybody else."[8]

How did it happen that the Romans, without any predecessors or templates for the project, set about the task of equipping themselves with a vernacular literature on Greek models?—and not only a body of texts with claims to literary status, but an array of accompanying phenomena that define and convey those texts, so that one eventually sees in Rome a heavily Greek-style education and apparatus of literary scholarship, together with a developed historiographical tradition about their past and a mythological network that connected them to the inheritance of the Greeks. None of these projects was predictable, and none had any clear parallel. Looking at the Mediterranean world in 250, no observer would conclude that an empire needed to have a widely disseminated vernacular literature, or that a state of non-Greeks should have intimate reciprocal links with Greece through a systematically interconnected historiography and mythology, or that another linguistic group should commission literary works to be translated from Greek into their own vernacular. It had never happened before or anywhere else in the Mediterranean that one culture should set out to take over the prototypical literary forms of Hellas in order to create its vernacular equivalent, and for a parallel of any substance we have to wait until the Late Middle Ages, when the Latin forms became in their turn one of the new interactive catalysts for the emerging European vernacular literatures. We are used to thinking of Greek and Latin as the "classical" literatures, with later traditions as the "vernacular" literatures, but from the standpoint of the Western tradition, at least, Latin is the first "vernacular" literature.

As we shall see throughout, the process of working with Greek culture had always been part of Roman life, starting hundreds of years before the first Latin poet on Ovid's list, Ennius, put pen to paper, and this remained the case for as long as a Roman culture existed. But a crucial century can be picked out as distinctively transformative for the categories of literature, historiography, and mythology. The conventional starting date for this process is the reform in the year 240 of the great annual festival of the Roman state, the *Ludi Romani,* to allow for the staging of a Latin play translated from a Greek original.[9] We shall be considering at various junctures what is at stake in focusing on this as a "beginning moment," but if Latin literature did not begin within four days of the Ides of September 240, then the Latin translation project did—and as we shall see, what we call "Latin literature" is inconceivable without the translation project. Between 240 and 140 the Roman engagement with Greek culture underwent a series of fundamental redefinitions, even if these were in many ways continuous with earlier developments, and it underwent these redefinitions as part of a larger process involving many different cultures, in Italy and beyond.

This century is a crucial segment of a longer process of unprecedented expansion and change. In 320 the Romans were a powerful city-state with control over a substantial swath of territory in the western flank of central Italy. Fifty years later, by 270, the Romans had completed their conquest of the peninsula of Italy up to the Apennines. One hundred years later still the Romans had become the unquestionably dominant power in the Mediterranean, with their armies having broken ancient empires and monarchies from Africa to Greece and Asia. Within this explosion of activity, the century that is the main focus of this book takes us from the *Ludi Romani* of 240, the victory games over Carthage, celebrating their final victory in Sicily the year before, after twenty-three years of war, down to a period about a century later when the Romans had the only "other" vernacular literature in the Mediterranean.

Everything about this project is problematic, starting with the definition of all the terms I have been using so far, "literature" and "translation," "historiography" and "mythology." Justifying the use of a term

such as "literature" in an ancient context is a notoriously unstraightforward thing to do.[10] These terms are still occasionally treated as self-
evident categories, reified concepts that apply across time and space,
but they are not givens in nature; instead, in the Roman middle Republic
all of them are interactive frames in which Romans, Greeks of different
heritages, and many other peoples, encountered and reshaped each other
in unprecedented ways. The sheer scale of the transformation in Roman
life in these years is so great that we can tend to take for granted the fact
that the Romans would take the paths that they did, yet their cultural
strategies were unpredictable, and in a number of aspects they are hard
to parallel.

The object of the exercise is not to congratulate the Romans upon their
exceptionalism for having undertaken this strange experiment. There
are ways in which their experience was, I think, genuinely unusual, and
there are ways in which it tracked or overlapped with other currents in the
ancient Mediterranean: it goes without saying that it is meaningless
to describe any of these options as inherently either praiseworthy or
blameworthy, superior or inferior. I shall be trying to be as precise as
possible about the differences and the similarities between what the
Romans did and what their contemporaries did, but I intend no value
judgments, although I shall identify their value judgments when I think
it is possible. I am not trying to mark Rome up and other societies down
because the Romans set out on their peculiar path. For certain purposes
and in certain contexts we may well want to describe particular cultural
practices in early Rome, or in Etruria or Samnium, as "literature," and
I am certainly not claiming that interesting and important results could
not be gained from investigating those other cultural practices through
such a lens. In constructing an argument that the Latin translation
project led to an institution of Hellenizing literature unlike anything we
appear to be able to reconstruct from other contemporary societies, I am
not saying that the cultural practices of those other societies fail to
make some imaginary grade. We shall study such comparison cases
in Chapter 8, and there I shall be suggesting that it is not patronizing or
Hellenocentric to conclude that it is unlikely that these other societies

had literary practices that tracked those of the Greeks; in fact, it would be patronizing and Hellenocentric to assume that a developed society in the ancient world had to possess such a supposedly superior institution. The Greek model appears to be the default mode when scholars attempt to reconstruct what must have once filled the gaps in our current evidence about the cultural life of ancient societies known to the Greeks and Romans, with the assumption that if only something had survived it would have looked not very different from what does survive from Rome. I shall be arguing that we should be very cautious about assuming any such thing.

I am not, finally, interested in the issues of this book as a question of value or status within any of our own contemporary frames of reference. I am very happy to have the *Aeneid* and *Metamorphoses* to read, and on those banal terms I may be a partisan of the movement I am charting. But I am perfectly happy to imagine a counterfactual world in which the *Aeneid* and the *Metamorphoses* never got written, a more likely world, in fact, a world in which Rome still rose to be a major power without their élite having access to a vernacular literature—as was the case with the Achaemenid Persians and the Parthians, for example, or the Carthaginians, so far as we know.[11] My objective is to defamiliarize the terms of comparison and of reference we use in describing the Roman experiment so as to bring the strange developments of the period into perspective.

Engaging with "Hellenization"

I have been stressing that the Roman project of equipping themselves with a vernacular literature was a process profoundly implicated in dialogue with Greek culture; it is important to bring to the fore a number of problems of terminology and approach that face anyone exploring this process.

First, it is not at all the case that the Romans were suddenly introduced to the Greek world when they began their literature project—even if the later Romans themselves could talk like this at times for their own reasons, romanticizing some notional prior uncontaminated moment.[12] The idea that the Romans only met Greek culture when they began their literary project is actually a straw man in modern debates: it is very remote from the pioneering studies of Leo (1895/1912) and (1913) or Fraenkel (1922/2007). Interaction with Greek culture was, from the start, a distinctive feature of the Romans' relentlessly energetic modernism, marking them out from their peers as early as the seventh century, when "Rome, perhaps alone among the native communities of central Italy, began to take on some of the features of the Greek *polis*."[13] We shall investigate the nature of these interactions repeatedly throughout this book, but it should be taken as read from the beginning that there was no period in Roman history when they were not interacting in one way or another with Greek culture, in art, religion, and social practice. As Wiseman memorably sums up, after itemizing a host of examples of interaction with the Greek world on the site of archaic Rome, from the altar of Hercules to the Grecizing cult of Ceres, Liber, and Libera, with their priestesses imported from the Greek cities of Velia or Naples—"All this, before Herodotus was born."[14]

Further, when we talk about "Hellenism" or "the Greeks" or "the Romans," we are of course not describing one entity, but a mobile and varying target, as we are in any discussion of any "culture": "Large-scale cultures that are named and that therefore tend to be taken for granted (for example 'Egyptian,' 'Greek,' 'Phoenician') in practice consist of many different cultural spheres that may or may not compete with one another."[15] Who "the Romans" are keeps changing from generation to generation, as they interact with or amalgamate many different groups, redefining citizenship and inter-state relations in the process.[16] In their turn, as we shall see, the "Greeks" with whom the Romans come into contact in our period represent a variety of experience and opportunity across a wide tract of space and time, as the Romans move out from their first zones of contact to take control of most of what the Greeks called the *oecumenē*, the habitable world within their ken. The "Greeks" for them also have a diachronic as well as synchronic dimension at any given moment, with different imagined or represented Greeks potentially in play in their own constructions.[17] Nor are primary speakers of Greek the only groups with whom the Romans are coming into contact, or the only groups from whom the Romans are adapting and appropriating: in fact, as we shall see, particularly in Chapter 4, "Hellenism" itself is often being mediated to the Romans through non-Greeks, participants in the interactive zones of contact that characterized Italy from the archaic to the middle Republican periods. The processes I shall be tracing in this book are part of a complex series of exchanges and confrontations involving many different cultures in addition to the Greeks, for Rome was involved in interactive competition and exchange with a wide range of societies.

From the first remains of Roman life that we can trace, the culture of the people we call the Romans is continually being reinvented and redescribed, in a process of ceaseless interaction with new groups with whom they are always coming into contact. This assimilative impetus is a vital part of Roman mythological sense of identity, signaled in the *asylum* set up by their first king, Romulus, as a haven for any person who wished to come to sign up to the Roman project (Liv. 1. 8. 5–6). As Dench's major study makes clear, this myth is emblematic of the Roman conception of their identity as being constantly formed and re-formed by "immigration, mobility, and cultural fusion."[18] Assimilation is constitutive of Roman identity, marked by their self-conscious advertizing of how they took over their characteristic short sword from the Spaniards (Plb. 6. 23. 6), their distinctive *toga* from the Etruscans (Liv. 1. 8. 3), and their very name as citizens, *Quirites,* from the Sabines (Liv. 1. 13. 5).[19] According to Cornell, in a—justly—commonly quoted aphorism: "an independent or autonomous Latin culture never had a chance to emerge."[20]

In fact, it is becoming more and more evident that there is no such thing as an independent or autonomous culture at any time or place.[21] As Bayart puts it in his important study, "There is no culture that is not created, and . . . this creation is usually recent. Moreover, the formation of a culture or a tradition necessarily involves dialogue, and occurs in interaction with its regional and international environment."[22] We shall see the significance of this perspective especially in Chapters 4 and 5, when we investigate the development of the Romans' primary state festival within its always changing regional and international environment, with the assimilation of Greek drama marking another distinctive moment of Roman cultural appropriation.

The Roman interaction with Greek literary culture remains a key focus throughout, for this zone was the source for the literary models of the translation project, and for the personnel as well, the bi-and tri-lingual individuals who began the process by providing the translated Latin scripts for the dramas at the Roman games.[23] The preferred umbrella term for discussing such a process has long been "Hellenization," regularly paired with "Romanization," the term used to describe the corresponding impact supposedly made on the Western Mediterranean by the Romans. These terms have for some time been under suspicion, and for good reason, since they have so regularly been used in ways that beg important questions about the nature and direction of cultural interaction, and that make historically unjustifiable assumptions about the inherent superiority of certain peoples or practices. Wallace-Hadrill well expresses what is at stake in the use of these two terms: "The vocabulary is implicated in a whole view of the place of Greek and Roman culture in the building of modern Europe, for which Greek culture is the foundation of western civilization, the transmission of this culture appears a necessary step, the value of which to the Romans must be self-evident, just as the value of Roman civilisation to the western barbarians is self-evident."[24]

The more mobile and interactive models of intercultural exchange that we discussed above have enforced a profound rethinking of the traditionally understood terminology of "Hellenization."[25] The Roman expropriation of certain aspects of Greek dramatic and literary culture is not a case study in "culture flow[ing] downhill, from high to low, to fill a vacuum, introducing culture where no culture had been."[26] We are not watching a superior Greek culture naturally rushing in to fill a void in a more "primitive" culture, nor a "primitive" culture naturally seeing its deficiencies and scurrying to remedy them. Apart from the unhistorical value-laden judgment that there just are higher and lower cultures, with the Greeks always occupying the "higher" position and with predictable results coming from their meeting with those in a "lower" position, a major difficulty with such approaches is that they tend to characterize the parties as "active" Greek agents versus "passive" native recipients.[27] It is important to restore agency to the various participants in the transformations that overtook central Italy in the period we shall be considering. The Romans, as we shall see, were actively seeking out particular features of Greek and Greek-inflected life, and they certainly did not have the deferential attitude many models assume.[28] In the middle of the third century, these self-assured and confident people were emerging from a stunning series of transformative military and political successes going back three generations, and they suffered from no kind of cultural cringe. Nor, in their turn, were the Greeks passive partners, providing a tool kit and no more; the Roman experience in Sicily, in particular, shows a genuine dialogue taking place, as long-standing power relationships within the island are radically reconfigured.[29] The nuanced and always mobile relationship between "Romans" and "Greeks" will be a major focus throughout our investigation, especially in Chapters 4 and 5, and we shall see in Chapter 3 that the act of translation exposes a range of complex bi-directional asymmetries between Latin and Greek, Romans and Greeks.[30]

Such reconsiderations of models of cultural interaction have had a wide and salutary impact.[31] Students of the ancient world are now wary of the term "Hellenization," on the grounds that, as Keay says, it "is an asymmetrical term that privileges the Greek over other traditions, such as Carthaginian and Iberian, in the history of the Mediterranean, on the implicit basis that Greek cultural traditions were somehow superior and, as a consequence, the cultural standard to which peoples around the Mediterranean aspired."[32] The case study in this book presents a particular challenge, however, because we are dealing with a period in which some Greek cultural traditions certainly did become the cultural standard to which some peoples aspired. If we must avoid the chauvinism of assuming that Greek culture just was what people were naturally and helplessly drawn to because of its self-evident superiority, we must likewise avoid the lack of historical perspective that would blind us to what is at stake when certain Greek cultural products became salient objects of appropriation.[33] In the evolving *koinē* of fourth-century central and southern Italy, Hellenism was the major shared term, "*the* cultural language,"[34] and some aspects of Greek culture, especially the glamorous stage shows that were so popular throughout much of the Mediterranean, were indisputably high-status and high-prestige items in Italy in our period. They were the object not just of desire but of mimetic desire—to adopt the language of René Girard, according to whom we desire things not so much on their or our own account, but because someone else desires them.[35] For the Romans, the "someone else" in this case will be the Etruscans, the other Latins, and the Italic peoples in a widening circle. In Chapter 4 in particular we shall be tracing the competition over access to this high-status item, one dimension of a general competition among the Italian peoples that was in part channeled through the appropriation of Greek culture for reasons of prestige and differentiation.[36]

Modern observers, then, must always be careful not to impose hierarchies of cultural value on the ancient actors; at the same time, we must recognize that they themselves are regularly dealing with hierarchies of cultural value in their own terms, privileging some cultures and cultural features and downgrading others. We should not subscribe to and reproduce their priorities and hierarchies, but we need to recognize them when they exist and to take stock of their effects.

Before and After 240

A counterfactual world without a literature in the Latin language is actually—if it is allowable to say—what really should have happened, for the Romans had built an extensive empire, together with a developed panoply of cultural resources, before they turned to the expropriation of certain marked features of Greek dramatic culture in their *Ludi Romani*. It is absolutely not the case that Rome before 240 was a "cultural wasteland."[37] They had, for a start, been literate for centuries, and the first surviving Latin inscriptions go back to the seventh century.[38] Quite what kind of culture of song, poetry, drama, and speech the Romans had at any period before 240 is a keenly debated topic, to which we return especially in Chapter 8, yet there is no controversy whatever about certain fundamental points. The Romans, for a start, had *ludi scaenici,* "stage games," before 240, scenic displays as part of their pre-eminent public festival, the *Ludi Romani.* We return in Chapter 4 to address the vexed question of what the Romans might have been watching at those "stage games," but the *ludi scaenici* were part of a major reform of the *Ludi Romani* in 364, and they involved elements from Etruscan and Campanian practice as well as Greek. Colleges of Roman priests were singing hymns to their gods for centuries before 240, and they continued to do so for centuries afterward. And whatever other kinds of crafted verbal displays Romans were producing in the years before 240, the members of their élite were certainly making speeches, to the Roman people and to the Senate, to law courts, to their troops, and to representatives of other states.[39]

Before 240, then, the Romans were not strangers to other cultures, including Greek; nor were they strangers to a range of highly developed and socially important forms of verbal craft. But I agree with those scholars who nonetheless see a decisive shift in the years immediately after the first war against Carthage (264–241), as the Romans began the process of establishing a literature and a literary tradition in their own language on Greek models. In investigating this phase, we have to start with the problem of translation, since the process that led directly to the institution we now label "Roman literature" is generally thought to have begun with translations into Latin of scripts of Attic drama and of Homer's *Odyssey* in the 230s. Translation is a phenomenon it is easy to take for granted, and in Chapters 1–3 we shall attempt to recover what a peculiar thing translation is and how rare certain kinds of translation were in the ancient world, so as to restore a sense of what a strange operation it was that the Romans embarked upon in the systematic translation of the scripts of Attic drama. It was Friedrich Leo, a hundred years ago, who stressed the importance of translation for understanding the Roman enterprise, and my continuation of his initiative will no doubt appear reactionary to some. Certainly, there are long-standing institutional reasons one could point to for Latinists' "focusing on translation and transference, not on appropriation and reuse";[40] yet I hope that if we denaturalize our assumptions about translation then we shall see that Roman translation *is* "appropriation and reuse." It was certainly translation that made possible the later work of Latin literature, as we shall see in Chapter 3, through creating linguistic resources and new frames of reference, as if anticipating the role that translation was so often to have in other periods of world literature: "Periods of great productivity in literature are preceded by a generation of intensely active translators."[41]

In Chapters 4 and 5 we turn to the revolution in the *Ludi Romani* that occasioned the translation project, examining in particular the successive transformations in the international arena to which the various reforms in the *Ludi* were responding. Throughout the argument to this point, we shall to some extent be taking for granted the category of "literature." The investigation of "translation" will progressively illuminate some of the issues we need to consider in using the term "literature," and in Chapter 6 we consider what is at stake in using this term in an ancient, and specifically a Roman, context, in an attempt to isolate what ways of thinking about the category of "literature" will be most helpful for the Roman case. In Chapter 7, we then assess what the impact and reach of the new literature may have been within the expanding Roman world of the second century, as a widely diffused body of texts shook up the set of cognitive and imaginative possibilities for the growing number of people who had access to those texts in an empire with a very unusually literate élite. In Chapter 8, we shall be comparing the Roman experiment with other cases, in the ancient and the modern world, in order to try to clarify what was, and what was not, distinctive about what they ended up producing. As stressed above, the aim here is not to mark the Romans or Greeks up and anyone else down, but rather to try to be as precise as we can be about the particular circumstances that resulted from the Roman experiment. The Conclusion will assess the implications of the Roman achievement within a larger Mediterranean context, describing how they became part of the web of history, chronology, and mythology within the *oecumenē*.

None of what we are investigating in this book would have happened without the Romans commissioning translations into Latin of scripts of Attic drama for performance at the *Ludi Romani*. Let us begin, then, with translation.[42]

CHAPTER 1

Translation:
Languages, Scripts, Texts

JUST AS STUDENTS OF ROME often think that it was more or less natural and inevitable that Rome should develop a literature in the vernacular, one might assume that it was more or less natural and inevitable that Greek literary texts should one day be translated into Latin. Yet there is no evidence that the Greek texts translated by Rome's first translator-poet, Livius Andronicus—Homer and Attic drama—had ever been translated into any other language before he translated them into Latin. In fact, the Attic dramatic scripts had never even been adapted into other Greek dialects; according to Taplin, there is no evidence that any performances of originally Athenian tragedy or comedy occurred in the western Mediterranean "in any dialect other than Attic."[1] The Latin project of systematically translating literary texts is not a natural or inevitable thing to happen, and analogies for it in the ancient world turn out to be hard to find.[2]

The Strangeness of Translation

The perspective on translation assumed by most members of modern Western societies is naturally conditioned by our everyday experience of how normal translation is in the modern world. We take it for granted that we can go into any sizeable book store and buy English translations of Russian literature, or French literature, or German and Chinese and Japanese literature. This is, however, a comparatively recent state of affairs, and an exceptional one, in terms of the longer view of history. I first began properly to grasp this point when I attended the 2006 Columbia University conference on translation organized by David Damrosch and Wiebke Denecke. The number of participants was such that all speakers were held strictly to fifteen minutes each, but when Harish Trivedi (University of Delhi) rose to speak on translation in India he handled the problem of time pressure in a novel fashion. He faced the opposite dilemma of all the other speakers, so he said, since they had so much to say and had to cram it all into fifteen minutes, whereas he had only one thing to say and had to spin it out to fill his whole time. Eventually, after glancing at his watch a number of times to see how much of his fifteen minutes he had managed to use up, he had to say his one thing: "There is no translation in India."

Now, he immediately went on to gloss and qualify this remark. There have been periods of intense translating activity in India. Between the thirteenth and sixteenth centuries the literary traditions of most modern Indian languages got their initial impetus from translations of works from Sanskrit, usually the epics, *Ramayana* and *Mahabarata,* and many of the literary works of the regional languages were at that time translated into Persian or Arabic.[3] But since then translation across the boundaries of the different written literatures of India has been extremely rare: "until very recently, nothing was ever translated directly between Urdu, Hindi, Kannada, Tamil, Marathi, and so on."[4] Right up until today, most of the translation that goes on in India is into and out of English, and even the vernacular literatures are for the most part accessed by users of other languages via English translation rather than via translations into another vernacular.[5]

It may appear bizarre that in "a multilingual country with flourishing literatures in at least a dozen languages, there is singularly little translation between them."[6] There has never been such a thing as an impermeable culture, but a group is able to represent itself as being its own knowledge-world to one degree or another, and this is particularly the case with forms of textually encoded knowledge. As Jack Goody has demonstrated, literacy's codification of systems of knowledge and belief within a culture can in itself encourage the apprehension that there is a defined boundary between this knowledge system and the ones codified by other groups.[7] From this perspective, it is not, on reflection, obvious that even a bilingual group will need to set up a dialogue with outside traditions of knowledge and power by importing vernacular versions of texts that matter to those outside traditions.

The example of India shows us that the practice of translation can begin, tail off, resume: it is not a mechanism that ticks along at a steady rate once activated. The example of India also vividly brings home the point that translation does not have to happen, even in an multilingual environment with mutually interpenetrating literate societies who are each in possession of a vernacular literature.[8] The practice of translation is historically neither a necessary nor a constant feature of cultural interpenetration; translation does not automatically follow even from extensive bilingual or multilingual interaction. Instances of translation have their own distinctive rhythms and modalities, interacting variably according to differing political, social, and institutional pressures.

The Case of Ptolemaic Alexandria

A case study from the ancient world that we could put in dialogue with the Indian example is that of Alexandria under the Ptolemies (305–30). Here a Greek-speaking Macedonian monarchy presided over a very cosmopolitan society including Egyptians, Jews, and Greeks from all over the Mediterranean world, while at the same time working continuously in close collaboration with the highly literate Egyptian priestly, administrative, and scribal orders.[9] Yet in Alexandria we see these sophisticated literate cultures living in conditions of intimacy at the élite level for a long time without a systematic translation project getting under way—and even without the Greek-speaking élite developing an engagement with the languages or writings of their new subjects.

It is, of course, regularly claimed that the Ptolemies commissioned translations into Greek of all kinds of texts, eventually including even Roman texts.[10] The evidence, however, is late and misinformed, with much of it being part of a retrospective conversion of Ptolemy II Philadelphus (reigned 283–246) into a culture hero of librarianship and patronage.[11] As Most puts it, "it is only scant, unreliable, and late evidence that provides any support at all for the view . . . that the Ptolemies took care to include numerous translations from foreign works in the Library at Alexandria."[12] We shall consider shortly the apparent exception of the Septuagint, the translation into Greek of the Jews' Hebrew scriptures, together with the translation into Greek of Egyptian chronicles by the Egyptian priest Manetho; for now, overall, I concur with Rajak: "It is doubtful whether any other large-scale translation enterprises apart from the Septuagint were undertaken in Ptolemaic Alexandria."[13]

Translation into Greek of Egyptian works in Demotic does occur in Egypt as early as the second or even third century BCE;[14] but it develops real momentum quite a bit later than the period of the first Ptolemies, becoming suddenly especially important—for reasons that are hard to recover—in the second and third centuries CE.[15] These translations appear to be the work of Egyptians translating into Greek rather than of Greeks translating out of Demotic, regularly as part of an anti-Greek impetus.[16] Importantly, we do not find translation of literary texts in the other direction, from Greek into Demotic.[17] Further, it is likely that Egyptian and Near Eastern animal fables and similar elements of popular culture had already been available to Greeks earlier, under the Ptolemies, in oral as well as written form, regularly mediated by non-Greeks into Greek formats; material that is ultimately of Assyrian origin, for example, will have circulated in Aramaic, and through that medium become known to Jews in Alexandria.[18]

The Indian case alerted us to the fact that translation is not something we should just expect to happen whenever literate cultures overlap with each other, and the case of early Ptolemaic Alexandria bears this out. The Macedonian monarchs and their advisors instituted Janus-faced ideological programs carefully designed for the comprehension of their diverse subjects,[19] but the government of the kingdom depended on Egyptians learning Greek rather than vice versa. Faced with new administrative demands for the new monarchy, and with Greeks evincing "reluctance at the top for learning Egyptian," the Ptolemies tried hard and with real success to produce a new generation of trained Egyptian scribes and administrators who were bilingual and biscripted.[20] It was this specifically trained Egyptian bureaucracy who produced the bilingual and triscripted inscriptions most famously represented by the Rosetta Stone.[21] As is often noted, the first member of the Ptolemaic dynasty to be able to speak Egyptian was apparently the last member of the dynasty, Cleopatra VII (Plut. *Ant.* 27. 4–5), and it is highly unlikely that she could also read or write it;[22] before her, the Ptolemies will have addressed their troops through interpreters.[23] In the early years of the Ptolemies' reign, interaction at the top between Greeks and Egyptians appears to have been limited: there was no élite intermarriage in the first generations of the Ptolemaic kingdom, and Egyptians were at this stage still excluded from the Greek cultural institutions of the *gymnasion* and *ephebeia*.[24] This situation became much more mobile fairly quickly, as we see with the intriguing example of the Egyptians who become officers in the Ptolemaic army, learning Greek and acquiring double names, leading the way in the process that eventually makes labels of ethnicity moot by the time of the Roman Empire.[25]

These administrative protocols go a long way to explaining the "striking asymmetry" in the "relation between Greeks and Egyptians" remarked upon by Jan Assmann: "Whereas the Greeks showed an eager interest in the culture and the land of Egypt without, however, making the effort to study the language, the Egyptians learned Greek without getting interested in Greek culture and geography."[26] This is not to say that no élite Greek before Cleopatra ever learned Egyptian: some certainly did.[27] It is a matter of scale and reach, and of the avenues of access. Proximity and even sustained administrative cooperation do not necessarily lead to predictable patterns of knowledge transfer or of translation: we find translations from Demotic into Greek, for example, but not the other way around.[28] As Goldhill puts it in discussing the interfaces between Alexandrian literature and Egyptian mythological ideology: "There are different potential negotiations at each interface between cultures, and we must remain as sensitive to where the border controls are being enforced as to the apparent border crossings."[29]

Two Ptolemaic "Exceptions"

There are two very important cases of translation into Greek that we know of in the Ptolemaic sphere, and neither of them is, as one might perhaps expect them to be, an example of the Greeks reaching out into another culture for knowledge in translated form.

Some time early in the third century, the Egyptian priest Manetho of Sebennytus wrote a history of Egypt in Greek.[30] Major portions of this now lost work are said by our principal source, the Jewish priest-historian Josephus, to have been "translated" from Egyptian sources (*Ap.* 1. 228). Josephus uses the verb μεταφράζω, which can denote a range of practices, including paraphrase, and it is hard to know precisely what is meant here, since neither the original Greek text of Manetho nor the Egyptian sources behind it survive.[31] Manetho's effort is symptomatic of a widespread energetic engagement with the challenge of Hellenism on the part of peoples conquered by Alexander and his successors.[32] At about the same time as Manetho was writing, a Babylonian priest, Berossus, under the rule of the Seleucids, was writing a history of Babylon in Greek; Demetrius the Jew, writing in Alexandria about fifty years after Manetho, under Ptolemy IV Philopator (ruled 221–205), composed in Greek a history of his people from Adam to his own time.[33] We observe a related phenomenon in Italy around the same time as Demetrius, for the first Romans to write histories of their own people follow in this same track, writing in Greek and not their own language; as we shall see, a crucial difference is that the Romans were the conquerors, not the conquered.[34]

The impact of Hellenism is remarkably powerful and remarkably quick. Manetho and Berossus are producing their hybrid works, unimaginable without dialogue with Greek historiography, within half a century of the conquest of their countries by the Macedonians; as Dillery very tellingly observes, "a similar history of Egypt was not produced in Aramaic, the official language of the Persians, during the roughly two hundred years of Persian occupation."[35] The histories of Berossus and Manetho are not part of a Greek drive to learn about their new subjects at a more economical price than that of learning their languages and scripts.[36] Rather, these works are an independent response to the new situation from a high-ranking Egyptian or Babylonian who is attempting to mediate his culture's knowledge to a new kind of audience, both external and internal. Each author is linking a Hellenic system and his own inherited traditions in a way that will ideally make new sense both to a recently dominant Greek readership and also to fellow-members of his own priestly élite who are having to adapt rapidly to a totally unexpected reconfiguration of power; in the case of Manetho, independently generated synchronisms between his Egyptian material and key events from Greek tradition were an important part of this attempt at linkage.[37] So far as we can tell, Manetho's initiative failed in at least half of its apparent ambition, for "the Hellenic class continued to prefer other writers, such as Herodotus, for basic reading about Egypt,"[38] and Manetho's work really came into its own only when its chronologies were put into the service of Egyptian, Jewish, and Christian polemic, as various traditions argued over the priority of their peoples' inheritance.[39] Berossus' work likewise had a minimal impact on a Greek audience, who preferred to consult Greek authors such as Ctesias for lore on Babylonia.[40]

The other major translation of Ptolemaic Alexandria, the Septuagint, is of far greater importance in terms of the transformations it eventually made possible. The Septuagint is easily the most significant translation in human history, for, as Rajak points out in her magisterial study of the translation, if the Hebrew Bible and its Messianic prophecies had not already been translated into the *lingua franca* of Greek, then Christianity could never have developed outside Palestine—at least, not in any conceivably recognizable form.[41]

The Septuagint was not commissioned by a Greek king who wanted a complete collection of what the world had to offer, as the "Letter to Aristeas" and much modern scholarship would have it; instead, it was carried out by Alexandrian Greek-speaking Jews whose ability to read their Hebrew or Aramaic texts was becoming less and less secure.[42] The translation was not so much a transference from one culture into another as an internal realignment within an already multilingual and heterogeneous religious community.[43] Further, there were various versions of Hebrew books available for the translators to work on, and the production of the Septuagint was by no means "a concerted effort to produce a homogeneous Greek translation of a pre-established canon of Hebrew books";[44] in addition, various new versions of the Septuagint kept being produced from the second century on.[45] Paradoxically, it may have been the very existence of the Septuagint, with its appearance of being a "translation," that in time produced the impression that there must be a unified "original" to which this translation referred, thus engendering a new kind of pressure to canonize a hitherto more disparate body of sacred texts. Here we may have a case of a translation generating an original, instead of the other way around.[46]

The kinetic power of the young Macedonian monarchies was immense. The impact of the Greek powers in their interaction with their new subjects produced new possibilities for interaction. The Macedonian monarchy may not have directly commissioned the Septuagint, for example, but it is impossible to imagine the Septuagint being produced without the reconfigurations provided by the transformational environment of Ptolemaic Alexandria. Similarly, as Assmann says of Manetho's history, "Without Hellenism, such an encounter between Egypt and Europe by means of a common cultural form of expression would have been impossible."[47] Still, the patterns of interaction are not necessarily of the kind that modern observers might naturally expect, and not even of the kind that the Byzantine scholar Tzetzes found it natural to envision looking back some fourteen hundred years later. The Greek élite did not in an inquisitive spirit commission translations for their own consumption, and they were less receptive than one might have expected them to be even toward those Greek translations written by non-Greeks to which they did in theory have access. As we have seen, Manetho's history left no trace of an impact among Greek scholars and historians, and even though the Septuagint leaves more of a mark in our sources, it only became properly current among Greek readers as a vehicle for the diffusion of Christianity.[48]

The Variability of Translation into Greek

There is a larger context for the apparent general reluctance of the Greek-speaking Alexandrian élite to learn the Egyptian language and themselves to translate Egyptian texts into Greek, or Greek texts into Egyptian. In general, as has often been remarked, translations into Greek are not common in the pre-Christian Mediterranean outside of official contexts, and the ones we do know of from the pre-Roman period tend very much not to be written by Greeks.[49] The non-Greek authorship of these translations into Greek represents a striking asymmetry, one that should interest scholars of translation studies, for whom the direction of translation is always an important consideration. To identify the primary language of the translators is not necessarily a reflection of "a confident cultural 'ontology' born of modern nationalism," as argued by Whitmarsh, although his general point that the whole sphere of interaction should inform us "[i]f we wish to understand how 'Greek culture' operated" is a very important one.[50] The direction of translation can have important consequences for our understanding especially of the power-structures underpinning the interactions in the intercultural zones. The impact of Hellenism repeatedly involves local élites trading "up" by learning Greek, without any necessary reciprocal movement from primary Greek speakers.[51]

Indeed, Greek élite knowledge of other languages in the Classical and Hellenistic periods is itself harder to document than one might imagine.

The scholarly glossaries that we know of from the Hellenistic period, for example, are not the product of a bilingual Greek world, nor are they designed to assist Greeks in reading or speaking Near Eastern languages. Overwhelmingly, they are lists of recherché words in Greek dialects. The so-called *Oxyrhynchus Glossary*, which does uniquely contain considerable numbers of "Persian, Babylonian and 'Chaldaean' words transcribed into the Greek alphabet and translated into koine Greek," never cites non-Greek sources and is clearly "a bookish collection, written by someone who has read widely but has never been in touch with the original sources."[52] As the recent editor of this *Oxyrhynchus Glossary*, Francesca Schironi, puts it, "Glossaries on papyrus . . . do not show any interest in dialects and languages *per se,* but only in connection with literary evidence."[53] According to Schironi, the evidence of the glossaries tends to confirm the general skepticism, memorably voiced by Momigliano, about élite Greek knowledge of non-Greek languages in the time of the Macedonian monarchies.[54]

It is in fact very difficult in general to assess how many Greeks learned other languages, and how much variability there was according to social standing, region, or period. It is an interesting part of Greek élite self-definition that they should in many periods exaggerate their ignorance of other languages, when we so often observe people exaggerating their linguistic competence, and we always have to be alert to the possibility that a monolithic construct presented to us by our sources is masking a much more complicated picture. In the Roman Imperial period, for example, élite Greeks tended to affect no knowledge of Latin or of Roman history and politics, although they certainly did possess it.[55] In the fifth century BCE, the Athenian anti-Persian rhetoric following the Persian wars masked a genuine receptivity to Achaemenid culture in a variety of domains, as Miller has compellingly demonstrated; nonetheless, according to her account, the extant literary evidence points to Themistocles as the only élite Greek of the fifth century of whom we can confidently say that he could speak Persian.[56]

There undoubtedly were other Greeks apart from Themistocles who spoke some Persian in the fifth century,[57] not least while acting as intermediaries in the wide "variety of pragmatic interactions" involved in "commerce, diplomacy, travel and warfare."[58] D. M. Lewis has recovered from Persian documentation concrete evidence for Persian- and Elamite-speaking Greeks in the Persian administrative service as early as 510, so that "there should be no reason to doubt their availability to the King, and to satraps, particularly in the west, in all relevant periods."[59] Even in these spheres of pragmatic interaction, however, it is bi- or trilingual non-Greeks who are the ones better attested in the literary evidence, such as the Carian Mys in Herodotus (8. 135. 3), the Lycian Pigres in Xenophon's *Anabasis* (1. 2. 17), or the Carian Gaulites in Thucydides (8. 85. 2): this is further demonstration of the protocols that must always be allowed for in our assessments of the various types of evidence with which we are presented.[60]

Learning a language is one thing; reading and especially translating a text is quite another. Capacity in the one domain by no means leads automatically to capacity in the other, however natural it is for products of modern education systems to assume that bilingualism and biliteracy go together. It is observable that those who grow up speaking, for example, French at home while being schooled in English will be fluent in spoken French while finding it difficult to read and especially to write French. Even Lewis's bilingual Greeks in the Persian administration are not necessarily biliterate: "They only dictate so they do not need to be literate themselves in Elamite; they do need to have enough spoken Persian and Elamite to do their jobs."[61] It looks as if Maurice Sartre was basically right to say of the Hellenistic period: "No Greek author felt it necessary to learn Aramaic, Egyptian, or some other language spoken in the world that emerged from the Alexandrian conquest in order to have direct contact with the culture that it transmitted."[62] The reverse was not the case: "After Alexander, many Easterners learned to read, write, and speak Greek, but they had always been biliterate, or triliterate, and understood the need to master foreign scripts and languages."[63] Berossus and Manetho are important cases in point, as are the Egyptian and Babylonian administrators who worked with the new Macedonian monarchies to forge the joint ideologies that so distinctively mark the self-presentation of the Successors.[64]

The Greek élite tendency to monolingualism and especially uniliteracy in the Classical and Hellenistic periods appears to be curiously exceptional in the context of the time, reminding us once more of how "the Greeks of the Classical period . . . did everything differently from all other peoples around them."[65] The Greeks in this regard resemble the overwhelmingly monolingual Americans and British of the contemporary world: if your language is the default language of international culture, and if there are plenty of people to interpret and translate for you in the domains of diplomacy, government, and trade, why not be monoglot? Again, we take it that there is more Greek bilingualism operating in the interstices of the interacting cultures of the eastern Mediterranean than our élite Greek sources allow; yet the élite pose of exclusivity itself remains a distinctive and arresting cultural feature, whatever it may be cloaking. In any event, we certainly see no systematic élite educational program for Classical or Hellenistic Greeks designed to deliver bilingualism and biliteracy, of the kind that we shall see in place in the Roman sphere.[66] Nor do we observe élite Greek authors in the Hellenistic kingdoms developing biliteracy in order to translate texts either into or out of Greek, even if some of them will presumably had some oral knowledge of other languages; again, the difference in the Roman case will be very great, for there we shall see not only non-Romans translating from Greek into Latin but also, in due course, Romans as well. Of course, in the Roman sphere we can identify with confidence at least one primary speaker of Greek who learned another language, Latin, well enough to write epic and drama in his new language—Livius Andronicus. In the following chapters we shall be examining the remarkable circumstances in which this became possible.

Powerful political, social, or religious pressure was necessary for texts in other scripts and languages to break through the barrier systematically into the world of Greek culture via the medium of translation. We have already remarked that a considerable period of sustained intermingling was necessary before translation on an appreciable scale developed momentum in Egypt.[67] Even the Roman conquest of the Greek world did not lead straightforwardly to any translation project from Latin to Greek, although a good number of Greeks certainly became able to deal with Latin, and not only at the level of the élite who were interacting with the Roman power structure.[68] In due course, we find bilingual Latin/Greek glossaries in use under the Empire, and even Greek translations of portions of Virgil and Cicero on Egyptian papyrus.[69] But it took the shattering impact of Christianity to produce a truly significant reshaping of the patterns of written as opposed to spoken interaction, so as to produce large-scale translation into Greek of texts in other languages. The translation of Syriac Christian texts into Greek beginning in the fourth and fifth centuries CE is a telling case in point. Many inhabitants of Syria at this period were bilingual in Greek and Aramaic/ Syriac, but "it was Christianity which provided Syriac with the necessary prestige to enable it to compete as a literary language (in specific spheres) with the language of contemporary political power."[70] The mobility and diffusion of the new religion, which transformed the previously low-caste language of Syriac into a vehicle of religious power, shook up the age-old hierarchies in the Near East, rather as in the West the new religion led to new dynamics of translation, as a canonical body of religious texts, unlike anything the pagans had ever possessed, needed to be universalized for new readerships.[71]

The range of possibilities in the history of translation into Greek shows that translation is not something we should just expect to happen whenever literate cultures overlap with each other. It is, in fact, more normal in the ancient world to find what Greg Woolf has called "parallel literatures," all with "their own rules of play."[72] The case of Ptolemaic Alexandria in particular shows that prolonged intimacy between two literate cultures can produce asymmetric and unpredictable traffic across social, linguistic, and textual lines, with any kind of frequent translation outside the realm of chancellery and court developing in different phases, in one direction (Egyptian to Greek) and not the other, taking time to come into play. Further, not all texts are the same, and different categories of text vary in their susceptibility to movement in translated form:

as we shall examine in detail shortly, élite texts (and especially drama) have far less mobility than fable, novel, and romance.[73]

As we shall see, the impact of the new Roman empire in its interaction with its new subjects likewise shook up the kaleidoscope and produced yet more novel variants of possibility. The Roman case will prove to be very different in important respects, most strikingly in the fact that proficient knowledge of a second language, Greek, increasingly became the norm among the Roman élite. We shall need to attempt to isolate the enabling factors behind this phenomenon, for, as the case of the Ptolemies and Seleucids shows and as we shall see in more detail in Chapter 3, it was by no means normal in the ancient world for conquerors to learn the language of their subjects.

Ranges of Possibilities

If we consider the Indian, Ptolemaic, and Greek scenarios, it appears that there is a large set of possibilities for interaction between different groups across and among the zones of spoken language and written text, with many different kinds of possible contacts and adaptations. It is always important to guard against the fallback idea that certain predictable kinds of transference and commerce are to be expected when different language groups, equipped with different texts, are in contact with one another.

"Translation" to an English speaker will convey the impression that the activity is a matter of "carrying across" some content from one language to another: one can fall into positing a monolithic culture of monoglots on either side of a divide, which the translator penetrates by carrying across something from one side to the other, compensating for a language deficit.[74] This is in fact a reasonably rare scenario historically, although something like it can occur, as we saw in the case of Manetho's Egyptian history, but even here we are dealing with traffic from a bilingual sphere into a monolingual one. One can even find large-scale translation activity taking place across language borders when there is no sustained bilingualism in play. The case of translation from Greek to

Arabic is particularly striking, since for centuries after the Islamic conquest of Byzantium's eastern provinces there were intensive translations of Greek medical and scientific and philosophical texts into Arabic, even though, as Adams and Swain put it, "There was no Graeco-Arabic bilingualism. Indeed, there is no better example of an absence of bilingualism."[75]

Much more common is a scenario in which bilingual or multilingual communities interpenetrate, with translators operating "from the intersections or overlaps of cultures."[76] This is the kind of world that is familiar to students of the *Alexander Romance,* for example, which from the fourth century CE onward found its way from Greek into Latin, Syriac, Armenian, Arabic, and many other languages.[77] In these circumstances, labels of "source" or "target" cultures can prove to be very misleading, for translators can partake of both as they negotiate the in-between spaces.[78] Bi- or multilingualism provides a dynamic environment in which, as De Crom well puts it, "the linguistic defects of a community are hardly the most important, let alone the *only* motivation for translation. More often than not translation in a multilingual context has to do with languages' differing statuses and with strategies to influence and change hierarchies of languages, texts, and traditions— in short, with the *prestige* of a language, a text, or even of a translation itself."[79] The situation in Rome in the middle Republic, as we shall see, is much closer to this scenario than to the concept of "compensation for deficit," which our word "translation" almost automatically connotes. The translations of John Dryden provide a convenient modern example of how misleading "deficit" can be as an explanation of a translation project, for they were written for an audience who were, for the most part, perfectly capable of reading the originals for themselves.[80]

We are concentrating on textual adaptation here, but bilingual environments can of course also provide a venue for oral mediation, even if "translation" is not the appropriate term. This is what happened, for example, in the case of Near Eastern works such as the Gilgamesh epic in the orientalizing period of the eighth to the seventh centuries BCE, when Greek singers must have heard versions of the epic from oral presentations of some kind: Homer and Hesiod were certainly not reading cuneiform tablets.[81] Similarly, in the period after the eventual end of the cuneiform culture in the wake of the Greek conquest, the mechanisms behind similarities in surviving Aramaic or Akkadian works and Greek counterparts are more usually explicable as oral than as textual.[82]

We are left with the problem of the frequent mismatches between the charts of bi- or multilingualism and of translation. We can have translation without bilingualism and bilingualism without translation, and more or less any scenario in between. Why is there not more symmetry between the frequency of shared language use and the frequency of textual exchange through the border zones between and among communities?

Translating Is Not Interpreting

This large question would require many test cases and a much longer book in order to receive any kind of adequate answer, but it is worth addressing it here, however briefly, in order to set the scene for what we observe in Rome in the middle Republic. To see how the charts of interaction in language and text do not always match up, I find it useful to go back two hundred years and pick up a crucial distinction, which Friedrich Schleiermacher already drew upon—and already put under his own kind of pressure—in his foundational essay of 1813, "On the Different Methods of Translation." Schleiermacher begins this essay with a discussion of the difference between "interpreting" and "translating," and it is a difference that it is important not to gloss over.[83] The view that translating and interpreting are fundamentally the same thing seems to be regularly taken for granted. Wilss, for example, in a standard book on translation, speaks of "interpreting, i.e., the oral form of *Translation*, . . . its written counterpart."[84] But this way of looking at the relationship between interpreting and translation is radically misconceived. Giving an oral version in one language of what someone has just produced orally in another language is not a process we can transfer to what is happening when a written text undergoes a transformation into another, corresponding, written text. Bluntly, interpreting is oral, and translating is textual, and the differences between the two can be extremely important.[85] As we pursue the strangeness of translation and the distinctiveness of the Roman case, then, it is provisionally worthwhile to keep open a difference between interpreting and translating.

"Interpreting," when bilingual people interact orally between representatives of different languages or even dialects, is everywhere in human experience and must always have been, ever since different language-groups evolved—whenever that was.[86] Interpreting was very familiar to the Romans and Greeks.[87] It was so familiar that—as is very well known—they hardly ever refer to it.[88] Homer never mentions interpreters, although language difference is clearly acknowledged in the *Iliad* (2. 803–4 states that the many allies of Priam each have their own languages, and 2. 867 refers to the "barbarophone" Carians).[89] Odysseus and Aeneas wander all over the Mediterranean conversing freely with everyone they meet. The only direct reference I know of in the epic tradition to problems caused by language difference is the wonderful moment in the *Homeric Hymn to Aphrodite* when Aphrodite, disguised as a Phrygian, tells Anchises that she happens to know Trojan because her nurse was a Trojan (113–16).[90]

Epic has its own economy of narrative, but even histories seldom make mention of what was certainly a ubiquitous feature of warfare and diplomacy.[91] In the *Anabasis,* for example, Xenophon seems to adopt the subtle strategy of mentioning the Persian leader Cyrus' interpreter, Pigres, when he is first on the scene (1. 2. 17), and then leaving unmentioned and understood his presence in later episodes when he will have been on the spot and doing his job. Accordingly, Pigres' function is not mentioned at the moment when Xenophon first introduces himself into the narrative, stepping out of the Greek line and having a brief conversation with Cyrus (1. 8. 15–17): this conversation must have been mediated through Pigres, who has just been mentioned as riding in Cyrus' company (1. 8. 12), but his role is not explicitly signaled.[92] Plutarch makes special, and unusual, mention of the role of the interpreter when Themistocles meets the Persian king, Xerxes (*Them.* 28. 1): this is because he is setting up the remarkable story of how Themistocles then went on to take a year to learn Persian himself so that he would not need to rely on interpreters in the future (*Them.* 29. 3).

In stressing the ubiquity of interpreting, I do not mean at all to imply that interpreting is a "natural" activity that we can take for granted and leave unexamined. In fact, in the way of these things, "Interpreting Studies" is becoming a field of its own.[93] We shall return in Chapter 2 to the symbolism surrounding the interpreter in Rome, but it is worth acknowledging at this point that interpreting is never something that just naturally happens when you need to know what people are saying and cannot understand their language; rather, interpreting always comes hedged about with significant cultural protocols. For now, all I want to establish is that oral interpreting is everywhere in human history, and very much part of life in the ancient Mediterranean.

"Translation," on the other hand, is a different matter. Interpreting is ubiquitous; translation is not. If we understand translation as the transferring of textual material from one technologically encoded instantiation to another, then we see that it was sporadic, not normative, in the ancient Mediterranean, with different phases of intensity in different places and times. Yet we tend to think of translation as natural because we confuse it with interpreting. Wilss's conception of interpreting and translation as two faces of the same coin is symptomatic of the way our thinking on this issue has been muddled up by a variety of influences, not least European structuralist linguistics, which has it that spoken utterance is primary while writing is a parasitic way of capturing speech.[94] It may come naturally to users of an alphabetic script to assume that the purpose of writing is to capture speech, but in most writing systems in the world there is no necessary relationship between speech and writing of the kind we take for granted as inheritors of the Greek alphabet.

One sees this point clearly in the case of Chinese writing. In origin, the Chinese writing system had a phonographic component according to the rebus principle, a hint as to the pronunciation of the written character; yet the passage of time and the increasing differentiation of the various spoken languages of "Chinese" have combined "to reduce the phonological component of the modern Chinese script and to strengthen its logographic nature, as the phonological component has become increasingly imprecise."[95] The script is not invested in capturing the sound of a spoken language, so that speakers of different Chinese languages or dialects will be able to read a written text out aloud in their own tongue, even though nowadays literate Chinese will favor the phonology of Mandarin.[96] The script has many great advantages, especially in unifying a multilingual nation by allowing for mutual literate comprehension among the speakers of the many different languages within China.[97] Indeed, until quite recently it used even to be possible for speakers of languages from completely different language families, such as Korean, Vietnamese, and Japanese, to interact within the "Sinographic sphere" without knowing how to speak any of the languages of China, communicating via "brush talk" by "writing . . . messages up in literary Chinese and passing sheets of paper back and forth in the fashion of an oral conversation."[98]

The permeability between different textual formats is quite different from the permeability between spoken languages. The same script can occlude differences between languages, as we see in the case of Chinese characters: conversely, the same language can become opaque through being written in different scripts. What are today called Standard Urdu and Standard Hindi are essentially the same language, still mutually intelligible (even if drifting further and further apart, especially as a result of intense pressure on the Urdu side to "Arabize"), but Urdu is written in a Perso-Arabic script and Hindi is written in an adaptation of the Devanagari script used for transcribing Sanskrit, so that they are mutually unintelligible on paper. This example shows how literacy is regularly "a barrier to communication."[99]

So far from being parasitic upon speech, then, writing is in fact a symbolic tool in its own right: "Symbolization is a faculty and speech, which is ephemeral, is only one possible tool for its expression; writing, which is material and potentially eternal, is another."[100] As such, writing is not an elidible part of the process of translation; it is not a mere vehicle for conveying what was originally "said," as if there is a natural oral expression, which the writing is merely mediating into another form for oral expression. The transferring of textual material is particularly marked when the scripts of the source and target texts are different, as they of course regularly are in the ancient world. There is, as we have seen, normally a strong connection between a culture's script and its religion and knowledge-world, making the exercise of translation into another script and cultural system extraordinary and remarkable.[101] As Rajak well puts it, "translation is not just a negotiation between languages but also a connection between two systems of thought and being"[102]— and those "systems of thought and being" can be embedded within individual writing systems with their own talismanic charisma and power. The combined viewing/reading experience of Egyptian hieroglyphics, for example, relying as it does on a complex interaction between images and signs, cannot be reproduced in other media.[103]

We certainly do find examples of transmission across the barrier between different writing systems, especially in government and diplomacy, for the chancelleries of the Near Eastern Empires were regularly operating with numbers of different languages and different scripts. In this environment we can envisage situations that will modify my provisionally strict dichotomy between oral/textual, interpreting/translating. We glimpse a fascinating scene in a relief surviving from the reign of the Assyrian king Tiglath-pileser III (c. 725): here someone is dictating (speaking, presumably, Assyrian) and two scribes are transcribing his words, one in Akkadian with a stylus via cuneiform on a clay tablet, and one in Aramaic with a brush via the West Semitic syllabary on a scroll.[104]

Still, even if Near Eastern chancelleries were the venue for interpreting and translating on a large scale, distribution patterns are not identical, for, in addition to the always crucial cultural or political factors, different writing systems can have a tendency to enable or disable different varieties of translation.[105] Schneider remarks that "the neighbouring civilizations of the Ancient Near East [Egypt and Mesopotamia] display almost antithetical patterns when it comes to translation."[106] As he says, pre-Greek Egypt has far less translation from outside than one might have expected; instead, one finds systematic "intralingual" translation, as earlier forms of scripts are superseded and their contents adapted to successive newer forms.[107] There is only one surviving text that looks as if it is a translation into Egyptian from a literary text in another language and script—the so-called Astarte papyrus, dating to around 1420 BCE, which may well be a translation from a poem in a West Semitic language.[108] Even outside the literary realm, only one example survives from preconquest Egypt of the kind of bi- or multilingual inscription so common in Mesopotamia, and that is the peace treaty between Rameses II and Hattusili III, king of the Hittites (c.1258), where the hieroglyphic text is clearly a (rather imperfect) translation of an original in Akkadian, the Near Eastern lingua franca (not the native language of the Hittite-speaking Hattusili).[109] The scribes of the Egyptian court corresponded regularly via Akkadian with their counterparts in Babylonia and Assyria, but it seems that the extra step of translating Akkadian material into Egyptian script was extremely rarely taken. Egypt, then, is a prime example of Woolf's "parallel literatures."

In contrast to the situation in Egypt, however—to return to the antithesis of Schneider—translation in Mesopotamia is regular, especially from Sumerian to Akkadian.[110] Here, however, we are dealing with a special case, that of the cuneiform script, the vehicle for the astonishingly adaptable and long-lived cuneiform culture, in which the cuneiform writing system was repeatedly remobilized to accommodate the needs and demands of new masters and new subjects, providing a field of communication throughout the Near East for millennia. Cuneiform was used to record and to translate between a variety of languages—originally Sumerian, which is a language isolate, with no known relatives, to East Semitic Akkadian (Assyrian and Babylonian) to Indo-European Hittite and to the language of the Elamites, another language isolate. The remarkable cuneiform script enabled a "cuneigraphic sphere" that was very roughly like the later "Sinographic sphere" in the Far East, and it represents a different kind of translation medium from the Egyptian script, as noted by Warburton, who contrasts the permeable cuneiform world with the Egyptian scene: "Real Egyptian thought was expressed in a different language and a different form of writing which was basically inaccessible to the rest of the ancient world, and the Egyptians saw no reason for others to master the system."[111]

It is important to take into account the impact of the script as well when we consider translating from Greek into Latin.[112] The commerce in textual encoding between Greek and Latin is very different from the commerce conducted via the textual opacity of logographic Chinese characters, where you can read and translate without necessarily knowing the original language: a text in Chinese characters "might be pronounced differently depending on whether a Chinese, Korean, Japanese, or Vietnamese person voices it in their vernacular language."[113] In the Japanese case, one may be biscripted but monolingual, and Japanese literature was indeed developed by people who could read Chinese texts but who, virtually without a single exception, spoke only one language, Japanese.[114]

If you are looking at an alphabetically encoded text, however, it is impenetrable unless you know the language.[115] The Greek writing system has a different basis from Chinese characters or cuneiform or hieroglyphics, since it "inform[s] the reader, in a rough way, of the actual sounds of speech."[116] The alphabet did not suddenly reveal the true nature of human speech, laying bare the hidden fact that humans had been using "vowels" and "consonants" all along without knowing it, but it did make it possible for someone who had learned the letters to read back aloud an encoded piece of text.[117] This is a transferable principle, which enabled the alphabet to jump across to encode Etruscan and Latin probably within one generation of its invention.[118] The oldest piece of alphabetic writing so far discovered, dated to around 775, was in fact found about ten miles from Rome, in the Latin town of Gabii—where Dionysius of Halicarnassus says Romulus and Remus went to school (*Ant. Rom.* 1. 84. 5).[119] Adaptations of letters were made to suit the different sounds of the various non-Greek languages;[120] in addition, rather as the individual Greek states did, the adapters of the Greek alphabet in Italy will have made comparatively slight orthographic innovations in order to differentiate their version and mark it out as distinctively theirs.[121]

In time, what we call the "Latin" alphabet and what we call the "Greek" alphabet end up looking distinctively different, but it is the same technology, and our modern printing conventions can exaggerate the differences very much. A modern printed text of the opening words of Homer's *Odyssey* will look like this: Ἄνδρα μοι ἔννεπε Μοῦσα πολύτροπον. If we transliterate that sequence of letters into the modern "Latin" alphabet, we have: "Andra moi ennepe Mousa polytropon." But if we perform the same exercise using the scripts in use in the middle of the third century, we have something like this:[122]

ΑΝΔΡΑ ΜΟΙ ΕΝΝΕΠΕ ΜΟΥΣΑ ΠΟΛΥΤΡΟΠΟΝ
ANDRA MOI ENNEPE MOVSA POLVTROPON

In the case of translating from Greek to Latin, the comparative transparency of the script highlights sameness and difference, unlike what is happening when a Japanese speaker reads Chinese characters, where the script is opaque and hides the way the language is different. The alphabetic script makes the differences between the languages immediate, but for a fluent speaker of the source language, the access to the original text highlights the sense of contact with what the original writer was attempting to communicate and enforces an attempt to find equivalence. As we shall see, this heightened awareness of the relationship between the languages at play, their differences and their similarities, has a deep impact on the strategies adopted by the men who translated Greek literary texts into Latin.[123]

Again, there is no question of knowing only the script and not knowing the language, in the way a Japanese speaker is able to read Chinese characters without actually knowing Chinese as a spoken language. Translating from Greek into Latin, then, can only be done by someone who knows both languages. This observation may appear so obvious as to be pointless, but if we follow Denecke's important argument of comparison with the Japanese example we see that it matters a great deal. As she puts it, "the Greco-Roman linguistic constellation was bilingual and monoliterate, while the Sino-Japanese constellation was monolingual and biliterate."[124] The consequences are profound: "Latin literature started with the *translation* of Greek models, whereas Japanese literature began as a *continuation* of Chinese literary production, supplemented by literary production in vernacular genres that had no Chinese precedent."[125]

What Does Not Get Translated

Before we turn to discuss the techniques, dynamics, and consequences of the Roman translation project, together with the conditions that may have enabled it, we need first to use the discussion so far as a background against which to take stock of a particularly important way in which the Romans were distinctive, even anomalous, in what they were doing when they started commissioning translations of Euripides and Menander. The priorities of the Romans in fact represent a highly unusual set of choices within the context of translation in the ancient and late antique world. What difference does it make that the Romans were translating these particular texts, and not others? Even in an environment where regular translation does occur, as in modern Europe, it is obviously not the case that everything gets translated: "Of course you can never translate anything and everything."[126] Discussion of this question will incidentally help us get some first purchase on an issue we shall address systematically in Chapter 6, of what it means to use the extremely loaded term "literature."

For it is interesting that in the ancient world we can normally use the practice of translation to define "literature" negatively. A rough and ready first working definition of literature in the ancient world turns out to be "that which does not get translated." We have already observed that there is virtually no trace of translation of literature into Egyptian from other languages and scripts (though we must always allow for the contingency of survival). Andrew George, in his monumental edition of the Babylonian Gilgamesh epic, points out that all kinds of other material was translated from the cuneiform script into different scripts and languages, such as Aramaic, and eventually indirectly into Arabic—medicine, divination, astronomy, astrology.[127] But the epic of Gilgamesh, and related literary texts, did not survive in this way, despite the fact that they had previously been translated within cuneiform.[128] Once again we encounter the potential significance of the writing system in considering the potential for translation: certain material which could be adapted from culture to culture and from language to language within the script world of cuneiform could not necessarily be moved as a textual entity out of the social and educational traditions and constraints of that script environment.

As George says, then, "the epic that we know died with the cuneiform writing system, along with the large proportion of the traditional scribal literature that was of no practical, scientific or religious use in a world without cuneiform."[129] Here it is important to stress George's phrase "the epic that we know," since the spectacular figure of Gilgamesh certainly left important traces in other cultures even after the demise of the cuneiform culture, as did numerous other aspects of the Babylonian literary heritage.[130] The vitality and importance of the continuing impact of Babylonian literature, and of the iconic figure of Gilgamesh in particular, are not in dispute. What counts for our present purposes is that these traces have been left by oral means or by incidental forms of transmission through Aramaic writing;[131] the mechanism was not systematic translations from the cuneiform text of the epic, such as could have preserved, for example, the distinctive plot and characteristic themes and tones of the Babylonian Gilgamesh epic canonically transmitted in cuneiform: "The epic itself, with its sombre, introspective tone, does not seem to have continued beyond the demise of Mesopotamian culture."[132]

We observe a very similar pattern many centuries later with the transmission of Greek writings into Arabic. In an astounding two and a half centuries, from around 750 to 1000 CE, Greek science, medicine, mathematics, and philosophy were translated practically wholesale into Arabic.[133] But there was no translation of "literature": no Homer, Sophocles, or Theocritus found its way into Arabic. Nor was there any translation of history, either because it was bracketed generically with "literature," or because it was regarded somehow as too culture-specific, just as "literature" presumably was. In his valuable appendix giving a bibliographical guide on Greek works translated into Arabic, Gutas has this note under the category of "Literature and literary theory": "High Greek literature was not translated into Arabic." Intriguingly, as he goes on to remark, "[w]hat was translated of Greek literature was what may be loosely called 'popular' and 'paraenetic' literature" (fables, Aesopica, novels, the *Alexander Romance*):[134] we see here a (very rough) analogy to the comparative mobility of such texts in Egypt under the Roman Empire. We observe the identical pattern during the creative burst of translation from Arabic and Greek into Latin in the early medieval period: here too it is the science and philosophy of the Greek world that is translated, while the literature of Byzantium and earlier Greece is left untouched by the transformative process.[135]

Scholars of all types are now far more open than they were a generation ago to the interactions between cultures, and even to the concept that cultures are formed in interaction; but we need to remain alert to the cases where this interaction falters, where traffic is regulated or choked. "Literature" is often one of these cases, as we have already seen in our discussions of India, Egypt both preconquest and Ptolemaic, and Greek receptivity to translation. As Denecke puts it, "literary texts are among the cultural products most resistant to travel and to successful diffusion."[136]

This preliminary finding only throws into higher relief the strange nature of the case of the Romans' interaction with the Greeks. In the first generations of the translation project, what the Romans translate from Greek is precisely what we call "literature," and what they leave untranslated is precisely what we call "science," together with mathematics, divination, and music. It is hard to say exactly when the first translation of a Greek scientific or medical text into Latin took place, but it was probably over a hundred and fifty years after Livius Andronicus first translated Homer: this is when Pompeius Magnus, as part of his role-playing as an imperial patron of culture and benefactor to the

Roman people, assigned to his freedman Pompeius Lenaeus the task of translating into Latin the Greek medical texts captured in Mithridates' library.[137] Strikingly, while the Romans did not translate astronomical texts from Greek into Latin,[138] they did translate, repeatedly, Aratus' *Phaenomena*, the major poetic treatment of astronomy in Greek.[139] This one example is a reflection of much deeper cultural choices on the Romans' part, to which we return in Chapter 5, where we shall see them negotiating complicated boundaries of differentiation in deciding which parts of Greek learning and education to appropriate for themselves, relegate to others, or reject altogether. For now, we observe only that a translated Aratus appears to have provided the Roman élite with all they felt they needed in this entire side of Greek intellectual culture, with the text somehow remaining exempt from the category of "science."

The Roman choice of what to translate and what not to translate, then, is curiously at odds with more regular patterns in the ancient world. The oddity of the Roman emphasis is further highlighted by the fact that the only texts that we know to have been translated from Etruscan into Latin were manuals on brontoscopy and haruspicy—watching thunder and inspecting entrails—important technical aspects of the divinatory branch of the religious wisdom of the Etruscans, their *Etrusca disciplina;*[140] and the only text that we know to have been translated from Punic into Latin was the twenty-eight-volume work of Mago on agriculture, which was somehow considered so important that the Senate drafted a committee, including a Punic-speaking senator, Decimus Silanus, to do the translation after the sack of Carthage in 146.[141] These examples fit much more closely the normal distribution patterns in the ancient world and its aftermath, since they are precisely the kind of materials that were translated out of Akkadian and into Aramaic (divination), or out of Greek and into Arabic (agriculture).[142]

The Romans' concentration on "literature" as an object of systematic translation in the first generations of their enterprise is looking more and more anomalous. We clearly need to put this category of "literature" under a lot more pressure. We shall do so below, particularly in Chapter 6. For now, however, some potentially interesting lines of stress are coming into view. When it comes to translating Greek texts, the Romans appear to seize on a category ("literature") that is left untouched in most other salient instances of translation in the ancient world, while leaving alone the major categories ("science," "mathematics," "divination") that those other salient instances seek out; yet on the very rare occasions when it is a question of translating texts in languages other than Greek into Latin, those other major categories are just what do receive attention.

Choosing what not to translate, then, is as revealing a question as choosing what to translate: these choices are two faces of the same coin, dialogically involved with the same complex cultural pressures. Again, we return to this important point in Chapter 5, where we shall need to investigate the social and political forces at work in patrolling the borders between Greek texts and a Latin audience, in order to tease out why some categories of text were given a pass to enter while others were not.

The discussion so far has aimed to denaturalize the idea of translation, to remind us of how odd and variegated and unstraightforward a phenomenon it actually is. "Translation," in the sense of the word I am using—and above all translation of "literature," a term we are still leaving somewhat unexamined at this stage—is not normative in the ancient Mediterranean, especially not in the areas of it known to the inhabitants of Italy under the rule of the Rome in the middle Republic. The issues I have been sketching here help explain why that is the case.

CHAPTER 2

The Roman
Translation Project

I N THE LIGHT of the discussion in Chapter 1, it looks as if Friedrich Leo was not overstating by very much when he wrote a hundred years ago that "Livius Andronicus invented the art of translation."[1] Livius will not have heard of the first first, the translation of Sumerian literary texts into Akkadian, but at least within the world he and his audience knew the translation of a literary text into another language would have been an event without precedent. There is no reason to doubt that his translations represented the first translations of Greek literature into another language, and, as Leo puts it, for Andronicus "es war nur eine Literatur."[2]

Not the "Faithful Interpreter"

There was therefore no model available for the new practice.[3] The first practitioners of the new translation movement were all people who grew up speaking Greek as a first or second language, with Latin as a second or third, and their background in Greek literature gave them no training or background whatever for the task of translating literary texts, as McElduff well points out: "they came from a [Greek] literary system that did not just relegate translation to a secondary status, but denied it existence, despite being part of a cosmopolitan region that held other literate cultures."[4]

Further, Livius' mode of translation, which became paradigmatic for his successors, was very different from what we can surmise about what had previously been the case at the linguistic interface between Romans and Greeks. If we imagine what kind of templates Livius Andronicus may have had available to him as he began translating Homer or Euripides into Latin, then one certain template will have been the work of the interpreter, for interpreting must have been a very common feature of Roman life as they expanded their domain to include the peninsula of Italy and the island of Sicily.[5]

Here I must stress that we have no direct evidence for the norms of interpreting in Roman Italy in the middle of the third century; inevitably, we extrapolate back on the basis what we know from later periods, which is always a risky procedure. But if we may project back from better-documented later periods, there will already in the third century have been all manner of symbolic protocols associated with interpreting in contexts involving the Roman state and its representatives. Later sources stress that originally only Latin could be used before the Senate, so that an interpreter will have been regularly present;[6] further, we are told that Roman officials followed the same protocol and that they would speak in Latin to Greeks, through an interpreter, even though in many cases they could perfectly well have spoken in Greek.[7] The reality will have been considerably more fuzzy than this received version has it, as Horsfall well points out;[8] and from the generation before Livius Andronicus, in 282, we have the diverting tale of the Roman envoy L. Postumius Megellus making such a mess of the language when addressing the people of Tarentum in Greek that he aroused derision, and worse, from the audience.[9] Yet the symbolic impact of speaking via an interpreter is very great. As Gruen and Adams have demonstrated, for the audience of Greeks who have to sit through a largely incomprehensible harangue before they hear a version they can understand, the impression of subservience to Roman power is unmistakable.[10] The interpreter is not simply "useful," in that he makes communication possible: just by virtue of being there, the interpreter becomes a visible token of mediation up a hierarchical chain.[11] A similar atmosphere is captured with the very common religious dimension to the word *interpres,* which was regularly applied to the priests who mediate "down" to humans what the gods are saying via their own semiotics of communication.[12]

In the religious context, it is certainly crucial that the *interpres* should get it absolutely right, and it is a given in Roman discussions of the job of the interpreter that he should be literal and "word for word" *(uerbum e/de/pro uerbo)* in his rendering.[13] Roman authors regularly distinguish between the activity of the interpreter and that of the translator of literature on precisely these grounds;[14] and when they talk about the style of the "interpreter" they will also have in mind the operating procedure of the state officials who produced analogously literal and "word for word" versions of *senatus consulta,* treaties, and so on.[15] Here is another case where my provisional dichotomy between textual "translating" and oral "interpreting" needs qualifying, for the idealized techniques of official oral interpreting and chancellery translating appear to track each other very closely.

Cicero, in a well-known passage (*Opt. Gen.* 14), claims of his own versions of Aeschines and Demosthenes that he has not translated like an interpreter, but like an orator *(non conuerti ut interpres sed ut orator),* not considering it necessary to render word for word *(non uerbum pro uerbo necesse habui reddere),* but preserving the overall style and impact of the words *(genus omne uerborum uimque seruaui).*[16] Elsewhere (*Fin.* 3. 15) he says that it will not be necessary for a word to be squeezed out from its corresponding word *(nec tamen exprimi uerbum e uerbo necesse erit),* the way interpreters without fully trained skill in expression do it *(ut interpretes indiserti solent).*[17] Cicero is not talking here about the difference between two models of literary translation but about the difference between literary translation and the interpreting or translating performed in official contexts.

The most famous enunciation of the dichotomy between the literary composer and the interpreter is in Horace's *Ars Poetica,* where he tells his reader not to take pains to exchange word for word the way a faithful interpreter does (*nec uerbo uerbum curabis reddere fidus/interpres,* 133–34).[18] Despite the enormously influential afterlife of this phrase in all European languages, Horace is not talking about "faithful translation," either as a good or a bad thing; as Bettini has well shown, Horace is talking about a specific cultural practice, that of the interpreter, whose job it is to mediate between two parties without distortion and to give a word for a word with utmost scrupulosity.[19] Horace's point is that this is not what the literary artist is doing, as he goes on to demonstrate a few lines later with his creative rewriting of the first words of Homer's *Odyssey;* here Homer's "after he sacked the holy city of Troy" is drastically rewritten via Hellenistic chronography to capture the post-Homeric understanding of the fall of Troy as a world-historical moment, the beginning of a new phase in Mediterranean history: "after the epoch of the capture of Troy" (*captae post tempora Troiae,* 141).[20]

According to these accounts, then, the Roman official interpreter, unlike the literary artist, aims to produce a word-for-word version, and the office that produces translations in Greek of Roman *senatus consulta* or treaties is likewise aiming at a word-for-word version. Horace had himself worked in that office, so he knows what he is talking about when he disparages the efforts of the "word-for-word" *interpres:*[21] as a *scriba quaestorius* attached to the *aerarium,* he will very probably have been directly responsible either for producing translations of official documents into Greek himself or for overseeing others who did so.[22] In surviving Greek-language versions of original Latin *senatus consulta,* we observe precisely the kind of highly literal word-for-word rendering to which both Cicero and Horace object. As Sherk remarks, there is an extraordinary stylistic consistency in these documents: "The texts span a period of two hundred years, yet one sometimes feels that a single individual has done them all."[23] The first of Sherk's Documents dates to 189, and already fully embodies this characteristic style, so that one has some confidence in positing a bureaucratic procedure that predates the first appearance by some considerable period of time.

Sherk thoroughly analyzes these in-house stylistic practices, where highly Latinate phraseology is imposed upon the Greek, and Adams gives examples from Augustus' *Res Gestae*, where we have, for example, ὤμοσεν εἰς τοὺς λόγους for *iurauit in mea uerba,* and εὐχὰς ἀναλαμβάνειν, instead of Greek idiomatic ποιεῖσθαι, for *uota suscipere.*[24] One even finds Greek versions with a "dative absolute," instead of the regular Greek genitive absolute, for consular dates, since this is as close as the ablative-less Greek can get to the original Latin ablative absolute.[25]

Such cases used sometimes to be regarded as mistakes of some kind, but they are instead classic examples of translating "down," from a language of higher power and/or prestige into a less powerful or prestigious language, with foreignizing traits being left in the translation as a marker of dominance.[26] The Latin/Greek case is of course a peculiarly vexed one when it comes to assessing relative power and prestige, as we shall see below, but in these official contexts the symbolism of Roman dominance is plain to see: "If the documents were given in this way a distinctive Romanness, so much the better: the non-Greek idioms bring out the Roman indifference to the sensibilities of their subjects."[27] This is another example of the domineering use of Latin remarked upon above in connection with the deployment of the official interpreter: the Latinate Greek of the official inscriptions is a corollary to the aggressive staging of encounters with foreigners who are obliged to use an intermediary to communicate with Romans or to tolerate listening to Latin before they get a version they can understand.[28]

Word-for-word fidelity is also to be found much later in pedagogical contexts, with bilingual texts of Virgil and Cicero, for example, being used in the Roman Empire to train Greek-speaking students who needed to learn Latin.[29] Above all, literal fidelity in translating texts, rather than in interpreting, or in its associated governmental contexts, comes to be of extreme importance with translations of the Hebrew Bible, from the Septuagint to Syriac and Latin versions.[30] This topic takes us too far from our path; we need note only that this highly influential and important tendency in world translation is a completely misleading model to have in mind when considering the techniques of the first translators of Greek literature into Latin.[31]

There is, then, good reason to think that Livius Andronicus' model of what happened at the interface between Latin and Greek in interpreting or in official interstate translation was that of a faithful attempt to reproduce as closely as possible what was said, or written, by the other party—and this is, as we shall soon see, very far from what we observe in his own literary translations, or indeed in any Latin literary translations. Further, as we shall also see, the hierarchical and aggressive foreignizing, which may already have been a feature of official Latin translation in the Middle Republic, is itself a very different model of linguistic and cultural relationship from what we observe in the Roman literature translation project. What the translators of Greek literature into Latin are producing entails a completely different way of thinking about the relationship between texts, and between languages and cultures as well.

The Bilingual Classroom

If we are trying to find a more productive contemporary environment in which Livius might have hit upon his variety of translation, we should probably be looking at teaching. The tradition as transmitted in Suetonius (*Gram. et rhet.* 1. 2) says that Livius Andronicus was teaching the sons of his patron Livius in Rome, and if he was following what his own experience had been and what was to be the experience of many generations of Roman schoolboys afterwards, then once he had got them past the basics he will have been teaching them Homer.[32] Now, *can* you teach Homer to pupils whose first language is not Greek without "translating"? In the process of explaining Homer's language, Livius will necessarily have provided equivalents in Latin: this is the force of the verb used by Suetonius to describe his procedure with his Greek texts, *interpretari*, which, as Kaster puts it, in this context "should connote neither 'explanation'/'exegesis' alone nor 'translation' alone, but some combination of the two that cannot be more precisely defined."[33] Livius will also have inevitably brought to his new challenge in Rome the formation he had himself undergone as a pupil in a Hellenistic classroom, presumably in Tarentum, where he would have followed the exercises outlined by Jocelyn: "The schools of third and second century Greece employed two exercises akin to the translation of poetical works from one language into another. In the one poetic texts were interpreted word for word in the everyday language. In the other a rhetorical equivalent of the substance of a poem or prose work was sought."[34] Both of these models had a clear utility to Livius when he turned to translating Homer or Sophocles into Latin: in one case, you have to find a word from a different register, or language, that has an equivalent meaning, and in the other case you have to find a way of recasting the original while preserving its gist.

The point is not to write a chapter in a biographical novel, or to invent a Just So Story. Nor am I trying to resurrect the old idea that Livius wrote his translation of Homer's *Odyssey* as a school aid, designed to help boys who found the original hard.[35] In this connection, it is worth disposing of another regular modern preconception about translation that does us no service in the Roman context: it is important to note that translation was not conceived of as serving a utilitarian function or providing a service. Kaimio well remarks that Livius' translation of Homer's *Odyssey* "was intended to open up a new genre for Roman literature, not primarily to help people with poor Greek to read Homer."[36] Even the translation of Mago's Punic work on agriculture in 146, picked out by Kaimio as the first translation into Latin undertaken for the reasons so many manuals are translated in the modern world, is not so easy to categorize. We cannot say why the Roman Senate undertook such an enterprise, but it is unlikely that the translation was meant to provide a helpful boost to Italian farmers who were behind the times:[37] Libyan farming techniques are anyway not directly transferable to Italian conditions (Columella, *Rust.* 1. 1. 6). Perhaps this was the most effective and economical way that the Roman Senate had of giving a picture to the Roman people of what this land was like that they had just conquered and made their own, with a view especially to eventual colonization.

We do not commit ourselves to any particular view of the motivation or purpose of Livius' translation if we hypothesize that he may have gleaned conceptions of translinguistic interpretation from a pedagogic experience of intralinguistic interpretation.[38] For the following discussion, the most important aspect of this hypothesis is that we should envisage Livius' pupils having an education that was bilingual. A certain number of people in Latium had been learning Greek somehow or other for centuries before Livius Andronicus turned up in the city of Rome, and we do not really know what that experience was like.[39] The tradition about Livius is our first reasonably secure evidence for the bilingual education that was to become so characteristic in the Latin-speaking world: "The curriculum of *grammatica* was Greek, and Greek seems to have been used metalinguistically as the language of instruction."[40]

It is important to take stock of how unusual a situation this is within the ancient world, or indeed beyond. A very small and select group of scribes in Mesopotamia and Egypt, for example, was schooled in reading and writing in more than one language and often in more than one script, but at Rome we eventually see that anyone who progresses beyond the basics is expected to master some spoken and written Greek and is instructed, at least in part, in Greek. The comparatively widespread ability of educated Romans to master these skills has a great deal to do with the script in use, since the alphabet "was so simple that it could be used by all people of normal intelligence even outside the circles of learned professional scribes."[41] Again, if we follow the comparative lead of Denecke, we see how very different the Roman experience was from the Japanese. At the time that the first Japanese literary works were being crafted on the Chinese model, "there was no instruction in conversational Chinese . . . and native speakers of Chinese played no part in Japanese education."[42] As Denecke points out, the difference is largely a result of the utterly divergent geopolitical realities underlying the interactions; Rome conquered Greece, Japan did not conquer China, so that the Roman domain is "a world where actual people and not just cultures embodied in imported texts collide and coexist."[43] Every classicist is used to the fact of Roman bilingual and biscripted education, but it is not at all a normal thing to happen. And it has important consequences.

The Originality of Translation

As we have seen, the kind of fidelity that was expected from an interpreter or a state translator (or, much later, from a Latin translation of the Bible) is not what is understood in the Latin translation project of the Middle Republic. Livius Andronicus leads the way in a new kind of endeavor.[44] From the time of Friedrich Leo onward, scholars have stressed the free and creative way in which the Roman model of literary translation works. The translations claim to be artistic works in their own right, not just representations of some other entity.[45] The regular word for this kind of translation is *uertere*, "to turn," a word with connotations of metamorphosis, of magical transformation, not of ferrying across from one place to another;[46] as Bellos points out, in comparing the normal English metaphor of "transferring," "the history of translation . . . might have been significantly different in the West had the job always been thought of as a 'turning.' "[47] In this connection, it is telling that the translation of Homer's *Odyssey* by Livius Andronicus, for example, is not referred to as a translation but as "Livius' book," whereas many modern translations of novels into English do not even have the translator's name on the front cover.[48] The self-assured and even combative attitude of the Roman translator is caught in an anecdote concerning the declaimer Arellius Fuscus; he took over a Greek epigram from an Asian rhetorician, and when challenged with what he had done, he said, "I strive to rival the best epigrams; I don't try to spoil them but to beat them" (*Do . . . operam ut cum optimis sententiis certem, nec illas corrumpere conor sed uincere*, Sen. Con. 9. 1. 13, tr. M. Winterbottom).[49]

This self-assuredness and boldness is present in the first fragments of the new translations—perhaps disconcertingly for those moderns who are stuck with a patronizing attitude toward the supposedly parasitical nature of translation, and also toward "archaic" poets, who should know their place.[50] Livius' self-consciousness about the novelty and power of his operation is clear from the surviving fragments.[51] Among these fragments, very fortunately, is Livius' translation of the first words of Homer's poem:

Ἄνδρα μοι ἔννεπε Μοῦσα πολύτροπον
The man to me tell, Muse, of many turns

Virum mihi, Camena, insece uersutum
The man to me, Camena, tell, a turned one

As Hinds has wonderfully shown, Livius produces a pun on his own operation when he translates Homer's πολύτροπον, "of many turns." This
word is itself ambiguous in Greek, meaning "full of shifts," "cunning,"
or else "full of physical turns," "well-travelled"—and this second meaning
could be thought to be glossed with Homer's immediately following
words ὃς μάλα πολλὰ/πλάγχθη, "who was made to wander very much"
(*Od.* 1. 1–2). The Homeric scholia are already debating the issue of the
meaning of the word, and Livius is volunteering a philological judgment
here, for the Latin *uersutum*, literally "turned," is opting for the meta-
phorical meaning, "wily."[52] At the same time, as Hinds shows, since
uersutum comes from *uertere*, the Latin word for "translate," Odysseus/
Ulysses is now presented as the "turned/translated" man, with the "turn"
from Greek into Latin becoming the latest in the many "turns" undergone by Homer's hero, giving him even an extra degree of accomplish-
ment in adaptability as a result of this latest transformation:[53] as Hinds
puts it, "our poet introduces a Ulysses in whom the very linguistic switch
to which he owes his textual existence has been made part of his pro-
verbial versatility."[54] This fortuitously surviving first line already exem-
plifies the observation of the contemporary translation theorist, Sukanta
Chaudhuri: "Whatever a translated text might be 'about,' it is always simultaneously about itself, about the working of language within it, on a
plane that the original text was not."[55]

Scholars have called attention also to the power of what Livius is doing
with his renaming of the Greek Muse. Homer calls on Μοῦσα, *Mousa*,
but Livius does not call his goddess of song "Musa"; he has found in Latin
culture an equivalent, a kind of calque.[56] His *Camena* is a water divinity identified with a spring outside Rome's city walls, and since the
Muses were closely identified with the spring of Hippocrene on Mount

Helicon in Greece, this is a deft choice, especially as Livius is also suggesting the idea that the word *Camena* is connected with *carmen,* the Latin word for "song."[57] Many of the equivalences that Livius uses throughout his translation ("Zeus/Jupiter," "Hera/Juno") will have been already available to him as a result of centuries of intercultural traffic that had incrementally built up "the great dictionary of equivalences."[58] A good number, however, are very likely to be his own invention, and, as Leo points out, his choices reveal a high degree of boldness and self-confidence.[59]

If Livius can highlight culturally specific difference within equivalence as he performs a turn of Homer's Greek Muse into a different religion, he can also make us aware of the point—now forever associated with Borges' "Pierre Menard"—that even an identical element can contain radical difference.[60] The second word of his first line, *mihi,* is as "faithful" a translation of the Greek word μοι, "to me," as you could possibly give: in fact, they go back to the same pronominal root. Yet the identity of that "me" becomes problematic if we pay it any more than mundane attention.[61] It is, and it is not, Homer, while it is, and it is not, Livius. We glimpse here the gulf between a poet composing in Greek in the eighth century and a poet composing in Latin five hundred years later.

If we are very lucky to have Livius' version of Homer's first line, we are very unlucky not to have his version of the tenth line:

τῶν ἁμόθεν γε, θεά, θύγατερ Διός, εἰπὲ καὶ ἡμῖν
From whatever point you will, goddess, daughter of Zeus, tell us too

The scholiasts are already debating the force of the word καὶ, "too."[62] Is the meaning "'Tell us too, share your knowledge with us' or 'Tell us as well as others,' an appeal to precedent?" Livius' Latin will presumably have simply been *nobis,* "to us," and the force of the second interpretation will have been very strong: "You have told Greeks this song before, so now tell it to us as well."

We observe the same bold self-consciousness about translation technique and dynamics in the dramatic prologues of Plautus and Terence.

The most original parts of a Plautine or Terentian play are the methodological discussions of the translation process;[63] this interest in translation carries through into a range of metatheatrical staples of the plays, especially the figure of the comic cook, with his new recipes and blends for his new market.[64] For what it is worth, I imagine that when Livius Andronicus puns on Ulixes as the "turned" man in the first line of his *Odyssey,* he is drawing upon his own (now lost) dramatic prologues, for this is where his audience will have first heard this usage of *uerto,* as the Prologue ambled forward to set the scene for the comedy to come.[65]

Sameness and Difference

An important part of the project of appropriating these texts, then, is not just finding the right degree of sameness, but finding the right degree of slippage, to accommodate and to represent the differences between the cultures and their languages. The entire translation project together with its consequences, leading down to the *Aeneid* and Juvenal, is involved in adjudicating this sameness and difference, and translation places a particularly clear and accurate lens on this process.

Scholars of translation studies regularly use the vocabulary of "foreignizing" and "domesticating" to analyze this dynamic.[66] Ever since Schleiermacher, theorists of translation have been very interested in the two broad options available to translators: "Either the translator leaves the writer alone as much as possible and moves the reader toward the writer ['foreignizing'], or he leaves the reader alone as much as possible and moves the writer toward the reader ['domesticating']."[67] As Umberto Eco puts it, "given a translation from Homer, should the translation transform its readers into Greek readers of Homeric times, or should it make Homer write as if he were writing today in our language?"[68]

The "foreignizing/domesticating" distinction is, as we shall see, more fuzzy than it is sometimes presented as being, but the broad extremes are recognizable. The Septuagint is a classic example of a "foreignizing" translation, as Rajak demonstrates, in that it systematically "reproduces in the target language [Greek] the form and structure of its equivalent in the source language [Hebrew]": the effect is to make the text feel as if it is somehow "foreign," as if it still has palpable traces to the original, instead of reading seamlessly as a piece of Greek, to the extent that the translation "can be trying to read, sometimes obscure, and occasionally unintelligible to those accustomed to literary Greek, be it classical or Hellenistic."[69]

Rajak has made a compelling case for these features in the Septuagint being part of a thought-out strategy of appropriation and accommodation, but there can be cases where a foreignizing stamp is present because the translators do not have the resources to cope in any other way with the text that is given to them. Such is regularly the case when a dominant external literature is impinging for the first time on an emergent literary system, imprinting markedly foreignizing traits onto the new translations.[70] Here a striking example would be the first Europeanizing dramas ever staged in Russia, commissioned from German-speakers in Moscow by Tsar Alexis, father of Peter the Great, starting in 1672. Translated by Russian officials in the foreign office "into the only written Russian idiom they knew, an archaic mix of Church Slavic and the legalese language of official treaties," the play scripts were "clumsy, . . . often incomprehensible," and riddled with Germanisms "such as the use of German-style auxiliary verbs, which are redundant in Russian."[71] This example conjures up a hair-raising counterfactual scenario in which the first Latin dramatic scripts are translated from Greek by the *scribae quaestorii* in the style they themselves use for their "legalese language of official treaties."

If "foreignizing" translations leave the mark of the original in plain sight, then the "domesticating" approach aims for the opposite effect. John Dryden gives a classic statement of the "domesticating" stance when he states his objective in translating Virgil's *Aeneid*: "I have endeavoured to make Virgil speak such English as he would himself have spoken, if he had been born in England, and in this present age."[72]

Livius Andronicus, as we have already seen with his programmatic choice of *Camena* for Μοῦσα, is very much siding with Dryden in taking the second of Schleiermacher's options.[73] He is systematically domesticating "as part of an overall translation strategy which brings the source text closer to the linguistic and cultural world of the translator's audience."[74] Even in the first line of his *Odyssey,* we see Livius avoiding a formation such as **multiuersutum* to translate the compound *polytropon* of the original: this would have been too foreignizing a move, resulting in something with a non-Latin feel.[75] The excellent summary of Possanza gives key examples, which I reproduce here, of how Livius is Romanizing in "expression, style, and form."[76] The distinctively Greek idiom of "fence (ἕρκος) of the teeth" is not reproduced, but replaced with an image of speech escaping upwards out of the mouth, an idiom that privileges the idea of verbalization as "liberation" of the willing sound (*quid uerbi ex tuo ore supra fugit,* fr. 3). Odysseus' knees are "loosened," following Greek epic idiom (Hom. *Od.* 5. 297), but Ulixes' "heart froze for fear," so that the focus is now on the first origin of fear in the mind rather than on one of its symptoms (*Vlixi cor frixit prae pauore,* fr. 30);[77] *frixit,* "froze," rhymes with the Latin name *Ulixi,* to focus on the hero's new Latin identity, while still preserving the internal rhyme of the original λύτο γούνατα.[78] Homer's Nestor says the dead hero Patroclus was a "counsellor equal to the gods" (Hom. *Od.* 3. 110), but when he speaks in Latin Nestor uses "a more restrained expression familiar to Romans from its use in elogia of members of the socio-political elite," referring to Patroclus as *uir summus adprimus Patroclus* ("a man supreme, the very first," fr. 10).[79] Such choices are especially striking since, as we have seen, the model of governmental interpreting would incline Livius toward stricter fidelity, even at the cost of cultural garishness, of the kind that both Romans and Greeks appear to have tolerated perfectly happily in those official contexts.

Social institutions of the world of the Greek poem are Romanized.[80] The king's daughter, Nausicaa, rides in a *carpentum,* a special two-wheeled carriage used by elite Roman women (fr. 15).[81] Ulixes does not wear a "purple cloak of thick wool, two-folded" as in Homer (χλαῖναν πορφυρέην οὔλην . . . διπλῆν, *Od.* 19. 227), but a "dark, purple garment, large" (*uestis pulla purpurea ampla,* fr. 27); *laena,* the Latin derivative of χλαῖνα, has misleading ceremonial associations for Livius' audience, while *pulla* is a familiar term for them, which helps to domesticate the image of Ulixes at this point.[82] Most strikingly, the disparate fates and homecomings of Homer's heroes are focalized through the imperial view of the Roman state, so that their longed-for destination becomes "Greece," a geopolitical concept that was not available to them or to their original poet: *partim errant, nequinont Graeciam redire* ("partly they wander, they cannot return to Greece," fr. 11).[83] In all of these ways, the persons and perspectives of the Greek heroic age are modernized and adapted wholesale to the cultural frameworks of the new audience.

The meter of the new *Odyssey* is likewise a meter of Rome, for Livius chooses to write in the Saturnian meter, not in the original dactylic hexameters of Homer. Although the use of the Saturnian has regularly been regarded as a sign of Livius' backwardness ever since Ennius first stigmatized the meter as "verses which once upon a time the Fauns and bards sang" (*uorsibus quos olim Faunei uatesque canebant*, fr. 207), we are under no obligation to sign up to the teleological program of Ennius, the first person to compose Homeric dactylic hexameters in Latin.[84] Livius' credentials for metrical transformation are solid, as evidenced by his adaptations of Greek dramatic meters for the Latin stage.[85] His use of the Saturnian is not a default move, forced upon him haplessly because he had the bad luck to be born in the early third century, but rather a conscious choice that is part of an entire transformational strategy: he is deliberately choosing a Latin rather than a Greek meter just as he is deliberately choosing Latin rather than Greek diction and terminology.[86] The Saturnian's history and even nature remain mysterious and controversial, but there is every reason to believe that within Roman society it will have had ritual, sacral, and even prophetic associations:[87] these were the resonances that Livius was seeking out in his attempt to reproduce the elevated atmosphere of the Greek original. How much change Livius brought about in the meter in the process is very difficult to recover, given the controversy over what the criteria are for defining a Saturnian verse.[88] Certainly, the literary and epigraphic remains that can conceivably be bracketed as "Saturnian" form a pretty rough category, and it is possible that Livius and his successor Naevius were not simply taking over a ready-made template but imposing a defining shape, one that was then embraced by the élite.[89] It certainly appears to be the case that Livius and Naevius were the first to use the Saturnian for such extended compositions.[90]

We touched above on the significance of Livius' choices when it came to names in his poem, as he gave *Camena* for "Mousa," and "Ulixes" for "Odysseus." The problem of the names is a crucial one for any translator, and it is even now indicative of deep cultural choices and assumptions. The days are long gone when it felt natural in English translations of Homer to have "Jupiter" or "Jove" for "Zeus," but decisions over how to represent Greek names in English are still not neutral. Those who transliterate instead of giving Latin equivalents are performing a variety of Hellenizing that imparts an air of the authoritative exotic (even though no Anglo-Saxon goes so far as to write "Platon" or "Aristoteles"). Fraenkel protested against this brand of foreignizing, in favor of more domestication: "Scholars who, whether in Germany or in Britain, propagate such artificialities as 'Horatius,' 'Akhilleus,' 'Arkhilokhos' are guilty of widening the gulf between their countrymen and the classics."[91]

On the whole, as we have seen, Livius does not transliterate, but gives equivalents in Latin, either from established cultural equivalences or from his own calques.[92] Sometimes the existing Latin equivalent is itself already a transliteration, or a virtual transliteration, as with the centuries-old "Apollo/Apollon," or "Hercules/Heracles." When no equivalent is to hand, Livius will certainly naturalize, with, for example, "the nymph Calypso, daughter of Atlas" (*nympham Atlantis filiam Calypsonem*, fr. 13). The transliteration of "Circe" (*ad aedis . . . Circae*, fr. 24) is mediated by the nearby place-name of Circeii, which for centuries had been thought to be the home of the Homeric Circe, despite the fact that Homer places her in the far East, and the coincidence has assisted a domestication.[93] Deities of full standing will ideally have a Latin equivalent, even if it has to be calqued or improvised, which is why we find *Camena, Morta, Moneta*. In the dramatic genres also, we find the gods translated and human names transliterated. In Plautus' great play of transformation, *Amphitryo,* we see "Jupiter" and "Mercurius," not "Zeus" and "Hermes," but the human names of "Amphitryon" and "Sosia" remain the same in the Greek or the Latin version, with minimal adaptation (*Ampitruo* for Ἀμφιτρύων)[94]—although Sosia puns on the counterfactual possibility that his Greek name might change to the Roman name *Quintus* when he reacts to Mercury's boast about having beaten up four men with the fear that he might change his name and become Quintus, Number Five, instead of Sosia: *formido male/ne ego hic nomen meum commutem et Quintus fiam e Sosia* (304–5).

For the Roman audience, the constant reiteration of the claim that the Greek and the Roman deities have a convertible quality is part of a wider developing imperial self-consciousness, in which Rome is a newly crucial center for a long-standing habit of cultural exchange.[95] The practice of translatability of divinities is a widespread phenomenon in the ancient world, and Romans, Greeks, Etruscans, and Phoenicians had been claiming an identity in certain deities for a very long time before Livius Andronicus. This divine *interpretatio* is an important part of intercultural traffic and foreign policy, with ideological and theological consequences that are by no means trivial.[96] What we see in Livius' systematic practice of domesticating identification is a new phase in this process of mapping out a world of equivalences. In time, as we shall see in Chapter 7, he and his successors will create a terrain in which new universalizing claims can be made, in the self-conscious knowledge that the Roman deities have a dominant status of a transformative kind.[97]

Livius' epic and dramas begin the systematization of this process, mapping out a world of equivalences, but his works inevitably also call attention to the slippage and failure to mesh that we find in equivalence. Livius' gods combine Greek and Roman dimensions, which are not always readily compatible. His Mercury, for example, will have appeared in Hermes' role of escort of souls to the Underworld in the finale of the *Odyssey,* despite the fact that as a mercantile deity in Rome he had no such function in Roman religion.[98] Such self-consciousness about incommensurability in the process of translation is regularly part of the religious *interpretatio,* and we glimpse a wonderful example of this self-awareness in a fragment of Accius' *Tereus.* The Athenian woman Procne, living in Thrace, proclaims that "Here holiness is different, here the name and nod/divine power of Jupiter is different" (*alia hic sanctitudo est, aliud nomen et numen Iouis,* fr. 646). On the face of it, she is bitterly saying that among Thracian barbarians there is no piety, and in the original Greek, which is now lost to us, she will have been playing upon the widespread conception that there are many local manifestations of "Zeus," each with their own epithets *(nomen)* and prerogatives and areas of influence *(numen).* Speaking to Roman barbarians from a Roman stage, however, she is correct in saying that "name" of the supreme god, *nomen . . . Iouis,* is indeed different "here," in a new kind of way. Where once she was remarking on the comparability of different manifestations of "Zeus," now she is remarking on the translatability of two different religious systems. Her words raise the key question of how much translatability of *numen* ("divine power") there is behind the translatability of the *nomen* ("name"): to what degree is it in fact the same divinity behind the different names?[99]

Translated tragedy and epic, then, are highly self-conscious about how much adjudication of sameness and difference is necessary in these textual negotiations between cultures. A comic counterpart to this insight is available in Plautus' fondness for the figure of the monkey, illuminatingly analyzed by Connors. As she shows, whereas for the Greeks the monkey is a symbol of a failed attempt to attain a higher status, for Plautus the monkey becomes an emblem of a creative inventiveness in imitation of the Greek: "his monkeys mischievously embody in an especially literal way the wider cultural processes of imitation and adaptation and insistence on difference which are central to the development of Roman culture."[100]

In the case of one particularly telling and conspicuous nonhuman name, Livius opts for transliteration and not adaptation. Even though "Odysseus" became "Ulixes" as a character in the narrative, when taking over the title of Homer's epic Livius seems to have given a transliteration, so that his poem was known as ODVSSEIA, barely distinguishable from ΟΔΥΣΣΕΙΑ.[101] Ever since Knoche (1928), it has been regular to give the supposedly authentic original Latin spelling of *Odusia,* on the basis that double "s" did not become normal in writing Latin until well into the second century. Yet this is a misleading piece of faux-archaizing, designed to have the gratifying effect of making Livius look craggily and hoarily archaic. All such orthographic decisions are value-laden. We might compare, as an example, the consequences of the orthographic treatment of Shakespeare's and Spenser's texts. We do not write "Shakespeare's *Tragedie of Hamlet, Prince of Denmarke,*" as was originally printed, any more than we update to produce "Spenser's *Fairy Queen*" instead of *Fairie Queene:* Shakespeare keeps being modernized, while Spenser remains stuck in the late sixteenth century.[102] I am not advocating a global return to Livius' hypothetical original spelling for the sake of it, with, for example, *numpam Calupsonem,* or NVMPAM CALVPSONEM, for the conventionally printed *nympham Calypsonem.*[103] But the title is a special case. Just as with the majority of his dramatic titles, Livius opts for something very close to the Greek original.[104]

At the head of the scroll stands something like LIVI ODVSSEIA. The title of the epic foregrounds the Greekness of the product, while the author's name and the actual language of the work itself are domesticating in the deepest sense, making Rome the new center of a previously Hellenic discourse. In this respect, the Roman translation project runs markedly against the findings of contemporary polysystem translation theory, according to which one should expect first translations in a weak literary system to be strongly foreignizing, just as we saw in the case of Tsar Alexis' first dramas.[105] On the contrary, Livius is domesticating strenuously. The landscape and the seascape of Homer's poem, with the Sicilian and Italian locales so carefully identified by Hellenistic scholarship, have a newly topical identity for Livius' readership, recent victors in titanic land and especially sea warfare against the Carthaginians in and around Sicily.[106] The very choice of the *Odyssey* as the Homeric poem to translate is telling evidence of its topicality, for the *Iliad* was much the more popular of the two Homeric poems in the Hellenistic

period and far more important in the standard curriculum.[107] Livius'
comprehensive strategies of domestication and accommodation are tokens of an assimilative imperial ambition. His epic is making Homer's
Odyssey, the common inheritance of the Hellenic world, into a Roman
possession, peopling it with Roman deities, capitalizing on its action
in an Italian and Sicilian setting, and accommodating it to Roman
customs.

CHAPTER 3

The Interface between
Latin and Greek

BUT WHAT IS ROMAN, and what is not? Who is "Roman"? In speaking of "foreignizing" versus "domesticating," we need to inject more nuance into the distinction, not least in light of the unusual situation of the first composers of a literature in the Latin language. The murky boundaries between the language zones were negotiated by individuals who commanded unusual perspectives and allegiances.

Inside the Intercultural Space

Livius Andronicus was not a Roman, or at least not straightforwardly a Roman, even though eventually he became a citizen. His name, "Livius Andronicus," is as much a hybrid as the superscription to his epic, *Livi Odusseia*. The situation in which Romans will most usually have encountered the change of name and identity from Greek to Latin/Roman will have been in manumission, when a Greek slave was set free: here the original Greek name remained, but it became an addition to a Roman name. This is quite possibly what happened in the case of "Andronikos," who, according to the usual tradition, became a slave when his native city of Taras, Roman Tarentum, was forced to terms by the Romans in

272, and who was later transformed into Livius Andronicus when set free by his master, a Livius. It is in fact just as likely that the Greek Andronikos came to Rome as a free man, an entrepreneur who spotted a niche, and had citizenship eventually bestowed on him, as happened with Ennius in 184.[1] It is interesting to reflect on what is at stake in deciding which of these alternatives we find more compelling—dependent freedman or professional on the make.

In any event, the identity of all the first participants in the translation project was fascinatingly complex, since none of them was born into the status of being a full Roman citizen; instead, they occupied the volatile interstices between the cultures of central and southern Italy, especially Greek, Roman, and Oscan. Suetonius describes Livius and Ennius as *semigraeci*, "half-Greeks" (*Gram. et rhet.* 1. 2), and in a loose sense this description applies to all the first practitioners of the new translation literature, who normally inhabited the interstices between three linguistic cultures, with Greek and Latin as numbers two and three, and the first being Oscan (Naevius), Oscan or Messapic (Ennius, together with his nephew, Pacuvius), Umbrian (Plautus), Gaulish (Statius Caecilius), or Punic (Terence).[2] The first native-born Roman citizen *optimo iure* to take part in this project by writing poetry in Latin is the low-born Accius, son of ex-slaves, who was thirty years old in 140, a century after Livius' first dramatic production of a translation from Greek.[3]

If Livius Andronicus, the Greek who became a Roman citizen, was bilingual, then Naevius, who began producing plays and writing epic shortly after Livius, was trilingual. He was from Campania, born around 270, no doubt into the citizenship *sine suffragio*, and he grew up speaking Oscan, the main language of Campania and of the lower Apennine spine of Italy, as well as Greek and Latin. Ennius, the greatest figure of early Latin literature, was born in 239 at Rudiae, on the heel of Italy, and did not become a Roman citizen until 184, when he was fifty-five years old. He was almost certainly *quadri*-lingual. At the time of his birth, the local language in the region of Rudiae was Messapic, which was presumably his language as a child; he will then have learned Oscan, Greek, and finally Latin. Messapic was not a language of any pan-Italian or literary status, so that when he grew up he claimed only to be trilingual, in the famous dictum reported by Aulus Gellius, *Quintus Ennius tria corda habere sese dicebat quod loqui Graece et Osce et Latine sciret* ("Quintus Ennius used to say that he had three hearts, because he knew how to speak Greek and Oscan and Latin," *NA* 17. 17. 1).[4] In all of these cases, language choice will have been determined for the speaker according to mobile codes that depended on what Adams and Swain refer to as "the *domain* of language use," which they illustrate by referring to Langslow's example of the Austrian poet Grillparzer, who "used Italian for talking of music, French for polite conversation, Greek for philosophy, and Latin for rhetoric."[5]

The environment in third century Italy was a potent mixture of intersecting and competing languages and cultures. It is not surprising that the person who has responded most vividly to the fertility of this period is Mikhail Bakhtin, who closes *Rabelais and His World* with a memorable evocation of the liberating potential of the intersection of Greek theatre, Oscan improvisational farce, and the new power of the Latin theatrical presentations in Rome.[6] In this world, people like Livius Andronicus and Ennius were the indispensible cultural brokers who were able to parlay their skills across linguistic and cultural interstices, and to benefit from the vitally enhanced creative potential that came from inhabiting two or three linguistic cultures at once.[7] These men had the intimate knowledge of the Greek language, and they had the experience of a Greek education from their upbringing in the schools of Magna Graecia, equipping them with the skills that were so hard to come by in an era before dictionaries, encyclopedias, or concordances. They had the Greek books—I find it hard to imagine that you would have had much success if you went to Rome in 240 and tried to locate a copy of Euripides' *Medea*.[8] It was normal Roman practice to import foreign professionals in this way to supplement a gap in home-grown expertise; our culture brokers are part of a pattern.[9]

We return in Chapter 4 to explore in more detail the dynamic potential of these intercultural spaces or contact zones in the last decades of the third century. For now, we note only that this kind of interstitial space is where one historically finds rich terrain for translation, as we saw above;[10] this is the kind of competitive world of interpenetrating cultures out of which emerged the Septuagint, and, later, the *Alexander Romance,* and the Egyptian/Greek traffic of third-century CE Roman Egypt. Translators, as we have seen, are not normally carrying material across from one monoglot and monocultural domain to another, but mediating between bilingual or multilingual environments. The Roman case remains distinctive in that the Greek cultural zone that is the source for the texts to be translated does remain comparatively monoglot in important respects. It was a native speaker of Greek, Livius Andronicus, who first turned his hand to the translation of Greek texts into Latin, yet the educational and literary environment from which he came was, as we have seen, not one that had a tradition of bilingualism in education, literature, or translation. In rather the same way as the Egyptian priest Manetho is part of a response to the disruptive energy of Hellenism, a response that generated translation of Egyptian documents in the process, so Livius is part of a response to the innovatory impact of Roman expansion, one that generated translation of Greek literary texts for the first time.

Situating the translator-poets in this intercultural contact zone helps us to orientate ourselves when we consider the directionality of their translation. We perhaps automatically tend to think of the translation project from a Roman perspective, so that it seems—to use one of the two German adverbs for "out"—to be operating "heraus," as the importation inwards of something *from* outside. From the point of view of the artists, however, the project operates "hinaus," from their position inside Greek culture *to* outside. When Livius translates a Greek poem into Latin, in linguistic terms he is not positioned within Latin culture and reaching out into Greek culture to import something back into Latin culture, he is positioned within Greek culture and exporting something out of it into Latin culture. Or rather, he is both importing and exporting, he is operating both "heraus" and "hinaus"; he participates in both Greek and Latin linguistic cultures, even if, as far as he is concerned, there is only one *literary* culture at the moment he begins his work.

When talking of Roman familiarity with Greek myth or literature as evidenced in Livius and his peers, we need to think of these people making their way into a Roman cultural orbit and finding points of recognition and familiarity and difference there, rather than of Romans looking "out."[11] We are used to thinking of the process of Roman translation as "Hellenizing," and from the point of view of the audience this makes some sense, but from his own point of view Livius is not Hellenizing, he is "Latinizing," or "Romanizing."[12] Indeed, the translation project itself is part of a larger process in which "Hellenization" and "Romanization" are inextricable and mutually implicated aspects of the expansion of Roman power throughout the peninsula. As Wallace-Hadrill has shown, "Hellenization" is the medium "that made the diverse populations of Italy more similar in taste, economic relations and politics" from our period on, yet it is the "Romanization" of the peninsula that is of course the indispensable vehicle for this process.[13]

L1 and L2

If we use this vantage point to consider the options facing Livius (and Naevius, Plautus, and Ennius as well, who were all likewise "Latinizing," as it were, rather than, or as well as, "Hellenizing"), certain of their choices come into a rather different focus, especially as regards the applicability of the terms "foreignizing" and "domesticating."

It is a very unusual situation, at least in the modern world, for translators to work in the direction of Livius and Naevius, since translators "traditionally and now almost by iron rule translate from a foreign language into" their native language.[14] An example of this "L1" translation—translation into the first language of the translator—would be when a native English-speaker translates from French into English, where French is the "source language," and English is the "target language." But Livius Andronicus is a native speaker of the source language, Greek, and not of the target language, Latin. A modern example of this "L2" translation—translation into a *second* language of the translator—would be when a native English-speaker translates from English into French: again, this is very much not the norm in the modern world. L1 translation eventually became the norm at Rome, with Cicero, Catullus, and Germanicus translating into their native language of Latin; but in the first generations L2 translation was the norm, with native or near-native speakers of Greek translating out of Greek into Latin, which was their second or third language.

Grasping this point helps us understand, for example, the distribution of so-called Grecisms in early Latin literature. This term covers a range of phenomena in Latin.[15] The most straightforward category is that of borrowed Greek words, or at least words that are still marked as Greek, unlike words such as *nauta* or *nauis*, which are so thoroughly domesticated by the third century that native speakers do not consciously consider them "non-Latin." Here it is helpful to follow Gitner in using "the German distinction between a *Lehnwort,* an integrated loanword, and a *Fremdwort,* a borrowing still perceived as foreign."[16] Greek morphology can also be marked in Latin, as when Latin authors use Greek case endings, giving, for example, the Greek accusative singular—*a* in names such as *Hectora,* or—*en* for *Cybelen.*[17] Word order can also have a Grecizing effect, as when Latin poets follow Greek models in, for example, postponing co-ordinating conjunctions.[18] The most challenging category of Grecism is the syntactical. When students of Latin begin reading Catullus and Virgil one of their biggest hurdles always comes when they have to grapple with syntactical features in Latin that are borrowed from Greek—the accusative of respect, for example, when phrases such as *percussa mentem* or *restrictus membra catena* have initially to be "translated" into dog-English along the lines of "struck as far as her mind was concerned" or "bound by a chain in respect of his limbs."[19]

It is an arresting fact that all of these Grecisms, which become a regular feature of Classical Latin verse and eventually high prose as well, are extremely rare in the first texts of the poet-translators. Leo put it a little too strongly when he said that "There are no Grecisms at all in the early Roman poetic language" ("Gräcismen gibt es in der altrömischen poetischen Sprache überhaupt nicht"), for one does encounter the occasional example, as when Livius takes over the Greek adverbial use of

a neuter plural adjective in his translation of Homer.[20] But Leo's gener-
alization holds, especially for the Saturnian epics of Livius and Naevius—
even if they can have had no concept of "Grecism" of the kind modern
scholars deploy: their Greek grammatical training naturally had no corresponding category to cover taking over such features from another
language, since Greek writers did not at this time consciously adopt alien
linguistic features.[21]

At the lexical level, "[t]he only Greek words in the epics of Livius and
Naevius seem to be ones already domesticated in the language"[22]—
Lehnwörter, in other words. As for morphology, we have already observed Livius using Latin terminations for Greek names (*Calypsonem,*
Od. fr. 13), and this procedure is the norm in early tragedy as well as
epic.[23] In this regard, the first poets are following the usual procedure
that Latin speakers had followed in assimilating Greek names into
the declensions and morphologies of their own language, producing
Hercules,–ei to be declined like *res.*[24] We see this procedure at work already in "the oldest Greek loanword in Latin," the word *qurois* on the
dedication to Castor and Pollux in Lavinium from the end of the sixth
century, three centuries before Naevius' dramas; the word is obviously
Greek, κοῦροι, describing the *Dioskouroi,* "Sons of Zeus," yet the "ending
is an Old Latin dative plural, not a Greek one."[25]

One first encounters morphological and syntactical Grecisms on any
scale in Ennius' *Annales,* where there is a definite shift in approach,
giving such marked Grecisms as *perculsi pectora* (fr. 310) and *uicit*
Olympia (fr. 523).[26] This is an aspect of the new self-consciously Homer-
izing style in Ennius, which he deployed as part of his overall strategy
of providing a fully modern national epic, in the "correct" meter of Homeric hexameter, invoking the "correctly" named "Muses" instead of
the *Camena* of Livius.[27] Even for Ennius, the *Annales* are an outlier,
and we do not find such Grecizing syntactical features in his tragic
fragments; nor do they occur in comedy.[28] Only fifty years or so after
Ennius' *Annales,* in the tragedies of Accius, do we find the use of Greek
terminations in a name such as "Hector," giving the Greek accusative
Hectora instead of the normal adapted Latin form of *Hectorem,* as

was explicitly remarked upon in a hexameter work of criticism by one Valerius Soranus, around the year 100: *Accius Hectorem nollet facere, Hectora mallet* ("Accius wouldn't want to produce 'Hectorem,' he'd prefer 'Hectora,'" fr. 1 Courtney).[29] And even Accius is fundamentally staying with the norms of the traditional developed tragic style, showing many fewer Grecisms in his tragedies than in his other works on literary history and criticism.[30]

It may strike us as very odd that there is far less Grecism in Livius and Naevius, and even in Ennius, than there is in Catullus or Virgil, given that Greek was the first language of Livius and a childhood language of Naevius. There are certainly a number of factors at work behind this phenomenon, and they are not all recoverable. First of all, it is important to follow Mayer (1999) in seeing that these features of Latin literary diction were genuinely felt by the audiences of these texts to be "exotics." Modern scholars may explain many of these syntactical Grecisms as developments or extensions of existing features of the Latin language, but from a stylistic or literary-critical point of view, what counts—as Mayer crucially sees—is how it appeared to the Latin speaker, and here there is no doubt that Mayer is right to say that "this syntax was unmitigatedly foreign in feel."[31] Nor are we dealing with an inevitable feature of linguistic interaction and of Roman bilingual education. Such foreignizing impact is not something that just naturally follows when you happen to have bilinguals writing; as we have seen, we are dealing with an observable shift over time, and it is a question of conscious choices being made for specific reasons, with control being exercised according to genre and setting.[32]

If we consider the problem from the point of view of the composers, it is important to see that the urge to create a foreign-sounding effect in a translation is a feature of L1 translation, where writers are regularly trying to reproduce in their *own* language something of the effect of strangeness or exoticism that hits them when they read or hear the *other* language. This is going to be true of L1 translators such as Cicero, Catullus, and Virgil in a way it is not true of L2 translators such as Livius and Naevius. The L1 composers are striving for a defamiliarizing effect, as they aim to "make it new" by introducing items that heighten the language in a novel and even disconcerting manner.

In addition, reproducing a foreignizing effect in translation "is only a real option for a translator when working from a language with which the receiving language and its culture have an established relationship."[33] The less foreign the other language feels, and the more accommodating and extensive the existing cultural codes for that brand of foreignness are, then the easier it is to represent its foreignness. As Bellos shows, there are all kinds of accepted ways of representing Frenchness in an English translation, because English and French cultures have a long inter-related history, and English readers of such a translation can be relied upon to have enough French to get the point. It is harder to represent, for example, German-ness in an English translation.[34] It is harder yet to represent Hungarian-ness, and it is more or less impossible to represent Yoruba-ness.[35]

Grecisms eventually become an indispensible element of high Latin literary style, and in this respect there is a big difference from what we can recover of language-learning further down the social register. Here side-by-side Latin and Greek texts show a conscious effort to smooth over constructions that are challengingly different from any equivalent in the other language: on the Latin side, for example, there are no *quin* clauses or ablative absolutes with understood part of *esse* (the "*me consule* construction"), while on the Greek side, there are no participles of the verb "to be" and πρίν + infinitive constructions.[36] But even in élite Latin literature this distinctive brand of representation of foreignness takes a considerable time to develop momentum. It depends partly on the eventual transition whereby the writers of Latin literature are no longer native speakers of Greek but of Latin, and partly on the audience becoming more and more acculturated to Greek literary norms, as the culture develops increasingly systematic codes for representing "Greekness," so that they can intuit the "Greek" behind the Latin.[37] After all, a translator may well want to have a certain confidence that the audience will understand that he is not simply incompetent before he will try on foreignizing effects: "translators are instinctively averse to the risk of being taken for less than fully cultivated writers of their target tongue."[38]

A Literary Language for Rome

As Adams observes, primary speakers of Classical Latin may favor Greek morphology for Greek names in high poetry as a result of wanting to "use the sounds and inflections of Greek to evoke an exotic world."[39] He goes on to draw a contrast with the first composers of Latin poetry, "who persistently Latinised such names." We may now see that part of the explanation for the different choices of the first composers is that these individuals were Greek or primary speakers of Greek rather than of Latin, who will naturally not have perceived Greek as "exotic" in the same way. Yet the factors suggested by Adams as important for these authors are certainly also crucial, namely, that the first poets are motivated "by a sort of linguistic nationalism . . . or at least by a desire to establish a specifically Roman literary language."[40]

The apparent paradox of this variety of "linguistic nationalism" being mobilized by non-Romans who are not primary speakers of Latin takes us back to our earlier discussion of the first translations' radical domesticating strategies, which have been the object of study for over a hundred years. The avoidance of Grecisms highlights yet more vividly how astoundingly deep the first translations are in their domesticating, Romanizing strategies overall. These strategies are based on an intimate knowledge of the language and society of their target culture. In the course of their interstitial shuttling, the first translator-poets have acquired an extraordinary feel for the workings of Roman society, so that the overall knowledge of Roman culture on display in the first translator-poets is very remarkable.

Such cultural knowledge is evident in their feel for the values and the religion of their host society. We have already seen how Livius turns Nestor's praise of Patroclus as "equal to the gods"—language shocking to Roman political morality—into phrasing akin to that used in Roman epigraphs and funerary orations (*Od.* fr. 10). The understanding of Roman religious practice and sentiment in the first epics and dramas is very striking. Naevius, for example, modernizes Greek heroic practice by making the father of Aeneas consult books when he performs prophecy, acting like one of the college of the *decemuiri* (fr. 4).[41] Similarly, the translated figures on the Roman stage ventriloquize Roman ideology and morality even as they mediate the words of the Attic dramas. Ennius' character Andromacha describes Priam's palace as a *templum,* referring to the Roman conception of the Senate's meeting-place as a space established by augury (fr. 88);[42] Hecuba uses the language of Roman political discourse when she remarks that the words of the *opulenti* ("those with *opes,* with social power and influence") have more weight than the words of the *ignobiles* ("those without a *nomen,* of obscure and humble family") (fr. 173);[43] the heroes of Euripides' *Medea* are said to have rowed the Argo themselves (4–5), while "Ennius abandons this detail, perhaps thinking it inappropriate for men of the first social rank to perform such a menial task" (fr. CIII).[44] We shall see in Chapter 5 how these adaptations always bring with them traces of difference, for the "Other" can never be fully domesticated in such translation;[45] yet the fundamental work of domesticating accommodation is very striking and needs to be registered.

The poets' knowledge of their host culture is evident also in their feel for the Latin language and its range of possibilities, which formed the base point for the revolutionary project that faced them: "What the first writers of Latin poetry had above all do to was to develop the resources of their language, and so far as possible create the impression of a poetic medium out of what lay to hand."[46] Of course, it was not straightforwardly "*their* language," a fact that gives an extra edge to the challenge that faced them as they performed this work with and for the Romans, using their Greek training in style and rhetoric to build upon the resources they discovered in their target language.

In the tragic fragments, for example, it is clear that the poets exploit with assurance the diction of the Roman élite's religious, legal, political, and diplomatic discourses in order to start creating a counterpart to the marked language spoken or sung by the characters of the Attic stage: alliteration, anaphora, and ceremonial and ritualized diction are examples of features of the élite's existing discourses that could be capitalized upon by the poets.[47] As Adams remarks in the course of demonstrating the continuity of the style of military reports from the time of his first case, Plautus, it is possible to recover the traces of a range of sophisticated legal, sacral, and oratorical registers that had evolved before what we label "literary prose."[48] The stylized language of hymns and other *carmina* has likewise left its mark on the evolving literary language.[49] "Colloquial" language, however slippery in definition that term may be, has also made some contribution to the language of Republican tragedy.[50] This range of linguistic possibilities forms the base for the "considerable stylistic variation within the tragic register,"[51] and it is the departure point for exuberant innovation and bold experimentation, as the poets "created artificial patterns of words and phrases to a much greater extent than any of the classical Attic poets."[52] Such stylistic effects regularly attracted the censure of a more classicizing age, as when Quintilian criticizes Pacuvius for making up compounds out of a preposition and a pair of words, citing his description of dolphins as *Nerei repandirostrum incuruiceruicum pecus,* "Nereus' back-splayed-snouted in-curve-necked flock" (fr. 408, Quint. 1. 5. 67): Pacuvius' description is itself meant to trump Livius Andronicus' already energetic, though less transgressive image of dolphins as *lasciuum Nerei simum pecus,* "the frisky snub-nosed flock of Nereus" (fr. 5).[53]

In remarkably short order, we see in place "a uniform, firmly-established literary style, namely the style of Roman tragedy, the foundations of which were probably laid by Livius, but which in any case was fully developed and fixed by Naevius."[54] It is precisely the Latin of the élite in the metropolis that is the substratum of the evolving literary language, and this idiolect had itself been developing in response to unprecedented pressures for a century before the translator-poets came on the scene.[55] The poets are keying into the momentum built up by a sharp shift toward a standardization of the Latin language, a process that acquires particular impetus from the moment of Rome's establishment of hegemony over the other Latin states in 338 and her expansion into central Italy directly thereafter.[56] From the mid-fourth century on, the Roman version of the language spoken by all the people in Latium became more and more the prestige version of Latin, although this was a long process that was still work in progress in the time of Cicero and Varro.[57] We observe Plautus, for example, making fun of the Latin spoken by the people of Praeneste. Exactly how different "Praenestine" Latin really was from Roman Latin is irrecoverable, but what counts is the activity of marking off "our" way of speech from that of a possible competitor for status, since Praeneste was a proud and still nominally independent Latin state down to the time of the Social War.[58] In short order, Latin likewise became the language of power in central Italy. One immediately obvious result of the translator-poets' treatment of the Roman dialect as the received standard form of Latin, *tout court,* is that we observe no literary dialects in Latin of the kind that make learning how to read Greek literature such a demanding pleasure, for the literary language created by the interstitial non-Roman translator-poets was vectored on to this one specific form of Latin, the dialect of the élite of the metropolis.[59]

We may look to the well-studied example of archaism in the early poetry for a case of how successfully the translator-poets can manage the expressiveness of their target language as they work to "create the impression of a poetic medium out of what lay to hand."[60] Livius is able to capitalize on the existing resources of Latin in order to convey to his new audience the distinctive aura of antiquity and sublimity that he, as a native Greek speaker, intuited in Homer. For the Roman audience, as for a modern learner of ancient Greek, learning to read Homer is a painful process of coming to grips with what appears at first to be a vast mass of undifferentiated idiom, a panoply of forms and a welter of diction; but for Livius, as Waszink has finely argued, "Homer" is a specifically ancient form of his own language, one very much differentiated from contemporary Greek and from other forms of literary Greek, and he is able to use Latin archaisms along with other techniques in order to "convey to his Roman hearers and readers the impression which the original text had made on himself."[61] Accordingly, the fragments of Livius' epic contain a remarkably high number of archaisms, such as the genitive in —*as* of the first declension, which was centuries obsolete in the spoken language when Livius was writing.[62] The prominent verb *insece* in the first line of his *Odyssey* is already archaic in the third century, with a flavor akin to "impart unto me" in contemporary English.[63] Naevius follows suit in his Saturnian epic, the *Bellum Punicum,* where the archaizing style is an indispensible element in his conception of the appropriate mode for a Roman epic, both in the "mythological" and the "historical" portions.[64]

This is an extremely difficult operation for the pioneers to pull off. Imagine a contemporary translator of Shakespeare into French, who wants to mimic or evoke the somewhat archaic atmosphere that is now part of the experience of Shakespeare for an English audience. One first recourse could be to find a French author, with archaic stylistic characteristics, from an earlier period of literary history and to use that author as a model. But Livius could not do this, since there just were no Latin authors from an earlier period of literary history to use as a model.[65] His points of contact in his target language are more diffuse, and he needs to concentrate them in a marked way in order for his effects to come off.

Crucially, Livius and Naevius are not "archaizing" because they simply happen to be archaic.[66] This archaizing style is deliberately cultivated, and it is genre-specific, for it is associated particularly with epic, no doubt as a result of the L2 poet's initial attempt to find a domesticating counterpart in the target language for something he sees as distinctive in his source text. Livius and Naevius affect a far more archaizing style in their Saturnian epics than they do in their tragedies, and Ennius follows suit, with a much heavier load of archaism in his epic *Annales* than in his dramas.[67] As Fraenkel observed in the case of Livius, this distribution shows not only that Livius had a clear idea in his mind, acquired from his Hellenistic education, of sharp generic distinctions between epic and drama, but it also shows that he had some kind of diversity in Latin to work from, varieties of different registers and discourses, as we saw above, that could give him some traction as he developed his different generic idioms.[68]

Such domesticating strategies are by no means normal in historically comparable scenarios of a prestigious foreign literature being translated into an inexperienced vernacular. A generation after Tsar Alexis' failed first attempts at founding a Europeanizing Russian drama based on translation from German, the similar initiatives of his son Peter the Great were still being handicapped by the same difficulties in forging a literary style in Russian. Peter's translators were still using "the same hybrid of archaic biblical style and equally archaic legalese" of his father's initiatives three decades earlier, while in addition "many unassimilated foreign words invaded the official language, hampering understanding still further"; even more profoundly, when faced with the challenge of translating Molière into Russian in the first decade of the eighteenth century, Peter's commissioned authors had to grapple with the fact that Russian culture did not have the concepts, let alone the words, corresponding to the "pretensions, affectation, flirting, or *préciosité*" of French drama and society.[69]

The convertibility in the interface between Greek and Roman culture in the time of Livius and Naevius is far removed from the difficulty in cultural exchange between Peter the Great's Russia and France. However different the societies of Rome and Greece were, there was enough common ground in their *mores* for the translation project to gain a purchase, and this is not a situation—or a belief—that we should take for granted. This translatability and interpretability of the two cultures is not a universal, and every case has to be taken one by one, for the assertion that translatability can occur is a highly ideologically charged one.[70] The Roman case is particularly interesting, given that "the central, essential, paradox of [Roman] culture was precisely its simultaneous *incorporability* within Greek norms and its insistent *refusal* to construct itself in those terms."[71] Further, as Momigliano argues for Polybius and Posidonius, Greeks could tend to exaggerate the compatibility of the Roman fit with the Greek world.[72] Still, translatability could gain a purchase, and the degree of translatability between the source and target cultures of our study is not something we should take for granted, for there is regularly far more grit in the interlocking gears between source and target culture. The Romans' deliberate engagement with so many aspects of Greek culture did eventually mean that "they put themselves and the Greeks in a unique reciprocal situation."[73]

The paradox of these outsiders being the ones responsible for the creation of a literary language becomes less marked when we reflect on how frequently translation is a spur to precipitate changes in the target language. Livius and his peers are not just responding to or exploiting capacities in the target language, in other words: collaboratively and cumulatively they are effecting systemic changes in Latin, in ways that are analogous to other well-studied cases. As Wardy well puts it, "when translations are influential—for example the translation of Greek philosophy into Latin, the Bible into the Greek Septuagint or the English King James version, or indeed Shakespeare into German—they are quite capable of profoundly changing the languages into which they are put. People all too unreflectingly conceive of the language into which the translation is made as a fixed system to which the alien matter must conform, if it is to earn acceptance. On the contrary, the act of translation can effect a real transformation of the target language."[74] This continued to be the case throughout the history of Classical Latin for translations from Greek, which were "constantly provoking or instilling redefinition of what is possible as written Latin, or indeed as *Kunstprosa*."[75] Again, the situation of the first translators into Latin is piquantly different from the majority of modern examples, and different too even from the case of someone like Cicero, because Livius and Naevius are not working in a tradition that has a received idea that a store of translation is the way to enrich "their" own language.

The new translations and the literature they are building are transforming and redefining what Latin is and what Latin can do. They are doing this not so much by mechanically injecting foreignizing elements into Latin, although lexical items in particular are constantly shifting across from Greek.[76] As we have seen, the first poet-translators avoided

an overtly foreignizing strategy, and when Grecizing became an important part of Latin literary style, it remained confined to that register
and appears to have made little impact on the language more broadly.[77]
The impact of translation on the target language was more diffuse—
enforcing the distillation of existing elements of Latin, encouraging
formal differentiation of register, requiring the creation of new words
and patterns of words, and opening up possibilities for experimentation
that had not existed before, as Latin became a vehicle for epic, tragedy,
comedy, satire, and philosophy. The very study of Latin as a system was
based on the theories and patterns developed for the Greek language.[78]
The whole conception of Latin as an entity, with boundaries and with a
purity to be defended—a phenomenon that gathers real momentum already in the second century—is the result of the translation project. It
is a perspective formed by the process of interlinguistic traffic, which
creates boundaries by appearing to transgress them: the idea of *Latinitas,*
"proper use of Latin," is modeled upon the Greek concept of *Hellenismos,*
"proper use of Greek."[79]

The success of the Roman enterprise in co-opting a widening
circle of collaborators into their developing imperial project is a remarkable phenomenon; and a fine example of this success is provided
by the participation of the cultural brokers, middlemen like Livius and
Naevius, in the sequentially collaborative project of equipping Rome
with a literature and a literary language to be its vehicle.[80] It is basically
a figment of modern nation-state ideology that a nation or a group has a
language that fits snugly onto the political or cultural unit, for historically this is seldom the case.[81] If we should not look for such a circum-
stance in third-century Italy, it remains the case that the Latin language
has an important part to play in the development of an identification
between the Roman state and its army and its allies, as the first stage in
the process that leads to the emergence of Latin as an imperial language, with more and more Italic people trading up to acquire the language of the ruling power.[82] This is not a part of any "language policy"
on the part of the Roman state, and it took centuries, down to the

death of Augustus, for Italy to become a domain of primary speakers of Latin.[83] But it is not possible to imagine the process of Latin developing into such an instrument of power and a language of culture to rival Greek without the developing consciousness of the Latin language as an entity, as an item of status; and part of *that* process is the development of the new literature and of the new idiolect that was its vehicle.[84]

It is worth stressing that the changes undergone by Latin in response to the translation project took place in relation to the Greek language and Greek literature. This may seem so obvious as not to be worth remarking, but it is always important to denaturalize what we take for granted, and the role of Greek in the transformation of the Latin language seems so inevitable that we need to register that other contact languages appear not to have played a comparable role. It could, after all, have happened that authors of Latin texts should reach out to other Italic languages, especially since many of them grew up speaking various of those other languages (Oscan, Umbrian, Gaulish), but such interactions were not part of the formation of the evolving literature in Latin.[85] The evolving relationship between Latin and Greek, given new momentum and direction by the translation project, was an exclusive one in terms of the formation of a literary language. Greece was *the* other language, as evidenced by the phrase *utraque lingua*, "either language," and "for Latin literature, Greek and Greeks were the only reference culture."[86] Earlier on, Etruscan and Punic seem to have been special cases for the Romans, and we have seen that at least one Roman senator knew enough Punic in 146 to be able to chair a committee to translate the Punic agricultural work of Mago, while the extensive passage of Punic spoken by the Carthaginian character in Plautus' *Poenulus* (940–49) presumably meant something to some members of the audience, although this is very controversial.[87] Yet these conditions yielded to the normative situation of the period from the third century on, where we observe a strong Roman reluctance to learn any language other than Greek.[88]

"UP" and "DOWN"

Translation very seldom occurs on a level playing field. There is almost invariably some kind of disparity in prestige or inequality in power to tilt the surface, and these disparities tend to have an effect on the kinds of translations that result. Interestingly, the first literary translations into Latin do not fit neatly into the normally observable patterns of asymmetry. The whole operation is, for example, very unlike the projects of translation in the field of postcolonial and subaltern studies. As Hose (1999a) has pointed out in a bracing counter-factual argument, by the tenets of postcolonial theory the development of Roman culture looks for all the world as if the Romans had actually been conquered by the Greeks instead of the other way around, as they mimic various Greek master-discourses and accommodate themselves to Greek templates and paradigms. In postcolonial translation theory, "the 'foreign' language [the language being translated from] belongs to a politically or culturally dominant nation and the 'native' language [the one being translated into] to a subordinate or subjugated one."[89] The Roman case is much more complicated; the "native" language, Latin, is politically and militarily dominant, to an ever-increasing degree, yet the "foreign" language, Greek, still commands high cultural prestige.[90] The work of someone like the Egyptian priest Manetho is different again in its asymmetries. Taking texts in your own language and putting them into the dominant culture's prestige language of Greek is quite different from taking texts in the dominant literary language of Greek and putting them into a vernacular that has next to no international prestige as a cultural item, no matter what power that vernacular has as the language of a growing imperial force.

Further, as we have already seen, especially through the example of the attempts to bring Europeanizing drama to Russia, newly emerging or weak vernacular literary systems are usually the object of heavily foreignizing styles of translation. The first translations into Latin, by contrast, are strongly domesticating and minimally foreignizing in terms of diction, syntax, and cultural atmosphere. The heavily foreignizing translation style that we can observe for our period is one that runs in the opposite direction, from Latin to Greek, as the official jargon of the Roman state leaves its tracks on the Latinate Greek versions of senatorial decrees.

The relative prestige and status of Latin and Greek are in flux as the Roman translation project gets underway, and the status relationship between Romans and Greeks is itself not one that can be neatly imposed onto the diagram of the relative status of their languages. We must remain alert to the fact that "Greek" is not just "Greek" for the Romans of our—or any—period. The status and prestige of the Greek shimmering behind the translated surface of tragedy or Saturnian epic is very different from the flavor of the Greek employed by the code-switching characters of Plautus: "The Greek in Plautine comedy is not the Greek of the originals he adapted but rather the Greek spoken in Rome and the rest of Italy, and its connotations are not prestige and education but servile status and frivolity."[91] These extremes reveal the peculiar range of the connotations of the "same" language, which was associated with ancient prestigious cultural artifacts and practices at the same time as it was an everyday language of low status, spoken in Rome by slaves, freedmen, and practitioners of professions not held in high regard by the élite, such as medicine and pedagogy: Greek "was, paradoxically, both a lower-class and an upper-class language within the same society."[92]

A helpful road map through the terrain of such interfaces is provided by Bellos's discussion of the UPs and DOWNs of translation. As he puts it, "[t]ranslation UP is toward a language of greater prestige than the source. . . . At other times UP may be toward a language with a larger readership. . . . It may also simply be the language of the conquerors, or of a people with greater economic power." Conversely, "[t]ranslation DOWN is toward a vernacular with a smaller audience than the source, or toward one with less cultural, economic, or religious prestige, or one not used as a vehicular tongue."[93] As an example of translation DOWN, Bellos points to the Austro-Hungarian Empire, where "laws, regulations, official announcements, and daily news were translated from German, the language of the court and imperial administration, into the seventeen official languages of that ramshackle state." Another clear example is to be found in the Spanish Philippines, where "the direction of translation was always downward, from Latin into Castilian, and from Castilian into Tagalog."[94] Literary texts, together with "philosophical and mathematical treatises, and religious texts" tend not to accompany the official communications to the same degree, because the speakers of the lower status vernaculars who might be an audience for such texts tend to trade up by learning the dominant language, as was the case with German in the Austro-Hungarian Empire.[95] This is essentially what happened with Greek in the Hellenic Mediterranean and Near East, where local élites traded up to join the mainstream by learning Greek, obviating the need for translation of such material into their vernaculars; here we have a classic case of how "the prestige language functions as the mediator of modernism."[96]

As Bellos argues, the type of translation one tends to find in each case is rather different. Translations UP "toward the more general and prestigious tongue are characteristically highly adaptive, erasing most of the traces of the text's foreign origin; whereas translations DOWN tend to leave a visible residue of the source, because in those circumstances foreignness itself carries prestige."[97] From this perspective, in the third century Latin is UP in relation to Greek. The translations of literary texts into Latin are indeed "highly adaptive, erasing most of the traces of the text's foreign origin," so that we have a case of translating UP into Latin, while the aggressive leaving of Latin traces in official texts translated into Greek is a classic example of translating DOWN. The L2 poet-translators are treating Latin as a language of prestige, to which they must make accommodations, and the Roman state is treating Greek as a less prestigious language, to which their agents and officials need to make minimal accommodation. Considering the immense contemporary prestige of the Greek language and culture in general, this is a striking phenomenon, and it is testimony to a remarkable self-assurance commanded by the Romans: one would otherwise have assumed that the Greeks who are translating Greek literary texts into Latin would have done so in a characteristically foreignizing manner.

The turns adopted by the translation project look rather like a way of pushing back against that potentially threatening cultural dominance; they are part and parcel of the assertiveness and even aggression with which the Romans could negotiate their interactions with Greeks and the Greek language.[98] At the same time, the very existence of the translation project is of course evidence of admiration for and envy of the other culture: otherwise, why adapt some of the most prestigious of its monuments? A much later, but still relevant, body of evidence sheds some light on what was at stake in the late third century. Eleanor Dickey's fascinating study of the Imperial school language-learning texts reveals a striking disparity in focalization: "whereas Latin speakers learned Greek in order to gain access to Greek literature and culture, Greek speakers learned Latin because it was useful."[99] As she says, "Romans would have wanted vocabulary related to philosophy, sculpture, painting, literature, literary criticism, scholarship, and the history and culture of Athens in the archaic and classical periods; these are all topics that a Greek speaker would have little interest in discussing in Latin."[100] Rather similarly, the élite who commission and pay for the new translated dramas of the third and second centuries are responding to a view of Greek culture as a high-status possession, which they are attempting to appropriate and access in novel ways.

We return in Chapter 5 to consider in more detail the dynamics of imitation and distancing behind the Roman appropriation of Homeric epic and Attic drama. For now, we note that the translators of Greek literary texts into Latin are modeling a relationship between the languages and cultures that is considerably more nuanced than we observe in many other cases. It could have been easy for them to patronize the target language as they adapted their high-status artifacts for local circumstances, yet their work has no such features. In a fluid environment, they skirted the obvious hierarchies and asymmetries and produced something like a level between the flows of UP and DOWN.

A Bilingual Governing Élite

The immediate target audience for the new translations comprises the inhabitants of the metropolis, especially the élite, who supplied the magistrates responsible for commissioning them. This élite is becoming more and more bilingual as our period goes by, since the norms of Roman education increasingly rely on bilingual instruction, with a recognizably Hellenistic education syllabus in place for the élite by the end of the Hannibalic war.[101] It is, of course, important to recognize that there is not one thing that is "bilingualism," as Horsfall has pointed out: "It is unproductive to consider bilingualism as a phenomenon single, whole and unitary; to read, to write, to comprehend and to speak a second language are four distinct, though related talents."[102] Bilingualism, then, is not the same as being able to write two languages or scripts: most bilinguals can write in only one language (or in none, especially in an ancient context). Yet the Roman élite during our period became not only bilingual but also literate in two languages, although not in some globally competent sense. Even a highly educated Roman of the second or first century did not swim as naturally in philosophy or poetry as he perhaps could in oratory and history, to cite the case of Cicero's character M. Antonius (*cos.* 99).[103]

The Greek that such people heard spoken around them was the *koinē* of the Hellenistic world, which did not provide a clear window onto the Greek of Demosthenes, let alone Thucydides, let alone Homer or Archilochus.[104] Further, this group was not in the least homogeneous in their attitude towards the "other" language, its speakers, and its texts.[105] Still, even given this varied range of sympathy and competence, it is clear that already in the third century the poet-translators could rely upon their audiences knowing enough Greek to be able, for example, to catch reasonably sophisticated translingual puns. These are, after all, the same people who could savor the translingual pun in the name Aemilius Lepidus, a pun which depended on the *cognomen* of *lepidus*, "charming," "graceful," evoking the Greek word αἱμυλία, "a wheedling way with words," that could be detected lurking behind the *nomen* of *Aimilius* (the middle Republican spelling).[106]

Plautus has been closely studied in this connection, with Fontaine recently making the most far-reaching claims for the depth of the knowledge of Greek language and literature on the part of a Plautine audience whom he characterizes as "enthusiastic, philhellenic, and aristocratic."[107] At the very least, Plautus expected that he could, for example, land a punch with a pun on the Greek root for "lie" in his slave-hero's name "*Pseud*olus" (*Pseud.* 403, 927). Ennius attracted censure from Varro for following Euripides in saying that "the shepherds now call Paris 'Alexander,'" after he warded off robbers from their herds (*quapropter Parim pastores nunc Alexandrum uocant*, fr. 64); in the original Greek, the etymology of "Warder-off of Men" within the new name *Alex-ander* was clear, according to Varro, but not in Ennius' Latin (*LL* 7. 82). This is not a mistake, however, as Varro would have it *(est lapsus),* but a knowing piece of translingual lore, as is the declaration in *Andromache,* likewise criticized by Varro in the same passage, that "He who gave her the name Andromache named her correctly" (*Andromachae nomen qui indidit recte ei indidit,* fr. 99); here the audience needs to know the Greek etymology of her name, ἀνδρὶ μάχεται, "she fights against man."[108] Wordgames of this kind are constructing the audience as masters of the translinguistic field; it is interesting that a person like Varro, who could have read Virgil's *Georgics,* where such plays abound, is doggedly missing the point of Ennius' procedures. Again, when one of Pacuvius' tragic heroes proclaimed from the stage that "what our people call 'sky' the Greeks call 'aether'" (*id quod nostri caelum memorant Grai perhibent aethera,* fr. 89), he was not telling his audience anything they did not know already; these words are not didactic, but part of a consistent destabilizing strategy, of decentering assumptions about who "we" are within the translating space.[109]

This is a very remarkable state of affairs in an ancient context. We have already observed that extensive élite bilingual education was not a normal condition in the ancient Mediterranean. We take the fact of élite Roman bilingualism so much for granted that it is easy to overlook how extraordinary it is that the Roman élite learned not only to speak but to read and even to write, at some level, the language of one of the groups they had conquered.[110] The Greek ruling class of Egypt did not have a bilingual education in the language of their subjects: we have seen that the Ptolemies had been ruling Egypt for over 250 years before someone came to the throne who could speak Egyptian, and there is no reason to think that even she could read or write it. The Seleucids did not learn Persian or Aramaic as they ruled over their conquests. In their turn, the Persian royalty and nobility did not undergo a bilingual education that schooled them in one of the many languages of their far-flung empire, although some of the Persian ruling class will certainly have learned other languages during their tours of duty in various satrapies. The evidence is disconcertingly patchy, and is based in part on inferences from naming practices, for Persian nobles sometimes have patronymics that are Egyptian, Babylonian, Greek, or Lycian, so that one assumes intermarriage and some degree of bilingualism.[111]

In the case of Persian knowledge of Greek, we have snippets of evidence. Herodotus gives us an anecdote of a Persian speaking in Greek with a man from Orchomenus called Thersander, whom Herodotus meticulously cites as his informant (9. 16); Xenophon describes Pategyas, a trusted adviser of the rebel Cyrus, shouting out a warning to everyone of the king's army's approach καὶ βαρβαρικῶς καὶ ἑλληνικῶς, "both in Persian and in Greek" (1. 8. 1); Quintus Curtius says that Darius III was not a novice in Greek (*haud rudis Graecae linguae*, 5. 11. 5), in a context where another high-ranking Persian, Bessus, is explicitly said not to know any Greek (5. 11. 7). Darius still had a Greek interpreter (5. 13. 7), and as his case shows, there is nothing to stop someone who has some functional command of another language using an interpreter.[112] Indeed, it can be a positive advantage, as in the modern case of the French president François Mitterand, who had very good German but still found it useful to have the extra time for reflection provided by the interpreting pause when he was meeting with Chancellor Kohl.[113] The Persian élite could of course manipulate local texts, or local knowledge, without necessarily knowing the local language or texts at first hand. Xerxes could stage a visit to Priam's Troy (Hdt. 7. 43) at the beginning of his invasion of Greece in 480 and then desecrate the tomb of Protesilaus, the unjust man who began the attack on Asia (Hdt. 9. 116);[114] this does not mean that Xerxes knew the text of Homer in any form (the role of Protesilaus is clearly news to him), but it is evidence that the Persian staff knew local traditions and took an interest in working with or against them.

Some Persian nobles, then, appear to have learned Greek, Egyptian or Aramaic. What stands out in the Roman case is the scale and systematic nature of the bilingual education that was evolving during our period. I am not trying to give the Persian ruling nobility a bad grade because they did not have the foresight to realize that texts in Greek would one day form the basis of curricula for introductory Western liberal arts education courses. The point is that ruling a polyglot empire in the ancient world did not necessitate learning any of the subject languages, any more than it does nowadays: the contemporary American dominion is likewise run by monoglots. The self-consciously hard-nosed Gaius Marius enunciated the normal ancient attitude, the road not actually taken by the Romans, when he said that "it was ridiculous to study a literature when its teachers were subjects of another people" (Plut. *Mar.* 2. 2).

The Roman élite's command of Greek had direct political consequences, in that it eventually enabled them to have control over the Eastern portion of their empire, where Greek could be a common language of government and administration. In time, two languages sufficed for Rome to rule her polyglot empire: bluntly, they could rule the West by means of the local élites trading "up" to learn Latin, and they could rule the East by virtue of the fact that their own élite learned Greek.[115]

Yet the audiences of Livius' and Naevius' first dramas did not know that their grandsons would one day be ruling the Eastern Mediterranean, and even if they must certainly have found some command of Greek an asset in their control of their new dominions in Magna Graecia and Sicily, other factors are also at play. Their annexing of these new aspects of Hellenism is a decisive intensification in a long-standing relationship with Greek culture, which had always represented a very special case for them. Paul Veyne exaggerates, but not by very much, when he claims that, for the Romans, "Hellenistic civilization was . . . not Greek civilization or foreign civilization, but civilization pure and simple."[116]

What were the new circumstances that produced a new kind of appropriation of this familiar civilization on the part of the Roman élite? At the beginning of our period, no Roman military force had ever gone east of Italy, and their direct acquaintance with the Greek world was as yet confined to Magna Graecia and Sicily. We need to turn to the interfaces within this world in order to begin addressing the question of what it was that they might have thought they were getting out of this new orientation towards Greek culture, and in order to put more context into our discussion of the translation project. It is a cliché of contemporary translation studies that in translating "we bring into play not only two languages but also two cultures."[117] It is time to investigate the broader interactive cultural conditions that brought into being the new translations and their unpredictable cascade effects. The translator-poets were working from within the interstices between groups who were undergoing profound change, and within institutions and protocols that were likewise in rapid transition. In the next chapter we examine the Italian and wider Greek setting for the revolution we have been investigating.

CHAPTER 4

Middle Grounds,
Zones of Contact

NOTHING COMES FROM NOTHING. When Livius Andronicus was commissioned in 240 to translate an Attic dramatic script into Latin for a tragic performance at the *Ludi Romani,* the greatest Roman state festival, this was a revolutionary moment, one that would have remarkable consequences, but it did not come out of nowhere. In Chapter 8, we discuss the range of possible scenarios for literary or verbal artistic culture in Rome before the translation project, but here we concentrate on the stage shows. The new translated dramas that became part of the Games from 240 on were certainly an innovation within the conventional format of the *Ludi Romani,* but there was an existing slot for a stage performance already in place as part of the Games. *Ludi scaenici,* "stage shows," had been introduced as a new component of the *Ludi Romani* in 364, more than 120 years before Livius and his collaborators first staged a translated version of an Attic script. These earlier shows were themselves inconceivable without the influence—however mediated and indirect—of Greek drama, which had made its impact felt in southern and central Italy for many years before the reform of 364. In order to contextualize the new developments of 240, we need an idea of this deeper background, both in terms of what use the cultures of Italy were making of Greek drama before 240 and also in terms of what use the Roman state was making of its major festival, the *Ludi Romani*.

As far as the *Ludi* are concerned, it is clear that Livius and his peers are not just translating random texts that happen to strike their fancy. Virtually all of the early translations from Greek into Latin are of drama, commissioned by magistrates of the Roman state for performance at state religious festivals, and the innovations in the *Ludi* were the result of political decisions taken by the Senate and the responsible Roman magistrates and fostered by their successors.[1] All of the major reforms of the *Ludi Romani* came in response to large-scale political changes, perhaps even as far back as the expulsion of the kings: certainly the Roman political revolution of 367–366 was, as we shall see, a key context for the reform of the *Ludi* in 364, and the innovation in the *Ludi* in 240 was likewise part of a response to unprecedented transformations undergone by the Roman state.

As I shall argue in this chapter, the reconception of the *Ludi Romani* that we observe in 240 was not just a matter of internal negotiations between members of the Roman élite but part of a new kind of international dialogue as the Roman state repositioned itself in response to new possibilities and commitments in the immediate aftermath of the Great War with Carthage in Sicily (264–241).[2] This is an environment in which both the poet-translators and their commissioning magistrates have a heightened self-consciousness about what is at stake in the meetings between cultures, not only between languages or texts. In thinking of the Romans' interactions with other cultures, we are not dealing with a self-contained core Roman culture that is bolting on an optional accessory, for Roman culture is itself not a defined self-contained entity in the first place; what counts as Roman culture is continually being reinvented and redefined as a result of the mutual interaction between the Romans and other peoples with whom they progressively come into contact.[3] Translation highlights this point in a particularly vivid way, since the translators are the classic go-betweens, creating difference between cultures even as they mediate.[4]

Greek culture is of course a key "other" culture for the Romans to be in dialogue with, and the degree of their receptivity to Greek culture appears always to have been especially avid.[5] Greek drama is an essential part of the dialogue that particularly engages us here. In order to set the scene for the switch in receptivity toward this specific aspect of Greek culture that we see in 240, we need a picture of the larger context of the various forms of impact that Greek drama had previously had on their sphere of knowledge.[6] Here we are fortunate to be able to draw upon the results of the recent revolution in the study of Greek drama outside Athens.

Greek Drama, from Magna Graecia to Central Italy

After decades of scholarship focusing on what Athenian drama meant for Athenian civic culture, we now have a distinguished body of work on the rapid and widely diffused impact of Athenian tragic and comic drama outside Attica and even outside the zone of primary Greek speakers.[7] Aeschylus already travelled to Sicily in 476/5 to oversee a production of his *Persae*, as part of the Syracusan tyrant Hieron's attempts to show that his part in the defense of Hellenism against Carthaginian barbarism deserved to be ranked with the achievements of the mainland Greeks' defeat of the expedition of Xerxes (*Vita* 9). Aeschylus also wrote and directed in Syracuse a performance of a new tragedy, *Women of Aetna,* to honor Hieron's foundation of the city of Aetna (*Vita* 18). From a Sicilian perspective, even speaking of the "impact of Athenian drama on Sicily" could look too Athenocentric, for they had their own story to tell about the Sicilian origins of tragedy and comedy.[8]

During the fourth century theater-building took off throughout the Greek world; there is evidence for over ninety-five permanent theaters being built outside Athens by the end of the century, and there will have been temporary and *ad hoc* venues for performance in addition to these.[9] These new theaters were used. Dramatic performances proliferated outside Athens in escalating fashion from the late fifth century onward, and found a receptive audience not only in Sicily, where drama was big business even earlier, but also in Magna Graecia.[10] Many Greek states introduced dramatic components to existing festivals or founded imitations of the Athenian Dionysia, while the Macedonian monarchs Philip II and Alexander the Great, together with the Successor kings, were adept at the staging of great festivals, including drama, to celebrate military victories and weddings and so on:[11] the Macedonian attempt to lay claim to the patrimony of Athenian and especially Euripidean drama is a very important chapter in the reception of Athenian drama, and it has direct relevance, as we shall see, to the Roman experience.[12] Local playwrights also started to write plays, both for production at the Athenian festivals and also, conceivably, for local production as well: we know of a tragedian called Patrocles from Thurii, together with the Syracusan tyrant Dionysius, who won at the Athenian Lenaea in 367, while the comic playwright Alexis was born in Thurii around 375.[13]

Sicily was to take on a new kind of importance for the Romans when it became the cockpit for the Great War with Carthage, but the southern Italian context is the world from which the first translator-poets came, and this area was the seedbed for the first contacts that central Italy had with the performance of Greek drama. The flourishing dramatic culture of Taras/Tarentum in particular had a knock-on effect in the zones of contact fringing out from the southern Italian coast. Numerous surviving vases, produced for the local southern Italian market, have detailed representations of scenes from drama. Even if some of them may conceivably depict plays written by poets from Magna Graecia, they remain evidence of an enthusiastic audience for travelling players' productions of canonical Greek comedy and tragedy right up into Apulia, in areas inhabited by people who were not primary speakers of Greek.[14] Although some have argued that only Hellenophones could have appreciated Attic drama in the original language, and that the vases must therefore not be intended as representations of staged performance, there is no reason to doubt that there was an Italian market of non-Greeks who were keen to watch Greek performances of Attic drama. After all, what range of command of German and Italian is there in an American or English audience of Wagner or Verdi? There will have been a wide spectrum of competence in Apulia as well, and we do not have to choose between a scenario where everyone is fluent in Greek and can therefore get everything out of the play or a scenario where no one knows any Greek and can therefore get nothing.[15] What is needed is for enough people to get enough of it to make it worthwhile, and it would seem that this was regularly the case in the contact zones of southern Italy.[16]

The frequent performance of Greek drama in southern Italy led to the creation of novel fusion forms as the various local cultures reacted in their different ways to the charismatic appeal of the new medium and adapted their own existing musical and dance practices in the process. As Robinson puts it, speaking of the fourth century, "New interpretations of theatre, and new hybrid forms of performance were emerging in Italic centres."[17] Wiseman has collected a range of fascinating material, especially from central Italian and Latin bronze caskets and mirrors, that appears to be evidence of "a common fourth-century culture of mimetic representation extending far beyond the Greek cities of southern Italy and into Etruria and Latium."[18] These shows represent a medley of styles, from tragedy to strip-tease, "mix[ing] hero-tales with erotic farce," and they play freely with the received figures of myth, issuing from "an imaginative mythic world in which the characters of Greek heroic legend, known not from texts but from oral story, might be combined in quite uncanonical ways."[19]

None of this divergent response to Greek dramatic culture necessarily means that the people involved knew Greek, or knew it well—although it does not mean that they did not. The modern example of the impact of Japanese art on nineteenth- and twentieth-century European art, or the ancient example of the geographically much more intimate interaction between Classical Athens and Persia, both show that enthusiastic reception which is very sophisticated in the receiving culture's terms can take place despite deep ignorance of what the items in question signify in the other culture, and certainly despite complete ignorance of the other culture's language. Again, there will have been a spectrum of knowledge and expertise, and a wide variety of agendas.

The Italian peoples' varying responses to the drama of Hellenism are characteristic of the way in which different groups participated in the evolving *koinē* of central and southern Italy, where Hellenism was becoming "*the* cultural language."[20] The Italian scene is part of a much larger picture: as Burkert puts it, by about 500 "Greek style had become a model for the whole of the Mediterranean world."[21] In this respect, Greek culture was like American culture in the contemporary world, the accepted common international medium for entertainment and consumer products.[22] The "common culture" denoted by *koinē* does not by any means imply that all of these cultures are engaging with Hellenism in the same way, but there is a remarkable degree of shared artistic expression in fourth century Italy, with "no radical difference in quality or concept of either artistic or material culture between Southern Italy and Central Italy or between Magna Graecia and the Italian 'natives,' from Lucania to Rome and Etruria."[23] Hellenism is a key medium through which these groups meet and define each other, so that the *koinē* is a kind of zone of exchange.

Such zones of interaction are highly dynamic, and the flow of energy is not all in one direction. It is not just a matter of "native" cultures passively accepting what the Greeks have to offer, nor even just a matter of "native" cultures reacting creatively and independently—it looks as if the Tarentine theater itself underwent significant changes as a result of the feedback loop linking them with their neighbors.[24] The tantalizingly intriguing figure of Rhinthon has attracted speculation in this vein. A native of Syracuse, he came to Tarentum some time before 300 and became known there for a new form of Greek drama, written in Doric, the dialect of both Syracuse and Tarentum, not in the Attic of the spoken portions of Classical Athenian drama. These new dramas appear to have been in a medley of styles, grounded in parody of tragedy, and they were referred to by later authors as φλύακες "farces," or ἱλαροτραγῳδίαι, "cheerful tragedies."[25] It is quite possible that this new form was itself some kind of fusion, arising from dialogue with local traditions.[26] It is likewise conceivable that some non-Greek Italian peoples adapted Greek plays into their own languages to one degree of fidelity or other. It cannot be ruled out, although there is no evidence that they did do this, or that such adaptations were scripted if they took place, or that such scripts were transmitted, if they were ever written. We remain in the dark on this possibility, although we should bear in mind the general rarity of translation of literary texts, as presented in Chapter 1, when we entertain its likelihood.

The Italian peoples' adventurous work with Greek myth and performance that we glimpse in the fourth-century evidence represents a model of cultural interchange that is very familiar, one where fidelity or even understanding are not necessarily at issue at all, or only tangentially. A rich "mutual creative misunderstanding" can flourish in such a "middle ground," as White has termed these areas in his case study of the cultural space created in the Great Lakes region through the interaction of Indian, French, and then British participants.[27] Characteristic of such spaces is the absence of marked power asymmetry. The players are not all of equal strength by any means, but a "middle ground" ceases to be such when one of the actors is able to move to an assertion of real dominance, as the French and then the British were eventually able to do against White's other protagonists.[28] Within the broad area of central and southern Italy in the early fourth century, when Rome had not yet established hegemony over even her immediate neighbors and was recovering from the Gallic sack of 390, we are indeed dealing with a competitive cultural space without a single presence that commanded preponderant military and political authority. That would not remain the case for very long.

The New *Ludi Scaenici* of 364

The central Italian interactions with Greek performance traditions stemming from Magna Graecia are an indispensable context for thinking about the introduction of the very first *ludi scaenici* as part of the *Ludi Romani* in 364. As we look forward to 240, it is worth our while to consider the introduction of the first formal stage shows in Rome. It will help us gain some idea of what the Romans were watching at the stage games before Livius Andronicus' first staged translation, in order to put more precisely into focus what was new about the reform in 240; it will highlight how crucial an instrument of public policy the *Ludi* were in the Roman Republic; finally, it will highlight the international character of the *Ludi,* so as to sharpen our apprehension of the new international environment for which the *Ludi* were once again reformed in 240.

If we are to put any stock in our sources, the introduction of stage shows to the *Ludi Romani* came at the end of a period of comparative peace and just before an explosive decade of warfare that set Roman power on its path to becoming by far the strongest state in Italy by the end of the fourth century.[29] A main driver for this sudden expansion was the resolution of the long-standing internal political strife that had resulted from the existing élite's refusal to admit "plebeian" competitors to the highest commands and offices. The details of this process do not concern us here, but the new accommodation within what was to become the Roman Republican nobility was clearly an important setting for the reform of the *Ludi Romani.*[30] During the years 367/6, especially as a result of the so-called Licinio-Sextian Rogations of 367, the distinctive features of the classic form of Republican government came into being: new magistracies were created (the praetorship and the "curule" aedileship), while the large college of consular tribunes was abolished and the highest command was now to be shared between two consuls, one each from the patricians and plebeians. Sure enough, the first plebeian to become consul was L. Sextius Lateranus, in 366, the year after he and his fellow tribune of the plebs, C. Licinius Stolo, had the Licinio-Sextian Rogations passed.[31] The consequences of this realignment within the élite were very great, enough to justify Flower's identification of this watershed as the moment when her "second Republic" came into being, the immediate precursor of the "Republic of the *nobiles*" that was to lead Rome to dominion over the Mediterranean.[32]

The events of 367/6, with the election of the first consul from the *plebs,* were already marked out by the first Roman historian, Fabius Pictor, as a crucial moment in the city's history.[33] Livy highlights the pivotal significance of these events and of the concomitant changes to the *Ludi Romani* through a skillful piece of book composition across the boundaries between Books 6 and 7. Book 6 closes with the great hero Camillus brokering the deal that leads to the acceptance of the first plebeian consul's election; the Senate decide to celebrate the new concord by adding a fourth day to the traditional three days of the *Ludi,* and new magistrates are elected to oversee these special Games (6. 42. 9–14). Book 7 opens with the first plebeian consul taking office (366) and with the filling of the various new magistracies (7. 1. 1–2). Very quickly Livy passes to the next year, 365, when a pestilence breaks out and claims the life of Camillus, who is hailed as being "the second founder of the city of Rome after Romulus" (*secundum a Romulo conditorem urbis Romanae,* 7. 1. 10). Immediately thereafter, in the year 364, with the pestilence still raging, the state attempts to appease the angry gods with a *lectisternium,* a special Greek-style banquet for the gods, and finally they resort to the introduction from Etruria of *ludi scaenici* to the *Ludi Romani* (7. 2. 1–3). For programmatic reasons of his own, Livy refers disparagingly to this innovation, and even introduces the year with dead-pan irony as a year when "nothing worth preserving in memory took place" (*nihil dignum memoria actum,* 7. 2. 2); but his very organization of the ending and opening of his Books 6 and 7 has marked the new games as a watershed, with the death of Camillus demarcating the restoration of the city's fortunes after the Gallic sack from this revolutionary moment (*res nova,* 7. 2. 3).[34]

A number of important reforms are in train during these turbulent years, and the *Ludi Romani* are involved intimately in them. A significant rethinking of the *Ludi Romani* took place, just as appears to have been the case after the expulsion of the kings almost a century and a half before, when the formerly intermittent *Ludi* first became fixed as an annual event in honor of the supreme god of the Republic, Jupiter Optimus Maximus, anchored on his special feast day, the Ides of September, the day of the dedication of his Capitoline temple.[35] As we have seen, in 367, the same year as the Licinio-Sextian Rogations, the *Ludi Romani* had another day added to make a total of four (Liv. 6. 42. 12), thus setting the scene for a change in format.[36] Yet two new sets of personnel needed to be in place in order to enable the introduction of the *ludi scaenici* into the *Ludi Romani* three years later.

In 368 or 367 the College of Two Men for the Performance of Sacred Rites, *IIuiri sacris faciundis,* had its membership multiplied by five, to become the *Xuiri sacris faciundis;* instead of two patricians in the college there were now to be five patricians and five plebeians (Liv. 6. 37. 12, 42. 2).[37] The opening up of a major priesthood to plebeians was seen as an indication that the consulate would follow (Liv. 6. 42. 2), and the new plebeian members of the college would be eager to make a mark.[38] The college was responsible for the care and consultation of the Sibylline Oracles, Greek hexameter texts stored in the temple of Jupiter Optimus Maximus, and also for any action involving the *ritus Graecus,* ritual involving anything categorized by the Romans as "Greek." These priests were associated especially with religious innovation in Rome, for religious change regularly came marked as "Greek"; they were soon to be involved in the run-up to the reform of the *Ludi Romani.*

The magistrates in charge of actually running the *Ludi* were the aediles, who up until 366 had been exclusively plebeian officers. Now they were to be elected by the whole citizen body. Things did not go smoothly at first, it seems, because the plebeian aediles baulked at the prospect of paying for the newly augmented games in 366. As a result, the people elected new patrician equivalents to run the games, named "curule" aediles, as they had the right to sit on the special curule chair otherwise only used by the consuls and praetor (Liv. 6. 42. 13);[39] in short order, the curule aediles were alternately patrician and plebeian (Liv. 7. 1. 2). These new aediles, like the new plebeian *Xuiri sacris faciundis,* would be anxious to make a mark, and they could do so by exploiting their prerogative of mounting the upgraded *Ludi.* It was these first curule aediles who ran the new, extended, *Ludi Romani* for the first time in 366, and two years later it was the plebeian M. Popillius Laenas, holding the curule aedileship, who together with a colleague whose name is now lost to history took the decisive step of introducing "stage shows" to the augmented Games.[40] As one of the most prominent rising plebeian stars, destined to be consul four or five times from 359 on, Laenas appears to have seized his chance to capitalize on the opportunities for self-promotion provided by the recently reorganized *Ludi* as he introduced a popular new dimension to the Games.[41]

It is, as we shall repeatedly see, a feature of Roman innovation that it should be tied to the creative "solution" of a great crisis.[42] In the years surrounding these reforms of the *Ludi Romani*, the Romans negotiated a high-stakes political crisis in an environment of religious experimentation and innovation. Pestilence, the death of the state's father-figure, an apparently intractable constitutional impasse—all these threats are creatively turned into an opportunity to wipe the slate clean and to deliver solutions that could not otherwise have been accepted. The showcase for the resolution is a reform in the state's principal religious festival, and the mechanisms for that reform are ostentatiously attributed to outside powers that can be harnessed by the state's experts in religious negotiation with the world beyond the *pomerium*, the newly enhanced college of the *decemuiri sacris faciundis*. Just as the state can harness Greek and Etruscan ritual knowledge for resolving a crisis, so it can harness technical expertise from outside, in the form of the Etruscan professionals who know how to put on stage shows of the desired standard.

The introduction of stage shows in 364 is part of a Greek-style innovation, however mediated the Greek dimension may have been. Immediately before the reform the newly enhanced *Xuiri sacris faciundis* ordered a *lectisternium,* a special banquet for the gods, a procedure marked in Roman tradition as part of the *ritus Graecus:* this was only the third such ceremony since the beginning of the Republic, and it will have been ordered by the *Xuiri* after consulting the Sibylline books (Liv. 7. 2. 2). The subsequent commissioning of "stage shows" is a Roman attempt to put on a new, modern, and Hellenizing, face to their neighbors. As we saw above, the introduction of stage shows to an existing public festival is something that a number of Greek states had themselves been doing for some time, and other central Italian, especially Etruscan, cities must have been experimenting in the same way.

Physical evidence of possible theatrical performance spaces in Rome's periphery in the fourth century is scarce, but not altogether absent. Excavations at the Etruscan city of Caere, thirty miles northwest of Rome, have revealed an "orchestra" space dating to the fifth century, with steps that could be used for seating facing it; further afield, the impressive second-century Etruscan permanent stone theatre at Castelsecco, outside Arezzo, certainly had a more rudimentary precursor of some kind, with wooden seating and stage.[43] It is extremely likely that in fourth-century central Italy temporary stages were the norm. At the time of the introduction of the Roman *ludi scaenici,* after all, there was not yet a permanent stone theater even in Athens, and the Athenian authorities were still putting out contracts every year for the installation and removal of temporary wooden seating on the southern slope of the acropolis; the construction of a stone theater in Athens began only in about 350, to be completed in 320/19.[44] Temporary structures of this kind leave no mark in the archaeological record, but their existence has been hypothesized for Etruria, Magna Graecia, and Sicily in this period.[45] The Romans used makeshift wooden stages for their *ludi scaenici* all the way down to 55, when Pompeius Magnus built Rome's first permanent theater, and they presumably took this model—along with so much else—from the contemporary Etruscan practice of the fourth century.

The Roman games, then, were not the only show in Central Italy, and they will have been in dialogue with other, competing, games, especially in Etruria. As Rüpke puts it, "There can be no doubt about the 'international' character of such games, mirroring the Greek institution and involving members of middle Italian elites."[46] As we have seen, the very introduction of the Etruscan-style theatrical games is part of a Roman pattern of soliciting religious intervention from outside in response to the kind of catastrophic failure of their own traditional techniques that they had witnessed during the uncontrollable pestilence: Greek rites are tried out by the *Xuiri,* and then, as often, Etruscan resources are called in to assist.[47] The *ludi scaenici,* then, are formally marked from the start as part of a process of interaction with a neighboring power.

This international perspective also enables us to see that the Licinio-Sextian Rogations were not just an accommodation within the city of Rome but a way of allowing for horizontally mobile elites from outside to get access to a comparable status in Rome without necessarily having to abandon their local base.[48] M. Popillius Laenas, the curule aedile who introduced stage shows into the *Ludi* in 364, may be just such a case. His *cognomen,* "Laenas," is originally an Etruscan clan name: if he is a product of horizontal mobility within an élite Etruscan/Roman network, he is perhaps able to be a mediator for Etruscan culture into a Roman space.[49]

We do not need to fall back on a particular individual's biography in order to explain why the new stage shows in Rome had such a strong Etruscan dimension, as all the evidence suggests they did.[50] Going "Etruscan" looks like the most accessible way to go "Hellenic" in this environment. For the Romans, the Etruscan scenic tradition was the most immediate and prestigious of the time, as Etruria had been a leader in the Central Italian work with Greek stagecraft.[51] Etruscan influence had of course been present from the beginning of the Roman *Ludi* during the last years of the monarchy and the transition to a Republic, for the holding of circus games with horse and chariot races, together with boxing contests, is a feature of Etruscan culture domesticated by the Romans over a hundred and fifty years before 364.[52] The innovation of stage shows, however, represents a new kind of dialogue with Etruscan work on Greek culture. Crucial indirect evidence for the Etruscan filter for a Grecizing stage tradition at Rome lies in the terminology of stagecraft in Latin, since the language of the stage in Latin consistently bears the traces of having come into the language from Greek, but via the intermediary stage of Etruscan. The words for "stage" *(scaena),* "mask" *(persona),* and "dancer" *(ludius/ludio)* are all loan words from Etruscan, which first took them over from Greek.[53]

We return in Chapter 8 to consider what kind of theater the Etruscans may have been performing themselves at this period, and later. For now, we may note that what the Romans took over from the Etruscans in an institutionalized way in 364 was a musical performance, a spectacle involving singing and dancing to the double reed-pipe *(tibia)* together with masked performers engaged in mimetic movement.[54] Obviously there had been music and singing and dancing in the city of Rome before 364, not least as part of the major procession leading up to the Circus games that were the highlight of the *Ludi Romani*.[55] But the introduction of a stage—even if a temporary and *ad hoc* one—was the marker of a key innovation.[56] Etruscans had already made their own adaptations of Greek performance culture, and now the Romans were reaching out into their neighbors' orbit in order to begin in turn their own version of a prestigious Hellenic institution, using Etruscan expertise and probably Etruscan performers in the process.

On the Roman Stage, 364–241

In addition to these new Etruscan-inspired performances, what else might Roman audiences have been watching on their makeshift stages in the *ludi scaenici* slot of the *Ludi Romani* between 364 and 241? This is a very hard question to answer, for the evidence is so thin and patchy that investigators operate mainly by processes of analogy and backward projection from better-documented periods.[57] If such retrojection is an inevitable part of any enquiry into fourth- and third-century performance culture in Rome, we need to be on our guard against its dangers. Features of Roman performance culture that appear not to fall into the categories of the post-240 translation project may naturally seem to have preceded the changes that began in 240, yet it is possible that the new kinds of dynamism unleashed in the last third of the third century were themselves responsible for other innovations and experiments.

The Romans presumably continued to watch the kind of improvisatory medley that had been engrossing them, along with other central Italians, for some time, and one may readily conjecture that the new *ludi scaenici* still found room for these popular riffs on Greek myth, with all their inventive musical and dramatic energy. It is regularly assumed that the Romans were also watching versions of Oscan slapstick farce, of the kind that later scholarship called "Atellan," after the Oscan town of Atella in Campania where this tradition was supposed to have arisen.[58] As these were originally unscripted, quasi-improvisational shows, they have not left a secure trace; yet we know that "Oscan shows" *(ludi Osci)* were popular at Rome in later, better documented periods, even down to the time of Augustus, and it is readily imaginable that as the Roman armies came into regular contact with the peoples of Campania from the late 340s on, the shows of the Campanians could travel the hundred and twenty miles northwest to the city of Rome and make that hub into another part of their Italian circuit.[59] On the other hand, just because the Oscan farces look satisfyingly "primitive," we should not automatically assume that their appearance in Rome predates the revolution initiated by Livius and Naevius; it is on balance more likely that the Oscan farces were known in Rome before the translation project, but it is conceivable that it was the expansion of Roman dramatic horizons after 240 that led to the Oscan *atellana* entering Rome, "parallel to Greek drama rather than as a precursor to the latter."[60] Further, we should remind ourselves that the Greek dimension is already inextricable from this popular improvisational art form: as always, we are not dealing with a pre-Hellenizing phase as opposed to a Hellenizing phase, but with two different varieties of interactive responses to Hellenism.[61]

If the Romans could enjoy watching slapstick farce in the Oscan language, it is possible that they also had the opportunity to watch stagings of Greek drama performed in Greek by Greek companies, just as people in southern Italy did, even if they were not primary Greek speakers either: again, we may think of a rough analogy with Anglophone audiences today attending Italian operas performed in Italian.[62] This is controversial, and the secure evidence for performance of Greek drama in Greek at Rome is considerably later than the third century.[63] The highly organized and prestigious companies of the "craftsmen of Dionysus" *(hoi Dionysiaci technitae)* did not come into the Italian picture from the Eastern Mediterranean until much later, in the first century: the "Greek artists" *(artifices Graeci)* who are said to have performed before that time, at the games celebrated by M. Fulvius Nobilior or L. Cornelius Scipio Asiagenus in 186, or by L. Anicius in 166, need not have been actors at all, but, for example, players on the *aulos* or *cithara*.[64]

If the prestigious professional theatrical organizations of the East, the *Dionysiaci technitae,* did not become part of Italian life until considerably later, this does not in itself preclude the possibility that other bands of Greek wandering players could have made their way to Rome before 240, as they had been finding their way into Apulia since the fourth century.[65] It is entirely possible that troupes of Greek players had Rome on their travelling circuit before 240 but left no trace in the sources, while the big stars from the established *technitae* in the East in the better documented later period did manage to be noted by historians.[66] It is difficult to assess how likely or unlikely it would be for an aedile in 300 or thereabouts to decide to have a troupe of Greek artists put on a Greek play at the *Ludi Romani*. I shall shortly be arguing that the mid-third century in Rome saw a new kind of direct engagement with canonical Greek dramatic culture, and stagings of Greek dramas in the original Greek could be either a catalyst for that change in perspective or a consequence of it. Perhaps Sicilian troupes were making the journey to Rome toward the end of the Great War with Carthage, adding Rome to their circuit as they capitalized on the market they had helped create with their performances for the Roman military personnel on the island.[67] At the very least, we should take seriously the argument that the new Latin productions beginning in 240 will have required skilled and trained personnel, and that the most likely source for them will have been Greek dramatic companies from Sicily or southern Italy; Livius knew where to go to get his players, even though the players may never have been to Rome before.[68] In the fallout from the continuous warfare in Magna Graecia, regular festival occasions for performance may have been scarcer, with an extra incentive for the players to seek out new fields of opportunity.[69]

A final category for us to consider is that of dramas about the Roman past. It is regularly argued that Romans must have been watching historical dramas of some kind both before 240 and after, in a continuous tradition; in these pageants, so the argument goes, the Roman gods and heroes of the past were put on the stage before the Roman people, providing a venue for the work of collective memory.[70] This attractive hypothesis is extremely controversial, since direct evidence for such dramas is lacking for the pre-240 period of Roman drama, while the plays on historical subjects that are attested from the literary period do not much resemble the hypothesized pageants. On the available evidence, Rome's second dramatist, Naevius, was the first person to stage at Rome a historical drama (*fabula praetexta,* as they came to be called, "play in official magistrates' costume").[71] Naevius established a pattern followed by later dramatists of setting such plays either in the legendary period (with his *Lupus* [Wolf] on Romulus and Remus) or in the contemporary or near-contemporary world (his *Clastidium,* on M. Claudius Marcellus' winning of the *spolia opima* in his victory near that town in 222, was perhaps staged in 205, when Marcellus' son fulfilled his father's vow at Clastidium and dedicated a temple to Honos and Virtus).[72] If Naevius' plays are an innovation, then they fit very well with the development of the *fabula togata* ("comedy in Roman costume"), which took off from the translation-pieces of the *fabula palliata* ("comedy in Greek costume"), probably early in the second century; it looks as if, after a generation of translated Greek comedies and tragedies, some poets took on the challenge of presenting both comic and serious dramas in Roman costume that did not have a Greek original as their basis, with the inspiration for the serious dramas being material from very recent events or from the deep past of the period of the kings.[73] Naevius is the right person to be the innovator for historical drama, if such is the case; just as he took the translation of the *Odyssey* by Livius as a model for his new task of writing an epic about Roman history in the *Bellum Punicum,* so too he took his own and Livius' translations of Attic tragedy as a model for his new task of writing a serious drama about Roman history.[74]

The hypothesis of a now lost tradition of historical drama cannot be definitively proved or disproved. The historical *praetextae,* however, were rare, with only ten attested titles for the whole Republican period; it would appear that the near-contemporary ones were controversial and too disruptively linked to the powerful individuals whom they celebrated.[75] This fits with the apparent pattern whereby plays on the earlier (and hence presumably less partisan and controversial) periods were staged at public *ludi,* while the more individually slanted contemporary plays tended to be staged by nobles at personally funded votive games.[76] So far from being the first visible trace of a submerged popular tradition, the historical *praetextae* actually attested are "boldly innovative and daring pieces," not a manifestation of the people's shared view of the past but part of interaristocratic competition, "staged in a highly politicized atmosphere."[77]

Things may have been different a century earlier, but we do not know. We cannot say whether or not dramas about the past had been staged before Naevius, nor can we be confident what the venues might have been for them if they were.[78] If we apply Occam's razor, the most economical explanation of our surviving data is that the new literary formats of the late third century, in a dynamic relationship with the heightened political competition among the great families of the *nobiles* from the late third century on, encouraged experimentation with a new kind of drama, one that did not in the end really take off as it might have. The form of the *praetextae* appears to have been the same as that of the translated tragedies in meter, diction, and (probably) dramatic structure;[79] if there is a relationship with earlier historical dramas, the transformation has been very systematic indeed. The topical political dramas celebrating the achievements of great individual *nobiles* are most readily explicable as part of the post-240 revolution, rather than as a continuation from before it.

There were many venues for spectacle and musical performance in the city of Rome apart from the single day given over to *ludi scaenici* in the great games celebrating Jupiter every September. The great procession that opened the games, the *pompa circensis,* was itself an extraordinary spectacle of music and dance (Dion. Hal. *Ant.* 7. 72. 1–13); the priestly colleges had their regular *carmina* ("hymns"), some of which were performed in public; neighborhood festivities of all kinds were a regular part of urban life, and it is imaginable that travelling troupes mounted their popular farces at such venues. But the day set aside for stage performances at the *Ludi Romani* every September was special, and performances there were highly marked, as a demarcated part of the city's most elaborate religious festival, honoring the city's supreme deity. Although, as we have seen, many of the details remain frustratingly obscure, on this day the Romans were watching Etruscan or

Etruscan-inspired performances, with masked performers singing and dancing to the double reed-pipe *(tibia),* while the earlier impromptu performance tradition perhaps continued in tandem; probably, they were watching "Atellan" farces in Oscan;[80] possibly, part of the proceedings involved stagings of events from Roman myth and even celebrations of the deeds of Roman commanders.

As we conclude before turning to the changes set in train from 240 on, it is crucial to remind ourselves that the *Ludi Romani* were an international event. This aspect of the games will have changed register in significant ways as the city moved from being a major player in Central Italy, as it was in 364, to being the ruling power in Italy and a real presence in international affairs by 272, to being a major Mediterranean power after the conquest of Sicily in 241. From their origin, the *ludi scaenici* came marked as bearing features of this international aspect, for they provided a showcase for the evolving Roman power to an expanding series of contact zones, and they embodied a form of spectacle that emerged from Roman dialogue with their neighbors—proximately Etruscan and, ultimately, Greek. Here, as so often, we see the Roman fascination with the hybrid nature of their culture on display: the evolving spectacles are not only "borrowing" from the neighboring cultures, they are staging the way that Roman culture is an assimilative and hybridizing phenomenon.[81] The dynamically evolving international context will be vital to bear in mind as we consider the new developments of 240 and the immediately following years.

A New Kind of Fidelity

We have seen that the interactive work done with Greek drama in Central Italy was extremely free-form, ranging exuberantly in its "creative miscomprehension." The shows put on in the Romans' *ludi scaenici* after 364 are one example of this independent and innovative kind of work with Greek drama, mediated through a predominantly Etruscan filter. The productions of the 230s, on the other hand, are categorically different from this improvisational occasionality, however much of a trace may have been left on the new scripted dramas by the musical and acting styles of the previous spectacles. The translation project that began in the late third century is quite new, for it is carried out by people who are putting a new kind of premium on a new kind of fidelity. They are writing translations of canonical Greek scripts, observing Greek generic demarcations between tragedy and comedy by avoiding free-form combinations, and using verse forms that have successfully adapted Greek metrics to the very different language of Latin.[82]

Any program of fidelity has, of course, infidelity and distancing built into it. Translation looks as if it is establishing contact and similarity, and in certain important respects it clearly is: but it is also establishing a fundamental degree of distinction, down to the level of the individual word, where there can be difference even in the for all intents and purposes identical words μοι and *mihi,* "me."[83] If we have seen this similarity and difference being worked out at the micro level of diction by the translator-poets, we shall see in this and the following chapter that the micro level is a fractal of what is happening at the macro level, where similarity and difference are likewise in dynamic dialogue with each other.

The fidelity to the language and form of the Greek originals is, certainly, inflected by distinct traces of the earlier performance traditions and by contemporary tastes in music and dance, which combine to create quite different visual and dramatic effects from those of the model plays in their original Athenian performance. In order to appreciate these different effects, we need to remind ourselves that Athenian tragedy and new comedy exhibit markedly diverse styles of performance.[84] Tragedy has spoken iambic trimeters, together with longer lines in "recitative" with musical accompaniment, and elaborate lyric song, both in the sung and danced choral odes and in shared lyric exchanges between chorus and characters; new comedy limits the role of the chorus in comparison with tragedy and old comedy, has very minimal interaction (if any) between actors and chorus, dispenses almost entirely with lyric song, and is conducted mainly in spoken iambic trimeter, with some chanted longer lines. The Roman plays sound and look quite different from these

Greek originals in some important respects, not least in having tragedy and comedy resemble each other to a marked extent. Unlike their counterparts in the Greek tradition, the first dramatists composed both tragedy and comedy, and this must be a large part of the explanation for the fact that at Rome the two forms looked much more alike in their presentation, with similar musical and metrical patterns, and with far more sung or recited verse than the originals: "Plautine comedy was more musical not only than its model, the prosaic New Comedy, but also than Greek tragedy."[85] Again, it is attractive here to detect the popularity of music and song at the existing *ludi scaenici* at work.[86]

The comic chorus, however, was not revived at Rome, as the characters did all the singing—differing in this regard from contemporary Greek performances of new comedy, where the chorus continued to provide sung interludes, even if the current *communis opinio* has it that these choral interludes of Greek new comedy were not scripted and were not connected to the action.[87] As in comedy, the tragic characters on the Roman stage will have provided a good deal of the sung element of the performance. The role of the Roman tragic chorus, however, is extremely controversial. The titles of many tragedies make it overwhelmingly likely that some kind of chorus was present (for example, Ennius' *Eumenides*, Accius' *Bacchae, Myrmidones, Troades*);[88] but it seems that they cannot have danced, since Roman theatrical spaces gave up the Greek dancing area (the *orchestra*) to members of the audience, and the first tragic performances will have been located entirely on the temporary stage, with the audience sitting directly in front on the steps of a temple.[89] It is not even agreed whether the sung choral odes of the originals were retained in any significant way.[90] Strzelecki has established beyond any doubt that Ennius, for example, did translate portions of Euripidean sung lyric into Latin lyric, although it is not therefore certain that these songs were sung by the whole chorus as opposed to an individual *coryphaeus*.[91]

If we look for comparative evidence from elsewhere in the Hellenistic world in order to shed light on the treatment of the chorus in Rome, we could perhaps turn to the peripatetic professional theatrical troupes in south Italy. It has been suggested that these troupes travelled light, with three actors and a *coryphaeus* who would train locals to do some kind of choral performance without necessarily reproducing the full sung and danced effect of the original.[92] If this is the case, then it is possible that such a model was familiar to the first translator-poets at Rome, who may also have gone to such troupes for their personnel. Further, at the Hellenistic dramatic festivals of the Sarapieia at Tanagra (late first century) and the Soteria at Delphi (mid-third century), it appears that revived old tragedies were put on without a chorus, and this may have been the norm known to Livius and Naevius.[93] In this case, however, as in so much of what we want to know about theatrical performance in third-century Italy, one must in the end agree with Jocelyn (here speaking of the problem of why the metrical and performance conventions of tragedy and comedy are so similar to each other at Rome): "The paucity of our knowledge of what went on during the third century in the theatres of Etruria and the Greek and Oscan speaking cities of the South makes it incapable of settlement."[94]

For all of these important differences between the performance style of the Roman translations and that of the original plays as staged in Athens, it remains the case that the program of the new translation project, with its ambition to go directly to particular sources for sustained adaptation, was qualitatively different from what had happened before at the *ludi scaenici*. The authors' new program of fidelity is in no worthwhile sense qualitatively superior—or inferior—to what preceded it. But it is one that modern observers, so familiar with the Roman case, can too readily assume to be natural or inevitable, when in fact, as we have seen throughout, it is a peculiar innovation in an ancient context. This act of appropriation was no weak act of deference, as became clear in our discussion of the massively domesticating thrust of the translation project. It was an enabling move, part of a larger project of cultural translation that is our focus for the rest of this chapter, a project that made it possible for the interstitial middle men to capitalize upon their skills and produce something that in time began to look like some kind of equivalent to the performance culture and the literary traditions of the Greeks.[95]

The distinctive change represented by the new translation project is not a shift toward an engagement with Greek traditions in comparison with an earlier period free of engagement with Greek traditions. There never was a period of Roman culture free from interaction with Greek culture, and the *ludi scaenici* before 240 are, as we have seen, no exception to this rule: in their conception as an international showcase, in their Etruscan-derived technical terminology for the stage, and in their very use of stage, mask, and music, the *ludi scaenici* of 364–241 are wholly inconceivable outside of dialogue with Greek festivals and performance traditions. It is quite incorrect, then, to think in terms of a "pre-Greek" phase being superseded by some kind of Greek phase. But there are two major, and closely inter-related, changes observable with the revolution begun in 240 in comparison with what had gone before. Firstly, the international setting for the *ludi scaenici* has been transformed out of recognition, while, secondly, the nature of the Romans' engagement with Greek theatrical traditions has changed, shifting from an indirect, free-form, and Etruscan-mediated adaptation of Greek forms to a more direct and canonically informed model of engagement, with a new kind of determination to "get it right" in transposing from the model culture.[96]

From *Koinē* to *Imperium*

Both of these phenomena—the transformed international setting and the shift to a more direct kind of work with Greek drama—are intimately related to the profoundly disruptive impact on the long-standing central and southern Italian *koinē* generated by Rome's extraordinary trajectory of military success in the scant century between the abolition of the old "Latin League" in 338 and the victory in Sicily over Carthage in 241. The comparatively level playing field of the "middle ground," with its remarkable shared *koinē*—the environment that first gave birth to the Romans' *ludi scaenici*—is transformed by the suddenly predominant impact of a power that generates a new kind of centripetal force.[97] Magna Graecia, which had been the ultimate source for the dissemination of

Hellenic dramatic culture up the peninsula, had already fallen on hard times from the 370s on, with only Taras and Naples as major exceptions to a general decline into second-rate power status;[98] the near-contemporary and later rhetoric of the "barbarianization" of the region should not be taken straightforwardly at face value, but it must betoken at the least some loss of self-assurance and sense of identity.[99] Yet the region as a whole saw a particularly sudden and abrupt decline in its cultural influence on Central Italy in the years immediately following the capitulation of Taras/Tarentum to Rome in 272. This decline was part of the breaking-up of the Hellenic-inflected *koinē*, as the various regions no longer participated jointly in that distinctive shared culture but found themselves increasingly responding in atomized fashion to the new preponderance of Roman influence: "Roman intervention apparently destroys meticulously the former equilibrium of Italy, and replaces it with a new infrastructure, a new Roman framework."[100] This is by no means to say that regional variety disappeared as all the local units succumbed to some new homogeneous format of "Romanization," since vigorous and differing responses to the new realities are observable throughout the peninsula:[101] but the comparative cohesion of the former shared "middle ground," one not centered on Rome, was a thing of the past.

The mid-third-century context is one in which the Romans are digesting their conquest of the peninsula and formulating increasingly coherent views of the integrity of their new conquest, with the development of a new "Italian" reality. By providing the first overseas province, the conquest of Sicily—a momentous watershed, to which we return in the next chapter—must focus their minds in an even more sharpened way on what "Italy" is, but already at the time of the crossing into Sicily in 264 the Roman Senate is operating with a concept of Italy as an entity that is "theirs."[102] The battle of Sentinum in 295, the battle that "sealed the fate of Italy,"[103] gave particular initial impetus to such conceptions. The pervasive tentacles of the developing road network, the siting of colonies at strategic nodes on that network with the accompanying spread of Roman ideological and religious agendas, the transplanting of entire populations from one part of Italy to another, the development of Latin as the language of power—these inter-related features, with gathering momentum throughout the third century, all follow from and in turn cumulatively contribute to a new sense of what the Roman state is and what its relationship is to the rest of Italy.[104]

Relations between the Roman center and the Italians are radically reconfigured in the light of these transformations, during which we see the breaking up of the old *koinē* that had served the peoples of Italy—including the Romans—so well for so long. The new shows that are staged from 240 on—Latin and Roman appropriations of Greek theatrical classics into a new kind of dramatic festival—are part of a new competition over status in relation to Hellenism, as the Romans attempt to rusticize the other Italian peoples by setting themselves up as the only people in Italy who have a counterpart to a distinctively Greek institution, one of immense cultural prestige.[105] Jonathan Z. Smith's powerful work on comparison reveals that "'x resembles y'" really means "'x resembles y more than z with respect to . . .'" or "'x resembles y more than w resembles z with respect to . . .'"[106] From this perspective, then, the *Ludi Romani* are staging more than the claim "Rome resembles Greece": they are claiming "Rome resembles Greece more than the other Italians do with respect to international high culture."[107] As Wallace-Hadrill puts it, "Culture does not just say who you are. It says who you are *in relation to others*."[108]

The experts who provide the scripts for the new shows are themselves examples of the new power dynamic, for there is no more striking aspect of the impact of the new Roman power on the peoples of Italy than the Italian origins of the providers of the new literature.[109] They come initially from Magna Graecia and its penumbra, attracted by the gravitational pull of the new center. The case of Ennius in particular shows the way that the impact of Rome is transforming long-established patterns: as Purcell points out, it is significant that Ennius' native territory was Messapia, on the heel of Italy, which had "so long resisted the influence of nearby Taras," but which now "came to form part of the Roman *koine* as it never had of the Hellenic."[110] The central power of Rome provides the force field that drives the changes, but the participants are, eventually, a pan-Italian constituency.

The reorientation away from the superseded Hellenic-style *koinē*, as part of a new relationship with the various Italian peoples, needs to be contextualized within the larger state-sponsored Hellenism that we can observe operating at full throttle all through the third century. This new phase is a sign of Rome's strenuous efforts to modernize in this period.[111] Roman horizons are expanding fast at this time, and a perceptible re-orientation away from Magna Graecia to mainland Greece is part of a developing self-consciousness about their newly imperial status. Their receptiveness to the victory ideology of Alexander is one aspect of their embracing of a new range of ways of conceiving of their new role and status.[112] Alexander's example even taught the Roman elite, and their gods, to start shaving: Varro records the arrival of the first barber in Rome in the year 300 (*RR* 2. 11. 10), and the god Mars on Roman coins from this time resembles Alexander in being "beardless, side-whiskered . . . with unruly hair."[113] The Romans are also looking to Athens for imperial prototypes at this period. The goddess Roma, on coins dated by Burnett to the early third century, is modeled with great fidelity on the goddess Athena (and in one type she is also wearing Alexander's Phrygian helmet).[114] The Romans appear to be keying into the widespread fourth-century interest in "the complexities of the vast and singular Athenian state."[115] As we shall see in the next section, it was specifically the dramatic canon of the Athenian state that was the target of the new Roman translation project.

Around this key year of 300, the Romans set up two statues beside the Senate house in the Forum, of Alcibiades and Pythagoras, as respectively the bravest and wisest of the Greeks (Plin. *HN* 34. 26). Alcibiades' presence surely owes something to the impact he made on the Western Greeks during the meteoric few months he spent in their zone at the beginning of the Athenian expedition against Syracuse in 415;[116] yet his commemoration by the Romans at this juncture must also betoken a quickened interest in the history of the Athenian state. The pairing with Pythagoras, firmly part of the world of Magna Graecia as far as the Romans are concerned, complements the range of options available to Roman perspectives in these years of rapid change.[117]

The newly modernizing Hellenism is especially conspicuous in the religious domain, where we see an explosion of Hellenizing adaptation and innovation beginning around 300, signaled especially by the introduction of the cult of Aesculapius in 291, and going down to the importation of Cybele, the Magna Mater, in 204.[118] The Romans show a discriminating religious knowledge in these two choices, for both of these cults are already marked within the Greek world as ones that get imported and arrive from elsewhere.[119] Cybele in particular was a controversial cult, whose status within the Hellenic world was the focus of intense debate: the Romans' modernizing here is taking them into contentious contemporary terrain.[120] It is telling that this intensified program of Hellenization in religious experimentation was marked by a more direct recourse to the Greek world outside Italy. As Gallini importantly observes, in contrast to the earlier phase of religious Hellenization as far back as the early post-regnal period, when Magna Graecia or Campania were the source of Roman outreach, Asclepius/Aesculapius, for example, was brought to Rome directly from Epidaurus in 291, while the Magna Mater came from Pessinus in Asia Minor in 204.[121]

The principal state-sponsored religious festival, the *Ludi Romani,* itself became, in the middle of this century of Hellenizing religious importation, the venue for an analogous kind of religious experimentation with a newly direct access to Greek sources. Importing Greek drama is not the same as importing the cult of Aesculapius or of Nike/Victoria, but it is related—it is an attempt to ramp up the prestige and attractiveness of the state's main religious festival by reaching out to the Greek world for the right kind of charismatic importation, which could be adapted to the language and culture of the host society, just as new deities and cults could be imported and adapted.[122] The personnel who made this possible—Livius and his immediate successors—were men from Magna Graecia, products of the reconfigured relationship between Rome and the south of Italy; they were now agents in a new phase in Rome's relationship with Greek games and stage productions. When the Senate, as the body ultimately responsible for the *Ludi,* announced the reform for the year 240, it will have used a formula like the one suggested by

Wissowa: *ludos scaenicos/graecos esse faciundos* ("Greek stage games are to be performed").[123]

Again, it is important to remind ourselves that the reform of 364 was already one that we can construe as a Hellenizing initiative, within its own distinctive international setting.[124] The difference is between a comparatively mediated access to Greek dramatic culture, conditioned by a world—the *koinē*—in which many players were participating in a shared enterprise of experimentation, and a comparatively direct access, in which the Roman state transformed its principal religious festival by doing something quite without precedent, commissioning translations straight from canonical texts. The *koinē* has broken up under the newly disruptive impact of a suddenly predominant Rome, now a state with Mediterranean status—in effect, an imperial power, with a different kind of agency in a different kind of international setting.

Accessing the Canon

An important aspect of this newly direct access to Greek sources is the canonical nature of the texts taken over for the translation project. A strongly classicizing and canonizing urge is evident from the beginning of the translation project.[125] Livius translated one of the ultimate classics, the *Odyssey,* and he and Naevius and their successors translated dramas from the accepted golden age of tragedy (the fifth century) and comedy (the time of Menander), not contemporary texts. New plays were still being produced in Athens as they wrote, while the fourth century had been "a time of extraordinary vitality"[126] in Athenian theater, but the Roman dramatists translated no contemporary tragedies and very few fourth-century ones; nor, despite their upbringing in or near Magna Graecia, were they adapting Italian or Sicilian drama.[127] Among the sources for Roman translation drama, there are few names in addition to the "classical six" (Aeschylus, Sophocles, Euripides in tragedy, especially in the first generations; Diphilus, Menander, and Philemon in comedy).[128] As Potter puts it, "Roman poets were aware of Greek literary 'brands,' and were able to exploit that 'branding' to attract audiences."[129]

The canonizing momentum in Hellenistic performance tradition and scholarship to which the Roman poets were responding ultimately traces its way back through popular taste—in the case of tragedy all the way back to the fifth century, where we see Aristophanes' *Frogs* already treating the Big Three as in a league of their own, and in the case of New Comedy to the early third century, as attested by victories for revivals of plays by the accepted masters of the genre.[130]

Our poets, then, were working with canonical texts, and their way of apprehending those texts was not free-floating. It was mediated through Hellenistic taste in performance and through contemporary Hellenistic conditions of scholarship and education.[131] Further, it is highly likely to have been indebted to the prototype of the Macedonian appropriation of Athenian drama, for the Macedonian kings and their successors had focused on precisely this canon as a vehicle for their pursuit of the claim to be worthy inheritors and masters of Hellenic culture, given that Athens was so successful at projecting herself as "the Hellas of Hellas," (Ἑλλάδος Ἑλλάς, Ἀθῆναι, *Anth. Pal.* 7. 45. 3).[132] These canonical texts were being received in a contemporary frame, as canonical texts always are. Euripides, to someone like Livius or Naevius, was not the Euripides of Jean-Pierre Vernant, the archetype of the Classical Athenian democratic moment, but rather the international melodramatic Euripides of the Hellenistic travelling players, the school teachers of the Greek *oecumenē,* and the Macedonian pretenders to the mantle of *hellenismos.* The first creators of Latin literature were products of the mid-third century, so that Naevius was an almost exact contemporary of Eratosthenes of Cyrene, while Callimachus was perhaps still alive, only just, in the year in which Livius put on his first translation.[133] This is a time when Hellenistic scholarship is codifying and organizing the canons of drama and the other genres, creating a newly fixed institution of literature. Here we see the crystallization in the Greek world of what Whitmarsh has called the "archival sensibility," "an awareness that individual texts belong in a vast constellation of works—a library, whether real or virtual—that constituted the Greek tradition."[134] This is the sensibility and the institution upon which the Roman equivalent is calqued from the start, and we shall pursue the implications of this calquing systematically in Chapter 6.

A vital aspect of the new program of fidelity, then, was that it entailed a turn not to what was recent and close but to the prestigious classical texts that defined the Hellenistic canon and that were the particular target of those non-Athenians who wanted access to the charisma and authority of the cultural center of Greece. The performance tradition of Greek drama at Rome is directly dependent upon an educational and literary tradition as well as upon the traditions of performance within the ambit of the Roman experience.[135] We are not dealing with "Greek" drama, but with Athenian classical drama as enshrined not only in the international performance tradition but in the canons and curricula of Hellenistic scholarship. This new development is inextricable from the dissolution of the *koinē,* which had originally provided the environment for Rome's encounters with Greek theatrical tradition. We see the organizers of the reform of the *ludi scaenici* in 240 aiming for a different kind of relationship with that theatrical tradition as they reposition themselves on an international stage that is unrecognizable from the one occupied by their predecessors in 364. And this newly Hellenizing reform is in its turn a feature of a new variety of religious Hellenizing, which itself self-consciously involves an emancipation from the outmoded *koinē* and a newly direct access to Greek sources of religious authority and charisma.

CHAPTER 5

A Stage for an Imperial Power

THE SCENIC REFORMS to the *Ludi Romani* in 364 had been part of a Roman strategy of self-staging within an international arena, and so were the reforms of 240. But the international arena of 240 was one that would have been unimaginable to M. Popillius Laenas and his colleagues of a hundred and twenty-five years earlier. In assessing this new international context, we need, above all, to take serious account of the impact of the victory over Carthage in the Great War of 264–241, with the accompanying conquest of Sicily.

The Sicilian Connection

The conquest of the largest island in the world known to the Romans at the time was an amazing achievement, which had a profound impact on the Romans themselves and on the Mediterranean world in general. Sicily had been a renowned cockpit for intermittent warfare between Carthaginians and Greeks for some two hundred and fifty years when the Romans crossed from Italy in 264, and yet in twenty-three years the Romans won uncontested control of the island. For a Greek world reared on stories of the endless wars with Carthage fought by the Deinome-

nids in the fifth century, and then by Dionysius I, Timoleon, and Agathocles, this was indeed something to take stock of. For the Romans, it
marked an unmistakable watershed moment, helping to fix the conscious
knowledge that they now possessed an empire, as Cicero much later was
to remark: "Sicily first taught our ancestors how wonderful it was to
exercise imperial power over external peoples" (*prima docuit maiores
nostros quam praeclarum esset exteris gentibus imperare, Verr.* 2. 2. 2).[1]
The historian Diodorus may have been biased as a Sicilian, but one
sees why he describes Sicily as "the fairest of all the islands, since it has
the power to contribute greatly to the growth of an empire" (Ὅτι
Σικελία πασῶν τῶν νήσων καλλίστη ὑπάρχει, ὡς μεγάλα δυναμένη
συμβάλλεσθαι πρὸς αὔξησιν ἡγεμονίας, Diod. Sic. 23. 1. 1).

As many scholars have stressed ever since Friedrich Leo first made
the point a hundred years ago, it is crucial to see the *Ludi Romani* of
240 in the light of this transformative experience.[2] First of all, at a perhaps comparatively banal level, we have to take seriously the impact of
the generation-long exposure of tens of thousands of Roman legionaries
and naval personnel to the Greek culture of Sicily, especially to that of the
Syracuse of Hieron II.[3] Certainly, the Romans' experience in Campania
and South Italy had already given them direct exposure to Greek theater
before they crossed to Sicily;[4] yet the years in Sicily afforded an opportunity for an intensification of a long-standing acquaintance. The island of
Sicily shared a remarkable theatrical culture as part of a more generally
diffused *koinē*, one that included the areas nominally under Carthaginian
control at the beginning of the war.[5] The Sicilian environment, with its
many local theaters, and especially the contemporary pretensions of Hieron II, with his determined boosting of Syracuse's status during the war
years, provided an unprecedented opportunity for the Romans to ac-
quaint themselves at first hand with what Hellenistic theater had to offer
in terms both of drama and of ideological display.[6] One of those looking
and learning will have been Cn. Naevius, the second translator-poet of
Rome, who tells us that he served in this war in Sicily (Gell. 17. 21. 45).

Sicily, then, provides an acculturation process for a potential theatrical audience back in Rome. We may note that this process is not without

a wider context, for the Romans were by no means processing theater alone during their many long years in Sicily during the Great War. The impact of Sicily on the Roman imagination was already strong even as the war was going on. Later Roman memory concentrated on the sack of Syracuse by M. Claudius Marcellus in 212, together with his subsequent transfer of vast amounts of artistic booty to Rome, as the tipping point when Sicily's Greek culture first penetrated the Roman sphere;[7] but the interaction goes back two generations earlier. Already at the beginning of the Great War the whole area of the Comitium in the Forum, the heart of public meetings and elections, was reconfigured into a new format that was probably Sicilian in origin: instead of the centuries-old rectangular space, there was now a circular one, with banks on the interior, designed to resemble Greek *ekklesiasteria*.[8] It was right by this Comitium, during the process of radical reconfiguring, that M. Valerius Messalla erected the sundial that he had taken from Catana, near Mt. Etna, in 263, the first sundial to be erected in the Forum (Plin. *HN* 7. 60). Coarelli is no doubt right to link these two initiatives, both quickened by the Sicilian experience.[9] One likewise observes Syracusan impact on the decoration of the sarcophagus of L. Cornelius Scipio Barbatus, from around 240: it is striking, in light of our earlier discussion of the Roman orientation away from the dissolving Italian *koinē* in this century, that not only the modern decoration but also the Greek-based presentation of the tomb as "analogous to an altar, and no longer to a house," are a sign of "an evident desire among the ruling class for a break with the Central Italian tradition."[10]

It is possible to trace a larger pattern for the way that the Romans inserted themselves into the extremely complex ethnic and political jigsaw of the island of Sicily.[11] In fighting the Carthaginians, they embraced the long-standing Syracusan model, itself calqued upon mainland Greek anti-Persian ideology, whereby the Carthaginians were cast as "barbarians," the enemies of Greek/Syracusan "civilization."[12] In his poem on the war with Carthage, Naevius appears to have insinuated the Romans into the Syracusan half of the civilization/barbarian paradigm, holding up the Romans as the inheritors of the Sicilian anti-Carthaginian

Greeks in their role as human counterparts of the gods, who imposed order upon the monsters of chaos in the Gigantomachy.[13] This was not an inevitable position to adopt, even if the Romans had been experimenting with it for over thirty years already before they entered Sicily.[14] The Romans' choice of this brand of Hellenism was in part a response to initiatives from Sicilian Greeks and others, such as the originally Elymian foundation of Segesta, whose people invited the Romans, at the very beginning of the war, to consider themselves as relatives on the basis of their supposed shared Trojan ancestry.[15] Other Sicilians, including many Greeks, sided with Carthage—the pro-Carthaginian histories of the Great War and, later, the Hannibalic War were written by Greeks, including the Sicilians Philinus of Acragas and Silenus of Caleacte.[16] "Hellenism" in Sicily was no monolithic entity, and the Romans were making conscious choices about which Greek paradigms and allegiances to identify with, and which to reject, in response to a variety of Sicilian initiatives.[17] Finally, Leigh (2010) has made a convincing argument for the impact of the Sicilian experience on the beginnings of Roman epic: Livius Andronicus' translation of Homer's *Odyssey* found newly rich resonances for a Roman audience who had sailed and fought in the *Odyssey*-rich geography of the island, while Naevius' *Bellum Punicum* gave monumental shape to the transformative experience of the Romans' becoming a major maritime power, as they followed in the sea-tracks left by the single ship of their ancestor Aeneas.[18]

If Sicily is transformative for the Romans' encounter with Hellenism, within fifty years of the end of the Great War "Greece proper" (*germana Graecia,* as Plautus calls it, *Rud.* 737) was to bulk larger in their imagination, with "colonial" Sicily losing status as the cultural model. Even so, the sidelining of Sicily did not happen overnight. Ennius' "minor" works, from around 200–180, are still all based on Sicilian models—Epicharmus, Archestratus, Euhemerus; and when, at presumably around the same period, Scipio Africanus Maior was asked whom he thought to be the most accomplished men of affairs in terms of wisdom and courage, he replied "Dionysius and Agathocles, the Sicilians" (Polyb. 15. 35. 6).[19] The edginess of the confrontation between Sicily and Athens

around the year 200 is glimpsed in the words of the Prologue to Plautus'
Menaechmi, about two Syracusan twins: "This plot," says the Prologue,
"is Greekish; still, it's not Athenianish, but Sicilianish" (*hoc argumentum
graecissat,/tamen non atticissat, uerum sicilicissitat*, 7–8).

If we focus on the Romans' reform of their *Ludi* in 240, it is important to note that Syracuse in particular represented a showpiece to the
Roman officer class of how an up-and-coming Hellenistic power stages
itself to an international audience—just at the time when the Romans
found themselves precisely in the position of becoming such a great Hellenistic power. The conquest of Sicily, after all, put Rome in a leading
position on the world stage in a distinctively new way. The *Ludi Romani*
of 240 marked this moment for an international audience, for they were,
in effect, the Victory Games to celebrate the end of the generation-long
war.[20] Following the war's climactic naval battle at the Aegates islands
on 10 March 241, the Gates of Janus had been closed for the first time
since King Numa, by a consul with the *cognomen* "Athenian," A. Manlius Torquatus Atticus.[21] The two commanders who had won this
battle, C. Lutatius Catulus and Q. Valerius Falto, celebrated their separate triumphs on 4 and 6 October 241 respectively, some twenty days
after the *Ludi Romani* of that year: the *Ludi Romani* of September 240,
then, were the first ones to be held after the victorious conclusion of
the war. As a Hellenistic-style victory celebration, these games follow
in the pattern established by Philip of Macedon and his son Alexander
together with the Successor kings, who had used dramatic festivals to
celebrate military victories.[22] When one considers how important
Macedonian victory-ideology had already been to the Romans for two
generations, as we saw in the last chapter, then it looks as if the Macedonian project of appropriating Athenian drama was likewise influential in 240, as the Romans set about their new kind of appropriation.[23]

The sheer scale of the new games, as they developed in succeeding
years, was itself a factor in their appeal to the Roman governing class,
for they represented another means of staging Rome as an world-class
hub, an international center of enormous wealth and power.[24] It was in

Sicily, above all, that the Romans learned how to play this kind of game, observing Hieron's varied monarchical displays. The Romans had never had the territories of a king fall under their dominion before, for Italy was an oddly king-free zone in the period of the Roman conquest. Having a king as an "ally" posed new challenges even to the Romans' keen political intelligence, especially when this king was himself experimenting all through these years at finding ways of projecting his own longed-for status as an equal to the Successor monarchies of the Eastern Mediterranean.[25] As Dearden well puts it, "For officers and officials, the celebration of official festivals with their allies, especially Hiero, must have been first a matter of courtesy and then acculturation."[26] The Romans were of course not only spectators of but participants in a web of Hellenistic power relations, as they learned how to be a great power. The Sicilian experience represents a new intensification of a "gradual process of international image-building" that Curti has traced down to the end of the century, involving the Romans' "development of an international vocabulary, in order to participate as an equal in the on-going dialogue between other leading powers."[27] Part of this new vocabulary was the spectacles. Theater, in Syracuse as in Alexandria, was part of the appurtenances of Hellenistic monarchical power, like coinage, war fleet, siege engines, and city fortification—many of which were likewise media for Roman self-promotion during our period.[28]

One of the clearest demonstrations of how implicated Syracuse was in the new developments in the Roman games is the famous incident in 237, reported by Eutropius (3. 1), when Hieron II came to Rome to watch the games *(ad ludos spectandos)*; scholars have inferred that Hieron may even have played a part in the planning of the new games and had come to judge their success.[29] Hieron brought with him a huge gift of grain for the Roman people. This donation was part of his use of the grain trade to create links to "all of Greece and the islands" (from an epigram by Archimelus, reported by Ath. 209e), with donations of grain to Rhodes after the earthquake in 227/6 as another example (Polyb. 6. 5. 88).[30] Such donations were a strategy pioneered by the Deinomenid rulers of Syracuse two and a half centuries earlier, and the provision of dramatic displays was also part of Syracusan international politics going back to the fifth century: both strategies are aspects of what Kowalzig has called "a greatly competitive commemorative culture, operative in local contexts and an immense bargaining tool in interstate relations."[31] Strikingly, it was precisely in the immediate aftermath of the Great War, in 238, that Hieron started work on his magnificent new theater in Syracuse, the one that visitors to the city now see, replacing an earlier one constructed of more humble materials.[32] Hieron is erecting his own victory monument, of course, but it is hard not to see the remaking of the theater as in part a reaction to the new Roman initiative, a strategy for reasserting Syracusan cultural preeminence. As often, intercultural dialogue is precisely that, a dialogue, not a top-down imposition.

The Romans by no means took over the Syracusan model *in toto*. Most tellingly, they did not go on to erect a permanent theater, and were not to do so—as we have already discussed above—until the year 55.[33] They carried on erecting their temporary structures as they had already been doing for over a hundred and twenty years, despite the fact that these were precisely the years when many West Greek cities were transforming their theaters into permanent stone monuments.[34] There are many reasons why the Romans would want to persevere in their time-honored practice.[35] The dramatic festivals were first and foremost religious rituals, which it was never desirable to change, and the use of temple-precincts as settings reinforced this instinct;[36] the Senate could continue to exercise control over the occasions, since building the temporary structures was expensive and time-consuming;[37] the prestige of having erected a permanent personal monument of this kind was too great to concede to any individual; finally, the permanent theater had many negative associations in the contemporary Greek world, as a site for popular demonstrations, riots, and lynchings.[38] It is utterly characteristic of the Romans' Hellenizing initiatives that they should exclude distinctive features of the phenomenon in question even as they appropriated and transformed others.

An International Festival

The victory games for the Great War, staged in the "imperial" capital, occasioned a reform in the scenic component. The commissioning of a translation into Latin of an Attic dramatic script for performance on a Roman stage marked out a certain kind of Hellenism for the *Ludi,* showing that Rome was competing with other international powers, aiming for a prestige like that attracted by the great Games of the Greek world, and vying with the attempts of the Macedonian monarchs to lay claim to Athenian cultural preeminence.[39] It can be no coincidence that immediately after the peace the Romans sent an embassy to Ptolemy III Euergetes of Egypt, offering to give him assistance in his war against Seleucus II of Syria (Eutr. 3.1); the king politely declined, as the war was over by the time the Roman embassy arrived, but the incident is another token of the Romans' consciousness of their new position within the international rankings.[40] Tellingly, later Roman accounts of early *Ludi* in Rome anachronistically make the city of Romulus already a focus for flamboyant staging of attractive Roman spectacles, designed to impress neighbors, as when Romulus puts on stage shows at the Consualia to entice the Sabines to visit, bringing those Sabine Women with them (Ov. *Ars* 1. 101–14). Such stories are radically unhistorical, but they show a keen understanding of how the *Ludi* work in an international context to stage Roman culture in alluring ways as part of an imperial strategy of the projection of "soft power": the Games are not just the fruits of imperial conquest, but a tool of imperial conquest.[41]

Scholars of the Roman *Ludi* rightly stress the personal ambitions and motivations of the individual magistrates who had charge of the festivities, while we must also allow for the element of contingency in this particular innovation.[42] Frustratingly, we cannot recover the individual dynamics behind the first shows, even if, on the basis of what we know from later periods, there is no doubt that thrusting young *nobiles* will have relished the opportunity to gain fame and popularity through the mechanism of the spectacles. Perhaps a one-off occasion proved contingently successful enough to generate sequels. It is easy enough to write a novel in which Livius Andronicus is commissioned for the special peace games because his former master, or his patron, L. Livius Salinator, is on the committee planning the games. Salinator could remark, "I have a *Graeculus* at home who might be able to do something special for us"; and after the performance was over we can imagine the *nobiles* walking away and saying to each other, "That was very worthwhile; let's do it again next year." All kinds of deep conditions of receptivity and familiarity would be necessary for an accident like that to stick, but they need not be determinative conditions.

Nonetheless, we must resist "the tendency to lose sight of the Hellenistic perspective in favour of a Roman-centred reading."[43] If we bear in mind the international nature of such festivals, and consider the radically new geopolitical circumstances of 240 in comparison with those of even thirty years before, then we should see this major reform, furthering the projection of Rome on an international stage in the guise of a Hellenistic power, as part of senatorial policy. It was with the Senate that ultimate responsibility for the Games lay, even if delegation of the management was their normal operating procedure.[44] The political culture of Flower's "third republic" (from 300 to 180), in which the roiling rivalry of the *nobiles* was somehow contained within the ring controlled by the Senate, provided the conditions that enabled the program of innovation from which emerged the translation project.[45] This is not to say that the Senate from the start had some kind of grand design of appropriating Attic drama, nor is it to deny that the individual *nobiles* who competed to mount the most appealing shows had a crucial role to play in developing the momentum of the *ludi scaenici*; but the initial impulse to transform the *Ludi Romani* was state policy, however contingent and unpredictable its knock-on effects proved to be.

The transformations of Roman culture that we can observe all through our period are a classic example of how important it is to see any given culture not as a closed and stable system but as something always being reformed in response to the regional and international environment.[46]

Roman culture is a particularly interesting case of how self-conscious this process can be. Their society is ceaselessly redescribed in response to new interactions and challenges, and their discussions of how their culture is formed are always sensitive to the interactive and hybrid nature of the process.[47] The international spectacles of the *Ludi* are the ideal place to stage this process of dialogue and fusion, with Greek tragedies in Latin, or with Plautine comedies, which are translations of Menander and Diphilus into Latin incorporating aspects of Oscan Atellan farce. If we think of the project of translation as a whole, the point is clear: the Roman games with their Latinized Menander and Euripides showcase the Roman ability to process and internalize difference, to make it their own, and the games also showcase their ability to turn that understanding back onto a continually changing audience of outsiders, including Etruscans, Latins, Samnites, Campanians, Greeks, and visiting Hellenistic monarchs.

Swimming with, and against, the Mainstream of Hellenism

In the victory games of 240, for the first time—and not just for the first time at Rome, but *so far as we know* for the first time ever—a translation of an Attic dramatic script into another language was staged. This did not have to happen, and any innovation in the *ludi scaenici* could have taken other forms. It is imaginable, for example, that the new drama could have been in Greek—either one taken from Sicily or from the Athenian canon. The state might even have commissioned a new play in Greek, freshly composed by Andronikos.[48]

In many ways, this perhaps apparently bizarre counterfactual possibility is in fact what we might have expected to happen instead, given the more normal patterns of responses to Hellenism that we observe in the world of the *oecumenē*. We have seen how representatives of different groups took over the Greek form of historiography for their own ends, and this is characteristic of the responses of groups conquered by Greeks or in close connection with them. The ways in which different groups swam in the current of Hellenism varied greatly, and fierce anti-Greek sentiment is at times easy to point to, as in Judaea and Egypt;[49] but a common feature of the response to Greek culture is the way in which ambitious upwardly mobile members of local élites could equip themselves with the education in Greek language and culture necessary to converse and write in Greek and to join the common current of the *oecumenē*.[50] This brand of Hellenism could become, as Bowersock (1990) has shown, "a medium, not a message, . . . provid[ing] a common language for local traditions and religions to express themselves," enabling differences to be smoothed down, "help[ing] to discover a common world and a cosmopolitan consciousness."[51]

Something like this might have happened with the Romans if they had not become an imperial power, because the great difference between them and most other members of the *oecumenē* was of course primarily that they were not conquered by Greeks but instead conquered them. Toynbee has an engaging counterfactual of his own to bring out what was at stake: "We may guess that, if the Roman Commonwealth had been confined to Central and North-Western Italy by Pyrrhus, or if it had been broken up by Hannibal, works of literature written by Romans would have been written thereafter in Greek."[52] Operating from the position of dominance that they actually occupied, however, this variety of participation in Hellenism was very much not what the Romans wanted. They did not want differences smoothed down or to allow themselves to be submerged in a common flow. That way lay the risk of cultural submersion, and they were aggressive and self-assured enough not to countenance that possibility.[53] Roman aristocrats did of course follow this variety of Hellenism in their writing of the first historiographical treatments of the city's past in the Greek language, as we shall see in Chapter 6, but even they switched to Latin for this purpose after one generation. To us, it may appear strange that Roman aristocrats should write in Greek when they turned to history, but within the comparative perspective of other élites' interaction with Hellenism, it looks very much like the expected thing to do, while the next stage, of writing in Latin, is the strange thing to do.

What actually happened under the Romans' aegis was the emergence of a mini mirror version of the *koinē* of the *oecumenē*'s Hellenism, with members of local élites trading up into the new language of power and culture, just as their counterparts in the East were trading up into Greek.[54] Latin in very short order became a *koinē* language for literature within its own imperial penumbra; if Syrians, Egyptians, Babylonians, and Carians could participate in Hellenism by writing in Greek, then Campanians, Messapians, Celts, and Umbrians could participate in Roman culture by writing in Latin, taking over Greek originals in the process.

From within this new *koinē* of their own, the Romans could negotiate their own relationship with the literary domain of Hellenism, in a pattern that tracked the guarded and nuanced nature of their overall relationship with Hellenism, in which Rome was committed to "borrow only what she wanted to borrow and only to the extent that she wished."[55] In a dialectic described as "mimesis and alterity" by the anthropologist Michael Taussig, interacting cultures are regularly selecting from each other characteristic features for disparagement or envy. A process of imitation most economically makes these features available for experimentation and analysis, allowing one to capture and control the strange power of the other culture. As the alien features are brought home, the resulting sense of anxiety or revulsion produces a backlash, in which the imitated characteristics are once again set at a distance. The competing cultures, then, oscillate between concentrating on otherness, by focusing on what is different about their rivals, and concentrating on similarity, by the imitative process that best enables them to define and master what makes up that otherness.[56] The regular Roman spasms of backlash against Greek culture, in other words, are a constitutive dimension of their Hellenization, not a momentary interruption of it.[57] This distanced and selective relationship with Greek culture is the general background for the vernacular adaptation of Greek literary models.[58] The translation project in particular represents this pattern at its most acute, becoming a kind of fractal of the larger relationship, since it put a focus, from the lexical level up, on sameness with difference, fidelity with innovation.

By having a literature in Latin the Romans were able to participate in Hellenic culture, but in a mediated fashion, on terms they could dictate.[59] One observes closely related strategies at work in the way that they adapted the Greek educational curriculum for their own élite. The studies of Rawson (1985) and Wallace-Hadrill (1988) bring to light how precisely nuanced the Romans were in their selection from the range of Greek *paideia*. We have seen how eccentric within an ancient context were the Romans' choices of the texts to target for translation, as they focused on "literary" texts rather than technical or "non-literary" texts;[60] analogously, from the panoply of *paideia* they were extremely selective in choosing what to take over for their own education program, introducing a marked differentiation into what the source culture regarded as a unified whole.[61] They embraced rhetoric, *grammatica* in all its glory, and certain elements of philosophy (ethics, dialectic, some physics); on the other hand, they "neither understood nor respected . . . the mathematical arts of geometry, arithmetic, astronomy, and music," all of which "were essential parts of Greek παιδεία."[62] As we have already seen, the verses of Aratus on astronomy were obsessively translated by the Romans from the late Republic on, and it is very telling that it was this poetic manifestation of a key aspect of Greek science that came through the portals.[63]

These choices were a reflex of deep social forces, as the Roman élite adjudicated which aspects of Greek knowledge could be accommodated to their systems of power or conceptions of dignity and which had to be shunned altogether as potentially disruptive or else left to Greek practitioners.[64] The aristocracy was able to adapt to those parts of Greek knowledge that could be made to work with their expertise in speech-making, law, and control of tradition, while filtering out the accomplishments branded as banausic or threatening to impinge on their monopoly status as authoritative experts.[65] The recurrent expulsion of philosophers and of teachers of formal rhetoric in Latin made especially visible the élite's determination to patrol the boundaries of their traditional prerogatives and authority as mentors of their heirs, even as they worked to incorporate the modernizing new system of education.[66] Yet this apparent assertion of ancestral values and morality against newfangled Hellenism is more complicated in its motivations than it may appear at first, for it is itself a mark of power in the Hellenistic world to expel philosophers.[67]

It still remains striking that the Roman élite should take over *grammatica* so obsessively, and that an acquaintance with Greek literature and, gradually, with Latin literature, should be regarded as indispensable for participation in a militaristic empire's governing class. At a basic level, the embracing of the fundamental school curriculum of the Hellenistic world is part and parcel of the developing pressure to have some command of Greek as a prerequisite for the exercise of power and as a necessary marker of the imperial status of the governing class that was now competing directly with the other great Hellenistic powers. Once the momentum for bilingualism in the governing class was underway, nonparticipants would be left behind. Taking over for their own use the linguistic schooling used by Greeks was no doubt the most economical way of achieving this objective, yet there is clearly a good deal more at stake. In the first generations, the deliberate embracing of Greek as the other language a Latin-speaker needed to know in order to retain or achieve status is part of the advancing of Latin as the language of power in the peninsula that we discussed in Chapter 3, with its accompanying "barbarianization" of the other Italians by Romans intent upon establishing cultural superiority.[68] Incrementally, the education system and the developing Hellenizing Latin literature were jointly advertizing the ideology that the other Italian languages did not count.[69] The phases were not in any kind of lockstep, as we see in the proud declaration of Ennius that he had three hearts because he knew how to speak Greek, Latin, and Oscan (Gell. *NA* 17. 17. 1): but we should note that Ennius did not say that he wrote in Oscan. Over time, the Roman élite no longer learned any language other than Greek, and the developing apprehension that Latin and Greek were the paired languages of power and prestige reinforced the distinctive status of the new imperial language.

Making an education of this kind necessary for participation in élite governance was clearly an exclusionary policy, regulating who could be admitted to the first circle.[70] In a sense, however, it was also an enabling and inclusive policy, since it granted a means of admission to prestige and rank that was not there before, and that could be exploited by men from outside the circle of the *nobiles* in the vertiginously expanding world of the Roman empire from the third century on.[71] Rawson draws attention to Cicero's view that "in his boyhood . . . Greek and Latin studies were more eagerly pursued in the Latin cities than in Rome."[72] Cicero had not carried out a sociological survey, but his impression must mean something, and his own career is itself the most spectacular example of how far someone who was not *Romano di Roma* could go as a result of training and education. As Dench puts it, "the prestige of Latin . . . actively encourages its literary use precisely by the 'new,' those whose urbanity and centrality is most questionable."[73] As we shall see in the next section and particularly in Chapter 7, the new literature was likewise a phenomenon that could not be ring-fenced: it presented its own challenges to the worldview of the *nobiles,* making profound re-adjustments necessary to their way of coping with their expanding horizons.

Remarkably consistent patterns of selection and rejection are observable in Roman education from the third century down to the first—and this is particularly striking because, even if there were periodic state interventions to ban undesirables, there was no state direction of education in Rome. The Romans could indeed be criticized by Greeks for this lack of state direction: Cicero has his character Scipio Aemilianus defend the Roman tradition against Polybius' censure on this score (*Rep.* 4. 3).[74] The Romans' consistent patterns of discrimination in their reaction to Greek *paideia* are related to their management of the translation project. It matters greatly that they should engage with Hellenism on their own terms, and the use of Latin rather than Greek for the new literature is an aspect of this larger phenomenon.

The case of Jewish interaction with Hellenism is an interesting *comparandum,* for here too we see a distinctive culture resisting the threat of submersion even while responding to the pressure to engage in dialogue.[75] The Jewish and Roman responses shed light on each other but are tellingly diverse. Especially in Alexandria, we observe a "creative

Jewish-Greek culture, which sprang from, and built upon the Septuagint, but expressed itself in all the major Greek genres—epic, drama, history-writing, philosophy, and rhetoric."[76] Ezekiel, for example, wrote a tragedy in Greek on *Exodus,* Theodotus wrote an epic in Greek on the events concerning Schechem in *Genesis* 33–34, and Demetrius' chronological treatise περὶ τῶν ἐν τῇ Ἰουδαίᾳ βασιλέων ("On the kings in Judaea") organized the events of *Genesis* and *Exodus* in a consistent chronology, systematically using Greek scholarly techniques in the process.[77] These intriguing ventures represent a Jewish attempt to mediate between authoritative texts from their own heritage and prestigious models from the other culture. For their part, the Romans had no such pre-existing authoritative Latin texts to bring to the dialogue; nor, after the first generation of Roman histories written in Greek, did they follow the path of Demetrius (or Manetho or Berossus) in writing their history in the Greek language. Rather, they used Greek models to provide templates for writing history in their own vernacular, just as they used Greek models for templates in many other literary forms. For this initiative, the only possible glimpse of comparability from the Jewish case would be the short stories in Aramaic going under the names of *Judith, Esther, Daniel,* and *Tobit,* which have some kind of relationship—albeit very indirect, and hard to recover—with evolving Greek literary forms, in addition to their own distinctive background.[78]

Yet no one wrote a Hellenizing tragedy or comedy in Aramaic, or a Hellenizing epic in Hebrew. Nor did anyone write Hellenizing history in Hebrew. 1 Maccabees, now preserved in Greek, was originally composed in Hebrew, but it is essentially a continuation of long-standing Jewish history-writing practices, and not the product of systematic engagement with Hellenizing historiography.[79] Nor is it likely—if we look ahead even as far as the first century CE—that there was the stamp of Hellenizing historiography on Josephus' initial Aramaic version of what was eventually transformed into his Greek history of the *Jewish Wars.* This now lost Aramaic work was sent, so Josephus tells us in the Preface to the extant *Jewish Wars,* to the Aramaic-speaking "Parthians and Babylonians, and the most remote tribes of Arabia, together with the Jews who lived across the Euphrates, as well as the people of Adiabene," just across the Tigris (*BJ* 1. 6).[80] Given this audience, and the traditions to which they were accustomed, the work is unlikely to have contained "characteristic formal features of Graeco-Roman historiography" such as "speeches and digressions," but was probably rather "in the nature of a plain report, with perhaps some passages of lamentation."[81]

More obliquely, the Romans' choice to maintain a distance from full participation in Hellenism has unexpected affinities with the strategy adopted by the LXX translators, who were also resisting being engulfed in the other culture even as they engaged with it. These translators, as we have seen, deliberately produced a "foreignizing" translation bearing many traces of the original language's forms of expression: "Septuagint language in its nature . . . reflects a kind of recalcitrance, a reluctance to accede totally to a Hellenizing 'project,' which by the same token could not be ignored. Cultural adaptation went only so far."[82] This particular Jewish response to Hellenism was to "go Greek" but in such a way as to preserve all the time the impression of an indigenous template shimmering just beneath the surface of the "other" language of the text; the Roman solution was to "go Greek" but in their own language, so that the template whose impression was always shimmering beneath the surface was the "other" language, not the indigenous one.

Acting Greek

Scholars have regularly debated what Roman audiences got out of the translated Greek dramas that they were watching, in ever increasing numbers, from 240 on.[83] Jocelyn offers perhaps the strongest expression of puzzlement over the relevance such dramas could conceivably have had: "It is hard to see how such performances could have been thought more pleasing to the Roman gods than those which preceded them, and doubtless still continued, or what pleasure they could give to the mass of the Roman citizenry."[84] As far as the gods are concerned, Rüpke is no doubt correct to say that the nobles wanted to ensure that the gods "were witnesses of cultural products of the highest quality, . . .

Greek or Greek-style cultural products, of the same provenance and style as those selected by the nobles throughout the Italian municipalities for their villas and libraries."[85] As for the pleasure the new performances gave to "the mass of the Roman citizenry," I can do no better than recommend Gildenhard's zestful list of elements from mythological tragedy that one can imagine appealing to a Roman audience—many of them overlapping with whatever list one would draw up for elements appealing to the original Athenian audience—including family dysfunction, "societal breakdown," and a "voyeuristic fascination with the uncanny and prohibited."[86]

Attempts are often made to find a more specifically topical or political reference point for the Roman audiences as they watched their translated tragedies about cannibalistic monarchs and sacked foreign cities: such attempts tend to stress a genealogical interest on the part of the Romans, who were supposedly anxious to see how their mythological Trojan ancestry fits into the larger patternings of Greek myth.[87] Identifications of this kind can certainly at times be too mechanistically precise, and more diffuse and general points of contact are regularly at issue.[88] Yet in standing back from the search for "a coherent political meaning and message" we must be careful not to set up a misleading dichotomy between a hierarchically stratified Rome where drama is for entertainment and a unified Athens where drama is a civic occasion for the working out of communal ideology.[89] The comparison we should be making is not so much with the original fifth-century Athenian performance context but rather with the international arena for multiple reperformances, which was by now the normal reception context for Attic drama, not only for the Romans but for everyone in the Hellenistic world.[90] This international character of Athenian tragedy is so important that it had already left its mark on Aristotle's *Poetics*, for example, in which the relevance of the tragedies to Athenian civic ideology is scandalously—to most modern scholars—absent: "What looks for us like a suspicious oversight in the *Poetics* is in reality a symptom of Attic tragedy's success abroad, success that had been set in motion when Aeschylus first landed in Sicily and perhaps even earlier."[91] The public venues of the stage performances at Rome allowed space for many kinds of work that we may identify as "political" in a broader sense, and in Chapter 7 we shall see how important the new drama was in assisting in the creation of new knowledge systems of myth, religion, and philosophy.[92] For now, coming from our discussion of the way in which the Romans' new literature was the product of a nuanced and selective form of engagement with Hellenism, I want only to suggest how important a political and social function the new tragedies and comedies each discharged in providing a framework for thinking with and about the Greeks.

The century after 240 witnessed the efflorescence of Roman drama and the extension of Roman power over the Greek world. During these disorientating and turbulent times, the Romans needed to know what the Greeks were like, and they needed to digest Greek culture in the process. The new spectacles were the crucial venue for working this out. As McElduff well puts it in connection with comedy (and the same point applies to tragedy): "at least one of the functions of Roman comedy was to explain, to enclose the Greeks on a stage and make them knowable."[93] In certain respects, this could be an objectifying process, presenting "a stereotype of Greekness that would fix the colonial subject as a category within Rome."[94] It could also be a very mobile process, allowing the opportunity to experiment with "being" Greek, for the masked performers of both tragedy and comedy enabled the audience to try out what it was like to look at the world like a Greek, to identify momentarily with Greeks and their perspectives, in order to refine what it was like to look at the world as a Roman did. Of course, Attic drama in the first place had enabled its audience to perform the same kind of maneuver, making it possible for the Athenian audience to experiment with "being" Persian, or Trojan, or Theban, in the pursuit of defining what it was to be Athenian; and this game of shifting identification had been played by proxy for many decades by audiences in Syracuse, Taras, and Delos. On a stage in Rome, such exercises in decentering are potentially even more disorientating, for the dramas are translations, and, as Gildenhard points out, "[t]ranslation . . . renders both the foreign familiar and the familiar foreign, generating an interesting oscillation between moments of perceived identity and moments of perceived alterity."[95] This is true on the linguistic level, on the level of the plot and characters, and on the level of the whole cultural setting.

From this point of view, the translated dramas have a powerful destabilizing potential.[96] Comedy enjoys reminding the audience of the game of transcultural identification they are performing as they sit in Rome pretending that they are "really" in Athens, or in Athens pretending that they are "really" in Epidamnus, or Thebes.[97] It is generically *de rigueur,* says the Prologue to Plautus' *Menaechmi,* for comic poets to do this: *atque hoc poetae faciunt in comoediis,/omnis res gestas esse Athenis autumant,/quo illud uobis graecum uideatur magis* ("Actually, this is what poets do in comedies, they say that all the action takes place in Athens, to make you think it's more Greek," 7–9).[98] The Prologue goes on to tell us (in the immediately following lines if we follow the transposition of Gratwick (1993) *ad loc.*): "This city is Epidamnus, so long as this play is being put on: when another one is put on, then it'll be made another town" (*haec urbs Epidamnus est, dum haec agitur fabula:/quando alia agetur aliud fiet oppidum,* 72–73). We can imagine Mercury speaking the Prologue in Plautus' *Amphitryo* to an audience sitting on, let us say, the steps of the temple of Magna Mater on the Palatine: with an expansive sweep of his arm he takes in the Circus Maximus, the slope of the Palatine hill, the shrine of Victoria, and the temple itself, before delivering his punch line: *haec urbs est . . . Thebae* ("this city is . . . Thebes," 97).

When the father Micio in Terence's *Adelphoe,* then, upbraids his wayward son Aeschines, his outraged question has a double bite: *in qua ciuitate tandem te arbitrare uiuere?* ("Come on, in what state do you think you are living?" 685). If something like these words had been in the original when it was first staged in Athens, then this question would already have had an extra degree of electricity in Syracuse, Taras, Naples, or any other Greek city in which it might have been performed outside Athens. In Rome, in Latin, a "barbarian" language by the codes of the original playwright, the question invites a heightened degree of self-consciousness about the compatibility of cultural norms, focusing the play's key interests in authority and fatherhood.[99] Do Athenian sons behave like Roman sons, or Athenian fathers like Roman fathers?[100] In what ways are these Greek "characters" like us, or we like them? The authors themselves, as we have repeatedly seen, are individuals who shuttle back and forth between these categories.[101] Apart from the Greek Livius Andronicus, the other authors of the translated dramas are genuinely interstitial figures, neither Greek nor Roman, but definitely "barbarian" by conventional Greek criteria: when Plautus' Prologue announces that "Plautus translated the play in barbarian" (*Plautus uortit barbare, Trin.* 19; cf. *Maccus uortit barbare, Asin.* 11), there are three, not two, points of reference potentially in play.[102]

In tragedy, likewise, the identity of "we" and "here" can be destabilized, as the characters' words decenter assumptions about who is who inside the translating space. We saw in Chapter 3 that one of Pacuvius' tragic heroes draws attention to linguistic difference in an arresting way, when he declares that "what our people name as 'sky' the Greeks call 'aether'" (*id quod nostri caelum memorant Grai perhibent aethera*, fr. 89). Cicero's character Balbus, our source for this fragment, expresses some baffled irritation at the apparent rupture of the dramatic illusion: *quasi uero non Graius hoc dicat! "at Latine loquitur." si quidem nos non quasi Graece loquentem audiamus* ("As if it weren't a Greek saying this! 'But he is speaking Latin,' you'll say. Well, so long as we weren't listening to him as if he were speaking Greek," *ND* 2. 91). Yet the play from which this quotation comes, *Chryses,* is itself about the apparent loss and then rediscovery of Greek identity, as N. W. Slater (2000) has demonstrated. The speaker is probably the eponymous hero of the play, Chryses, the son of the Greek Agamemnon and the non-Greek captive Chryseis; her father Chryses' embassy to recover his daughter triggers the action of the *Iliad.* Brought up by his grandfather, young Chryses only discovers that he is really of Greek parentage when his half-siblings Orestes and Iphigenia turn up in their flight from Tauris. When he speaks these words before the revelation of his new identity as a Greek, his use of *nostri,* "our people," as opposed to the Greeks, and his marked use of a Latin word as opposed to a Greek word as a token of his distance, both make an irrational kind of sense within the play: it is even possible that the stress on the language difference between *nostri* and *Grai* means that we are to understand him as speaking in "Trojan," rather than Latin (or Greek).[103] Chryses' remarkable declaration opens up the possibility for a Roman audience to identify with the person who needs to mark off distance from the Greek, with the criterion of language as a key element of that marking off of distance.[104] How their identification then readjusts as Chryses turns out to be a Greek after all is an intriguing question, with a range of possible responses: are they going to maintain their distance or follow Chryses in an attempt at accommodation?[105]

The figure of Medea is another fascinating case study for the Romans, who can identify with Greek rejection of barbarian freakishness or else recognize that they are themselves outsiders to the Greek, just as Medea is.[106] As Cowan well puts it, after treating the Medea of Roman tragedy as an exemplary case of the original outsider being transformed: "The appropriation of Greek tragedy . . . facilitated the exploration of issues of ethnic and cultural identity, centred on the familiar poles of Greek and barbarian but with the audience as likely to identify with the latter as the former."[107] Here the Macedonian experience is a most compelling comparison case, for the Macedonians, "of all recipients of Greek tragedy in antiquity," are "the *closest outsiders,*" who "desperately and unequivocally strive to be acknowledged as a fully-fledged part of Greek culture."[108] The Macedonians will themselves have experienced moments of disorientation in their play-watching as they pursued this goal of incorporation, seeing themselves as outsiders from an Athenian point of view, and having potentially different focuses of sympathy from those of an Athenian audience;[109] for the Romans, who have a far more distanced relationship with Greek culture, and who never wanted "to be acknowledged as a fully-fledged part of Greek culture," the potential to see themselves in the role of the outsider in an Athenian drama is going to be considerably higher.

A Roman audience, for example, is certainly going to incline to identify with the "barbarian" rather than the Greek when the Trojan Andromacha hails her father Priam's fallen palace: "I saw you with barbaric force at hand" (*uidi ego te adstante ope barbarica*, fr. 89). Here the "barbaric force" are the Asian allies of the Trojans, helping them against the Greek aggressors. It would be a mistake to draw the sting of the shock generated here, as the Roman audience are invited to identify with their Trojan ancestors, who are presented as the outsider in the Athenian original.[110] The issue is still very much alive a hundred and fifty years later in Virgil's *Aeneid*, where Aeneas imitates Ennius' Andromacha in his description of the palace of Priam as decked out with "barbaric gold" (*barbarico . . . auro*, 2. 504).[111]

The flexible appeal of the myth of the Romans' Trojan origin is especially clear at moments like this. The Romans could stress their affiliations with Hellenism or they could play up the degree to which they were un-Greek, or anti-Greek: the Trojan myth sums up this doubleness, for it could help make the Romans part of the Greek scheme of things or else cast them as opponents of the Greeks if necessary.[112] Such Janus moments are of particular significance at the turning point of the sack of Troy, when the Hellenistic construction of time tips the scales of world history away from Asia and toward Greece: the new Roman perspective allows another view, by which the heirs to the Trojan "barbarians" will themselves take over Greece and inherit the mantle of empire.[113] Virgil's *Aeneid* takes these global oscillations as a cardinal theme, and the challenge of identification presents itself from a new angle when the Eastern forces of M. Antonius at the battle of Actium in 31 are described in exactly the same words as those used by Ennius' Andromacha of her father's allies, *ope barbarica* (*Aen.* 8. 685), in disturbing resonance with the language earlier used by Aeneas himself to describe Priam's sumptuous palace (*barbarico . . . auro*, *Aen.* 2. 504). Virgil's self-allusion crystallizes the question of how far the Romans have succeeded in distancing themselves from their Trojan ancestors and identifying themselves with the Greek *mission civilisatrice*; but his initial allusion to Ennius should alert us to the fact that such problems of identification and appropriation of the role of the other are radically involved in the Roman translation project from the start.

As discussed in Chapter 2, the Athenian Procne likewise destabilizes the audience's focus of identification when she calls attention to the problem of who "Zeus/Jupiter" is in Thrace and what the religious and moral norms are "here." For the Roman audience, the exercise in decentering and defamiliarization is different from what it had been for the Athenian audience, since for the Romans "here" is actually a place where "Zeus" is "Jupiter."[114] The perspectives shift through the act of translation, as the marginal becomes central, and the outsiders become the masters. In all of the cases we have been surveying, we see another culture "writing back" against the Greeks' designation of them as "outsiders," decentering existing assumptions in order to claim a new kind of parity with Greek status.[115] The Romans are creating a new kind of interpretative space in the process, redefining the terms of Hellenism and forging "an active and dynamic transcultural sensibility."[116]

This "mobile sensibility" afforded Roman audiences a supple tool.[117] Working systematically with Greek culture through the medium of translated Greek drama gave the Romans an extremely economical and powerful way of assessing their ever-changing relationship with Hellenic culture and of reshaping their sense of national identity in the process.[118] Their Greek plays in Latin helped to focus their attention on similarity and difference at every level, discharging for them a function analogous to that which Jonathan Z. Smith describes Judaism discharging for the modern Christian student of religion, since it is:

> close, yet distant; similar, yet strange; "occidental," yet "oriental"; commonplace, yet exotic. This tension between the familiar and the unfamiliar, at the very heart of the imagining of Judaism, has enormous cognitive power. It invites, it requires comparison. Judaism is foreign enough for comparison and interpretation to be necessary; it is close enough for comparison and interpretation to be possible.[119]

The Romans had many opportunities to perform such cognitive operations, for the scale of the new theatrical culture in Rome rapidly expanded, with proliferating opportunities for the performance of drama. Within two generations, there were well over a dozen days available in the festival calendar for theatrical performances, as the Senate added more and more festivals with a scenic component, in large part as morale-building responses to the successive crises of this tumultuous period, in rather the same way as we observed in the initial reforms to the *Ludi Romani* in 364: *Ludi Plebeii* and *Ludi Cereales* (c. 220), *Ludi Apollinares* (212), *Megalesia* (194), *Florales* (173).[120] By the time Ennius died in 169, hundreds of performances had taken place. Rome could take on any city in the world, even Athens and Syracuse, in terms of scale of production.[121] Further, it is highly likely that the productions went on the road after their first showings at the Roman festival, giving yet more opportunities for Roman citizens, Latins, and allies to experience the translated worlds of tragedy and comedy in Praeneste, Venusia, Pompeii, or Capua.[122]

The Romans, then, quickly found themselves in a unique position, thanks to the culture brokers who emerged from the imperial zone created by the expansion of Roman power over the peninsula of Italy and the island of Sicily. These entrepreneurs had an indispensable role to play in the Romans' acquisition of this crucial part of their imperial domain. In comparison with the performances before 240, the new poets, with their revolutionary translations, were trying to get it right in a novel kind of way. As we saw in the case of Livius Andronicus' substitution of *Camena* for *Mousa,* however, "getting it right" can never mean getting it absolutely right: there is always slippage and lack of synchromesh in translation. The new translations in Latin allowed difference to be maintained, even as assimilation was practiced. This is true at the level of diction, and true at the level of the large-scale cultural interactions of the new hybrid *Ludi Romani*—or the newly hybrid *Ludi Romani,* we should say, since they had always been a hybrid, first Etruscan/Roman, and then, since 364, Etruscan/Oscan/Roman/Greek.

The Games of Anicius:
A Road Not Taken?

The old forms of the pre-240 *ludi scaenici* did not vanish overnight by any means, but continued to find stage-time. When all the actors in Rome were expelled for a period by the censors in the year 115, an exception was made for "the Latin pipe-player with singer and the song-and-dance équipe" (*praeter Latinum tibicinem cum cantore et ludum talarium*, Cassiod. *Chron.* 2 p. 131 f. Mommsen); as pointed out by Reitzenstein, it looks as if this exception was meant to protect the ancient forms of music seen in the great parade before the circus games and performed on the stage ever since 364.[123] In at least some of the available performance slots of the various *ludi scaenici,* these older shows co-existed somehow with the new Greek dramas in Latin. In principle, new forms of synthesis could have arisen out of this co-existence, yet there is no evidence that any such hybrids developed.

We may, however, have one possible case of an attempt at a hybrid form, combining professional Greek standards of musical performance with the old formats of the *ludi scaenici* and of other elements of Roman dance culture. In February 166, L. Anicius Gallus celebrated a triumph over the Illyrian king Genthius, and as part of his celebrations he held victory games, using a massive purpose-built stage in the Circus Maximus. These games have gone down in history as a wonderful fiasco, thanks to the disdainful account of Polybius, as reported to us by the equally disdainful Athenaeus (*Deipnosophistae* 14. 615a–e = Polyb. 30. 22). Since Polybius appears to be writing as an eyewitness, Anicius' show will have been one of the very first events Polybius witnessed in Rome, for he had arrived there late in the previous year.[124] Everything Anicius did in arranging his victory games was completely ridiculous, according to Polybius (ἀγῶνας ἐπιτελῶν τοὺς ἐπινικίους ἐν τῇ Ῥώμῃ παντὸς γέλωτος ἄξια πράγματα ἐποίησεν). The detailed account of what went on is too long to reproduce here, but the show began in the normal Greek way, with some superstar Greek *artistes,* specially brought in for the games by Anicius, playing on their pipes onstage, with their choruses accompanying them in song and dance in the *orchestra* below. Anicius wanted something different, however, and he sent his lictors to tell them to make it more of a contest (ἀγωνίζεσθαι μᾶλλον ἐκέλευσεν). The *artistes* were baffled, and a lictor indicated that they were supposed to wheel around and advance on each other and enact a kind of battle (ἐπιστρέψαντας ἐπαγαγεῖν ἐφ’ αὐτοὺς καὶ ποιεῖν ὡσανεὶ μάχην). The pipe-players and choruses did their best to follow instructions, and the audience went wild when one of the dancers did a neat spin and put up his fists as if to fight with a pipe-player who was advancing towards him. "While this group was still competing in a battle line, two dancers, accompanied by a group of musicians, invaded the dancing area, and four boxers got up onstage, along with trumpeters and horn-players." Tragic actors seem to have been part of all this somehow, for, says Polybius, "as for what I could add about the tragic actors, some people will think that I am joking."[125]

To the Greeks Polybius and Athenaeus this is a ridiculous fiasco, and from their cultivated perspective it shows up the Romans for the hapless philistines they need them to be. But what on earth did Anicius actually think he was doing? A range of suggestions have been made, from Gruen's proposal that Anicius was engaging in sheer parody of Greek norms, as a brazen act of confident self-assertion by the Roman conqueror, to Günther's proposal that he was mounting a mimetic display of his victories in Illyria, setting off the conquered Greeks in contrast to the victorious Roman spectators.[126] If we follow an old suggestion by Reitzenstein, however, we may apply a little hermeneutical charity and see Anicius as trying out a jazzed-up version of the kind of mimetic dancing to the *tibia* that had been part of the *ludi scaenici* since 364, together with boxing to the accompaniment of the *tibia* that also seems to have been part of games in Etruria and Rome.[127] If this hypothesis has any force at all, then the crowd are treated to something like the traditional choreography they are used to from the old *Ludi* and the *pompa circensis*, and Anicius is trying to modernize it all by blending in accompaniment from top Greek talent—who prove to have not the remotest idea what is going on, even if they will presumably have had some coaching in advance.[128]

Spectacles in International Dialogue

To the knowing eye of the accomplished Greek observer the result of Anicius' attempt at innovation is an utter farce, but it is possible that we have here a trace of a more experimental approach to engaging with Greek culture—in this case, an experiment that did not actually take hold. Whether this charitable interpretation of Anicius' program is right or not, we can at least be sure that his show was in competitive dialogue with the smoothly professional Hellenizing show that Aemilius Paullus had just put on at Amphipolis in the spring of 167, to celebrate his victory at Pydna the year before. According to Livy, Aemilius' games were all done in the Greek mode, with music and stage performances as well as athletic competitions and equestrian events: *ita factum est, ut non magnificentiam tantum, sed prudentiam in dandis spectaculis, ad quae rudes tum Romani erant, admirarentur* ("done in such a way that the Greeks were amazed at not just the splendid scale but the practical grasp of staging spectacles, at which the Romans at that time were inexperienced," 45. 32. 10). Aemilius is quoted in the same context for the famous remark that arranging a banquet and organising *Ludi* was part of being the same person who knew how to conquer in war (45. 32. 11; cf. Polyb. 30. 14; Plut. *Aem.* 28. 5).

Aemilius here is following in the footsteps of the Successor-kings, themselves following in the footsteps of Philip II of Macedon and his son Alexander, past masters at stage-managing Pan-Hellenic victory games.[129] Anicius is perhaps reacting against this suave imitation of Greek practice, and trying to co-opt the same kind of glamorous professional Greek *artistes* who were employed for Aemilius' games in order to give a new burnish to traditional Roman spectacles, aiming for some novel synthesis that never took off. Aemilius Paullus' own solution to the problem of cross-cultural dialogue was to give impeccably Greek games in Greece and then to come home and stage what became the template for the quintessential Roman triumph, the most famous Roman triumph until Pompeius Magnus' third triumph in 61.[130] Poor Anicius' triumph, celebrated less than three months after Aemilius', was doomed to be the loser in the comparison (Liv. 45. 43. 2).

The innovative rivalry over the staging of spectacles in Rome was intense, and it was being played out on an international stage, for other Hellenistic powers were watching Rome as much as Rome was watching them.[131] If we focus too hard on the mediation of Greek culture into Rome we can overlook the reverse traffic, as striking features of Roman life become the object of fascinated mimesis by Greeks, especially by Greek monarchs. Edmondson has clearly brought out the way in which the extraordinary spectacles put on by Antiochus IV in Antioch in the late autumn of 166 were intensely competitive both with Aemilius' Greek games at Amphipolis and also with his Roman triumph. Antiochus began his more traditional Greek-style festival games with a mock Roman triumph, continued with public banquets in the Roman style, and finished with Roman gladiatorial shows and wild-beast hunts (Polyb. 30. 25).[132] Antiochus, who had spent over ten years as a hostage in Rome from about the age of 27, was as fascinated by Roman electioneering as he was by the Roman triumph (Polyb. 26. 1), while Prusias II of Bithynia was intrigued by the Roman institution of the freedman (Polyb. 30. 18. 1–3).

Spectacles at home and abroad, then, staged both by Romans and by their competitors, were a mobile feature of the ever-evolving world of international politics. The new Greek dramas in Latin were a key part of the Roman spectacles, with opportunities for their staging being built in to each successive new festival that was added throughout our period. Yet the impact of the dramas was felt beyond the venues of the spectacles. Through the revolutionary act of translation, the translator-poets enabled the creation of a new force altogether. No one had mapped the Greek forms of drama onto another language in this way before, and the paradoxical result of this new attempt to translate or faithfully adapt the Greek models was to lay the ground for the unprecedented creation of the Mediterranean's second vernacular literature. We turn in the next chapter to consider the distinctive features of this new vernacular literature.

CHAPTER 6

A Literature in the Latin Language

T HE FIRST TRANSLATORS were not just "carrying across" material from one area to another: from within their interstitial spaces they were catalysts, transformative agents. Thanks to the effects of their productions, the culture of the Roman people and their allies underwent a decisive shift, as in surprisingly short order "another form of public communication had been developed: literature."[1] There had certainly been musical and verbal performances of various kinds at Rome before the translation project got under way, and we shall investigate the possible nature of those performances in Chapter 8, together with the contributions they may have made to the new literary culture. Yet the scale of the new developments is very striking, and betokens a decisive reorientation in a new direction. As we have seen, hundreds of translations of tragedy and comedy were commissioned in the decades following Livius Andronicus' first staged play in 240, since by the 180s the Roman state was providing "about fourteen official days for production, hardly less than the time available at Athens for dramatic competitions."[2] The translated dramas in turn provided the momentum for an expanding torrent of experimentation in other Hellenizing literary fields, both in verse and prose, producing works that were no longer necessarily translations or adaptations of Greek originals, but that extended the range of writing practices in novel ways—epic (following Livius' initial translation of Homer's *Odyssey*), history, oratory, satire, and literary history.[3] These works are lumped together in our handbooks as "archaic" literature, but in fact these years are the most overtly modernizing period of Roman cultural history.[4] The new literature had a kinetic impact on Roman life in many different spheres, and it set in train a process that in time transformed Greek literary and intellectual life as well: Plutarch's *Parallel Lives* and *Roman Questions* are a link in a chain that ultimately goes back to the Rome of the late third century.

What Does It Mean to Speak of "Latin Literature"?

Rome came to have a vernacular literature that had its departure points in the literature of the Greeks, and I have been arguing so far that this is a highly anomalous state of affairs in the context of the time. Scholars tend to assume in the first place that it is natural to expect a nation to have a vernacular literature with generic features broadly along the lines of what we see in Greece and Rome, but, as we shall see in Chapter 8, there is no evidence that any other contemporary non-Greek group in the Mediterranean had anything corresponding to such a Grecizing category of "literature" before the Roman experiment. This certainly does not mean that the cultural productions of those other societies are somehow beneath our notice, or that we could not analyze them through the lens of "literature" if we wished, just as we may in a great range of societies. After all, human beings began producing physical art 50,000 years ago at the latest, and verbal art, together with music, song, and dance, has presumably been part of human societies in one guise or another since at least that same time, and very probably long before. Within this impossibly large field of activity, definitions and criteria will necessarily be fluid and variable.

Scholars do not agree on very much when it comes to defining "literature" or the "literary," but one thing that is perhaps generally agreed is that "literature" is not an ahistorical category that applies across time and space: as Compagnon puts it, "literature has no essence but is a complex, heterogeneous, changing reality."[5] From that point of view, we have no need to define "literature" as an entity, or to assume that we can measure other societies by the criteria of the contemporary West, any more than when discussing "science" or "sport." Still, the modern Western institution of "literature" is regularly used as a benchmark when observing ancient conditions, and from that perspective it is often claimed that the Greek and Roman world does not show the features of modern literary systems.[6]

In certain senses, it is clearly correct to point out that historical developments in the modern world have created conditions that have no counterpart in the ancient world. It was only in the eighteenth century, for example, "that literature was redefined as part of the fine arts and the literary artifact was reconceived as an autonomous aesthetic object operating under its own rules and requiring a special kind of critical attention."[7] The full-blown apparatus of "literature" as a "differentiated social system" with its own autonomy and protocols is a feature of the modern Western world that cannot be imposed as a template on other times and places.[8] Nonetheless, emphasis on difference from the modern world can produce its own distorting affect, and can distract us from identifying features of Roman life that do eventually mark out a recognizable literary culture as a distinctive system within the society in ways that set the Romans apart from their contemporaries except for the Greeks. The Roman world in time has libraries, endowed professorships, a common educational track with a "core" and "periphery" of accomplishments (experience of which was indispensible for anyone with any pretensions to status), copying houses, transmission of authoritative texts together with the scholarship that accompanied them, and empire-wide circulation of texts in a great variety of genres:[9] texts of Virgil's *Aeneid* have been found at Hadrian's Wall and on the top of Masada, and Gallus' elegies resurfaced in the sands of Egypt.[10] Even by the early second century BCE, and possibly earlier, the men who produced the acting scripts for the Roman *Ludi* had their own marked-off status as a *collegium po-*

etarum;[11] by the middle of that century, the new texts they had been producing were on the educational curriculum and starting to be the object of critical work of various kinds.[12]

To speak of a modern-style "literary system" in place in Rome in the second century is certainly anachronistic in important respects, yet the features just cited can help to highlight how rapid and systematic the distinctive changes in Roman culture had been since the beginning of the translation project.[13] These cultural features were the product of very large-scale changes in Roman life, and they increasingly aligned the Roman experience with the Greek. Even within this process, in trying to pin down what may be distinctive about the Roman case, we have already seen that the category of what gets translated or not can help shed some light on how certain works were apprehended in the ancient world. The Romans look distinctly anomalous in this regard, in that they do the reverse of other groups, translating what most scholars would accept as "literary" texts and leaving alone technical or scientific— "useful"—texts. Some kind of definition of what counts as "literature" is in play in such cases, if only a negative one.

Writing within the Frameworks of Hellenistic Literary Culture

In addition to acknowledging that there is no one definition of "literature" that applies across time and place, we should also acknowledge that the production and reception of literature is a fragmented field—there is, after all, no necessary synchrony even to the development of modern Western literary systems, within which we observe different phases to different aspects of the process. Fundamentally, as Compagnon well puts it, "literature" presents us with "the contradiction of two possible and equally legitimate perspectives: a *contextual* perspective (historical, psychological, sociological, institutional) and a *textual* perspective (linguistic). Literature, or literary study, is always caught between a historical approach in the broad sense (the text as a document) and a linguistic approach (the text as an artifact of language, literature as the art of language): the two are irreducible."[14] Different historical phases will call for us to give different priorities to these perspectives.

As we shall see in detail later in this chapter, Compagnon's "textual" perspective is one that we may, or even must, bring to bear on reading the first documents of the translation project. From the point of view of the writers, operating within an evolving textual system, it can certainly make sense to talk of their consciousness of participating in a "literature" from early on, not least because the bi- and trilingual poets were bringing to bear assumptions about literary systems that they had learned in their first education, as students of the institution of Greek literature. The earliest Latin dramas and epics display a highly "literary" dynamic of marked language, with allegiance to models and distancing from them in the arena of intertextuality: these texts depend upon formal generic distinctions and choices of meter that are meaningless outside a space of literary-critical self-awareness.[15] The poets' self-consciousness about their novel role as translators heightens the sense of engagement with literary prototypes: as we saw in Chapter 2, the first line of Livius' translation of Homer's *Odyssey* puns on the fact that this is a new "version" of a classic. On the other hand, from Compagnon's "contextual" perspective ("historical, psychological, sociological, institutional"), we observe different phases in comparison with those of the "textual" perspective.[16] It was in no sense inevitable that this other kind of momentum would also develop in Rome, but, as we shall see in the next section, by the middle of the second century we observe the new texts featuring in Roman education and in various forms of literary-critical history and polemic: the development of social institutions to accommodate and work on the new texts is not one we should expect to come into view straightaway—or even necessarily to happen at all.

From both the textual and the contextual perspectives, we may be sure that the first producers of the texts in the translation project will have had a well-developed sense of what a certain kind of institution of literature was like, as a result of their Greek training and upbringing. We have already remarked above that the conditions through which Livius and his successors apprehended their Greek model texts were those of contemporary Hellenistic scholarship and education, in which the canons of drama and other genres were being codified, systematized, and commented upon.[17] In this regard, for Livius Andronicus "the category 'literature' was defined by and consisted of Greek texts."[18] For these writers, the texts they were producing were from the beginning calqued upon texts encountered within the context of the institution of literature in Greece: the models for the first Roman poets "were known and studied in the form in which Hellenistic scholarship presented them."[19] And within that institution, by the period of the late third century, a good working definition of literature could have been the one given by Roland Barthes: "Literature is what is taught, period, that's all."[20]

The first texts of Roman literature were translations, and their composers' decision to pick out certain Greek texts as the object of translation inevitably marked out the new Latin versions as having a special relationship with the source texts, as being in some sense participants in or continuators of that literary tradition. This deep background partly explains the intense self-consciousness Roman poetry displays from the start concerning "its place in its tradition . . . ; . . . it is metapoetical to a high degree."[21] Further, the act of translation out of a canonical body of ranked and organized texts engenders the apprehension that there is a lack in the target culture, a supplement that has to be filled.[22] Already the very first translator-poet, Livius Andronicus, is writing both comic and tragic scripts, revealing how comprehensive were the ambitions for the project of translation. Before Livius, it was practically unheard of for anyone to compose scripts for both comedy and tragedy, with the fifth-century Ion of Chios being the one exception as a candidate for this inclusiveness;[23] indeed, the professional divides between the forms were so strong that various guilds of actors of drama, the *technitae* of Dionysus, specialized in either tragedy or comedy.[24] Livius also wrote a translation of epic, so that the ambition of his work had a striking comprehensiveness across the major genres: the motivation is the urge to fill out the gaps and provide an attempt at a systematic supplement.

The Roman experiment involved the incremental construction of a parallel canon in the major genres of Greek (epic, tragedy, comedy, above all), upon which there followed—as we shall see in the next section—the emergence of a developing critical discourse, initially fostered by the poets themselves, and then of an educational and scholarly apparatus. The emergence of this secondary apparatus was by no means inevitable, but the conditions were conducive from the beginning, just as they were, for example, in the Japanese case: "Unlike Chinese and Greek literary culture, Japanese and Roman education developed on the basis of previous canonization efforts and scholarly literature of their reference cultures."[25] From this perspective, "the Roman translation project is a form of literary curatorship, a kind of calque upon the codification and organization being undertaken especially in contemporary Alexandria: by the Augustan age, with its twinned Greek and Latin libraries, the Latin side of such a library is in a sense double-curated, double-libraried."[26]

Although in epic and tragedy the models were archaic and classical, the new Roman literature was a child of its time in its relationship to the literary-critical modes and the reading techniques acquired through Hellenistic education:[27] after all, Livius and Ennius are recorded as having taught Roman schoolchildren (Suet. *Gram. et rhet.* 1), and their instruction was no doubt close to what they had themselves received. As Donald Russell well puts it, "There was no pre-scholarly epoch in Latin literature, as there had been in Greek. Criticism went side by side with creation from the start, and it was a scholarly criticism, involving close attention to linguistic and formal correctness."[28] This is not to say that Livius and his successors were anticipating a Catullus or a Virgil in deeply philological exploitation of Alexandrian scholarship—indeed, the standard exegetical commentaries on Homer, of which the scholia of modern editions are the fragments, had not yet been produced when Livius wrote his translation of the *Odyssey*.[29] Yet much exegetical material that later found its way into the commentaries was already in circulation and in use in the classrooms of the Hellenistic world, and just such material must lie behind the examples that scholars have detected of the first poets translating in the light of scholarly explanations of Homeric or tragic passages.[30] Scholars since Friedrich Leo have regularly been op-

posed to the possibility of the translator-poets being indebted to specifically "Alexandrian" influences, on the grounds of anachronism; but
for this period, as for the late Republican period, we should remember
that " 'Hellenistic' is not necessarily synonymous with 'Alexandrian' or
'Callimachean.' "[31] We do not transform a Livius Andronicus or a Naevius into a learned Alexandrian philologist or an early embodiment of
Catullus' aesthetic if we see him as a product of Hellenistic education,
and as bringing the preconceptions of such a background to bear on his
compositions in Latin.[32]

Such a conclusion about the educational and scholarly background
of the first translator poets is not as minimalist as it may appear to be.
From the point of view of the Rome of 250, it was not in the least predictable that a body of dramatic scripts and other texts in Latin should
soon be produced in conformity with Hellenistic understandings of
genre, meter, and diction. Further, in the case of Ennius, two generations later, we are faced with a poet who self-consciously strikes a pose
as a writer with more specifically refined and professional philological
skills than his predecessors. In his polemical "second preface" in Book
7 of his *Annales,* Ennius proudly claimed that before him no poet in the
Latin language (he means his predecessor in Latin epic, Naevius) had
been "devoted to the study of language" (fr. 209). The Latin phrase is *dicti
studiosus,* a calque on the buzz word φιλόλογος, *philologus,* and it sets
the bar high for the readers of Ennius' epic, and for his oeuvre as a whole,
which covered an extraordinary variety of genres in inventive and intellectual ways—epic, tragedy, comedy, epigram, philosophical essays,
satire.[33] This is the context in which to assess the nature of Ennius' bold
work with the opening scene of Callimachus' *Aetia* at the beginning of
his own *Annales* (frr. 2–3).[34] By having a dream of transplantation like
that of Callimachus (fr. 2), who dreamed of being transported from the
new land of Ptolemaic Egypt to the original source of poetry on Mt. Helicon, where Hesiod had met the Muses face to face (*Theog.* 22–34), Ennius was able to assert that he too could lay a mediated claim, from the
position of a new kind of outsider, to the patrimony of the homeland of
Greek culture. Callimachus' work was directed towards a "new center,"

of Alexandria and Cyrene, one that was represented as the new endpoint of the culture of "old Greece";[35] Ennius can represent Roman history as the next step and the city of Rome as the next "new center."

We need to remind ourselves that in the contemporary Greek world Callimachus, despite (or as well as) being a formidably learned operator, was not the icon of recherché taste that he became for the Romans of the late Republic and the Augustan period, and that he tends to remain for modern readers. The popularity of Callimachus' *Aetia* is attested by widespread papyri finds in provincial towns in Egypt, sometimes with reading apparatus of a kind to suggest that many of his readers were by no means learned.[36] By choosing to open his new epic with a clear allusion to this recent Alexandrian masterpiece, in other words, Ennius is not endorsing the dichotomies that were later constructed by a Catullus or a Virgil; rather, he is claiming that his new epic will be both Homeric and modern, a new chapter in an ongoing literary history that is shaped and informed by the critical standards of Hellenism.[37]

The Development of a Second-Order Institution of Criticism

If the Roman poets are operating within Hellenistic literary and critical frameworks from the outset, we may also see them constructing a second-order critical discourse within three generations, with a particular emphasis on literary history, in a way that helps to create a Roman equivalent of the Greek "archival sensibility."[38] The tragic poet Accius, born around 170, is a crucial figure in this new development. From some time around 140 on, he was producing, together with his tragedies, a range of works on literary history and theory, including discussions of grammar and orthography.[39] His major work here, the *Didascalica*, may well have been in prose, covering Greek as well as Roman theatrical history, with discussions of chronology, authenticity, and attribution. Composed in at least nine books, the work mentioned the relative dates of Homer and Hesiod (fr. 6), and may therefore have covered other genres besides drama in some detail.[40] His *Pragmatica*, of uncertain

scope, discussed issues of stage performance in the appropriately dramatic meter of trochaic septenarii.[41] Accius also had strong views on
orthography, trading punches with the satiric poet Lucilius on this question, as he suggested, for example, that Latin should follow Greek in
writing double *g* instead of *ng* in words such as *aggulus* (for *angulus*).[42]
In this regard, he was consistently sticking to his own Grecizing ten-
dencies in his tragedies, where he practiced taking over Greek declension forms instead of domesticating Greek names into Latin declensions; as we saw in Chapter 3, he was explicitly remarked upon for this
strategy by one Valerius Soranus, in a hexameter work of criticism from
some time probably around 100: *Accius Hectorem nollet facere, Hectora
mallet* ("Accius wouldn't want to produce *Hectorem,* he'd prefer *Hectora,*" fr. 1 Courtney).[43]

This part of the tragedian's oeuvre represents an implicit claim that
the new literary culture needs not only more additions but also an apparatus of criticism and historical organization. The conscious attempt
to create links with Greek literary history that we glimpse in the *Didascalica* is especially important, for it gives a literary-historical and scholarly contour to the ambition discernible in the translation project as a
whole, of producing a literature that would be a continuation of Greek
literary history by other means. From this perspective, the *Didascalica*
represents an extraordinary claim, one that could not have been advanced by any other contemporary culture.[44] Accius' attempts to construct debts to Greece at a cultural level in his mysterious hexametric
Annales are part of the same momentum, as he explicitly describes the
Roman festival of the Saturnalia as deriving from the Greek and especially Athenian festival of the Cronia (*nostrisque itidem est mos traditus
illinc/iste, ut cum dominis famuli epulentur ibidem,* "and from there that
custom was handed down to our people, that slaves should dine in the
same setting as their masters," fr. 3. 5–6 Courtney).

Accius' literary-critical and literary-historical work is not alone in the
world of the second half of the second century, for other writers produced analogous works in verse. We have a fragment of a variation upon
the Hellenistic "canon" format from the *De Poetis* of Volcacius Sedigitus,

who gives a swashbuckling ranking of the poets of the Latin comic tradition, from number one (Caecilius Statius) to number ten (Ennius), in the dramatic meter of iambic senarii.[45] The cocky poise Volcacius displays in his deft procedure—at once exploiting and playing with the norms of scholarship—is striking testimony to the sophistication of the poet and his audience.[46] One Porcius Licinus wrote some kind of literary history in verse (trochaic septenarii, the same meter as Accius' *Pragmatica*).[47] This work discussed the date of the arrival of the Muse in Rome, in a fragment that remains extremely controversial; it also had a lot to say about the life and work of Terence, with scurrilous and tendentious remarks about his relationship with the nobles Scipio Aemilianus and Laelius.[48]

Such quasi-scholarly writing by the poets—zestfully polemical and argumentative—anticipates the work of scholars such as L. Aelius Stilo, who first systematically set about constructing the apparatus of Latin scholarship within a curricular environment around the end of the second century BCE.[49] Stilo, like Accius, concerned himself with the problem of the authenticity of Plautus' plays, and he wrote a commentary on the hymns of the Salian priests, together with etymological studies, including the language of the Twelve Tables. We must not see Stilo as an Alexandrian librarian transplanted to Rome; the interests of Stilo and his peers "were in the compilation and identification of what manuscripts they had, not recension, collation, or emendation."[50] Yet their work represents the first recoverable systematic attempt to set in place a scholarly and educational apparatus for literature in the Latin language that would correspond to the existing apparatus for literature in Greek.[51]

It was not inevitable that this scholarly and educational institution should take root in Rome, however natural it now appears to us. In fact, it is an amazing development. Leo, as so often, pinpoints with terse eloquence how extraordinary and unprecedented was the Roman case: "It was something completely new that the Greek techniques of research should be applied to another language and to works written in another language."[52] After all, the "first-order," "textual" construction of a literary tradition based upon Hellenistic categories had been going on for a hundred years before we have secure evidence for any "second-order," "contextual" work on that tradition.

It was the poets themselves who generated the momentum for reflecting upon their tradition, first from within their own practice—as we have seen with Livius Andronicus' punning upon his "turning" of Homer, or with Ennius' polemic against his predecessor Naevius—and then in the more explicitly literary-historical and critical works we have just been discussing. It is striking that the first dedicated disembedded reflections on the history and nature of the new literature were written by practitioners—Accius, above all, but also Porcius Licinus and Volcacius Sedigitus. This intense debate over the Roman literary tradition and its relationship with the Greek tradition grows out of the self-conscious reflection of the practitioners upon their craft—a reflexive practice that, again, had been part of their poetic technique from the beginning.

The eventual role of scholars and educators in shaping the institution of Roman literature was clearly crucial, and the apparatus they constructed over time tracked that of the Greek model with extraordinary fidelity.[53] Yet they were building on a momentum set in train by the engagement of the practitioners with their own developing tradition, especially in connection with drama, which was still, in the middle of the second century, overwhelmingly the main bulk of Latin literature and the principal focus of critical attention. The eventual formation of canons and curricula is in dialogue with the poets' own vigorous debates over their traditions and also with popular taste as manifested in the acting companies' repertoires. In this way, the first canonizations and rankings are arising, as they had in Athens, from the esteem of audiences, performers, and fellow artists.

A Roman Literary Tradition

I have been stressing that the translator-poets are a product of Greek literary systems. The literature that eventually developed from their initiatives was not only calqued upon Greek literature but also generated in time an institutional apparatus of scholarship that was itself calqued upon the institution of Hellenistic scholarship. We now need explicitly to take stock of the important fact that, as we have already been seeing with the poets' debates over the status of the different Roman authors, the Roman poets were by no means operating wholly from within Greek literary traditions. Very quickly, the Greek literary tradition became only one arc of their horizon. From the start, Livius Andronicus is working with a different culture from the Greek, even as he is operating under the "conviction that Greek literature, for being the only literature known, is to be identified with literature as such"; yet the dialogue becomes significantly different the moment Livius' first successor, Naevius, starts producing his own dramas five years later, in 235, for "unlike his predecessor, Naevius did not see Greek literature as literature as such,"[54] inasmuch as there was now a set of Latin plays already there for him to take account of.

At this point, we are in a different kind of literary tradition, as the poets take on a challenge not faced by anyone within the ambit of the Greeks before, so far as we know: they must focus on what is at stake in not only translating Greek literary culture but also in developing an ongoing related literary culture in a different language, Latin. From early on, we detect the assertion that Roman literary culture is a successor to Greek, an inheritance of it, rather than a cadet branch of an ongoing development. In time, this assertion acquires solidity thanks to the remarkable sleight of hand by which the Roman literary tradition erects a "chronological fence . . . between Greek and Latin literary traditions," creating the (completely unhistorical) impression that "Latin literature begins at a point when . . . Greek literature more or less stops."[55]

Later Roman poets regularly mark their consciousness of this dynamic as they compulsively engage in the so-called "two-tier" or "window" or "double" allusion, signaling that they are imitating a Latin predecessor as well as a Greek passage already imitated by that predecessor.[56] We see the first surviving example of this practice in the epic tradition of Livius Andronicus, Naevius, and Ennius. First, Livius translates a line of Homer in which Pallas addresses Zeus: ὦ πάτερ ἡμέτερε,

Κρονίδη, ὕπατε κρειόντων ("Oh our father, son of Cronus, highest of the ruling gods," *Od.* 1. 45). We have Livius' version of the first half of this line, in which the Greek Cronus is characteristically domesticated as Saturn: *Pater noster, Saturni filie* ("Our father, son of Saturn," fr. 2). Next, in the *Bellum Punicum,* Naevius has Venus address Jupiter, and he translates the second half of the Homeric line (which may or may not have already been translated by Livius): *summe deum regnator* ("highest ruler of the gods," fr. 16). Almost certainly in that same context, in a climax of approximation to the Latin religious lexicon, Naevius introduces a deity addressing Jupiter in narrative; together with a synonym for the original Homeric ὕπατε, "highest," he also gives Jupiter—known in Rome as Optimus Maximus ("Greatest, Best")—half of his distinctively Roman epithet, *optumum: patrem suum supremum optumum appellat* ("she addresses her father, highest, best," fr. 15). In Ennius' *Annales,* when a deity (probably Venus again) addresses Jupiter, the poet gives a variation of Livius' original line, while adding in the *second* half of Jupiter's Roman cult title to supplement Naevius' initial *optumum: o genitor noster Saturnie, maxime diuom* ("Oh our begetter, son of Saturn, greatest of the gods," fr. 444).[57] Ennius' newly Homeric hexametric epic is alluding to the original Homeric line, yet Ennius is doing so via Livius' original translation of that line, while simultaneously blending in the work on Livius' translation already performed by Naevius, so as to produce a fully modern and Roman version of the heroic moment. This chain of Homeric and Roman links is a template for how Roman authors will continue to work off both Latin and Greek models.

The new Latin epic tradition is self-conscious about its dynamic internal relationship from the moment there is a tradition—in other words, from the moment that Naevius sets about working with his predecessor's epic. Naevius uses the Saturnian meter for his epic because Livius had already used it for his. Livius' version of Homer now becomes the "first" epic retrospectively, not just because it has a follower, but because it is indeed now the first in a tradition, the equivalent of the "original" Homer as the first poet in Greek. If we had more of the two poems surviving, we would very probably be able to track Naevius' use of the

"Homeric" Latin prototype to create a heroic color for his narration of how Aeneas and his descendants, the Romans, revisit the Sicilian seascapes and landscapes where Ulixes had wandered.[58] Ennius, as we have just seen, evokes his predecessors meticulously at times, yet he wrecks this Naevian narrative with his own claim actually to be Homer, reincarnated after hundreds of years in the body of a Roman citizen.[59] His rewriting of the pre-existing Saturnian epic tradition is drastic, for his new epic in Greek hexameters now becomes the beginning of the tradition, and Livius and Naevius are radically demoted, with Livius' claim to be the first Roman Homer disparaged and displaced.[60]

Whatever Ennius may have hoped, debates over claims to primacy continue as the tradition develops. An anonymous Saturnian "epitaph" on the death of Naevius, from around the middle of the second century, may be seen as pushing back against Ennius' triumphalism, vindicating Naevius' stature as Rome's first master poet.[61] The poetic history of Porcius Licinus had something to say about when the Muse first arrived in Rome, or perhaps when she arrived in her warlike guise, although interpretation of this fragment continues to be keenly debated; in any event, it is possible, or even likely, that Porcius was not signing up to Ennius' claims of primacy.[62]

We see debates surrounding the dramatic tradition as well, with the poets constructing their lineages for their own purposes. These lineages become more unidirectional as time goes on, because after the first pioneers, who embraced both genres, the Roman playwrights diverge into being specialists in either comedy or tragedy. Livius and Naevius were ambidextrous, but Plautus, the third participant in the translation project, already confined himself exclusively to one of the two genres, as did all the other playwrights after him, with the exception of Ennius, who was anyhow far more distinguished as a tragedian, with only two comic titles to his name as compared to some twenty tragedies. The poets' reflections on their generic predecessors may take the form of external comment, as in the supposed "epitaph" of the tragedian Pompilius, in which he traces a line of poetic descent back to Ennius via Ennius' nephew Pacuvius: "I am said to be the pupil of Pacuvius; he in turn was the pupil of Ennius, and Ennius of the Muses; I am called Pompilius" (*Pacui discipulus dicor: porro is fuit <Enni>, /Ennius Musarum; Pompilius clueor*, Varro *Men.* 356). This elegiac epigram (a form itself first domesticated in Latin by Ennius) makes Ennius Number One in tragedy as well as in epic, with no mortal predecessors, and only the Muses as inspiration.[63]

We find many discussions of how the comic poets see their literary predecessors embedded in the prologues to their plays, as a reflex of how the theatrical performances are becoming an acknowledged tradition, with authorities to wrangle over. Plautus often refers to the Greek prototypes for his plays, but the sense of literary background within a doubly Greek and Roman tradition is more dense in Terence, where the prologues regularly engage in literary-critical debate and polemic.[64] The prologue to Terence's *Andria,* for example, defends the poet against his attackers: "when they attack him, they are attacking Naevius, Plautus, and Ennius, whom this poet of ours counts as his sources" (*qui quom hunc accusant, Naevium Plautum Ennium/accusant quos hic noster auctores habet, Andr.* 18–20). The prologue to the *Adelphoe* gives a particularly elaborate back story to the current production, mentioning (6–7) a Greek prototype (Diphilus' "Partners in Death," *Synapothnescontes*) taken over by Plautus in an earlier adaptation *(Commorientes)*—Plautus, however, did not take over a particularly attractive scene from his model, and Terence will now adapt it into his own play (8–11).

In these various ways the comic poets are presenting their tradition as populated by named authors of particular texts, a tradition that they are continuing with their own writing of new texts based on those of their predecessors.[65] Even if the texts under discussion were not catalogued in libraries in Rome at the time, they were available to the poets somehow, for otherwise they would not have been able to write their own scripts. Availability will have been patchy, certainly in comparison with conditions in major Greek centers. Terence seems to have gone to Greece to get the complete works of Menander, but he clearly did not have a complete inventory of earlier Roman comedies at his disposal.[66] He says in the Prologue to the *Eunuchus* that he did not know of the existence of two earlier adaptations of his Greek model, by Naevius and Plautus (33–34), and he puts this down to *imprudentia,* "inadvertency" (27). This does not prove that he had no copies of earlier texts, only that he could plausibly claim that it was understandable if some had escaped him.

Certainly, interpolation and doctored *didascaliae* are evidence for the continued possession of the original Latin scripts by the stage companies, but it does not mean that texts were *exclusively* in the hands of producers.[67] Nor does it mean that poets and audiences were shut out from considering the "literary" qualities of staged works.[68] These plays were, after all, openly paraded as being adaptations of acknowledged classics of New Comedy, and this stance in itself invites critical judgment as to the success of the adaptation from anyone in the audience who knows what a Greek comedy looks like—a considerable number, on any view. Audiences are called upon to value and assess the plays' skill in plotting, their linguistic dexterity and power, their knowing relationship with other works of the same genre, or with the ever popular Atellane farce, or with the competing sister genre of tragedy, so often ironically called into view.[69] Early Latin literature in general, as finely argued by McCarthy, displays a keen attention to "stylization (using language for its formal properties as much as for the content it conveys), secondariness (embracing Latin literature's epigonal relation to Greek literature), and dialogism (juxtaposing comic modes to highlight the incommensurability of languages and worldviews)."[70] Each of these three factors is given sharper focus by being viewed through the translation project: the formal properties of the Latin language are highlighted by being systematically compared to those of Greek; the secondariness of the translation project is overt, reveled in, and dynamically exploited; the dialogism of the entire confrontation between Greek and Roman worldviews is fundamental to the "compare and contrast" atmosphere of cultural syncretism that translation brings to the fore.[71]

Not many definitions of "literary" would exclude the features picked out by McCarthy here. As I suggested above, there are different phases at work in any development of an institution of "literature," and the dynamics we have been examining encourage us to see the preoccupation with a first-order, "textual" literary tradition at Rome as being in place from the beginning, even if we certainly need to wait a century to see explicit, disembedded "contextual" literary institutions in place.

Remakes, Sequels, and New Departures

If the open discussions in the comic prologues call attention to the apprehension of an unfolding tradition going back to the masters of New Comedy in Athens, and if even the fragments of the early epics show meaningful allusion and explicit literary polemic in play, then the unfolding succession of tragedies likewise acts out the evolution of a dramatic literary tradition in Rome—in more implicit, though no less striking, ways. Roman tragedy, like Roman comedy, presented itself from the start as being a new version of Greek drama, and it made its new engagements with that canon a prominent part of its technique.[72] Characters in tragedy can deploy overtly self-referential language of remaking and repetition, as if to remind the audience that this is a restaging of something once staged before. Accius' character Atreus, activating the same old story of the feud between Atreus and his brother, Thyestes, does not simply say "Here we go *again*," but "This time it will be bigger [and better]" (frr. 198–201):[73]

> *iterum Thyestes Atreum adtrectatum aduenit;*
> *iterum iam adgreditur me et quietum suscitat.*
> *maior mihi moles, maius miscendumst malum,*
> *qui illius acerbum cor contundam et comprimam.*

Again Thyestes comes at Atreus to manhandle him; again he approaches me and riles me up when I am at rest. A bigger task for me, a bigger evil has to be concocted, to pound down and crush his cruel heart.

Accius' Electra, when speaking in the *Agamemnonidae* of how she is "renewing" the old hatred between Atreus and Thyestes, likewise uses highly self-conscious language of reperformance when she speaks of "bringing back to life the enmities of the sons of Pelops, now snuffed out and obliterated in memory" (*inimicitias Pelopidum/extinctas iam atque oblitteratas memoria/renouare*, frr. 42–4).[74]

From within the Roman tradition as well, we may see remakes at work, as the tragedians work more and more intensively with their Roman predecessors. It appears that all of Livius Andronicus' original tragic subjects, for example, were treated again at later periods by various of his successors.[75] Accius' character Atreus is no doubt already working with this dimension as well, since Ennius had already staged a *Thyestes* about the feud between the brothers: Accius is calling attention to the fact that his new play is, in part, a Latin reperformance of a Latin reperformance of a Greek original.[76] A particularly striking feature of this self-referential turn in the tragic tradition is presented by the tragedies of Pacuvius, the nephew of Ennius. As Fantham has demonstrated, Pacuvius is fond of plots that "not only continue mythical narratives from earlier tragedy, but . . . were conceived as sequels (spinoffs?) to his uncle's successful productions."[77] In following up Fantham's argument, Cowan has shown that these plays "are self-consciously inscribed with their own belatedness and secondariness, yet at the same time serve as commentaries on and, sometimes, confident corrections of more established tragedies."[78] As a test case of the dynamism of the evolving tradition, Cowan discusses the successive plays about Medea by Ennius (*Medea Exul,* based on Euripides' play), Pacuvius (*Medus,* concerning the fate of Medea and her son after the action of Ennius' play), and Accius (*Medea siue Argonautae,* staging the murder of her brother Absyrtus, from before the action of Ennius' play). As he concludes, "In the course of a century, Ennius, Pacuvius and Accius imported Medea from Greece and established a dynamic, self-conscious tradition which acknowledged and challenged not only its Greek forebears but its own earlier stages."[79]

Within this process of self-referential innovation, it seems that the tragedians were nonetheless still not writing independently of reference to a Greek model or models. Certainty is impossible, since no Roman Republican tragedy survives in anything but meager fragments, and some of the Classical or post-Classical Greek plays that might have been their models are not even fragments. Yet the likelihood is that completely independent composition was not a feature of Republican tragedy, any more than it was of comedy, however much the successive generations may have loosened up in their experiments.[80] Here we need to remind ourselves that their conception of how to use a model was from the beginning more free and capacious than is implied by our default idea of "translation," and it was conditioned by the Greek performance traditions of post-Classical drama, where plays were regularly reworked for restaging with additions, cutting and pasting, and renaming of characters.[81] In other words, our modern sliding scale between "translation" and "free composition" is not a very reliable one to apply to the Roman dramas, and a great deal of inventive incorporation can take place, even as "the model behind the 'new' plays was still there to be recognised by audiences and readers."[82]

Beyond the Translation Project

A distinctively Roman capacious understanding of "translation," then, is probably sufficient to accommodate the productions of Republican tragedy as far as Accius' work in the second half of the second century. But even if we accept that Pacuvius in the early second century may sometimes already be composing without a particular Greek tragic template as his base of operations, the first works within the new literature that were not translations are still, as argued in Chapter 4, the *Bellum Punicum* and the *praetextae* of Naevius, which certainly predate Pacuvius' first works by some years.[83] For a generation after 240 translated drama was virtually the only manifestation of the new literary project, with the exception of Livius' *Odyssey,* and it was Naevius who broke the mould, taking Livius' translation as the model for his new independent epic on Roman history, and taking his own and Livius' translations as the model for dramas of Roman history in conformity with the generic norms of the new Roman tragic form.[84] Naevius' Saturnian epic on the Great War with Carthage in Sicily, in particular, was a work of extraordinary originality. His poem was the first historical monograph ever written in the Latin language;[85] in its linking of the mythical Trojan origins of the city to events within the lifetime of many of his audience, including himself, the poem created a perspective of myth and religion within which to make sense not only of the victory over Carthage but also of Rome's new position within the Mediterranean great power network.[86]

Ennius represents the next decisive break. In his *Annales,* he presented a hexameter epic on the Roman experience from the fall of Troy to his own day, around 170. His epic aimed at being a universal history, as we shall discuss in the next section, using Homeric, religious, and historical perspectives to further an extraordinarily ambitious goal, that of presenting the Roman empire as "the hub of space and time, the primary focus of the cosmos in all its aspects."[87] The poem was the first comprehensive history of the city in the Latin language, and it was in close dialogue with the newly emerging prose historiography about the city, which we consider shortly below.[88] Besides this remarkable achievement and besides the dramatic works that had originally made him famous, Ennius produced an astonishing array of shorter works, including treatises on philosophy and religion (*Epicharmus, Euhemerus*), panegyric (*Scipio*), a spoof mini-epic on refined eating (*Hedyphagetica,* "Delicatessen"), and mixed short poems, including epigram.[89] Some of these works, such as the *Euhemerus* and *Hedyphagetica,* are translations of the usually free variety, and the *Euhemerus* was a prose text, the first such produced by a participant in the translation project. The range of possibility for writing in Latin had been remarkably extended by the time of Ennius' death in 169. The new literature had achieved escape velocity, even if no Latin poet after Ennius, apart perhaps from Ovid, ever approached his range and inventive versatility.

A crucial related development is the emergence of a large-scale prose literature in the Latin language.[90] Romans had been drafting laws, keeping priestly and family records, writing reports to the Senate, and giving speeches for hundreds of years, but the systematic and prolific publication of dedicated treatises, speeches, and especially histories, developing in momentum throughout the first half of the second century, was a new phenomenon, one that introduced a new dimension to the life of the city and its empire.

The most remarkable facet of this enterprise was the intense work on Hellenistic-style historiography that began with the first systematic prose history of the city written by a Roman, the history of Fabius Pictor, which appeared towards the end of the third century.[91] This history was written in Greek, as were the next two histories of Rome written by other members of the Roman senatorial order, L. Cincius Alimentus (praetor 210/9), and A. Postumius Albinus (consul 151). Two other senators also wrote Roman histories in Greek, C. Acilius (his work appeared around 142), and Cn. Aufidius (praetor 107), while the son of the great Scipio Africanus, who never entered political life due to physical weakness, wrote some kind of historical work in Greek before his death in around 160 (Cic. *Brut.* 77, *FRHist* 3 T1).

As we have already seen, the third century gave rise to a number of partially similar responses to the challenge of Hellenism, with national histories being written in Greek by high-ranking Egyptians, Babylonians, and Jews.[92] The fact that these first Roman senatorial histories were written in Greek is partly explicable as being a result of the same reactions to Hellenism as seen in Egypt and Babylonia, with all the range of responses from justification to explanation to accommodation. Yet the differences are substantial. First of all, these Roman Hellenizing histories were not written by members of newly subject peoples, but by élite representatives of an empire that had brought virtually all of the Greeks living west of the Ionian Sea under their control by the time that Fabius Pictor published his History around 205, and that had expanded its sphere of control to the whole of mainland Greece and into Asia Minor by the time the third of this sequence of authors, Postumius

Albinus, had finished his work around the year 150. Three of these writers of Roman history in Greek are documented as mediators in the interface between Rome and Greek culture in their public roles as well as in their writings. Fabius Pictor led an embassy to the Delphic oracle after the destruction of the Roman army at Cannae in 216, and on his return he read out to the Senate a Latin translation of the oracle he had received there (Liv. 22. 57. 4–5; 23. 11. 1–7).[93] C. Acilius interpreted for the three Greek philosophers who appeared before the Senate on an embassy in 155, while Postumius Albinus bantered with one of that group, Carneades, and later served on the commission that established the province of Achaea, earning honorific statues for himself in Delphi, Olympia, and the Isthmus of Corinth.[94] Such men's status as "experts" applies on both sides of the language divide.[95] The fact that their histories are in Greek means that they can be read by Greeks, Romans, and Italians, providing a field of exchange across a range of cultures.[96]

Another major difference between the Roman senators' histories in Greek and those of Berossus or Manetho or Demetrius is that the format of the first Roman histories is far more deeply indebted to Greek generic norms of historiography.[97] The other authors were mediating prestigious documentary texts or religious narratives of their own language and culture into Greek. The Egyptian priest Manetho, for example, is the end-product of a long and prestigious documentary culture with its own ancient narrative patterns for kingly history, so that the narratological forms of Greek historiography cannot be imposed on a blank field of "data," but are always interacting with another narrative mode.[98] Their Roman counterparts did not have such already organized material to transmute, and the transformational power of their Greek generic model was therefore more thoroughgoing, resulting in a historiography that is more recognizably Greek in its presuppositions about what a narrative of a city's past should look like. What Fabius Pictor was initially faced with was a welter of sources and traditions, from oral accounts to priestly and family archives, together with whatever material could be gleaned from the host of commemorative techniques honed by the competitive zeal of the great families: statues, dedications of spoils and temples, the displays of family history in the *atrium* of each noble family's house, the magnificent funeral procession and oration given to honor the dead noble who was going to join his ancestors.[99] Such a morass of material did not come with any pre-set structure. It was a massive intellectual and organizational challenge to frame a coherent chronological narrative out of the disparate items bobbing along in this "complex, multimedia memorial culture."[100] The organizational frame and method chosen was the obvious one, perhaps the only one: to write a history in the Greek mode.[101]

Fabius' historiographical format, then, is not a question of simply transposing material from one format to another, for history is not just a matter of writing down what people happen to be saying "anyway."[102] Literature is an institutional structure with its own transformative formal and social power, and historiography is a form of literature. The historiographical forms used by Fabius and his followers were inherited ultimately from Herodotus, and they entail ways of constructing experience that will not have come naturally to Roman senators. The specific form of encoding the past that we see in Greek historiography has its own transformational power as a tool of thought and as a system of representation. Fabius' narrative of Romulus and Remus, for example, is explicitly said by our main source, Plutarch, to be modeled on an existing Greek account by one Diocles of Peparethus (*Rom.* 3.1); this is the most economical explanation for the highly dramatic nature of the narrative, which has features characteristic of Attic drama, so that already a hundred years ago it was suggested that Diocles had modeled his version of the tale on a tragedy such as Sophocles' *Tyro*.[103] Certainly, as stressed by Momigliano, it goes without saying that Diocles' narrative must have had important points of contact with current Roman versions: "But the formulation, the presentation, was Greek."[104]

Besides such narratological debts, Fabius' history has numerous features that mark it as a Greek-style history. His date for the foundation of the city of Rome, for example, is a Greek one, "the first year of the eighth Olympiad," "748/7;"[105] the use of Olympiads for dating in Greek histories goes back some seventy or eighty years before Fabius, to Timaeus of Tauromenium, a major historian of the western Mediterranean, who remained central to the Roman tradition down to the time of Cicero.[106] Fabius likewise followed Timaeus in his antiquarian and religious interest in a phenomenon such as the *pompa circensis,* or in his analytical discussion of the causes of the outbreak of the Second Punic War.[107]

The construction of Roman history in the new Hellenizing historiography is a process of intercultural dialogue. When Romans started writing history, there was already a long Greek tradition of writing about the origin of the city of Rome and how it fitted in with their own versions of Greek and native interaction in Italy and beyond; further, there were a number of histories written by Greeks that gave a pro-Carthaginian version of the Great War, and then of the Hannibalic War.[108] The creation of a tradition about the distant and nearer Roman past is dialogic, even collaborative work, involving both Greek and Roman historians and poets.[109] Naevius, writing either shortly before or shortly after Fabius Pictor, is probably already engaging with Philinus, the pro-Carthaginian historian of the First Punic War;[110] Naevius' version of the Trojan origins will be drawing on Greek histories, presumably including Timaeus of Tauromenium, in addition to sources from Rome and Latium. At every turn in the ongoing process, the Greek and Roman writers are reacting to contemporary events, for work on origins and the past is always contemporary in motivation: Gabba crucially stresses that "the creation of historiography at Rome at the end of the third century was in response to political demands vis-à-vis the world of Magna Graecia and Greece that formerly did not exist. This is not a preconception, it is a fact."[111] Fabius Pictor's Olympiad date for the foundation of the city, for example, is not just a "fact" but a major ideological statement in its own right within this political context: the location of the foundation of Rome "within the panhellenic grid of the Olympiad system helps Fabius in his larger thematic plan of showing that Rome is not a barbarian outsider but an equal participant in the Greek cultural world of Italy, Sicily, and Greece 'proper'"; Rome was "not just a historical foundation but . . . a civilized *polis* from the start of civilization in Italy."[112]

Early Roman historians were engaged in an enquiry that reflected on the intriguing status of the Romans as simultaneously part of and not part of the Greek world, civilized yet non-Hellenic, comparable to Greek norms yet ultimately independent of them. From this perspective, their histories are performing work related to that of the translation project, where the ongoing development of the ever-shifting Roman cultural identity was likewise a process of dialogic interaction with Hellenic culture. As has become more and more clear over the last thirty years, it is emphatically not the case that Rome before Fabius Pictor was without a sense of history and a variety of ways of working with shifting constructions of the past; one may even wish to follow Purcell and see the institution of formal Grecizing historiography on the Roman past as "rather a pity," "superimpos[ing] on the lively Roman tradition a burdensome structure of Greek-style historiography, which eventually drowned out much of the earlier picture."[113] But the distinctive turn into Grecizing historiography entailed specific forms of representation and ideology, among which the relationship of Roman identity to Hellenism was one of the most important.

This major cultural project received an important re-orientation with the appearance of the first Roman history in Latin, the *Origines* of M. Porcius Cato. He began work on this history in the 160s, and he died in 149 or 148. Two senatorial histories in Greek had appeared before Cato began writing his history in Latin (those of Fabius Pictor and Cincius Alimentus), and one appeared just before or around the very time that his own *Origines* came out (that of Postumius Albinus). Histories of Rome in Greek continued to be produced even after Cato's work was published (by C. Acilius and Gn. Aufidius), but the momentum rapidly shifted to Cato's model, and we see many Latin histories appearing in the next half-century.[114] Cato's self-promotion as a new man is part of his choice of Latin instead of Greek, for he is using his own Latin speeches in his history in order to build a new kind of authority among his peers;[115] his strong emphasis on Italy as a concept in his history is also presumably at work, for it may have seemed fitting that the newly imperial language of Latin should be used for a history that aimed to account for

Roman preeminence as the leader of an Italian alliance;[116] and, finally, his aggressive posture towards the Greek language and its deferential use by his competitors is hard to disentangle from the choice of the Latin language.[117]

In noting the importance of this pose to Cato, I do not mean to sign up to any monolithic view of a supposed "anti-Hellenism" on his part. His history continued to be in sustained dialogue with Greek ideologies, origin myths, and narratological templates;[118] his other published writings, too, are in distinctively Greek genres, such as his *De agri cultura*, orations, and *De re militari*. Nonetheless, the shift in language from Greek to Latin entails ideological shifts of various kinds. Whereas Fabius Pictor, for example, had given a Greek Olympiad date for the foundation of Rome, Cato deliberately did not use Greek canons and did not give an Olympiad date; rather, he used the Trojan war as his benchmark, dating the foundation to "four hundred and thirty-two years after the Trojan war" (Dion. Hal. *Ant. Rom.* 1. 74. 2, *FRHist* 5 F13). He shifts the reference point from a Greek athletic festival to an event that can now be construed as the starting point of Roman history.[119] Cato's history is only one part of his production in Latin, and all of his works are important as signs of what could be achieved in Latin prose: new claims to knowledge and status were also being firmly advertised in Cato's publication of more than 150 speeches, together with treatises on agriculture *(De agri cultura)* and military science *(De re militari)*.[120]

By the death of Cato in 149 or 148 the new literature in Latin had acquired a crucial extra dimension. The production of independent dramas, epics, histories, and treatises had been underway for decades, and Latin had now been put into service in all of these departments. The inevitable question arises: what difference did this mass of production make to Roman life?

CHAPTER 7

The Impact and Reach
of the New Literature

G IVEN THE STATE OF OUR EVIDENCE before the late Republic, it
is a difficult task to assess the impact and the reach of the new
literature. Yet it is worth sketching some possibilities for what the interactive frames for the reception of the new literature may have been, and
how the new literature may have affected the worldview, imaginative capacities, and inter-relationships of its audiences.

Audiences

We begin with the reflection that there were a number of different audiences across time, space, and reception context. Social distinctions were
certainly at work in the stratifications of accessibility to education and
to the élite literature made readable by that education.[1] The constituency
of the audience for drama, which embraced a range of education, will
not have overlapped neatly with that of the readers of Ennius' *Epicharmus* or Accius' *Didascalica*. In the case of drama, if we are to believe
comic prologues, the audience at Rome included "free citizens *(liberi)*,
slaves *(servi)*, married ladies *(matronae)*, nurses with infants *(nutrices*
and *pueri infantes)*, prostitutes *(scorta)*, attendants on the magistrates

(lictores), and ushers *(dissignatores)*."[2] We should not conclude from such testimony that an audience for an Ennian tragedy or a Plautine comedy was a carnivalesque assembly, a cross-section of city life. Audiences for the dramatic performances at the festivals in Rome will usually have been quite small. Most performances in the first two generations took place in temple precincts, and the audiences who could be fitted onto the steps of Magna Mater on the Palatine, for example, cannot have numbered more than 2000, when the theater of Dionysus at Athens could at this time accommodate at least seven times that number.[3] Social stratification was at work in the seating for such performances, informally at first and then, after legislation in 194, codified by law: senators were guaranteed the best seats, at the front, in a move that proved quite unpopular.[4] Still, the numbers of potential spectators were raised by repeat performances, in Rome and elsewhere in the peninsula, and when plays were staged in the Circus Maximus or in the Forum, as regularly happened, then more people were able to watch than in the temple precincts.[5]

We do not, then, have a polarized choice between small élite groups with very sophisticated taste or large Bakhtinian throngs devoid of critical judgment. In the audiences of drama, as Horsfall has vividly shown, our modern distinctions between highbrow and lowbrow culture are not helpful, since the evidence from the first century, at least, shows drama being relished by a range of social groups.[6] A helpful comparison for the social role of drama in Republican Rome is perhaps to be found in the reception of Shakespeare in nineteenth-century America. Here the highly educated few certainly had access to literatures in the ancient languages and in the modern vernaculars, and they enjoyed more expensive seating in theaters, but the plays of Shakespeare provided a common theatrical culture all over the country: "Shakespeare *was* popular entertainment in nineteenth-century America."[7] Before the early twentieth-century demarcation that began to turn Shakespeare into a "classic," an increasingly exclusive possession of the educated, all sections of American society shared a passion for Shakespearean theater. This was an often burlesqued, excerpted, and parodied Shakespeare, part of a spectacular package that included "magicians, dancers, singers, acrobats, minstrels, and comics";[8] but it was an art form that anyone could attend, and the Roman experience was no doubt closer to this environment than to the reverential church-like atmosphere in which Shakespeare is normally experienced today.[9]

We have already discussed the important cultural work discharged by the translated tragedies and comedies in Latin, as they opened up an imaginative space for exploring the relationships between Roman and Greek experience.[10] It would be vacuous to catalogue ways in which the new dramas played their role in educating and challenging their audience about their ever-shifting roles on the world stage. I mention only one further case study as an example.[11] In the translated Greek comedies, the *fabulae palliatae,* as McCarthy (2000) has argued, audiences of masters and slaves saw their troublesome relationships enacted, and saw other troublesome relationships refracted in the process: young men's need for rebellion against their domineering fathers found expression through the figure of the slave, and the master's fear of his slave's uncontrollability found an outlet by fantasizing about the boundless ingenuity and impunity of the genre's star performer, the "cunning slave" *(servus callidus).* In dialogue with these translated comedies, from around the early second century, were the increasingly popular *fabulae togatae,* plays not based on the Greek models, in which the characters were in modern, Roman dress.[12] Very tellingly, as we are informed by the commentary of Donatus on Ter. *Eun.* 57, such fantasies about the power of the slave were curtailed when the characters were Romans, in Roman dress: *concessum est in palliata poetis comicis seruos dominis sapientiores fingere, quod idem in togata non fere licet* ("comic poets in the *palliata* had the license to represent slaves as wiser than their masters, which is normally not allowed in the *togata*"). Sadly, none of these "plays in the *toga*" survives, so we cannot track in any kind of detail how they formed a bicameral imaginary world in tandem with the *fabulae palliatae* written by Plautus, Caecilius Statius, and Terence.

The audience segments in the theater were not just Roman. The great *Ludi* of the Roman state were international events, as we saw

in discussing the *Ludi Romani* in Chapters 4 and 5. To our list of potential audience members we need to add newly enfranchised citizens,
Campanians with citizenship *sine suffragio,* citizens of independent
Latin cities such as Praeneste, members of Latin colonies, *domi nobiles*
from the various allied states, and visiting Greek or other foreign dig-
nitaries with their entourages. Whatever else these various spectators
were experiencing, they were all learning how to be Roman, or what
it is like to be a Roman, or to be in the Roman orbit. The evolving
sense of Roman identity that was so crucially molded by these performances was a dialogic one, inflected by the presence and interaction
of non-Romans, some of whom were from the states that contributed the
templates and the personnel for the dramas in the first place.

The knock-on effect of these performances continued when the
troupes went on the road.[13] Theatrical culture was enormously popular
among the Italian peoples, whose élite were developing an increasing
taste for the new Latin education and its accompanying literature, and
the impact of the Romans was disseminated by this means in addition to
the more obvious military, religious, and legal avenues.[14] Not only
drama travelled up and down the peninsula, and even beyond. The histories in Greek written by the Roman senators had potentially the widest
audience. Sure enough, we have firm evidence that Fabius Pictor was
being read in the east Sicilian city of Tauromenium in the second century, since a synopsis of Fabius' foundation legends has been found
written on the wall of a gymnasium there, as part of a catalogue of books
held in the gymnasium's library.[15] Lest we take it for granted that Greeks
would as a matter of course read histories in their language written by
a "barbarian" about his own people, we should remind ourselves that
the Egyptian history written by the priest Manetho left virtually no trace
of a readership among Greeks before its chronologies became an important resource for polemical debate between Egyptians, Jews, and Christians.[16] Sicilians, at least, needed to know about the new empire and how
it fitted into their own world-view.

When Ennius published the first book of his *Annales* sometime in the
170s, he announced that his audience would be "widely spread peoples":

latos <per> *populos res atque poemata nostra/ . . . clara> cluebunt* ("the subject-matter and my poetry will be spoken in fame through widely spread peoples," 12–13). Or perhaps he wrote that his audience would be "the peoples of Italy," <*perque> Italos populos,* if we follow the lead of Lucretius' adaptation of Ennius' prologue in his own opening section: there Lucretius said that Ennius brought down from Mt. Helicon a crown *per gentis Italas hominum quae clara clueret* ("to be spoken in fame through the Italian races of men," 1. 119).[17] Whichever reading we adopt, Ennius is explicitly envisaging a reception far beyond the metropolis and its élite. Half a century after Ennius, the satirist Lucilius, Cicero tells us, wrote that he was afraid of the critical judgment of people like Scipio and Rutilius, and was writing for the men of Tarentum, Consentia, and Sicily (*quorum ille iudicium reformidans Tarentinis ait se et Consentinis et Siculis scribere,* Cic. *Fin.* 1. 7, fr. 594 Marx). Cicero follows his gloss immediately by saying that Lucilius was being ironic, as usual (*facete is quidem, ut alia),* but it is telling in itself that someone writing in Latin in the late second century can claim even with his tongue in his cheek that his readership extended to the Greek city of Tarentum, the allied Bruttian town of Consentia, and the overseas province of Sicily. Again, this is testimony to a reception far beyond the aristocracy of the metropolis. This is an imperial readership, a reflection of the remarkable mobility of Italians all over the reach of empire from the third century on, in response to specific and unprecedented policies of the Roman imperial state.[18] As Scheidel puts it, while "short lives were common to all pre-modern populations . . . [b]y contrast, physical mobility far beyond one's native environment was a much more specific and culturally contingent determinant of what it meant to be 'Roman.'"[19]

New Horizons

To these large and growing audiences, in response to the dizzying expansion of the empire, the new Latin literature was making available systems of knowledge and ways of apprehending experience that were not in play before and that had a transformative energy of their own.[20] The

very first dramas, together with Livius' *Odyssey*, were already confronting the Roman audience with a newly coherent picture of mythology as a result of the systematization latent in the family relationships of the Greek divinities: this was not a pattern that emerged naturally
from the mere listing of equivalences of Latin names for Greek deities.[21]
Certainly, Romans had been avid consumers of Greek mythological
representations for a long time before 240, and the domestication of important cults and even of the proper names of Greek gods and heroes
was well underway before Livius Andronicus was born.[22] Yet the new
literature set out structures and relationships of a coherent kind, so that
a systematic picture of how this worldview operated was able to emerge:
"in the genealogical ordering and in the working out of the dramatic
character of the gods of Roman polytheism, a moment of theoretical rationalization can be detected."[23] Systematization of this kind gave
Roman audiences a distinct view of their connections to the world of
the past, with its contemporary ramifications in diplomacy and state-
craft. Accius in his *praetexta* entitled *Aeneadae siue Decius* gave an elaborate genealogical report on the Trojan royal house, meticulously going
from Jupiter to Anchises—and then presumably (in a portion now lost)
on to Aeneas, the ancestor of the Romans (fr. 653).[24] The system of networks in which the Romans figured is here given codified form.

The knowledge that came from increasing exposure to the tragedies
is memorably capitalized upon in Plautus' flamboyant jokes on Greek
mythology, and the developing education system will have had a role to
play as well, for mythography was a standard piece of the curriculum
for young students.[25] We should not underestimate how much cultural
work has had to be done in order for an actor to stand up in Rome and
impersonate Mercury, taking the audience into his confidence as he tells
them that his father Jupiter has made Alcumena pregnant (Plaut. *Amph.*
103), and then acknowledging that they "all know what my father Jupiter is like, how broad-minded he is in these numerous affairs, what a
mighty lover he is once someone has taken his fancy" (*nam ego uos
nouisse credo iam ut sit pater meus,/quam liber harum rerum multarum
siet/quantusque amator sit quod complacitum est semel,* 104–6). The

increasing professionalization of the Roman state in this regard is a closely related phenomenon. When the military catastrophes of the year 217 made the *Xuiri sacris faciundis* recommend a feast for the gods *(lectisternium)*, they laid out tables for the Greek category of the Twelve Gods, paired off male and female according to Greek practice (Liv. 22. 10).[26]

Not only mythology but religion and philosophy were being systematized in novel ways on the tragic stage. Rüpke has compellingly argued that Accius' tragedies made a particularly distinctive contribution to the way the Romans could systematize their religious system, by accommodating Greek theoretical reflections on key religious topics—theology, natural philosophical understandings of meteorological and astronomical phenomena, and divination.[27] Accius will have been intensifying and refining a tendency one may glimpse already in earlier authors. Pacuvius in particular is cited for some memorable philosophical turns.[28] One of his characters offers a prolonged meditation on Fortune (ten lines in the fragment cited by the author of the *ad Herennium*, 2. 36), beginning with six lines on what some philosophers say about the nature of Fortune *(perhibent philosophi)* and then going on to declare that "there are however other philosophers who say otherwise, that there is no Fortune, but all things are ruled by randomness" *(sunt autem alii philosophi qui contra Fortunam negant/esse ullam sed temeritate res regi omnes autumant,* 374–75). This is not bluster, but a precise reference to a contemporary technical debate, using a marked Greek loan word, *philosophi,* to set up the antithetical structure: the dichotomy corresponds to one familiar from Greek philosophy, between fortune/providence (τύχη) and accident (ταὐτόματον).[29] Again, the Pacuvian character Chryses discourses on the nature of *aether* as a sustaining force in nature, which works together with the maternal power of Mother Earth to create living things (86–92): the lines are indebted to the already philosophizing presentation of Euripides' *Chrysippus* (fr. 836 Nauck), but Pacuvius' presentation is consistent with the general way in which he "quite self-consciously intellectualised the genre, making it respond to the flood of ideas, philosophies and ideologies now entering Rome from the East."[30]

Ennius' translated treatises on natural philosophy and theology (*Epicharmus* and *Euhemerus*) are another addition to this mix. They are not meant to become any kind of orthodoxy—in fact, they are inconsistent with each other in their presentation of the gods, with the *Epicharmus* presenting the gods as manifestations of natural phenomena, and the *Euhemerus* presenting them as former human beings, given divinity by the peoples who nurtured their posthumous memories.[31] Instead, together with the other discourses we have been examining, they are a self-conscious attempt to annex foreign learning and to use it to extend the possibilities of thought and expression in Latin and at Rome. In the *Epicharmus,* for example, Ennius enjoys generating significant etymologies from the Latin names for the gods, as if to supplement the conventional etymologies that Greek poets and scholars had long been generating from the Greek names: he links *Iuppiter/Iouis,* for example, with the Latin verb *iuuo,* "to help" (*Var.* 57–58 Vahlen), and *Ceres* with the "bearing" *(gerit)* of crops (*Ceres quod gerit fruges, Var.* 50 Vahlen).[32] In all of these ways, religious and philosophical thought are becoming possible fields for Roman enquiry; they are emerging into categories, which are available for manipulation and exploitation in a range of genres.

Epic, too, was an important venue for the systematization of religious and other knowledge, and for the creation of distinctive frameworks for apprehending the Roman achievement.[33] We saw in Chapter 2 above that the domesticating strategies of Livius were already inviting fruitful comparisons and contrasts between the deities of Rome and Greece, capitalizing on modes of comparison and contrast that had been in place for centuries.[34] The most conspicuous example of this shift in apprehension is to be found in the new status of the Romans' chief god, Jupiter Optimus Maximus. Eventually, especially in the national epics of Naevius and Ennius, this partisan god will accrue to himself the supranational and potentially cosmic significance that his counterpart, Zeus, commands in Greek ritual and philosophy.[35] Such perspectives are not just a mirror of what everyone was thinking at the time anyway. Rather, they are a distinctive vision of Roman destiny, made possible only within the framework of the new literature, capitalizing on Greek epic strategies and Greek literary and philosophical scholarship in addition to Roman cult and practices of commemoration. The new Roman epic, with its distinctive religious vision, has its own contribution to make to the way the Romans were reconceiving their role on the world stage in these days of unparalleled expansion.[36]

There are undoubtedly important points of reference between the discourses of the epics and of the state's religious practices. It matters a great deal that Roman spectacles of all kinds, from the processions before the Circus games to the triumph, reveled in staging Rome as "the center of the world";[37] this perspective is a distinctively Roman one in the culture at large and in the new literature, since "Rome forms a centre for Italy and the empire, where Greece and the Greek world lack such a central point."[38] Nonetheless, the bold attempt of Ennius to plot Rome into a cosmic framework, in a universal history that makes Rome the end point of divine planning for the known world, is an intellectual and poetic achievement in its own terms.[39] Further, it is an achievement that had a substantial impact on later Roman thinking about history and the destiny of the empire, for the centripetal universal destiny of Rome is a crucial context for framing Roman achievement in Virgil, Livy, and Ovid, most obviously, but also in Vitruvius, Strabo, and Valerius Maximus.[40]

The New Professionals

All of the works we have been discussing so far, with the exception of the senatorial histories, were written by individuals of no particular social status, none of them born in Rome or even in Latium. Some of them were ex-slaves (Caecilius Statius, perhaps Livius Andronicus); none of them was born into the full citizenship apart from Accius, the latest of our authors, himself the son of ex-slaves, and some (for example, Plautus, Pacuvius, Pompilius, even Lucilius) probably never became citizens.[41] When Ennius addressed his audience as *ciues* in the opening sequence of his *Annales,* telling them that it was worth their while to learn what he had to tell them about the harbor of Luna (*Lunai portum, est operae, cognoscite, ciues, op. inc.* fr. ii 1 Sk.), he had held that status himself for only about a decade, having become a citizen in 184 at the age of fifty-five:[42] he proudly called attention to this moment of enfranchisement in his epic (*nos sumus Romani qui fuimus ante Rudini,* "I am a citizen of Rome who was formerly a citizen of Rudiae," 525). The audience of "citizens" that Ennius aims to reach has many circles, and we should not focus exclusively on the urban governing élite and overlook his own declared ambition of reaching a "widely spread" or "Italian" audience.[43] In his bold claim to have the power to address his fellow-citizens about their history, Ennius "models his authorial voice on that of an aristocratic speaker who addresses the people," arrogating to himself the right to incorporate the deeds of the whole of the SPQR into his epic.[44] It was perhaps an affront to some of the more distinguished members of his audience to be lectured in this way by such a person, and to have the history of their Republic organized, explained, and in a sense controlled by him. Yet Ennius' claims are based on a new kind of authority, grounded in his knowledge, control of tradition, and intellectual mastery of the literary resources that made his unprecedented *Annales* possible.[45]

The poets and their audience, then, are having to adjust not only to newly differentiated forms of knowledge but also to new social dynamics generated by the novel authority claims and status of those who asserted themselves to be the masters of such knowledge. In the career of Cato, in particular, with his aggressively staged disparagement of Greek professionalism, and his parading of his own knowledge of agriculture, law, and tradition, we catch a glimpse of the epistemological crisis that the new literature could pose to the traditional governing élite.[46] One cannot generalize about such a complex set of relationships in an ill-documented period spanning a number of generations of comprehensive political and social transformation, but particular case studies show that the relationship between a poet and the *nobiles* of his acquaintance called for novel solutions, both in social and poetic terms. Ennius, for example, was not able to pigeonhole himself within existing hierarchies or dynamics either in Roman terms (*patronus/cliens*) or in terms available in the Hellenistic monarchies (paid employment in a royal *Mouseion*). Rather, he plotted out his own terrain, and "realistically placed himself and his activities in an exclusive aristocratic milieu that was socially removed, albeit—or so he tries to insist—intellectually implicated in the concerns of the forum, the senate, and the lawcourts."[47]

The status of the poets was not easy to categorize for their contemporaries. They represented a novel kind of relationship for the élite to negotiate, given that there was no readily available framework for individuals of this expertise and mobile status to slot into. If we look to a larger background context, it is striking how very different Rome of the middle Republic was, even from Greece, in its lack of public institutions of support for intellectual or cultural activities. The dramas were virtually all staged as part of state-organized festivals, but the Roman state had no specific role in any other apparatus of support. As Rawson points out, there were no centers supporting education or learning of the kind that we see in the Museum of Alexandria or the Athenian philosophical schools; further, "there was no state-run training system (for the well-off) like the *ephebeia,* no public salaries or special rewards for individual teachers, doctors or engineers such as Greek cities often had. . . . There was no public patronage by means of competitions . . . for special skills at the great festivals. . . . There were not even public libraries, common in the Greek world, often in connection with the gymnasium and *ephebeia.*"[48] The poets appear to have been granted the right of a *collegium,* apparently in token of gratitude to Livius Andronicus for his role in the rituals of 207 before the battle of the Metaurus, but this honorific prerogative was no equivalent to the patronage of the Ptolemies.[49]

In default of such institutions, the literary and artistic entrepreneurs who came to Rome as professionals on the make were forging relationships with the wealthy and powerful individuals whom we regularly find providing the supportive network for artists in any premodern or early modern state.[50] There are numerous testimonia to the relationships between the poets and various members of the nobility, starting from Livius Andronicus teaching the sons of a Livius.[51] Yet the transformation in Roman life brought about by the impact of these individuals kept generating new scenarios as the poets accrued their own peculiar status, one that was marked in particular by the granting of the right for actors and poets to have their own *collegium,* which met in the temple of Minerva on the Aventine.[52] The new poets had a disruptive effect on established hierarchies.[53] Irretrievably murky traditions relate that the feisty Campanian, Naevius, feuded with members of the nobility; we shall never know what exactly lies behind these anecdotes, but they are at the very least testimony to the fact that it was thinkable for later generations that a poet of that period had enough standing to trade barbed remarks with powerful *nobiles.*[54] At the very end of our period, around 100, the poet Accius, born a citizen son of ex-slaves, is said to have ostentatiously refused to stand when the distinguished noble and would-be tragedian, C. Julius Caesar Strabo, entered the *collegium poetarum*—"not because he was unmindful of Strabo's status, but because he was quite sure that, when it came to a comparative ranking of the pursuits they had in common, he was considerably above Strabo" (*non maiestatis eius immemor, sed quod in comparatione communium studiorum aliquanto se superiorem esse confideret,* Val. Max. 3. 7. 11).[55] As so often in the study of the middle Republic, we have a handful of often unreliable anecdotes from which to generalize. Still, we observe a fluid situation in which the society has to adapt to the novel challenges presented by the entrepreneurial middlemen of the new literature. As Sciarrino well points out, the new poets represented a potential threat to the élite's prerogatives but also an opportunity; as she puts it, "poetry was a new medium and the prospects that it raised for the Roman elite were both enticing and disturbing."[56]

Texts in Circulation

The revolution in theater and in textual production that we have been considering is inextricably part of the rapid development of Roman society into a distinctively literate organization. The new literature itself depended fundamentally upon textuality, and, in general, as Habinek puts it, "the new culture of the late third century and early second century B.C.E. was intimately connected with the preservation, importation, and circulation of texts," with official documents also suddenly multiplying in number as the empire grew.[57] In the case of the publication of speeches, for example, which we see gaining in popularity throughout the second century, it is clear that even "traditional" forms of aristocratic expression are taking on new meaning and power as a result of the use of writing systems for new purposes.[58] The circulating texts are not just making more widely available words that only a few hundred would have initially heard: they are a new kind of social activity, with new consequences.

For the first generation of the new literature, as we have seen, production was almost wholly theatrical, designed for the great Roman festivals and also, very probably, for travelling performance afterwards. There were certainly scripts for these productions, and eventually those texts became objects of study and instruction, with an irrecoverable intermediate stage in which they must have achieved some circulation for interested readers, just as there was a market for texts of Menander or Euripides for interested readers. Yet the dramatic performances were for many years the primary contexts for the reception of the works of Livius, Naevius, Ennius, Plautus, and so on. The impact of the other genres, as they gradually emerged, was necessarily different, for they will have circulated primarily in writing.

The importance of writing for the dissemination of the new literature is regularly downplayed in much contemporary scholarship, often because scholars wish to recover an oral dimension to the reception of the new works so as to insert them into a supposedly more significant live social context than the one apparently automatically conjured up by the image of the solitary reader.[59] We do not need here to enter the dense thicket of discussions over orality and performance, or over the nature of Roman reading practices, which ranged from private reading to shared reading to being read to by professionals; their texts were certainly deeply enmeshed in aural habits of rhythm and rhetorical structure and just as certainly were regularly read in solitude by individuals.[60] But it is important to stress that writing and its dissemination have their own social power, which can be occluded by an overemphasis on oral venues for reception.

A recent test case may be found in Rüpke's arguments that the aristocratic banquet was the primary reception venue for the *Annales* of Ennius.[61] Now, I do not necessarily wish to deny that Ennius may have read out portions of his poem to groups of people at a banquet—although the findings of Parker for the late Republic and early Empire should give us pause even on this score, since it is clear that later poets may have read penultimate drafts to *recitationes* but did not perform at *convivia*: that was a task for slaves or freedmen, and a person such as Catullus or Propertius would not have wanted to be tainted by such association.[62] The *recitatio* did not exist as an institution before the late Republic, so that this option was not available to Ennius. The connotations of the *convivium* may have been very different in the Rome of 185 or 175, but we do not know. If the social norms of Catullus did apply in the time of Ennius, then the poet will not have welcomed being demeaned by himself performing at a *convivium,* even if other persons of lower status may have read his text out. In any event, more significantly, locating the reception context for Ennius at the banquet means that we overlook Ennius' demonstrable interest in the textuality of his work and its architectural organization, while also overlooking the dynamic impact of the public dissemination of a distinctively integrative and systematizing text.

Ennius refers to the text of his *Annales* as *poemata* (12), as written text.[63] One reference is explicit, referring to "sheets of paper" and using the verb *edere* for the first time in Latin in the sense of "publish/make public," corresponding to the technical Greek term ἐκδιδόναι: *neque me decet hanc carinantibus edere cartis* ("Nor is it appropriate that I make public this [matter] on sheets of paper that use abusive language," 458);[64] the other, the opening line of Book Six of the *Annales,* is a clear allusion to the physical act of unrolling a scroll: *quis potis ingentis oras euoluere belli?* ("Who has the power to unroll the mighty borders of the war?" 164). In a third reference, making himself part of a chain of written epic at Rome, Ennius speaks of his Saturnian predecessors in epic as *writing* in the meter in which the Fauns and soothsayers once used to *sing* (*scripsere alii rem/uorsibus quos olim Faunei uatesque canebant,* 206–7). These references to writing are in dialogue with intimations of future reading aloud, such as may be glimpsed in the metaphor of "being spoken" in the verb *cluebunt* that Ennius uses to describe the future fame of his verse (*latos <per> populos res atque poemata nostra/ . . . clara> cluebunt* ("the subject-matter and my poetry will be spoken in fame through widely spread peoples," 12–13).[65] It is interesting that the most explicit surviving references to written texts "speaking" in Ennius come not in the *Annales* but in other references to public monuments before which the people stand and read out the accompanying inscription.[66] The metaphor of "spoken" *(cluebunt)* in frr. 12–13, intriguing and important as it is in its "Homeric" evocation of future speech as an instantiation of the poem, remains an evocation of the reading of a fixed text that is in public circulation.

The self-consciously "written" text of the *Annales* was in service to an architectural organization that was a great intellectual feat in its own right, one intimately dependent on the technology of the book.[67] Ennius' shaping of Roman history into meaningful patterns through skillful use of the book scroll as a unit is a remarkable, possibly unprecedented, exploitation of what will have been a new technology in Rome—"the Hellenistic book-trade's average-lengthed papyrus roll."[68] His predecessor Livius Andronicus was working with a Homeric text that had not yet been uniformly accepted as divided into the twenty-four Hellenistic book units familiar to us today, and Livius' own version of the *Odyssey* was not organized in books, but comprised one volume.[69] The *Iliad* appears to have been read in its entirety in Hellenistic schools, while the *Odyssey* was excerpted;[70] if this was Livius' working model, then we may have some context for his amazing feat of compression. Naevius' *Bellum Punicum* circulated in a single volume like Livius' until it was divided into seven books by C. Octavius Lampadio, who was probably using Ennius' practice in the *Annales* as a template.[71] It is very frustrating not to have information on how many verses Naevius might have been able to get on his one volume, before it was divided by Lampadio: presumably, the total was reasonably high, unless Lampadio's seven volumes were very slim.[72]

The *Annales*, then, are certainly the first Roman epic organized in books. In fact, they may be the first work of any kind written in Rome that had the unit of the book scroll as an organizing principle, since it is possible that the already published histories in Greek of Fabius Pictor and Cincius Alimentus were following the old technology and did not have their material organized in book units of meaningful structure.[73] The crucial point about Ennius' book units is that they were the vehicle for an intellectual design, a presentation of epochs and patterns within the Roman past.[74] As single units, and as triads, the books had a role to play in isolating significant phases of the past: from the Fall of Troy to the end of the monarchy (1–3); the conquest of Italy (4–6, with the near-extinction of the city by the Gauls in 390 as a major end-point in Book 4, and the wars with Pyrrhus as a self-sufficient Book 6); the Carthaginian wars (7–9); the conquest of mainland Greece (10–12); the wars in Asia and Aetolia (13–15); reprise in 16–18.[75] Overall, one must conclude that "the *Annales* was designed to be read in large units."[76]

If Ennius' structuring of Roman history depended intimately on his writing technology, then the dissemination of his epic in textual form is inextricably bound up with its social power as a new kind of experience—one that carried to a new level the systematizing and integrating of knowledge that we have seen to be such an important feature of the new literature in general. When Rüpke identifies the banquet as the performance context of the *Annales,* he undersells his own insights on the way that writing was transforming the horizons of the Romans in this period. All the work of systematizing and integrating a new worldview for the élite, discussed so penetratingly by Rüpke, is already under way in the epics of Livius and Naevius, let alone Ennius, and Rüpke provides rich evidence for the intellectual linking-up function of the new epics, providing access as they did to newly coherent frames of reference.[77] It is only distracting to focus on the banquet as the primal scene for this activity on the assumption that this locale provides some kind of continuity with earlier oral forms of epic, of a supposedly more primal social power. As I shall argue in the next chapter, there was no such continuity— in fact, it is virtually certain that there was in the first place no earlier oral form of epic to be continued. Ennius' new epic acquired its social power through its dissemination as a text, one that he claimed would live long after him, with more enduring power than the statues and tombs of kings (404–6).[78] The self-awareness of the possibility of transcending the initial moment of production or reception is itself constitutive of the category of the "literary."[79] Ennius' stated ambition itself marks out his conception of the epic as a participant in a literary system.

In this form of dissemination, his epic, together with the growing body of other texts in the new literature, was able to play its important role in the creation of the Roman "imagined community," to borrow the phrase coined by Benedict Anderson to describe modern nationalisms.[80] Anderson's model is explicitly formulated to account for a different world from that of the Roman Republic, namely, the creation of nationalism from the late eighteenth century on; but his model is thought-provokingly apposite to the Roman situation, where, just as in the emergent modern nationalisms of his study, "substantial groups of people were in a position to think of themselves as living lives *parallel* to those of other substantial groups of people—if never meeting, yet certainly proceeding along the same trajectory."[81] This was a function that the new Latin literature helped to discharge, in a way that was only possible thanks to its mobility in textual form. Because of the salient example of Greek collective identity being forged in large part through their shared literary languages and texts, we can tend to take it for granted that this was a normal state of affairs in the ancient Mediterranean, when in fact it was highly unusual, as we shall see in Chapter 8. The Romans, like the Greeks, and also the Jews, developed a shared body of texts in a standardized language that helped sustain a sense of collective identity across large tracts of space and time.[82]

An Empire of Writing

We remarked above on the dramatic expansion of writing in a variety of official and nonofficial modes in our period, especially from the early second century on.[83] Not just the scale but the brand of literacy that we see in the Roman Republic at this time is distinctive in comparison with the greatly complex variety of literacies that we see in other premodern imperial states.[84] Many premodern empires, especially but not exclusively the "scribal cultures," had specialized writing techniques and differentiated spheres of competence that shut out non-experts who had not had their long professional training.[85] At Rome, we do not see such fragmented literacies. Rather, "Roman writing practices . . . were joined up."[86] In other words, alphabetic literacy was quite normal in slave-holding Roman households in the middle Republic, and the ability to read and write was a generalizable skill that enabled those who possessed it to have command of a range of different kinds of texts: literacy was not compartmentalized. This was the long-standing working base from which the state's uses of literacy took off: "the documentary explosion of official texts in Rome during the last two centuries B.C.E. represents an appropriation, for the needs of the state, of writing practices developed first of all to suit the private needs of its citizens."[87] Such a finding fits with the entrepreneurial and comparatively unsupervised atmosphere that we saw as the setting for the new literature: competence in literacy was not a caste preserve, either for those writing or for those reading.[88]

We have already noted that the bilingual and biliterate education of the Roman élite set them apart from other governing élites in the ancient world.[89] Within the larger comparative perspective we have just been considering, the Roman élite of the middle Republic now appear unusual in their degree of literacy altogether, let alone biliteracy. The Roman élite were heavily literate, and had processed through a rigorous educational process that formed the indispensable gateway to status distinction and to political and military success; by the mid-second century this education included not only Greek but Latin literary texts. The Greeks had a similarly comparatively diffused literacy going together with an intertwined educational and literary apparatus that determined élite identity, and they were obviously the model for the Romans; but then, as we have seen from the start, "the Greeks did everything differently from everybody else"[90]—apart from, now, the Romans, who were

themselves different again from the Greeks in having a normatively biliterate and bilingual élite. We take this situation for granted, but "[a]n
empire where the elite write poetry is a very unusual thing."[91]

In fact, an empire where the élite write at all is not necessarily so usual
a thing. Other empires in the ancient world were successfully governed
by a functionally illiterate ruling class working in tandem with a scribal
bureaucracy who commanded a variety of scripts and languages. The
Parthian and Persian empires are a classic example of "a society where
the top people need not be able to write at all. . . . Like many medieval
magnates, [the Persian nobility] saw no need to write themselves if
there was someone to do it for them."[92] The Persians are particularly
interesting in that they went to the trouble of commissioning a distinctive means of writing their people's spoken language, Old Persian, when
they came down from the Iranian plateau and took over the Babylonian
Empire; yet this script, dutifully produced by the inherited expert bureaucracy, had virtually no impact or usage outside monarchical display settings, and was soon left neglected.[93] "It is likely that very few individuals could ever write, or even read, Old Persian cuneiform. Possibly
the script was specially invented for Darius [I], and probably Darius himself could not read it."[94] As Tuplin tellingly concludes: "Written language was not part of the inherited sense of identity for Persian speakers;
changing that was not worth the candle."[95] The situation was different
for the predecessors of the Persians, among whom the Assyrian royal
family, for example, normally had some training in writing cuneiform;[96]
traditional views of a very low literacy rate in the pre-Persian Mesopotamian kingdoms appear now to be in the process of revision upwards.[97]
The ruling élites of Carthage and Etruria, to take another example, were
undoubtedly literate, although it is not possible to recover the nature of
their education: as we shall see in the next chapter, a number of the Carthaginian and Etruscan élite could at any rate read and write Greek in
addition to their own languages.

As Woolf stresses after a broad survey of the varieties of the uses of
literacies in premodern empires, "[n]o simple model of the relationship
between empire and writing can adequately capture this complexity."[98]

Against this manifold set of possibilities, the Roman case stands out as arrestingly *sui generis* in a number of ways. By the early second century the Roman Republic has an unusually literate society, with a distinctively "joined up" variety of literacy; the Roman and the Latin-speaking Italian élite have an unusually bilingual and biliterate education; they have at their disposal a vernacular literature formed by biliterate interaction with Greek literature and produced by bi-or trilingual middlemen; these middlemen can flourish in a mobile and fast-evolving environment in which their skills can earn them prominence and rewards; the new literature that they are producing is having a marked impact on the society's intellectual and imaginative horizons; and the new literature is firmly in place as a marker of status distinction and of the sense of identity proper to an imperial governing class.

Acts of Comparison

W E HAVE BEEN CHARTING the development of something corresponding to an institution of "literature" in Rome, beginning with the momentum provided by the "imperial moment" and the increasingly systematic adaptation of the scripts of Attic drama in the last third of the third century. In this chapter, we shall contextualize more precisely the Roman creation of a literature in the Latin language, through a number of comparative exercises. Each of the topics in this chapter could be a book in itself, and I do not aim to treat any of them in detail: I intend no more than to use various comparative frameworks to help us assess in a more fine-grained way what may have been distinctive about the Romans' initiative.

First of all, within the ancient Mediterranean context, precisely how unusual is the situation of the Romans with their Greek-based vernacular literature, one enmeshed within the educational and literate practices of the ruling order and diffused through an expanding geographical range? What cultural institutions may have been in place in other contemporary societies that mark them out as different from the Romans of the period after the Great War with Carthage? Secondly, in what ways did the new literature continue pre-existing artistic verbal and performance culture in Rome, and in what ways did the new literature depart from it? We shall need to assess what kind of artistic verbal and performance culture there was in Rome before the translation project, and what kind of continuity there may have been in this sphere once the developments we have been charting so far got under way. This exercise will further refine our understanding of what was distinctive about the revolution of the late third century. It will also bring into focus a third perspective from which to evaluate this large-scale change in the Roman sphere: in comparing the Romans before and after the watershed, we shall also be comparing them to the Greeks of the Archaic and Classical period, for it seems to be as impossible for us as it was for them to assess their achievement without making the Greeks, in one way or another, the other term of the comparison. What is at stake, then, in comparing Roman culture before and after the translation project with the culture of the Greek *polis?* Finally, we close the chapter by considering cases from the modern world that may shed light on the Roman experiment.

Comparative Cases of Other Vernacular Literatures

Let us turn to our first test case of comparison, and investigate how unusual the Romans might be by the early second century in their possession of a developed text-based vernacular literature. To begin with those closest to the center of the empire, we observe that other Italian peoples interacting with the Greeks appear not to have responded by developing a written literature. Indeed, part of the point of the Roman enterprise appears to have been precisely to enable the Romans to set themselves off against their Italian neighbors by creating a distinctively vernacular version of this prestigious Greek cultural product.[1] The Italians of the central and southern peninsula certainly had songs in their various languages, and we catch glimpses of that culture in a tantalizingly few epigraphic remains: the practice of inscribing epigrams on pottery or stone is itself one inflected first by Greek and then by Roman practice, although it remains controversial how much of the inscriptions' formal properties may be informed by knowledge of Greek or, later, Latin, verse.[2] Still, the summary of Jocelyn remains accurate: "The Sabellians, Umbrians and Messapians had been heavily influenced by Greek culture but although they used their respective languages in the Greek way for religious and legal purposes there is no evidence that they ever acquired a written literature."[3] In commenting on the popularity of writing in religious contexts in archaic Rome, W. V. Harris brings out the distinctive differences in the ways writing could be put to use: "Many of the archaic functions of writing in Rome and Italy resembled its functions in Greece. However this complex of religious uses is something of a distinguishing mark of archaic Roman and Italian culture, just as the preservation of poetic texts is a distinguishing mark of archaic Greece."[4] After 240, the preservation of vernacular poetic (and eventually not only poetic) texts became a distinguishing mark of Rome as well.

The Etruscans present themselves as an interesting comparative case for the Romans, for they appear never to have developed a "literature" as the Romans did, even though there were many points of contact between their relationship with Hellenism and the Romans'. The Etruscans did have a highly developed religious, especially divinatory, literature;[5] yet is very doubtful that "there was a considerable amount of other Etruscan literature not concerned with divination."[6] This kind of differentiation within ancient societies' writing systems is something with which we are by now familiar: if we observe the systematic use of writing in one department, then it does not at all follow that we may infer it was being used systematically in others.

The Etruscans were avid consumers of Greek artistic and scenic culture, with what appears to have been a sophisticated and independent acquaintance with Greek mythology.[7] As we saw in Chapter 4, their highly elaborated musical and dance performance culture became in the early fourth century the go-to model for the newly ambitious scenic games staged by the Roman state, yet we have no idea if there were scripts for these various performances—if indeed they included plotted dramas of the kind that might call for scripts in the first place, as opposed to balletic and musical shows—or if any such scripts were preserved and transmitted. It may appear natural to have scripts accompanying a scenic tradition, but the case of the Oscan farce, where the form appears to have flourished for centuries without a corresponding textual format, is a caution against this assumption. Conversely, the case of the mime and pantomime in Rome shows that you can have scripts or libretti for scenic performance without their entering wide circulation as literary texts or receiving the kind of critical attention that was paid to the *palliata*.[8]

Our only possible reference to written Etruscan dramatic texts comes from the first century, when Varro mentions one Volnius, "who wrote Etruscan tragedies" (*qui tragoedias Tuscas scripsit, LL* 5. 55). It is very hard to know what Varro means by this, and it has been suggested that he does not necessarily even mean that the tragedies were in the Etruscan language.[9] Volnius appears to have been someone Varro knew in person (Varro refers in this passage to something Volnius "used to say," *dicebat*), so that Volnius was writing a hundred and fifty years after Livius Andronicus. If these plays were in Etruscan, then, it seems they are not the last link in the chain of some kind of precursor of the Roman initiative, but rather the first—poignantly unfulfilled—case of another language group taking the Roman example as the model for a literature in their own vernacular.

Finally, we have scattered surviving references to *Tuscae historiae* or to Etruscan authorities for historical accounts.[10] None of these references need imply a developed historiographical narrative in the Etruscan language. The emperor Claudius, for example, once bragged obliquely about his learning by recounting a tale of early Roman history that included an obscure variant he had got from Etruscan authorities or sources: *si Tuscos [sequimur]* (*ILS* 212, line 19). These sources, as Cornell says, "need not have been a written historical work"; the sources could be an oral tradition, an earlier Greek or Roman writer reporting such an oral tradition, or a "book or document of some other kind."[11] If Etruscan writers were producing histories of their own peoples in the era of the Roman middle Republic, then it strikes me as more likely than not that they would have been following the mainstream and writing in Greek.[12] There are a number of avenues for historical traditions to have been passed down among the Etruscans and from there to enquiring Romans and Greeks, and it is no kind of value judgment to decide that free-standing developed historiographical narratives in the Etruscan language are unlikely to have been one of them.[13] As ever, we have to denaturalize our assumptions—in this case, the assumption that societies naturally write certain kinds of histories about themselves. As Baines points out in relation to Egypt, for example, "Egypt, like many civilizations, did not develop a genre of written discursive narrative or analysis of the past."[14] The Romans, after all, did not start writing systematic history about themselves for two hundred years after Herodotus, and then they did not do it in their own language for another half-century later still.

The Carthaginians present a second compelling comparative case. It is a common refrain in modern scholarship to lament the loss of a large-scale diversified Carthaginian literature, including histories, epics, lyric, and even drama.[15] Here one sees clearly the default assumption among many modern scholars that other societies must have possessed something analogous to the Greek or Roman model, even if it has perished. Yet there is every reason to think that there was no such body of Carthaginian literature lost when the Romans sacked the city in 146, and that Punic altogether had indeed "never been the vehicle of a significant literary culture":[16] "[t]here is—as yet—no direct evidence for myth, epic or poetry being written in the Phoenician cities of the first millennium BCE."[17] After the sack of Carthage in 146, the elder Pliny tells us that the Senate gave the Carthaginians' libraries to the local kings of Africa *(regulis Africae bibliothecas donaret)* and had a committee chaired by a noble, D. Silanus, translate the twenty-eight volumes of Mago's work on agriculture from Punic into Latin (*HN* 17. 22–23). Along with Mago's agricultural treatise, there were no doubt works on religion, corresponding to well-attested Phoenician works, with lists of traditional rites and conventional procedures.[18] Yet the bulk of the libraries' holdings, it has been cogently argued, were works in Greek, precisely the kind of treasure trove that would be appreciated by the zealously modernizing local kings who were the beneficiaries of the Roman Senate's bounty.[19]

When Roman and Greek sources, then, cite "Punic books" or "Punic histories," either from before or after the sack, we should always bear in mind the possibility that they were in Greek.[20]

There is ample evidence for the knowledge of Greek among Carthaginians.[21] Hannibal, for example, according to Nepos, learned Greek from Sosylus, who wrote a history of Hannibal's war against the Romans, and Hannibal himself wrote a book in Greek, addressed to the Rhodians, about the war fought in Asia by Cn. Manlius Volso (*Hann.* 13. 2–3).[22] A tantalizing story from Diogenes Laertius informs us that a Carthaginian citizen from the generation before the sack, Hasdrubal, "did philosophy in his own language in his homeland" (τῇ ἰδίᾳ φωνῇ κατὰ τὴν πατρίδα ἐφιλοσόφει, 4. 67). Whatever the basis for this report may be—and Diogenes may simply be drawing false inferences in claiming that Hasdrubal was philosophizing in Punic—Hasdrubal could not have done his philosophizing without excellent Greek, since he will have been studying Hellenistic philosophy at a high level: at the age of twenty-four, in the year 163, Hasdrubal moved to Athens to study in the Academy, changed his name to Clitomachus, embarked upon a Stakhanovite program of book production, with 400 volumes eventually to his credit, and in due course became head of the school. If he really was philosophizing in his own language before he moved to Athens, then this is remarkable testimony to what was possible at the interface between the two languages. He could not have picked up a book by Plato or Arcesilaus and started talking about it in Punic unless considerable familiarity had somehow built up: we have already seen how much intercultural work was necessary for anyone to start "doing philosophy" in Latin. I leave speculation on this possibility for those who actually know Punic.

If indigenous literary traditions are hard to find in Carthage, there were all kinds of predisposing factors of familiarity that might in theory have led the Carthaginians to take over Greek templates for literary forms in their own language and script. Traditional views of the surly and inward-turning isolation of the Carthaginians have crumbled before many studies of their active participation in the cross-currents of the Mediterranean, as they may be seen to have worked actively and independently with Greek elements of architecture, clothing, coinage, and epigraphy.[23] A fascinating example of their intimate dialogue with Greek culture may be found in their response to the catastrophe of their expedition against Syracuse in 396, which they interpreted as being the result of their sacrilege against shrines of Kore and Demeter; determined to adopt the rites of these goddesses in their own city in order to appease them, they turned to prominent resident Greeks to supply the knowledge, appurtenances, and even the personnel for the new cult (Diod. Sic. 14. 77. 4–5).[24] The similarities to the Romans' adoption from Campania of the cult of Ceres, Libera, and Liber on the Aventine a hundred years earlier, in 493, are striking, and give us a glimpse of a circuit of cultural traffic involving Latium, Carthage, and Magna Graecia rather than a top-down unidirectional "influence" from the Syracusans to Carthage.[25]

Carthaginians will have had opportunities for direct exposure to Greek drama in Sicily, and it is very likely that the great center of Carthage was itself on the tour for travelling Greek drama troupes.[26] Direct evidence is lacking, but a terracotta statuette of a comic actor playing a pregnant woman has been found on the site, dating to around 325; the figure may have been manufactured in Carthage, or it may be an import from Tarentum, and it is at the very least testimony to an interest in Greek comedy on the part of somebody in Carthage.[27] Yet there is no reason to think that anyone in Carthage ever took the step of trying to adapt the form into a Punic equivalent of any kind.

We have already seen that the Romans lived in close dialogue with various manifestations of Hellenic culture for centuries before a distinctive set of circumstances launched them on their strange experiment of taking over into their own vernacular one of the most prestigious aspects of that culture. It should therefore be no surprise that the Carthaginians, likewise living in close dialogue with various Hellenisms for centuries, should never have got around to doing something similar, but that they should instead have done the "normal" thing, and communicated with the *oecumenē* in the common language of the *oecumenē*, Greek.

The definitional issues in our enquiry continue to be very challenging, and other comparative cases from worlds unknown to the peers of Livius and Naevius only make the question more difficult. What is the status of the body of material that was turning into the Hebrew Bible, partly through the act of translation, at the very time when the Romans were working on their translation project? What is at stake in asserting or denying that this body of text is a "literature"?[28] The Jews certainly stand out as a group who develop a powerful sense of shared ethnic identity, one created in large part through their focus on a shared body of texts, and in this respect their experience has interesting points of contact with that of the Greeks.[29] Their approach to how their texts should be transmitted may itself owe something to the Greek treatment of canonical texts. The comparatively sudden transition to an attitude that mandated meticulously faithful transmission of the inherited Jewish texts is striking, for such an attitude to canonical texts is not normative in the Near East.[30] It has been suggested that the urge to stabilize and preserve the major texts in fixed form, which reached its definitive stage from around 50 BCE to 73 CE, is instead the result of interaction with Greek scholarship's determination that this is the way to treat high-prestige canonical texts.[31]

The question of dissemination is also an interesting one. How do we define and account for literary texts that undoubtedly have both the first- and second-order qualities of literature, which we discussed at the beginning of Chapter 6, and that nonetheless appear to have had an extremely limited circulation? Such seems to have been the case in certain phases of their history with the rich corpora both of pre-Demotic Egyptian literature and of the cuneiform literature of the last periods before the Macedonian conquest.

The number of literate élite officials in Egypt in the Middle Kingdom has been estimated at around 2000, in a total population of around two million.[32] The point is not to set up a *sorites* argument about how many literate individuals are needed to make up a community for "literature," but rather to highlight a case that throws a revealing comparative light on the situation in Hellenistic Greece and Rome, illustrating how the wide diffusion of texts in those societies is anomalous in an ancient setting. "In the surviving Middle Kingdom evidence, poetry is an invisible art, apart from the material presence of the poem's manuscripts"; unsurprisingly, in such a context, "[t]he social space for literature . . . remains deeply problematic," although it is possible to speculate about a larger audience being reached through some kind of public readings of the texts.[33] Later, in the New Kingdom, the copying and study of these texts became part of the training of scribes in the learning of Middle Egyptian, and we are in the dark as to what other reception contexts there may have been for this rich literature.[34] Again, wider audiences are imaginable through recitations of some kind, and we really do not know how many individuals may have had their own copies of works such as *The Tale of Sinuhe,* but the mainstream view in scholarship is that the texts themselves, "written in the esoteric hieroglyphic or hieratic scripts . . . can hardly have been accessible to anyone other than professional scribes."[35] This picture is transformed from the sixth century on by the development of the Demotic script and its accompanying literature, which was itself in many respects derived from the classical texts: here we see a much wider circulation of texts, involving a great variety of genres.[36]

In a rather similar way, the great texts of the Sumerian and Babylonian cuneiform literatures may have begun their lives in a context of performance, but the remaining manuscripts virtually all come from the environment of the scribal school.[37] As George puts it, "[t]here are exceptions, like the Babylonian Creation Epic *(Enūma eliš),* which was much studied and copied out by student scribes but also recited before the god Marduk by his priestly attendant on at least two occasions during the cultic year at Babylon. For the most part, however, the realm of pedagogy is the only proven context of the written literature."[38] Even in "library" finds there are very small numbers of literary texts.[39] In the eighth century, Aramaic gained ground in the Assyrian empire as a vernacular language and as an instrument of government, so that cuneiform was increasingly circumscribed within courtly and educational contexts: "[a]gainst this background it is unlikely that a written work of the old tradition such as the Standard Babylonian Gilgamesh epic had any life as literature outside pedagogy, where it was studied for its Old Babylonian quality as a good story and for its veneer of Middle Babylonian profundity."[40] Part of the rise of Aramaic was the development of a literature in the Aramaic language and script, of which very little survives since it was recorded on papyrus, not on clay tablets like cuneiform; there will have been oral performance of this Aramaic literature as well.[41] Where this new situation leaves the status of the old cuneiform texts is not an easy question to frame, let alone answer. As we saw in Chapter 1, the hero Gilgamesh survived the end of the cuneiform culture as a folk-hero in various contexts, so we must assume that there were avenues of reception, particularly from oral performance, no longer recoverable in any detail.[42] It is at least worth noting the uniformity with which scholars of cuneiform register "an essential difference between Mesopotamian civilization and that of classical antiquity. In Mesopotamia, there was no 'free' reading: no one is ever depicted reading for pleasure."[43] Nor does there appear to have been a "wealthy, leisured class for whom intellectual activities were optional, if challenging, pastimes."[44]

The societies we have been subjecting to this brief survey show a remarkable variety in the possibilities for the production, reception, dissemination, and use of texts. In all of the cases that we have been discussing, the question of missing evidence is obviously extremely problematic, and any chance find could mean a change in these provisional observations. At least, I aim to have denaturalized the category of "literature" in an ancient context sufficiently that the burden of proof is on those who would have it that the existence of developed, widely circulated, vernacular text-based literatures in the third century Mediterranean is something generally to be expected. The Greeks, the Jews, and the Romans, together with the Egyptians of the Demotic period, all in their very different ways, look unusual against the general background. If we do not find good reason to posit a developed poetic and prose literature in Punic in the highly successful and literate society of Carthage, or a literature in Etruscan, or in Oscan, then, as I argued above

in the Introduction, this is not a patronizing or Westernizing or Hellenocentric position. Rather, it could be described as patronizing and
Hellenocentric to assume that the Carthaginians, for example, must
have had this kind of literature, for such an assumption would itself
betray an *a priori* judgment that to qualify as a developed society in the
ancient world it was necessary to possess this supposedly superior
institution.[45]

Across the Watershed

We turn now to consider what kind of continuity there may have been
between the broad text-based literature of late third- to early second-
century Rome and the verbal and artistic culture that existed before the
watershed of the reform of the *ludi scaenici* in 240. My aim here is emphatically not to give some general account of Roman artistic and verbal
culture before the middle of the third century: for that, I refer the reader
to Horsfall (1994), still the best overall brief introduction.[46] Rather, we
shall concentrate on possible continuities in order to attempt to clarify
what may have been distinctive about the translation project and its
consequences.

As stressed in the Introduction and in Chapter 2, there is no doubt
whatever that the Romans were familiar with song, priestly hymns, oratory, and other forms of verbal artistry for a very long time before the
ludi scaenici of 240, and these practices may all be provisionally treated,
if we wish, as "literary" under one description or another. In general,
their word *carmen*, conventionally translated as "song," covers a wide
range of marked, stylized speech, and the "prayer" to Mars transmitted
in Cato's *De Agri Cultura* is as much a *carmen* as the "hymn" to Mars
sung by the Arval Brethren.[47] We may trace the Romans' spectacles of
music and dance with some confidence at least back to the first *Ludi*
under the kings.[48] They had been watching dedicated stage shows for
well over a century before the *Ludi* of 240, and it seems that the shows
available to the public in the original *ludi scaenici* continued to be staged
at least until 115, when the old Latin pipe players with their singers and

dancers were exempted from the general expulsion of actors from the city.[49]

Since, as we shall see, recent scholarship has been so interested in the possibility of an oral song culture of some kind in Rome before the translation project, it is also important to acknowledge the attention the Roman élite paid to a range of written discourses well before the mid third century. As we have already had occasion to observe, the Romans had known literacy for five centuries by the time Livius Andronicus' actors put on their masks and started reciting his lines. They had extensive public writings (laws, calendars, honorific inscriptions), with various kinds of archive at their disposal, and the élite must have been used to communicating important information in written form to the Senate and to their colleagues.[50] Finally, as ever, what is at issue in considering the departures of the years after 240 is not the difference between a period before Roman cultural engagement with Hellenism and a period after it, for Roman culture is always being formed in dialogue with Hellenic—among other—cultures: the Roman display of laws and calendars and honorific inscriptions, for example, is itself directly informed by Greek practices.[51] What is at issue are the different ways in which the dialogue is being conducted.

There are other hypothetical avenues one may envisage the Romans exploring apart from the translation project, in which case we would have been investigating different kinds of possible continuity. If there is a "lost" moment when the Romans might have been catapulted into a distinctively different kind of literary project from the one they did undertake, one could speculate that it might have been some sixty years earlier than the *ludi scaenici* of 240. Around the year 300, as we saw in Chapter 4, one observes a newly dynamic response to Hellenism gaining sudden momentum in the city.[52] A number of decisive religious innovations begin to take off at this period, and the Pythagoreanism of south Italy becomes important in a new way.[53] At this time a statue of Pythagoras was erected in the Forum (Plin. *HN* 34. 26), and the curule aedile Cn. Flavius dedicated a shrine to Concordia in the Comitium in 304, calqued upon the Greek cult of Homonoia, a concept of particular importance to the Pythagoreans.[54] Flavius had been a *scriba* of the great Appius Claudius Caecus, a figure who has suddenly attracted renewed attention, in particular as a focus for the aristocracy's interest in Pythagoreanism.[55] The charismatic Claudius has various testimonia attached to him in the tradition, which appear to show that writings of his were accorded importance and preserved, presumably by his family in the first instance.[56] A speech of his against peace with King Pyrrhus in 280 is repeatedly mentioned by Cicero, together with maxims described as *sententiae* or *carmina*, and a *carmen*—possibly, or possibly not, the same thing—described by Cicero as "Pythagorean," and said by him to have been admired by the Greek philosopher Panaetius.[57] Here we have the right kind of cultural nexus for a reorientation in verbal and textual production, yet it seems that this remained a road not taken, perhaps because it was too closely identified with the extraordinary figure of Claudius himself to become a template: as Rüpke puts it in discussing the speech of Claudius mentioned by Cicero, "what we see is a break with tradition, but not a trend."[58] The "trend" of publishing speeches did not gain real momentum until well into the second century, as we have seen. We must not underestimate the support network of copying and distribution and storing necessary for it to mean something to claim that Appius Claudius Caecus made public a *carmen* around 300 that survived and was read for generations.

The cultural reconfigurations around the great figure of Appius Claudius Caecus did not, then, have lasting consequences in the development of new forms of textual traditions. Yet Claudius and his peers sang and heard *carmina* as members of priestly colleges or as spectators of the *Ludi,* at the very least, and it is natural to enquire how such performances fed into what we now call Latin literature. The question of the connection between the styles and meters of Roman songs before and after the translation project is a difficult one. We are on surer ground with general traits of style, where it is possible to track the continuing impact of "many typical features of the traditional Latin *carmina,* such as assonance, parallel phrases, repetition, and alliteration."[59] The possible continuity of metrical forms is considerably more controversial.

Even in the case of the Saturnian, which is with increasing unanimity regarded as "a survival of an indigenous Italic poetic form," there is much debate over how standardized its form was before Livius Andronicus and Naevius took it over in order to use it to compose poems of very substantial length for the first time.[60] Certainly, however it was used earlier, the meter continued to be an important vehicle for experiment. Not only did Livius and Naevius use it for epic, but it was the base for inventive work in epigrammatic form in the sepulcher complex of the Cornelii Scipiones; the Saturnian verses on the various tombs, dating from around 240 down to 160, are clearly calqued upon the appearance and social function of Greek epigram, in dialogue with the conventions of Roman funerary oration.[61] By the time of the last burial, that of Cn. Cornelius Scipio Hispanus (praetor 139), the Saturnian has been replaced by the elegiac couplet, first used in Latin by the adaptor of the hexameter, Ennius: "Ennius' influence has now driven the Saturnian from the field."[62]

Again, a verse-form may have been influenced by Greek verse-forms and still predate the translation project. The form of the trochaic septenarius known as the *versus quadratus,* for example, used for all kind of popular songs in the surviving record, including children's and soldiers' songs, could be an originally Greek form, "since similar material is found in Greek and could have diffused into popular oral culture early on."[63] For the dramatic meters that were adapted with such flexible success by Livius Andronicus, majority opinion has it that there must have been some kind of precursors, since it seems incredible to most scholars that one individual could have come up with the panoply of solutions to adapting Greek dramatic meters into the very different language of Latin.[64] Yet it remains a compelling possibility that an individual was responsible, especially if Gratwick's interpretation of the Roman variety of iambo-trochaic verse is correct, for his theory posits a single intuition about how to adapt the quantitative metrics of Greek into a language with a strong word accent; if he is right, then that individual might as well be Livius Andronicus as anyone else.[65] Much, then, is uncertain: as Gratwick says, "we cannot even offer reasonable guesses as to how strange the early dramatists' music and quantitative polymetric lyrics sounded to audiences familiar with Saturnian verse and the cadences of the *tibicines* whose art was ultimately Etruscan."[66]

Comparing Greek and Roman Song Cultures

The only at all substantial surviving body of material that gives us any purchase on what Roman songs might have been like before the translation project is in the form of Roman priestly hymns; we shall be considering the nature of those hymns in the next section. Nonetheless, larger claims are regularly made for the possibility of reconstructing early environments for a wide range of song, depending almost entirely on testimonia from Cicero. The main focus of attention here has tended to be on what modern scholars call the *carmina convivalia*, "songs sung at banquets," from the songs that were once upon a time sung by Romans at banquets according to Cato in his *Origines*, according to reports by Cicero in his *Tusculan Disputations* (1. 3; 4. 3) and *Brutus* (75); Varro, in a fragment of the *De Vita Populi Romani* (fr. 84 Riposati) appears to be reporting the same custom, though without citing Cato explicitly as his source. Cicero has much more than this to say about the nature of early Roman culture, however, and on the basis of his statements, especially at the beginning of the fourth book of the *Tusculans*, a systematic picture has been created, above all by Nevio Zorzetti, of a diverse Roman song culture dating back into the early Republic or even beyond.[67] Zorzetti has argued for an organic archaic song culture at Rome, with performances both symposiastic and choral, explicitly in parallel with the oral song culture posited of the Archaic or Classical Greek polis.[68]

Among these various hypothetical forms of song, the one that has traditionally attracted most attention has been the so-called *carmina convivalia*. All that we know about these songs derives from three separate Ciceronian citations of the same passage from Cato's *Origines*, and also from a separate testimonium by Varro. At the beginning of the fourth book of the *Tusculans* Cicero reports that Cato in his *Origines* said that "amongst our ancestors there had been this custom at banquets, that those who were reclining would take it in turns to sing to the flute of the merits and glorious deeds of famous men" (*morem apud maiores hunc epularum fuisse, ut deinceps qui accubarent canerent ad tibiam clarorum uirorum laudes atque uirtutes, Tusc.* 4.3, *FRHist* 5 F113a, tr. Bispham and Cornell). At the very beginning of the *Tusculans* Cicero gives essentially the same information (*Tusc.* 1. 3, *FRHist* 5 F113b), while in the *Brutus* he laments the loss of "those songs that Cato has written about in his *Origines,* which were repeatedly sung many centuries before his time by individual guests at banquets concerning the merits of famous men" (*illa carmina, quae multis saeculis ante suam aetatem in epulis esse cantitata a singulis conuiuis de clarorum uirorum laudibus in originibus scriptum reliquit Cato, Brut.* 75, *FRHist* 5 F113c, tr. Bispham and Cornell). Varro has it that the songs were sung not by adults but by well brought-up young boys (*pueri modesti, De Vita* fr. 84 Riposati).

Now, I have nothing new whatever to contribute to the long debate over the actual historicity of these songs.[69] I agree fully with the view that Cato is already representing the custom as having died out long before his time, so that it becomes very difficult to accept what he says without independent evidence, which we do not have.[70] Archaeological remains of dining spaces in archaic central Italy have no independent evidentiary value for what was said or sung there. There is no doubt that the central Italian peoples in the sixth century eagerly embraced Greek dining and drinking customs and elaborated them in their own ways, and it would be extremely surprising if these settings did not witness song of some kind.[71] Yet we do not know what those songs were, if they existed; nor do we know what kind of continuity of practice and custom there may have been across the transformative years from 600 to 250.

If the Romans of 400 or 300 were singing songs at their *convivia,* they are not likely to have been mini-epics or "lays," but two- or three-line snatches like the *skolia,* "drinking songs," of Classical Athens.[72] This at least is what Cato appears to have in mind, not any kind of mini-epic solo performance, when he writes of the ancestors at feasts singing the praises and great accomplishments of famous men "in turn" (*deinceps*).

The deeper general background likewise makes developed heroic oral compositions unlikely for the early period: "There is no evidence that the preliterate Italic peoples possessed any tradition of extended oral poetry of the Greek or Sanskrit type (in spite of Romantic-era claims of oral historical 'lays')."[73] In other words, there is highly unlikely to have been any continuity of the kind that has been posited between this reported dining custom and an original performance context for the epics of Livius, Naevius, and Ennius.[74]

It is undeniably possible that independent knowledge of an aristocratic *skolia*-type custom came down to Cato, and to Varro, by some avenue or other, but the most economical explanation of the testimonia to my mind remains that of Dahlmann (1950) and Horsfall (1994), namely, that such accounts of the Romans' early "literary" history are fundamentally calqued upon Greek accounts of theirs. It is not a matter of accusing ancient writers of deliberately perpetrating meretricious fictions. Rather, on this hypothesis, faced with a more or less complete void, they did something not altogether remote from what their modern counterparts do, and looked across to Greece for comparison, in a procedure for which there are many parallels.[75] To quote Horsfall, then: "If from Cato on, our sources lament the demise of the *carmina* and if virtually all the details preserved in the learned tradition can be shown to conform to Greek usage and in almost all cases to derive from extant Greek scholarship on the συμπόσιον, then it seems to me incautious and ingenuous to say that we do actually know something about the *carmina*. Perhaps they existed. . . . But we have little choice but to admit that we really and truly do not know."[76]

Similar doubts surround the larger vision of a variegated symposiastic and choral song culture in early Rome, as based essentially on Cicero's evocation of a Pythagorean music culture dating back to the early Republic and going down to the time of Appius Claudius Caecus (*Tusc.* 4. 2–5). When we read what Cicero has to say about this early Roman culture, or in general about Roman cultural development vis-à-vis Greece in the opening sections of the work (*Tusc.* 1. 1–6), we need to be very cautious in taking what he says as "evidence," for he is not helpfully relaying information but pleading a very special case.[77] Quite apart from the basic question of what chain of information could allow Cicero to have worthwhile knowledge about conditions centuries before his time, we need to ask what his motivation is for advancing the claims he is making.

If we situate Cicero's remarks within the larger project of the *Tusculans* and of his philosophical writings altogether, it becomes clearer that his strategy is part of the peculiarly complicated stance he is adopting towards Greek culture at the moment that he is systematically taking over the commanding heights of Greek philosophy for Roman culture.[78] In a simultaneously defensive and aggressive move, he argues that Rome was perfectly capable of a broad range of cultural development from very early on, even if some of the more obvious tokens of cultural development—especially poetry (1. 3) and philosophy (2. 5)—might appear to have come along only at a late stage. In particular, Cicero is intent on proving that the Romans appear late in developing poetry for understandable reasons. At the beginning of the *Tusculans* he will have it that the Romans were for so long intent on more worthwhile pursuits, such as law and warfare, that they simply did not bother competing with Greece in this arena (1. 2–3). In his preface to Book 4, he has a more subtle and elaborate strategy, which involves postulating a sophisticated Pythagorean-based music culture at Rome well before the conventional watershed: in this way he can demonstrate that the Romans were indeed developing in their own fashion, as if preparing the ground for the sudden efflorescence of poetic culture when the time came: *facile ut appareat nostros omnia consequi posse, simul ut uelle coepissent* ("so that it is easy to see that our people had the ability to pursue everything successfully as soon as they wanted to do so," *Tusc.* 4. 5).[79]

In looking to Greek culture for analogies with which to plug the gap he perceives and tries to argue away, Cicero's procedure is rather like Cato's, and rather like that of the modern scholars who likewise feel that the Romans of the early Republic cannot simply have had no developed poetic culture, because it is somehow naturally to be expected that an ancient society should have such elaborated and diversified forms of performance and song. As Gildenhard remarks in assessing the position of Suerbaum on a supposed early Roman oral song culture, "[f]or Suerbaum it is simply a given that the Roman people had their own traditions of narrative, dramatic, and lyric poetry."[80] The comparative material we discussed at the beginning of this chapter, showing a great variety across a range of cultures in this regard, should make us cautious about assuming any such thing.

I am certainly not trying to argue that the Romans had no songs or music in the fourth or early third century, but we need to be as explicit as we can about what we have in the way of actual evidence and what we are inferring by way of analogy. We know that colleges of priests sang hymns, for example, and we shall investigate those hymns further in the next section.[81] We do not have such knowledge in the case of what, if anything, may have been sung in *convivia* or among the *sodalitates* of aristocrats, and we must be careful not to conflate the very different environments of the *convivium,* where our evidence is insecure, and the priestly college, where we have something more concrete to rely on.[82]

If the Roman writers were using Greek scholarship to help them construct analogies for what had been going on in the void that confronted them for the periods before the mid-third century, then modern scholars too are explicitly using analogies with Greek conditions for the same purpose.[83] When we consider the Greek side of the comparison used by Zorzetti, for example, we face difficulties—as he fully acknowledges—in pinning down which "Greece" we have in view, for there are enormous disparities over space and time in what we can all too easily lump together as "Greece of the archaic and classical period."[84] For men exchanging song (as in the putative *sodalitates*), do we envisage as a counterpart the mess halls of the Spartans and the Cretans, the symposia of Athens, the Pythagorean schools of Magna Graecia, or the great houses of Thessalian cattle barons? Further, comparing a supposed Roman oral song culture independent of texts with conditions in Archaic or Classical Greece is vulnerable to the objection that those Archaic and Classical Greek songs were not themselves independent of texts. The world of Alcaeus and Simonides is not an oral culture, but an oral-textualist culture.[85] Fowler, in criticizing "the desperate dogma that archaic Greece was an oral society," produces arresting figures: "By the late sixth century there were something like 200,000 epic and lyric verses, and early works of prose, circulating in writing."[86] No one is claiming anything remotely like this for the Rome of Coriolanus or Appius Claudius Caecus.[87]

Constructing a developed Roman song culture for the early and middle Republic appears to be a difficult project, as does the detection of significant points of continuity into the new project of translation and adaptation. Yet a test-case comparison between an example of early Roman *carmen* and equivalents from Archaic and Classical Greece will shed light, if from a perhaps unexpected angle, on points of resemblance in those earlier periods, and it will in the process help us refine our picture of what was different about the new situation that developed under the initial impulse of the translation project.

A Comparison Test-Case: Greek and Roman Songs for the Gods

Let us turn to an actual surviving text from before the watershed in order to see what kind of comparative work we may do with it. For a long time, especially since Norden's great book *Aus altrömischen Priesterbüchern,* a famous test case of comparison between Greek and Roman songs for the gods has been the *Carmen Arvale,* sung by the Fratres Arvales at their annual festival of the Dea Dia.[88] Our text was inscribed in the temple in 218 CE, but the *carmen* must go back in one form or another to the middle Republic at the latest.[89] It is "mainly written in cola which later crystallized into the Saturnian metre."[90] I give the text and translation of Courtney (1995):[91]

> *e nos Lases iuuate*
> *e] nos Lases iuuate*
> *e nos Lases iuuate*
> *neue lue(m) rue(m) Marma<r> sins incurrere in pleores*

neue lue(m) rue(m) Marmar [si]ns incurrere in pleoris
neue lue(m) rue(m) Marmar serp incurrere in pleoris
satur fu, fere Mars, limen [sa]li, sta berber
satur fu, fere Mars, limen sali, sta berber
satur fu, fere Mars, limen sali, sta berber
Sem]unis alternei aduocapit conctos
Semunis alternei aduocapit conctos
Simunis alternei aduocapit [conc]tos
e nos Marmor iuuato
e nos Marmor iuuato
e nos Ma<r>mor iuuato
triumpe triumpe triumpe trium[pe tri]umpe

Help us, Lares (x3)
and, Mars, do not allow disease and disaster to attack
　　　　　the multitude (x3)
Be sated, fierce Mars; leap (on to? over?) the
　　　　　threshold, stay put (x3)
In turn you [*plural*] shall summon all the Semones (x3)
Help us, Mars (x3)
triumpe! (x5)

As revealed by the intriguing detective work of Rüpke (1993), Norden began his work on the *carmen* in the expectation of isolating an element of Roman culture that came before Greek influence. Norden's text of the book was virtually ready for the press in 1926, and it must have been the appearance of Eduard Fraenkel's article "Die Vorgeschichte des versus quadratus" in *Hermes* 1927 that made Norden realize that his was a mistaken quest; it took him almost a decade to digest the implications.[92]

As Norden came to realize, the *carmen* exhibits features of Greek hymnody, starting with the anaphora-based structure itself.[93] Mars is commanded to "leap" (*sali*, 7–9), as Zeus is commanded to "leap" (θόρε) in the Cretan Hymn of the Curetes to Dictaean Zeus.[94] Mars is asked to be "sated" (*satur,* 7–9): Ares is already "insatiable" (ἄατος) in Homer

(*Il.* 5. 388). As Courtney observes, "[t]he assonance *lue rue* is of a type common in religious and magical formulae": he compares λιμὸς καὶ λοιμός in Hesiod, *Op.* 243.[95] Norden explicitly faced the theoretical problem of how to account for such similarities, using the then very modern terminology of evolutionary theory to ask whether the similarities were the result of "convergence" or "descent," "Konvergenz oder Descendenz."[96] He opted strongly for "descent," arguing that whoever wrote the *Carmen Arvale* did so in conscious knowledge of how Greek hymnic forms worked. After demonstrating that the *carmen* was not the original uncontaminated piece of ur-Romanitas that he had expected it to be when he began his study, Norden summed up the implications of his findings trenchantly: "This traditional classification: preliterary = national, literary = hellenizing, is no longer sustainable."[97]

There are, of course, major differences in social context between this Roman *carmen* and the Greek models to which it is, in whatever measure, ultimately indebted. An important one is personnel. So far as we can tell, in the fifth and fourth centuries Romans had delegated the tasks of singing such hymns to boards of priests, rather than to choruses taken from the citizen body, which is what we see as the norm in Greece:[98] the entrusting of singing and dancing for the gods to selected adult male citizens is an interesting exception to the general Roman disapprobation of Greek-style choric performance by the élite that we observe in the later period. This demarcation is a subset of a larger phenomenon in Rome, since one of the big differences between Roman and Greek priests in general is that Roman priests were always part of a *collegium* or a *sodalitas,* whereas Greek priests were not.[99] A related feature of this differentiation and compartmentalization may be seen in the Roman way of doing public sacrifice, for, unlike in Greece, the people as a whole did not normally participate in feasting after sacrifice, which was restricted to special groups of priests, and senators.[100] Various priestly *collegia,* then, had their own transmitted *carmina* but, as we shall see, we have no explicit evidence until the Second Punic War for songs to the gods in Rome being sung by choruses from the people, instead of by members of a board of priests.

The personnel may be different in important ways, but rhythm, structure, and even elements of phraseology all owe something to Greek norms. But which Greek hymns are we talking about when we say that the *Carmen Arvale* resembles Greek hymns, or that it benefits from being compared to Greek hymns? And what kind of image of hymns in the life of the Greek *polis* are we assuming when we make this comparison? If, for the purposes of comparison, we look across to Greece from the Rome in which we can posit a *carmen* such as the *Carmen Arvale* coming into being, then we face the problem that "the vast majority of archaic and classical cult hymns have vanished without trace,"[101] with the old cult songs being regarded by Hellenistic scholars as unsuitable for their attention and for subsequent transmission, "as not sufficiently interesting, or too unsophisticated, or downright of no literary value."[102] There are, however, some examples surviving from the Archaic or Classical period of a text that "has demonstrably been in practical use as (what we would call) a liturgical text."[103] It is striking that these songs are closer in style and ambition to the Roman *carmina* than they are to the verses of a Pindar or Simonides that perhaps automatically come to mind when we imagine a hymnic performance in classical Greece.

When the women of Elis, for example, invoked Dionysus, these were their words, according to Plutarch (*Mor.* 299B):[104]

ἔχει δ' οὕτως ὁ ὕμνος·
ἐλθεῖν, ἥρω Διόνυσε,
Ἀλείων ἐς ναὸν
ἁγνὸν σὺν Χαρίτεσσιν
ἐς ναὸν
τῶι βοέωι ποδὶ θύων.
εἶτα ἐπάιδουσιν·
ἄξιε ταῦρε,
ἄξιε ταῦρε.

The hymn is like this:
Come, Lord Dionysus,

to the sacred temple of Elis's people
accompanied by the Graces,
to the temple
storming on your bovine foot.

Then they sing the refrain:
Worthy bull,
worthy bull.

Rather more elaborated, and certainly more lengthy, is the Curetes'
Hymn to Dictaean Zeus, mentioned above as having a similar impera-
tive ("leap") to the one in the *Carmen Arvale*. Sixty-six lines long, the
Hymn is structured around a six-line refrain which opens the song and
is then repeated six times:[105]

Ἰώ, μέγιστε Κοῦρε,
χαῖρέ μοι, Κρόνειε,
παγκρατὲς γάνος, βέβακες
δαιμόνων ἀγώμενος·
Δίκταν εἰς ἐνιαυτὸν
ἔρπε καὶ γέγαθι μολπᾷ

Io! most mighty youth,
I salute you, son of Kronos,
almighty splendor, who stand
as leader of the company of gods!
Come to Dikta at this New Year's day
and take delight in the music.

As Cole remarks, these verses "are among the few pieces of extant Greek
lyric that might be translated, without significant loss of literary quality,
into Latin Saturnians."[106]

Here, I submit, is our real *comparandum*. This is the kind of cult song
that most inhabitants of the Greek world will have been performing, or

hearing, most of the time—and this is the kind of cult song that the Italic peoples, as well as the Romans, will likewise have been familiar with.[107] These Greek cult songs are anonymous, like the hymns of the Roman priestly colleges or the Iguvine priesthood. They come with no named author, since they are not part of the literary system and have no need to be: they are embedded in the traditional repeated ritual and need no other sanction.[108]

In this respect, as in the degree of literary self-reference, sophistication, and ambition, they are different from the hymns attributed to named poets that were eventually preserved through the channels of literary transmission.[109] It is important not to think of Pindar's *Paeans* or *Dithyrambs,* rather than the song of the Elean women, as the point of comparison for archaic Roman *carmina.* Here I agree very much with Zorzetti's distinction between Archaic Rome and Greece in terms of the range of songs that they could offer to the gods. Having pointed out that "archaic Rome did not produce texts that became classics—points of reference for tradition and literary research," he goes on to say that "even in the experience of the diverse Greek *poleis,* the levels of development in the literary sphere differed widely in quality, quantity, and time. Indeed, for the culture of the *polis,* literary development might be called an optional component, whereas the rites that literature presupposed were basic constituent parts."[110]

Zorzetti's important observation gives us the context in which to take proper stock of the extraordinary fact of the existence of that "optional component" in Greece—the amazing verbal artifact that a visiting professional like Simonides or Pindar might occasionally provide for a city's festival. Such a poem, as Griffith points out, once away from its original context, "is clearly no longer directly operating in furtherance of actual cult"; he goes on to speculate "whether the degree of allusiveness, narrative sophistication, and complexity of self-reference may not mark out several surviving poems as distinctively crafted art-poems (or even 'literature,' like the religious poems of e.g. John Donne and George Herbert), several cuts above the run-of-the-mill (actual) prayers offered up by ordinary singers and poets."[111] Poems such as the hymns of Alcaeus or Sappho, for example, are certainly in this latter category, for they were not composed for cult performance in honor of their addressees: when Alcaeus begins his hymn to Hermes by hailing the god and saying that he is singing of him because that is what he feels like (χαῖρε, . . . σὲ γάρ μοι/θῦμος ὕμνην, 308b. 1–2), he is using the language not of cult-song but of the rhapsodic *prooemium*.[112]

Even hymns of the kind written by a Simonides or a Pindar for performance within a ritual are, indeed, strictly, liturgically redundant, in that the ritual could "work" perfectly well without them: "hymns . . . were precious offerings, like any other consecrated work of art; they were not prayers."[113] This mentality explains why the words of the prayers of the priests are inscribed on the Iguvine Tables or on the inscription commemorating Augustus' *Ludi Saeculares,* but not the words of the hymn, only a reference to its singing.[114] Of course it is in the end hard to keep these two elements, "hymns" and "prayers," separated off into two watertight compartments in the Greek world, since a work such as Pindar's Sixth *Paean* can be intent precisely on breaking down these boundaries, situating itself, as it does, simultaneously within a specific cult context (to be performed by a chorus of young Delphian men at the Theoxenia) and also within a literary system embracing other lyric poems together with Homer and the Cycle: "Reading *Paian* VI means accepting a flexible compromise between the chorus and the authority of the author."[115] As Furley and Bremer put it, this poem "presents a rare and valuable glimpse of what one might call the high point of choral lyric serving a purely cultic purpose" (although I would dispute the adverb "purely").[116]

However we adjudicate in general or in any case between the porous and mutually defining categories of the "cultic" and the "literary," the key point is that in the world of Pindar we are faced with a category of the "literary" to be the subject of adjudication. As with the rest of the developing Greek literary system, the phenomenon of the elaborated Greek hymns looks more and more extraordinary—not necessarily part of any liturgical action, not necessarily part even of a ritual performance, capable of being disseminated widely as texts and sustaining an ongoing dialogue with other texts of the kind and with other literary forms. This is a truly remarkable development in comparison with what we can reconstruct in the experience of Italic peoples, and, as we shall see in the next section, there is no evidence that the Romans attempted to reproduce anything at all like it until the Second Punic War.

Rome of the middle Republic, then, was indeed similar to a Greek *polis* in fundamental ways when it came to providing songs for the gods, but it represented a kind of ground zero, practicing, as Zorzetti puts it, "the rites that were the premise for literary development in the *polis*," but without—on the basis of the available evidence—elaborating that "optional component" of "literary development."[117] Again, this is not at all far removed from the normal experience in the Greek world. For the most part, when it came to the kind of songs for the gods that they heard performed, the normal experience of the Greek citizens of the Archaic or Classical *polis* will have been close to that of the Roman of the early or middle Republic or to a member of one of the other Italic peoples of the same period.

Elaboration of Cultic Song: A *Carmen* for Juno

We can document an effort on the part of the Romans to take precisely this extra step of elaborating the "optional component" of "literary development" of cultic song. They began to supplement their priestly *carmina* with an extra Hellenizing dimension, commissioning a professional poet to compose a new *carmen* in honor of a deity, a *carmen* that would be sung by a chorus taken from the community, and not by a college of priests. This is a process whose beginning we can probably date with some precision, to late May or early June 207, as part of the buildup to the battle of the Metaurus on June 23 of that year.

The performance of Livius Andronicus' *carmen* to Juno Regina is part of an extraordinary sequence of ritual, given very high prominence in the account of Livy.[118] A terrifying series of portents, culminating in the birth of a hermaphrodite, was triggered by news that Hannibal's brother Hasdrubal had crossed the Alps to invade Italy with his army from

Spain. In response, Etruscan *haruspices* recommended that the hermaphrodite should be drowned at sea, and the poet Livius Andronicus was commissioned by the *pontifices* to compose a new *carmen* for a chorus of twenty-seven virgins to sing as they marched through the city (Liv. 27. 37. 4–7). As they were rehearsing the *carmen* in the temple of Jupiter Stator, the temple of Juno Regina on the Aventine was struck by lightning, whereupon the *haruspices* advised that the matrons should make donations to Juno (7–10). The *decemviri* took over at this point, arranging an elaborate procession of offerings and sacrificial offerings to the Aventine temple of Juno Regina, accompanied by the chorus of virgins, who sang their *carmen* as they went (11–15).[119]

The new ritual was, as Wissowa puts it, "Greek from beginning to end,"[120] although with major participation from the Etruscan *haruspices*.[121] As Scheid (1995) has taught us, what counts about the Roman *Graecus ritus* is not so much how "Greek" it actually may have been in fact, but rather how much and why it mattered to the Romans to mark a certain ritual as somehow falling under that rubric. On this occasion, it appears that it mattered a good deal. Although it was the *pontifices* who originally prescribed the singing of a hymn by twenty-seven maidens, after the temple of Juno was struck by lightning it appears that the *decemviri* took over. This college was responsible for the *Graecus ritus,* and they commissioned and oversaw the ritual on the day of the performance of the *carmen,* following the chorus of singing virgins, wearing laurel garlands in the Greek way (Liv. 27. 37. 11). The college contained a number of priests at this time with marked Greek knowledge and connections, including M. Livius Salinator, who was to win the climactic battle of Metaurus later in the month, and who had a close tie to the designated poet, Livius Andronicus.[122]

Livy does not explicitly name the deity for whom the song was originally intended by the *pontifices.* It was probably meant for Juno all along, in which case the lightning strike on her temple was a valuable coincidence, reinforcing the urgency of the commission.[123] In any event, there is ample evidence that Juno was an appropriate goddess to honor with choruses and music, both in the Greek world and at Falerii, about thirty miles north of Rome.[124] Further, it seems likely that Juno will have been chosen as an object of special attention because of the possible disaffection from the Roman cause that she embodied in the war, and in particular in Etruria at this juncture. Hannibal's religious propaganda aimed at stressing the links between Italic Juno and Carthaginian Tanit, and the Romans responded with marked honors to the goddess:[125] it is possible that the Romans were now trying to outdo musical rites in honor of "other" Junos in their innovative commissioning of a new *carmen* as part of an ostentatiously massive ceremony of expiation.[126] Long after the ceremony and the victory at Metaurus that it will have been seen as securing, it is extremely likely that this was the moment chosen by Ennius in his *Annales* as the turning point in Rome's fortunes, when Juno was finally reconciled to Rome and definitively joined Jupiter in favoring the Romans against the Carthaginians (Serv. *Aen.* 1. 281, 12. 841 = VIII xvi Sk.): Ennius will, on this reading, be picking up on the state's own motives in honoring Juno.[127]

The text of Livius Andronicus' new *carmen* was in the public domain.[128] Livy has clearly read it, and he famously records that it was "at that epoch maybe regarded as praiseworthy by unskilled minds, but now would appear repellent doggerel if quoted" (*illa tempestate forsitan laudabile rudibus ingeniis, nunc abhorrens et inconditum si referatur,* Liv. 27. 37. 13). This does not mean that it was in Saturnians, as is often assumed.[129] Livius will have learned the technique of composing a choral hymn as much from translating the choruses of tragedy for the *Ludi Romani* as from whatever Greek hymns he may have read, or heard in Magna Graecia.[130]

On the available evidence, the incorporation of the Greek-style *carmen* in the propiatory ritual was a new departure, one that was consciously modeled on the glamorous displays mounted in the cities of the Greek world.[131] The *carmen* that was commissioned by the organs responsible to the Senate, composed by Livius Andronicus, and performed before the Roman people by twenty-seven virgins as representatives of the community, not by a college of priests—this was a new text, commissioned from an individual composer, not an anonymous song transmitted in inherited books.

Zorzetti downplays the innovative nature of the rituals of 207, on the assumption that "nothing proves that Andronicus did not work within a liturgical frame that included the use of choral song."[132] Yet this assumption rather undoes the power of his own conclusions, quoted above, concerning the absence of classic texts from archaic Rome, together with the analogy between that situation and the usual state of affairs in the rituals of the Greek *polis,* where the rites did not necessitate the "optional component" of a "literary development."[133] Given the gaps in our evidence it is clearly impossible to assert that no one before Livius Andronicus had been commissioned to produce a Greek-style hymn for public performance by a chorus who were not priests, yet Livy's great emphasis on this moment makes it likely that he is marking the ritual as a decisive innovation.[134] Further, Cole is correct to respond to Zorzetti by stressing that the priestly hymns appear to have been sufficient hitherto, while importing an expert to provide an "accretion to the repertory of Roman musico-poetic culture" is wholly in line with Roman state practice.[135] As in the first scenic reform of the *Ludi Romani* in 364, and in the establishment of successive *ludi scaenici,* we see the state using the opportunity provided by a severe crisis to innovate in the cultural sphere of religion, using outside professional expertise in the process.

If we appreciate the novelty of the hymnic commission for the rites for Juno before the battle of the Metaurus, we see more clearly why the Roman state chose at this juncture to honor Livius and his peers, described as "scribes and actors" by our source (*scribis histrionibusque,* Festus p. 446. 25–448. 4 L), by granting them the right to meet and make offerings in the temple of Minerva on the Aventine.[136] It is, incidentally, very interesting that the Roman state did not have a specific term for these new professionals other than to bracket them with the *scribae* who worked for the quaestors: they are not called *uates,* let alone *poetae.* This grant is explicitly said by our source to be the consequence of Livius' *carmen* for the virgins, but it is also said to be in his honor "because he both wrote plays and acted in them" *(quia is et scribebat fabulas et agebat).* If we can put any weight on the wording transmitted by Festus, then, the special service of Livius Andronicus as composer of the *carmen* in the rites that saved Rome from Hasdrubal's invasion won him and his fellow dramatists official recognition, which was couched in terms of their playwriting. Livius' composition of the choral hymn will have occasioned the recognition of his status, but because the *carmen* was a one-off occasion, the "job-description" for the new guild had to be put in different language.

The next such occasion recorded by Livy comes seven years later, in 200 (31. 12. 6–10). Once again, the *monstrum* of hermaphroditism triggers the rite, overseen by the *decemviri*, who order a repetition of the rites of 207, with a hymn to Juno Regina performed by twenty-seven virgins. Livy repeatedly mentions the parallels between these events and those of seven years before (*sicut proxime . . . ; res diuinas easdem quae proxime . . .* , 31. 12. 8, 9), and he explicitly mentions the new hymn and its author on a par with the citation in 207: *carmen, sicut patrum memoria Livius, ita tum condidit P. Licinius Tegula* ("the author of the hymn, just as it was Livius in the memory of the senators, this time was P. Licinius Tegula," 31. 12. 10). The phrase *patrum memoria* ("in the memory of the senators") is perhaps striking when used to describe a gap of only seven years: this is no slip of the pen, nor a reference to any rites before 207, but a Livian ruse to expose the "invention of tradition" that is taking place with the second iteration of a spectacularly successful prototype.[137]

Although Licinius Tegula is mentioned only here in ancient sources, it is possible to establish that like his predecessor in Roman choral hymn, Livius Andronicus, he was a playwright and either the freedman or the client of a powerful Roman noble.[138] His wonderful *cognomen* of Tegula, "Flat *covering* rooftile" (from *tegere*, "to cover"), links him with a contemporary Licinius with the complementary *cognomen* of Imbrex, "Curved *waterproofing* rooftile" (from *imber*, "rainwater"). These two overlapping types of tile are inextricable pairs in architecture, and since there are no other Romans with these *cognomina* then the men should be an inextricable pair as well. According to Solin's study of "paired names" in Latin, Licinius Tegula and Licinius Imbrex will probably be brothers who were named together when made freedmen or given citizenship by a Licinius: the obvious candidate is P. Licinius Crassus Dives, consul in 205 and Pontifex Maximus at the time that P. Licinius Tegula was commissioned to compose his hymn in 200.[139] Now, Licinius Imbrex is known to us as a comic playwright (number four on Volcacius Sedigitus' list of the Roman top ten).[140] His brother Tegula must have been a playwright as well, and whoever gave these two professionals their names did so with his tongue in his cheek, playing on the nicknames for two paired and complementary types of applause used in the theater, with the palms flat or concave like the rooftiles the styles of applause were named after.[141]

The next such rite we hear of is in the year 133, following the murder of Tiberius Gracchus. By this time, we no longer have the text of Livy, which vanishes in 167, but Julius Obsequens in his Book of Prodigies, with Livy as his source, reports that twenty-seven virgins, singing, purified the city (*Prod.* 27a); once again, a hermaphrodite has been discovered, and once again Juno Regina is involved, since a baby was heard crying for two days behind closed doors in her temple, though it is not explicitly said that the hymn was in her honor, as it had been in 207 and 200.[142] Obsequens records hymns by twenty-seven virgins also in the year 119 (*Prod.* 34: again, a hermaphrodite; no mention of Juno Regina); in 117 (*Prod.* 36: again, a hermaphrodite; no mention of Juno Regina); in 104 (*Prod.* 43: twenty-seven virgins sang a hymn as they bore gifts to Ceres and Proserpina; no hermaphrodite mentioned); in 99 (*Prod.* 46: another hymn from twenty-seven virgins bearing gifts to Ceres and Proserpina, and two images of cypress wood offered to Juno Regina, as in 207; no hermaphrodite); in 97 (*Prod.* 48: another hermaphrodite; images of cypress wood offered to Juno Regina by twenty-seven virgins who purified the city; in this citation, no explicit mention of a *carmen* is made); in 92 (*Prod.* 53: two hermaphrodites; an offering to Ceres and Proserpina, and twenty-seven virgins singing a *carmen* purified the city).

Obsequens stops giving accounts of these commissioned hymns at this point (he continues down to the year 12). We always have to allow for the possibility that he simply stopped recording such commissioned hymns for one reason or another, but if 92 is the last such commissioned hymn in the Republic, it would appear to be a significant date, coming at the very end of the "third Republic of the *nobiles*" in Flower's periodization of the Republic (from 139 to 88).[143] As Forsythe points out, adducing the coincidence of many of these rituals with horrific civil bloodshed or serious military defeats, the procession and the hymn were mean to "purify the state" and "assist in the restoration of the *pax deorum*."[144] After the carnage of the Social, Marian, and Sullan wars, normal operating procedures come to an end, as the healing power of these purificatory rites appears to have been exposed as void. So far as we know, the next time a chorus of twenty-seven virgins would sing a hymn on behalf of the Roman people would be seventy-five years later, on 3 June in the year 17, when they were joined by a chorus of twenty-seven boys and went up to the Palatine to sing the *Carmen Saeculare* of Q. Horatius Flaccus.

It is an interesting problem whether or not the *carmina* mentioned by Obsequens will have had a named author in the now lost original text of Livy. We cannot now check this, since the surviving text of Obsequens only begins in 190, and between 190 and 167 (where Livy breaks off), there are no such ceremonies recorded either in Livy or in Obsequens. If the text of Obsequens had been preserved for the year 207 or 200, then we could have cross-checked to see if he mentioned Livius Andronicus or Licinius Tegula as the poets on those occasions. Were new poets, then, commissioned on each of these subsequent occasions? Presumably new poets were commissioned for the hymns to Ceres and Proserpina in 104 and 99, since they were new deities in this cult; otherwise, did the *decemviri* assume that they already had two hymns to Juno Regina—one by Livius Andronicus and one by Licinius Tegula—and could simply recycle them? Our inclination one way or the other will to some degree be based on our views about priestly conservatism and the possibilities for Roman cultural expression in the second century. It seems to me that if we take seriously the category of Hellenizing "hymn" as introduced in the rites of 207, then we should imagine a poet being commissioned each time for the successive expiations: as Scheid puts it, in general terms "[a] hymn . . . would be composed by a poet . . . , and would not be repeated from traditional texts controlled by the priests."[145]

Throughout the second century, standard rituals will have been regarded as perfectly sufficient most of the time, and the attested *carmina* in Livy and Obsequens will have been the exceptions, composed by experts in poetry for rare and specific occasions. This state of affairs is, as we have seen, extremely close to the situation in the typical Archaic, Classical, or Hellenistic Greek *polis;* there too the accepted traditional hymns will have been sufficient for most purposes most of the time, with a Simonides or some other expert professional being called in only very exceptionally, if ever.

In some ways it might appear surprising that this extra dimension came so late to Rome, when the very first Roman songs to the gods already show such marked Greek imprints. Yet the *carmina* of 207 and 200 find their context within the larger revolution we have been tracing in Roman life—pioneered by precisely such figures as Livius Andronicus and Licinius Tegula—a revolution that saw the aggressive adaptation of Greek epic, tragedy, and comedy in the generation leading up to the battle of the Metaurus. The Roman state had organized many rituals before, regularly involving priestly song, and regularly involving Grecizing elements under the care of the *decemviri*. Yet the decision to innovate with the adaptation of a Greek-style choral hymn shows the enthusiasm for new Grecizing departures that is so characteristic of the period as a whole. There are undeniable elements of continuity, but they go with an ambition to use their new professionals to reach out into the other culture for elements that will be yet more glamorous, charismatic, and effective. We do not have the *carmina* of Livius Andronicus or Licinius Tegula, but we may be sure that they will not have been a continuity of policy by other means. These works, like the dramas composed by these same men, did not come from nothing: but they are the products of decisive, planned, reorientations in their home cultures, even if the momentum unleashed by these reorientations took the Romans in undreamt of directions.

Inventing Vernacular Literatures

In the Classical world, it is very difficult to find parallels for the Roman experiment. Fine-grained analogies with the Roman case are not so easy to find in the post-Classical European world either, even though we see there many examples of the general template of a prestige language and literature—often Latin—providing models for adaptation into a vernacular.[146]

The invention of a vernacular literature in English, for example, is similar and dissimilar in arresting ways. The speed of the creation of a core for a new vernacular literature in English—a process that took a scant generation, from 1370 to 1400—is very reminiscent of the Roman case.[147] According to Catto, Chaucer and his peers (especially John Gower, William Langland, and the author of *Sir Gawain and the Green Knight*) were not continuing or developing an English literary culture that was already awaiting their attention, for the late Old English literature that might have performed this function was a closed book to them. Rather, they set about the bold project of creating a vernacular literature that could rival the vernaculars of French and Italian, using French language and literature in particular as an active partner, in addition to using Latin launch pads in the same way as did those other literatures—even if, as Catto shows, this new vernacular did not achieve its creators' (especially Chaucer's) ambition of forging another European vernacular literature to be widely read, along with French and Italian: that had to wait for another four centuries.[148]

Striking as this aspect of the parallel is, the linguistic starting point for the first Latin poets is quite different. As we saw in Chapter 2, the first Latin translator-poets had a rich linguistic field in their target culture from which to work, however much they supplemented and modified it. In England, on the other hand, "the English written language . . . far from being a natural development from early Middle English, . . . was effectively the artificial construct of a single generation of writers."[149] This "new literary language" then spread out to become the English of public business, supplanting the Latin and French/Latin formats that had been regular since the Conquest: "Nothing written in English in the preceding generation seems to prepare for its abrupt appearance and rapid adoption."[150] The new Latin literature certainly had a remarkable impact on the language, yet the relationship of the literature to the preceding linguistic environment is rather more like the medieval Italian case, where "practical literacy preceded the literary language."[151]

We have referred a number of times already to the remarkable deliberate creation of a national literature in the Russian language as a thought-provoking counterpoint to the Roman case.[152] In general terms, one is struck by the transformation in Russian life as Peter the Great (reigned 1682–1725) threw his country into modernity under the impulse of a new imperial self-consciousness, drawing on outside expertise, just as the Roman state had done, to equip the new Russia with contemporary literature, music, and architecture on Western European models to accompany its newly modern army, navy, and ports: the eventual end result was a nobility who were bilingual in Russian and French. Peter's success in laying the ground for a national literature in Russian was impressive, for the developments immediately after his death were dramatic: "If one compares the state of Russian literature in 1725 with that a mere half century later, the contrast is indeed staggering: in fifty years the Russians had successfully assimilated all the major forms of contemporary European literature—translated them, adapted them, and gone on to create independently in them."[153] Here one could substitute "Latin" for "Russian," "240" for "1725," and "Greek" for "European."

Nonetheless, there are important differences from the Roman case. Despite the transformations of the eighteenth century, by the early 1800s the body of literature in Russian was still such as to cause embarrassment to cultured Russians, as Figes remarks: "In the last three quarters of the eighteenth century some 500 works of literature were published in Russia. But only seven were of Russian origin."[154] The preparation time for a domestic Russian literary canon was even longer than the reign of Peter. As we have seen, Peter's father Alexis had begun the effort to foster Russian drama in the year that Peter was born, 1672, but his personnel encountered severe obstacles in the translation of European literary languages and cultural concepts into a starkly different cultural environment and into a written language with scant stylistic resources.[155] It took at least three generations, then, for this project to develop any real traction. The difference with the Roman experience is very marked. If the Russians were starting almost from scratch in terms of their language's resources and their familiarity with French, German, and Italian high culture, the Romans had a long-standing acquaintance with Greek culture, while the Latin language had been on a remarkable trajectory of expansion and change for over a century before the translation project began.[156]

For all that, the Russian case remains an important comparison. It reminds us that imperial states can succeed perfectly well without a literature, and that contingent circumstances can prompt them relatively quickly to re-orientate so as to trade up and supplement what they perceive as a lack by drawing on outside expertise. Although nothing seems more natural than that a nation should have a literature, there is nothing inevitable or predictable about it.

Conclusion:
Joining the Network

DURING THE SHORT CENTURY that has been our main focus, from the end of the Great War in Sicily in 241 to the destruction of Carthage in 146, the Romans experienced turbulent change in many spheres, both internal and external. In their acquisition of a literature, grounded first in drama and then in an increasing variety of genres, they were exposed to a range of internal realignments; their new literature, with the wider cultural ambit that sustained it, also enabled and enforced change in their relationship to the *oecumenē* that was progressively falling under their control. The most important of these changes came about through their increasingly coherent mythological and historiographical frames of reference, which in a reciprocal process were formed by the corresponding systems of the Greeks and simultaneously linked into them. Their Grecizing dramas, epics, and histories reshaped their own knowledge systems, enabling them to make a newly coherent version of their own past and of how they fitted into the time frames and historical structures of the Mediterranean world: as Rüpke puts it, "The connection to an expanded Greek mythology, chronology, and geography required a systematic reconstruction of the Romans' own corresponding fields of knowledge and also made their expansion possible."[1]

At the same time, this process fed back into how other peoples, especially the Greeks, saw the Romans' participation in their grids of myth, chronology, and history. The Romans were not only joining, but reconfiguring, the worldwide web.

Webs of History and Myth

Now, the Romans had long been linked up with other peoples via connections forged through imagined pasts. As Wiseman's fascinating work on the "legendary genealogies" of the Roman nobles revealed, some great Roman families seem to have been cultivating links with glamorous "ancestors" from the Trojan saga probably back into the fourth century, while arrivals from neighboring Latin cities trailed lustrous associations from their home bases, with the Caecilii apparently claiming descent from Vulcan's son Caeculus, who founded Praeneste, and the Mamilii from Mamilia, the daughter of Odysseus' son Telegonus, who founded Tusculum.[2] Romulus and Remus, Saturnus, Aeneas—these had all been linked up into Greek accounts "by means of a collaborative effort on both sides" even before Rome conquered the peninsula of Italy.[3] When the Elymian people of Segesta appealed to Rome for protection at the beginning of the Great War, in 263, basing their claim on their supposed shared Trojan ancestry (Zonaras 8. 9. 12), it will not have been news to anyone in the Senate that they had a connection to Troy.

Rome's historical consciousness had likewise been in dialogue with that of the Greeks long before any Roman citizen started writing historiography.[4] Their commemoration of Pythagoras and Alcibiades in the Forum around 300 showed an interest in major figures who connected Magna Graecia and mainland Greece;[5] from two hundred years before that, the cult of Jupiter Optimus Maximus, with Juno and Minerva, was being shaped partly in response to Greek civic ideologies that had their own past, while the cult site on the Capitolium kept tracking its counterpart in Olympia, in Western Greece, as a repository for historical memory.[6]

The development of formal historiography, however, together with an increasingly codified mythographical framework, provided something new in scale and systematization.[7] The first Roman writers of historiography were finding solutions to the problem of how to map the Roman past onto Greek grids of time, and their Greek counterparts, most spectacularly Polybius, were likewise engaged in the process of fitting the Romans into the intellectual frameworks that had been honed in order to accommodate the variety of calendars, eras, and time-reckonings available in the *oecumenē*.[8] The careful Greek/Egyptian synchronisms of Manetho had no impact whatever on the intellectual world of the Greeks until Christianity, but the Greeks found it much harder to ignore the pressing need to accommodate the ever more dominant Romans—even if the Alexandrian scholar Apollodorus still felt, when he published the first edition of his chronographic work in the 140s, that he could get away with not giving a foundation date for the city of Rome.[9] As we saw in Chapter 6, the progressive construction of Roman history in the new historiography was an intercultural process.[10] Greeks had written a good deal about the Romans' origins in particular, weaving them into their own connective filigrees, and it was a decisive moment when Fabius Pictor set the trend for Roman historiography by "unhesitatingly embrac[ing] a Greek perspective and accept[ing] what Greek authors had said about the past of Rome."[11] The existing grid of Greek tradition was the fundamental starting point for Fabius and his successors: "What the first Roman historians inherited above all was a coherent picture of world prehistory into which the origins of Rome could be fitted."[12]

This "coherent picture" was the product of centuries of work across the Mediterranean, by means of which travelling Greeks had fitted the various peoples they encountered, with whatever varying degree of dialogue, into an increasingly cohesive mythic framework.[13] Essentially, this is what we call "Greek mythology." It is often taken for granted that all societies have a "mythology," in the sense of a "mythic system," but we should be cautious about such an assumption. In the case of Egypt, for example, as I. Rutherford remarks, while "[a]nthropologists have taught us to think of mythology as a primary mode of thought among early peoples, . . . it is notable that in Egyptian literature continuous mythological narratives are surprisingly few";[14] as a result, according to S. West, "the lack of systematisation in Egyptian belief systems must have made it immensely hard for the Greeks to orientate themselves in the mythology."[15] For the Greeks already in the Archaic period, "myth" was not just something within which you could orientate yourself, it was the means by which you could orientate yourself: it was an ever-changing and developing network, a system of stories and genealogies that related to each other and allowed for the generation of significance across great expanses of space and time. "System" does not mean that there was not innovation, variation, and inconsistency, but these terms all have meaning within a linked-up complex.

As Erskine has recently stressed, this Greek systematization of myth arose from the scattered nature of the various groups identifying as Greek. The network of myth made it possible for people from the Crimea to Gaul to link their sense of identity to a shared and adaptable database, through the medium of connecting ties of kinship based on mythical and heroic genealogies.[16] This interactive mythology was woven into the overall network of Greek culture, itself created in response to and through the medium of the highly dispersed nature of Greek settlement, as Malkin has compellingly argued: "Greek civilization as we know it emerged . . . not in spite of distance but because of it. . . . [I]t was distance and network connectivity that created the virtual Greek center."[17]

There were diverse responses to this system from the many people who came into contact with the participants in it.[18] Some self-consciously "marginal" groups attempted to hook into the network via descent claims of their own, as we see in the case of the Elymian inhabitants of Segesta in their approach to their "Trojan relatives," the Romans, or in the case of a number of peoples in Asia Minor from the fourth century on, who were able to use the Arcadians as a point of access to participation in the web.[19] As we see with the Romans' response to the Greeks' emplotting them as descended from Trojans, the Trojan connection was a "shared myth," one that made it possible for the two parties to have "a common past that offered a basis for their relationship in the present":[20] from the Roman point of view, crucially, the "common past" of the relationship between Troy and Greece included both connection and antagonism, allowing them to keep their distance even as they embraced involvement.[21]

A crucial disparity, of course, between the Greeks and other parties was that non-Greeks were regularly accepting Greek versions of their past within these interactive frames, "yet this is not something that works in reverse. Greeks do not borrow their past from their neighbours. . . . No Greek, for instance, claims descent from Romulus."[22] As Erskine explains, the difference is that the dispersed Greeks have more at stake in allowing importation of local mythical traditions from other people into their inter-related system at any given point, whereas "their non-Greek neighbours . . . can adopt this Greek perception of themselves not because they lack a past or because they feel culturally inferior but because to do so does not threaten their sense of identity."[23]

Regularly the nature of our evidence makes it difficult or impossible to assess what kind of understanding of this Greek network was developed by those who came into contact with it.[24] The Etruscans are the most tantalizing case here, for there is no doubt at all that for centuries they worked zestfully and imaginatively with characters and templates from Greek myth.[25] This is clearly not just a matter of inserting some arresting images into an Etruscan context. Whoever, for example, designed the François tomb at Vulci (third quarter of the fourth century) had a deep understanding of the stratigraphic layering of time that underpins so many Greek mythic programs. The Athenian Parthenon, to take a famous case, displays mutually reinforcing images of events in different periods of time, from the birth of Athena at the beginning of the cosmic order, via the Gigantomachy, the birth of Athens, the Amazonomachy and Centauromachy, the sack of Troy, and then down to either the time of the battle of Marathon, two generations earlier, or the idealized contemporary world.[26] Such patternings are common throughout the Greek world,[27] and they have a correlative in the François tomb, where we see three distinct strata of time: first, events from the Trojan war, then fighting with "Romans" from a notional date of the early fifth century, and finally, almost two hundred years later, recent victories over the Romans.[28]

On the other hand, Central Italy of the Roman middle Republican period abounds in images that appear to show "creative miscomprehension" of Greek myth, with inventive juxtapositions used as the base for independent scenic and artistic representation.[29] Yet, as Wiseman acutely points out in discussing the figures from Greek mythology represented on one such artifact, produced by a craftsman named Novius: "Not that 'Greek mythology' is a concept Novius would have been familiar with. I imagine he didn't think of Amykos and Ajax as particularly Greek, any more than we think of Cinderella as Italian or Snow White as German; they were simply characters in stories everybody knew."[30] Accordingly, it is often hard to know in what ways any given image may be apprehended as connecting to a cultural world beyond itself. A striking image from a terracotta frieze on the *regia* in the Forum, for example, from around 550, shows a bull-headed man flanked by panthers.[31] Any classics undergraduate could identify this as the Minotaur, and a good classics undergraduate could tell you that he was the bull of Minos, the half-brother of Ariadne, and that he was killed by Theseus. But is this image in Rome in 550 *the* Minotaur in this way, part of a larger ramifying mythic system? Or is it a free-floating icon with exotic appeal, "a motif which might have travelled from southern Italy without the attached myth"— or something domesticated into a local myth or ritual in some way?[32] No possible answer to any of these questions entails a value judgment on our part: there is no "right" or "wrong" answer, and any response along this range has parallels in a variety of cultures. But it is frustrating not to be able to know which of these answers, or combination of them, might have been operative in archaic Rome.

The New Systematization

If we turn explicitly to consider the difference that the new literature made in the Roman engagement with Greek mythology, then we must begin, as ever, by reminding ourselves of how well acquainted the Romans appear to have been with many of the names and figures of Greek myths before the translation project got underway. We saw in Chapter 7 that the translator-poets were able to capitalize upon their audiences' possession of a good body of knowledge, which was part of a general familiarity with Greek cults and deities, such as Apollo or Hercules, whose names stand as an example of how much domestication of Greek mythic and religious nomenclature had already taken place.[33] Eduard Fraenkel first documented this familiarity and pointed out its significance; yet he also pointed out that before Livius Andronicus "the colourful Greek world of fable . . . was never represented as a coherent whole or contained in the framework of unified works of art."[34]

As we saw in Chapter 7, it was precisely this new "coherent whole" that was increasingly built up and made available by the activities of the poets, as the new dramas and epics fleshed out the family relationships of the Olympians and the structures of the great families of tragedy, opening up a newly systematic worldview in the process.[35] As always, if we consider the issue from the perspective of the composers, we think of them moving into the target culture from their own Greek background. These practitioners are coming to the project with a fully developed view of the ramifications of the Greek system, and they have the hooks ready-made from which to string the Roman connections. The period when this systematic literary appropriation of Greek myth develops momentum, in the middle to late third century, comes in the train of an intensive and systematic process of codification and organization of myth in the Greek world—one to which the translator-poets will have been exposed in their Greek schools. Of course, the process of codification had been going on in some form for a very long time, since Hesiod is the first surviving mythographer in a certain sense, with his *Theogony* and *Catalogue of Women*. Nonetheless, the first writers of Roman literature are working in an environment where the codification of myth and its formation as a system has fairly recently emerged as a serious scholarly pursuit in its own right, in large part as a result of scholarly commentary on the canonized authors.[36]

The knowledge of mythology that is obvious from Plautus' comedies brings home how rapid the process must have been. Although Fraenkel's predecessors had assumed that there was so much reference to mythology in Plautus because he had just copied it out from his Greek models, Fraenkel incisively demonstrated that "[i]n fact the interest in the content of Greek myth and the pleasure derived from it were much greater in Plautus and his audience than in the Athenians of the fourth and third centuries."[37] If we compare the comparatively illuminated cultural world of 200 with our uncertainties over quite what the bull-man represented on the *regia* three and a half centuries earlier, it is clear how much has changed. In the new Latin epics and tragedies and comedies, the world of Greek myth is absolutely understood as a world, as a system, one in which works of Latin literature are participating as knowing partners. Again, what is crucial is the understanding of myth in the sense of a network, a system of stories and genealogies that relate to each other and can be made to hang together so as to construct sense, or to allow sense to be constructed.

Such an understanding is coupled with the related project of historiography, which begins with slotting the Romans into this mythological system via the ancestry of Romulus and Remus. The overall effect is to give the Romans a new kind of "intellectual and diplomatic resource," and hence a new kind of power.[38] The Hellenic *oecumenē* offered to its participants "a common geographical, chronological, and historical framework that offered coordinates for every political community within it."[39] The Romans were able to enter into the collaborative project of weaving themselves into this project—and not as a marginal community hoping to find a niche of respectability, but as the ever more dominant player in the world of connection that the Greeks had created.

A Roman Dimension to the System

We may perhaps see this self-conscious mentality on display in the remarkable scene witnessed on the shores of the Hellespont in March 190, when a Roman army for the first time crossed from Europe to Asia, in pursuit of the retreating Antiochus III.[40] The main body of the army went over the straits without incident under the command of the consul L. Cornelius Scipio. His brother, P. Cornelius Scipio Africanus, was accompanying the expedition as the consul's legate, but he did not cross. As a member of the priestly college of the Salii, he announced that he was bound to remain stationary in one place during the thirty days that his colleagues in Rome were performing their sacred duties: these involved parading the *ancilia,* the twelve sacred shields, to key sites within the city, where they would stop to do their dance and sing their *carmen.*[41] Scipio must have kept campaigning in the month of March on previous occasions: his scrupulosity at this point had a purpose.[42] Whatever his diplomatic motives may have been for remaining isolated on the European shore for this period, it is hard to imagine that he was unaware of the ideological significance of the Romans' first encounter with this symbolically charged stretch of land and sea. Here was the crossing of Xerxes in 480, and the counter-crossing of Alexander in 334. Africanus was not called *Africanus* for nothing; as he prepared to move across this symbolic boundary onto the world's third continent for the first time, he may have used the staged connection with his colleagues' marking of the bounds in the urban center of the empire as a motivation to focus on the world-historical momentum that would be set in train as soon as he stepped outside his tent. He may have been concentrating, in his own terms, on the lessons to be drawn from the campaign, which are expressed by a modern historian in this way: "The essential unity of the Aegean basin, of the Greek world of Asia and of Europe as a geo-political system, had been revealed with dazzling clarity."[43] This is a symbolic delay for the benefit of the waiting legions, and the allies, and the people soon to be on the receiving end.

As soon as Scipio rejoined the main body of the army under the command of his brother, they moved down the coast to Ilium, the site of Troy, which Alexander the Great had likewise made his first stop after crossing the Hellespont (Plut. *Alex.* 15. 7). Here, if we are to believe the report of Livy, the consul sacrificed to Minerva/Athena (the same goddess to whom Alexander had sacrificed at Ilium), as the people of Ilium proclaimed the Romans as their co-descendants from the Trojans, and the Romans themselves rejoiced in their origin (*laetis origine sua*, 37. 37. 4). Following the destruction of the army of Antiochus III at Magnesia shortly thereafter, the consul took the *agnomen* of *Asiagenus* ("of Asia"), to complement the *Africanus* of his brother.

Africanus will almost certainly have read some Homer. He may even conceivably have read the close of Herodotus' *Histories*, with its heavily symbolic evocation of the Athenians' capture of Sestos, the arrival point on the European Hellespont of Xerxes' army; here the Athenians crucified the Persian governor of Sestos, Artyactes, for his violation of the temple of Protesilaus, the first Greek to land at Troy.[44] Yet the reciprocal European/Asian significance of the site and of the moment was available to Africanus even without these texts; as we saw above, in 480 Xerxes staged both worship at Troy and the violation of Protesilaus' shrine without needing to base his symbolic actions on direct knowledge of the text of the *Iliad*.[45]

Africanus' adoptive grandson, P. Cornelius Scipio Aemilianus, however, had certainly read his Homer before he stood and watched the final agonies of Carthage forty-four years later. In a famous moment, he turned to the historian Polybius, who was standing beside him, and quoted two lines of Homer's *Iliad* in which the fate of Troy is prophesied, adducing the quotation as a portent of the future fate of Rome: ἔσσεται ἦμαρ ὅτ' ἄν ποτ' ὀλώλῃ Ἴλιος ἱρὴ/καὶ Πρίαμος καὶ λαός ("There will be a day when holy Troy shall perish, and Priam, and his people," *Il.* 4. 164–5; 6. 448–49).[46] The younger Scipio is able explicitly to place his insight concerning the mutability of fortune and the transition of empire into a historical framework that can be traced back to the Homeric fall of Troy. This is an insight, and a text, that he can share as an equal with the Achaean citizen and Greek historian of empire standing beside him.

Yet the younger Africanus has another perspective available to him for the consideration of his empire's role and fortune. He was able to read works of literature in his own language, as well as in the Greek of Homer, in which the themes of world empire could be traced. He will presumably have read Naevius' *Bellum Punicum*, which began the Roman story with the fall of Troy (frr. 5 and 6). He will certainly have read the *Annales* of Ennius, a close connection of his family, who had died when Aemilianus was in his late teens. It was perhaps Aemilianus himself who was responsible for the redesign of the tomb of the Scipios in a period about ten years either side of the sack of Carthage, adding a gallery that had statues of the first Africanus and of his brother, Asiagenus, together with (probably) a statue of Ennius, who had commemorated them both in his epic.[47]

Ennius' *Annales,* like Naevius' *Bellum Punicum,* began the story of Rome with the historical turning-point of the fall of Troy, *quom ueter occubuit Priamus sub Marte Pelasgo* ("when old Priam fell under the armed force of the Greeks," 14). Other crucial moments of "Greek" history become part of Ennius' vision of Roman destiny. We know that Ennius mentioned Xerxes' bridging of the Hellespont (*isque Hellesponto pontem contendit in alto,* "he stretched a bridge on the deep Hellespont," 369). As Elliott points out, "it must be the case that the role of [this line] in Ennius' narrative was to promote an analogy between a critical moment in Herodotus' *Histories* and a more recent moment of Roman history as presented in the *Annales.*"[48] Skutsch suggested that the parallel was with the crossing of Antiochus III into Greece in 192, the ultimate cause for the counter-attack of the two Scipiones in 190.[49] Perhaps the parallel was with the first crossing into Asia of the Roman army under the Scipiones in 190, with the impious act of Xerxes being opposed to the righteous return of the Romans to their original home.[50]

We have spent a lot of this book in speculation, inevitably, so it is perhaps fitting to conclude with one last suggestion for the possible placement and meaning of a fragment from one of the great lost works of Latin literature. But it is not speculation to observe that the resources available to Scipio Aemilianus were qualitatively different from those available to his ancestors. In the possession of a large-scale literature in their own language, Aemilianus and his contemporaries commanded a crucial extra dimension to their relationship with the *oecumenē.* Their literature in time fulfilled a function akin to that of the Greeks, in creating links by which an increasingly dispersed language-group were able to maintain a sense of connected identity, especially as more and more different groups were cumulatively added to the set of primary speakers of Latin.[51] We shall never know the precise context in which Ennius referred to Xerxes' crossing of the Hellespont, but that should not distract us from acknowledging the remarkable fact that Ennius was inserting some moment of Roman history into a Greek historical matrix that charted the dynamics of power in the Mediterranean. That would have been extraordinary enough. The aim of this book has been to recover a sense of astonishment at the fact that this was taking place in a Homeric epic written in a language that was not Homer's.

Notes

INTRODUCTION

1. I give the excellent translation of P. Green (1982), without the Latin, partly for reasons of space, and partly to show how important translation is going to be in what follows. The poem in the form in which we have it must have been published after 19, for it mentions Virgil and Tibullus, who both died in that year: "Horace and, very probably, Propertius were still alive and therefore inadmissible to this catalogue of poets whose work survives their death" (McKeown [1989], 395).

2. McKeown (1989), 394, gives many poetic parallels for such catalogues; among the Roman authors, it is noticeable that they all list only other Roman authors apart from Statius (*Silv.* 2. 1. 250–55) and Ovid himself (*Ars* 3. 329–38, *Rem.* 759–65; *Trist.* 2. 363–466). Ovid is looking to Cicero in particular as the model for going through the Greek side and then the Latin (as with the orators in the *Brutus*); on this Ciceronian procedure, see Citroni (2003), 181–82.

3. Feeney (1991), 101–2. On Accius' work, see below Chapter 6, text accompanying notes 39–43. See Hutchinson (2013), 12–17 for an important discussion of the Romans' "division of literary history into two firmly separated histories, Greek and Latin" (12). Ovid is already exemplifying the pattern we see in Quintilian's reading lists in *Inst.* 10. 1. 57, according to which "Greek literature worth studying has more or less ceased by 240 or 200, as Latin literature is beginning" (Hutchinson [2013], 14): see below Chapter 6, text to note 55.

4. Lamberton (1986), 10.

5. Cf. Beard and Crawford (1985), 12–13: "We tend to take for granted the literature of the age of Cicero. . . . Yet less than two hundred years before Cicero
   literary production in Latin was something new."

6. Millar (2002–2006), 1. 27 (original emphasis); cf. Gratwick (1982a), 79; Jocelyn
   (1990), 597. For stress on the singular contingency of this phenomenon, see
   Toynbee (1965), 2. 433; Fantham (1989), 220; Mayer (1995), 300.

7. Millar (2002–2006), 3. 50: "We may well wonder why it was in Rome and not
   in Phoenicia that there evolved, entirely without the aid of a conquering Macedonian state, the only literary culture which really was a 'fusion' in Droysen's
   sense." The reference is to the notion of "Verschmelzung" ("fusion") between
   the cultures of West and East in the model of Droysen (1836), who coined the
   term "Hellenistic" to describe this result.

8. Bonfante (2011), 7 (quoting a "personal communication" from Otto Brendel).

9. Oakley (1997–2005), 2. 61–63.

10. As we shall discuss in detail in Chapter 6.

11. On these other cases, see Chapter 7, text accompanying notes 92–97, and
    Chapter 8, text accompanying notes 15–19.

12. Most famously, Horace, with his now clichéd claim that "captured Greece cap-
    tured her fierce conqueror and brought the arts into rustic Latium" (*Graecia
    capta ferum uictorem cepit et artis/intulit agresti Latio*, *Epist.* 2. 1. 156–57), on
    which now see Wallace-Hadrill (2008), 25; Citroni (2013), 202–4.

13. Cornell (1995), 118, quoted by Feeney (1998), 25–26; for overview, see Jocelyn
    (1990), 595–629; Cornell (1995), 81–118; Smith (1996), 225–28; Wallace-Hadrill
    (2008), 25–26. On the Greek dimension in cult from very early on, see now
    Forsythe (2012), 6–8, for the case study of the cult of Mercury, whose temple
    dedication day in 495 (Ides of *May*) was fixed by somebody who knew some
    Greek lore about the identity of Mercury's mother ("Maia").

14. Wiseman (1989), 132.

15. Ulf (2009), 89; cf. Wallace-Hadrill (2008), 17, on the "danger of monolithic con-
    structions of cultures and identities. Identities are multiple and overlapping."

16. Dench (2005), chapter 3; Eckstein (2006), 252–57.

17. Hutchinson (2013), 132 (summing up a long argument about Roman construc-
    tions of "Greece" in space and time).

18. Dench (2005), 103: see esp. 11–35 on Romulus' *asylum* as a template for "the
    important political, cultural, and social motifs of incorporation and trans-
    formation" (32); cf. Farrell (2001), chapter 1, esp. 26–27.

19. See Walbank (1957–1979), 1. 75 on Plb. 1. 20. 15 for much material on "the pop-
    ular *communis locus* that the Romans were especially successful at learning
    from, and improving on, their foes."

20. Cornell (1978), 110; cf. A. Barchiesi (2009), 109, on the hybridity that resulted from the Roman project of incorporation of Greek culture.

21. Ulf (2009), 81: "Parallel research on cultural contact in the modern world has cast serious doubt on one of the necessary presuppositions for comparison that cultures are clearly defined, essentially self-contained entities."

22. Bayart (2005), 59.

23. See the opening section of Chapter 3.

24. Wallace-Hadrill (2008), 10; cf. van Dommelen and Terrenato (2007b), 8–9, A. Barchiesi (2009), 99. Wallace-Hadrill's chapter 1 is a valuable survey of the issues in general.

25. See Millett (1990); Gardner (2013); and Woolf (1998), chapter 1, on the "Romanization" of Britain and Gaul; Gallini (1973); Dench (1995), 218–19; and Curti, Dench, and Patterson (1996), 181–88, on the "Hellenization" of Italy. See Whitmarsh (2013), 3–8, for an analogous criticism of traditional descriptions of Greek interactions with Near Eastern cultures.

26. Wallace-Hadrill (2008), 16, using the regular scholarly models for Greek interaction with the Near East to provide an analogy for the models often used for Hellenization in Roman Italy; cf. for the Roman case, Gildenhard (2010), 156–60; McElduff (2013), 40.

27. Curti, Dench, and Patterson (1996), 181–82 and Quinn (2013a) 191–92 have valuable criticisms of the active/passive dichotomy; see Ulf (2009), 89 for criticism of the assumption that "lower or less developed cultures adapt to higher or more advanced ones."

28. Gruen (1992), 270: "The attitude . . . was not simply one of respectful awe. Romans took care from the outset to project the primacy of their own interests and the subordination of Hellenism to national goals."

29. See Chapter 5, text accompanying note 32.

30. See Chapter 3, " 'UP' and 'DOWN.' "

31. I would subscribe to the view of Wallace-Hadrill (2008), 28: "Terms like 'hellenisation' and 'romanisation' are fraught with difficulties, though this is no reason for avoiding them completely, but rather for unpacking them carefully and not using them unreflectively."

32. Keay (2013), 318; cf. van Dommelen and López-Bertran (2013), 278–29.

33. To avoid any misunderstanding, I should say that I do not at all mean to impute any such "lack of perspective" to the convincing arguments advanced by Keay (2013) or van Dommelen and López-Bertran (2013).

34. Dench (2005), 166 (original emphasis).

35. Girard (1961/1965)—and subsequently elaborated.

36. Purcell (1994), 395, 403; Dench (1995), 29–66.
37. To borrow the phrase used as a straw man in the acute arguments of Farrell (2005) about the prehistory of Roman literature. The most compelling brief account known to me of the complexity and sophistication of the life of upper-class Romans well before 240 is Jocelyn (1990), 595–604, while the many works of T. P. Wiseman on the early and middle Republic bring to vivid life a range of evidence for the energy and creativity of "pre-literary" Roman culture. For surveys of the evidence and testimonia for early Roman writings, songs, and speeches, see the various contributions in Suerbaum (2002), 30–83.
38. Wiseman (2008), 1–7, has an excellent overview, importantly stressing the crucial importance of speech in conveying the content of the public inscriptions to the largely illiterate people. On literacy in early Rome, see Cornell (1991).
39. Jocelyn (1990), 598–99; Hölkeskamp (1995). On the evidence of Plautus in particular for the style of such now lost speeches, see Fraenkel (1922/2007), 162–64, 414–15; Jocelyn (1969), 172; Adams (2005), 73–74: discussion in Chapter 3 below, text accompanying notes 47–48. As a New Zealander I think of the example of the Maori, who were completely illiterate when the Pakeha arrived, but who had a highly developed and artistic tradition of oratory, with keen and expert judgment being given by seasoned practitioners; on Maori oratory, see Rewi (2010).
40. A. Barchiesi (2002); cf. Farrell (2005), 421.
41. Pavese (1961), 119. This theme is developed in Delisle and Woodsworth (1995), chapter 3 ("Translators and the emergence of national literatures"). Cf. the observation of Octavio Paz in Schulte and Biguenet (1992), 160: "The greatest creative periods of Western poetry, from its origins in Provence to our own day, have been preceded or accompanied by intercrossings between different poetic traditions. At times these intercrossings have taken the form of imitation, and at others they have taken the form of translation."
42. The general bibliography on translation is colossal: Gentzler (2001) and Pym (2010) provide accessible and enlightening introductions. The most helpful (and entertaining) introduction to the main issues is Bellos (2011); a great variety of essays in the multi-volume work of Kittel, House, and Schultze (2007). See collections of key essays in Schulte and Biguenet (1992) and Venuti (2012). For a classicist's contribution to the general debate, see Martindale (1993), chapter 4. For a bibliography on Roman translation, see Chapter 2, note 1.

Chapter 1 TRANSLATION

1. Taplin (2012), 227: he is not speaking of dramatic texts originally composed in Doric, by Epicharmus and Rhinthon, as opposed to the standard Attic of the Athenian stage.

2. The novelty of the Roman translation enterprise is a major theme already sounded by Leo (1895/1912), 78 and (1913), 59–60: there is an excellent account in Possanza (2004), 46–47; cf. McElduff (2013), 11–12 on "the unnaturalness of Roman translation."

3. Devy (1993), 117–18.

4. Bellos (2011), 12.

5. Chaudhuri (1999), 20–21.

6. Chaudhuri (1999), 36; he goes on to remark that "Indian literatures operate to an improbable extent in conditions of exclusivity. . . . In such a situation, the absolutism of each language within its territory can be near-total."

7. Goody (1987), 67.

8. See Bellos (2011), 215–17, for the preponderance of English, French, and German as the overwhelmingly dominating languages for translation into and out of in the modern world: these languages are the normative ones.

9. Selden (1998) is a wonderful introduction to this fascinating world.

10. Tzetzes XIa II 16–22 Koster is the key text: see Fantuzzi and Hunter (2004), 471; more cautiously, Fraser (1972), 1. 330.

11. See Bagnall (2002) for a deeply skeptical survey of the legendary foundation stories concerning the Library in Tzetzes and Pseudo-Aristeas, including reservations about the report of Ptolemy III Euergetes' purloining of books from visiting ships (353–54, referring to the account of Galen, *Comm. in Hipp. Epidem.* III (xvii a 606–7)).

12. Most (2003), 386.

13. Rajak (2009), 26; note her skepticism (26–27) about one of the cases regarded as possible by Fraser (1972), 1. 330, a translation from Persian of the writings of Zoroaster (Plin. *HN* 30. 2. 3–4). As we shall see, the Septuagint was in any case not commissioned by the Macedonian king.

14. See Moyer (2011), 137; I. Rutherford (2013), 27, 34 on the case of the *Dream of Nectanebo.*

15. S. West (1969), 183, for this as the period when "most of the papyri containing translations or adaptations of Egyptian works were written." See Hoffmann (2012), 557–58, on the sudden intensification of Egyptian-Greek translation around 300 CE, with speculation on the causes.

16. Fraser (1972), 1. 681–82; overview in Schneider (2011), 183–84; cf. Moyer (2011), 31, on how it was "probably" bilingual Egyptians "who were responsible for translating Egyptian texts into Greek." As John Dillery points out to me, the whole question of the social status of the producers and consumers of these texts is more open that it was for Fraser, to whom the romances and oracles were part of sub-élite culture; prophecy-literature, for example, is found in the Tebtunis Temple library, showing that the community of priests there was reading, and perhaps producing, such texts: see Quack (2005), 12; Ryholt (2012), vii.

17. Quack (2005), 5, 172.

18. M. L. West (1969), esp. 116–17 for mechanisms of transmission.

19. Koenen (1993); Assmann (2002), 374–76.

20. Thompson (1994), 75–78, with quotation from 74; cf. E. G. Lewis (1976), 167–68; Crespo (2007); Moyer (2011), 88–91. Interestingly, this is the kind of situation Herodotus envisages when he speaks of the Egyptian Pharaoh Psammetichus I (reigned 664–610) "provid[ing] Egyptian boys to be trained as interpreters for the Greek settlers in the Delta, thus establishing a profession that still flourished in the historian's own day" (M. L. West (1997), 608, with reference to Hdt. 2. 154. 2).

21. *OGI* 90 for the text of the Rosetta Stone. On the purposes behind such texts, different in kind from literary translations, see Gratwick (1982a), 79–80; Most (2003), 386; Rajak (2009), 25–26—also commenting on how often in such inscriptions "the two main language versions are markedly different": for the way that such inscriptions aim "to create *localized* texts addressing the needs and interests of each linguistic audience," see Larson (2011), 51 (original emphasis).

22. Fraser (1972), 1. 70–71; Pelling (1988), 191; Thompson (1994), 74; Asper (2001), 100–101.

23. Pelling (1988), 191, citing Plb. 5. 83. 7.

24. Asper (2001), 100; cf. Fraser (1972), 1. 70. On the exclusivity of the Hellenistic *gymnasion* in general, see Sartre (2009), 205–6.

25. Scheuble (2010). See Moyer (2011), 29–30 for further examples of this momentum towards breaking down the initially more separate domains.

26. Assmann (2005), 41; cf. Denecke (2013), 9, on "the puzzling disjunction between Greeks' enthusiasm about Egyptian culture and customs, but lack of interest in learning to read Egyptian texts." See Rochette (1994) on élite Greek resistance to learning Egyptian, and Torallas Tovar (2010), 21–24, on the sharp linguistic division between the Greek élite and their Egyptian subjects "during the first period after the conquest, the Hellenistic period." If there is ground

to the claims for Callimachus' direct knowledge of Egyptian regal mythology in, e.g., Koenen (1993) and Stephens (2003), the scenario I can most readily envisage is that of Callimachus having the contents of an Egyptian text explained to him by a bilingual Egyptian exegete: cf. Hunter (2003), 49 for this possibility. Hunter (2003), 46–53, gives a balanced general introduction to the issue of the "Egyptian dimension" to the court poetry of the Ptolemies.

27. Moyer (2011), 31–32.

28. Quack (2005), 172: "Dies dürfte auch damit zusammenhängen, daß Griechisch-kenntnis bei Ägyptern der Oberschicht weit verbreitet war, Ägyptischken-ntnisse bei Griechen aber wohl nicht in gleicher Weise."

29. Goldhill (2005), 102; cf. the picture sketched by Parsons (2007), 43.

30. Dillery (1999) and (2014); Verbrugghe and Wickersham (2001); Moyer (2011), chapter 2.

31. Most (2003), 386.

32. There are predecessors from another long-standing contact zone, Anatolia, in the form of Xanthus of Sardis, who wrote a history in Greek of his country, Lydia, in the fifth century, and of Menecrates of Xanthus, who wrote a history in Greek of his country, Lycia, in the fourth: Asheri (1983), 21–22.

33. There is a very large bibliography on all of these authors: see now above all, especially on Berossus, Manetho, and Demetrius, Dillery (2014). For orientation, see Momigliano (1975), chapter 1 (an avowedly Hellenocentric perspective); Dillery (2007) on Berossus and Manetho; Sterling (2007) on "The Jewish appropriation of Hellenistic historiography."

34. We return to the first Roman writers of history in Chapter 6.

35. Dillery (1999), 113. It is a major argument of Dillery (2014) that the works of Manetho and Berossus have no precise precedent as such in their own tradition and are formed in dialogue with Hellenism: see chapter 7 ("Conclusion to Narratives") in particular, with reference to the penetrating observations of Sartre (2009), 380; cf. Haubold (2013), 142–77, on the originality and independence of the new intercultural work formed by Berossus. Moyer (2011), 96–99, is correct to warn against colonializing narratives that cast Manetho as the passive partner, who could supposedly only do what he did thanks to being "civilized" by the Greeks, and he rightly stresses the cardinal importance of the Egyptian king-list as the organizing principle of the work (103–7); yet the new work is, after all, in Greek, and it is formed in dialogue with Greek representations, even as it is assuredly not an "imitation" of them (105–6): see Dillery (2014), 348–53.

36. Verbrugghe and Wickersham (2001), 119, argue against the claim that Manetho's history was commissioned by the Macedonian monarch.

37. On the synchronisms, see Verbrugghe and Wickersham (2001), 108; Moyer (2011), 110–14, stressing that from Manetho's perspective he is "subsum[ing] Greek chronology under the structure of the Egyptian king-list" (114); there is important discussion of Manetho's synchronisms in Dillery (2014), 97–117, to which I am here indebted.

38. Verbrugghe and Wickersham (2001), 119; cf. Dillery (1999), 94, on how the people reading Manetho were, "chiefly, other hellenophone non-Greeks such as Manetho himself."

39. Verbrugghe and Wickersham (2001), 115–19.

40. See Schironi (2013), with the comments of Heller (2014).

41. Rajak (2009), 1.

42. Fraser (1972), 1. 689; Momigliano (1977), 13; Rochette (1995), 254–55; Janse (2002), 383; Most (2003), 286; De Crom (2011), 86; Hunter (2011), 48–49.

43. On the complexity of the linguistic world of Hellenistic Judaism, see Rajak (2009), 94–97; De Crom (2011), 82–83.

44. De Crom (2011), 77; cf. Rajak (2009), 19, 212: "there existed no specific 'Alexandrian' canon of the Greek Bible, different in content from the evolving Hebrew corpus."

45. Rajak (2009), 16–17; De Crom (2011), 77.

46. A wild card, to be sure. But *something* generated a new pressure to stabilize the text of the Hebrew Bible to an unparalleled degree of uniformity within the period from the mid-first century to 73 CE, and the influence of Hellenism has been canvassed (see Young [2007], 183).

47. Assmann (2002), 424.

48. Rajak (2009), chapter 8 qualifies the outright statements of Momigliano (1975), 91–92, to the effect that "The LXX remained an exclusive Jewish possession until the Christians took it over." But she agrees, for example, that the Septuagint is unlikely to have been on the shelves of the Ptolemaic library (261; cf. Momigliano [1975], 92).

49. Momigliano (1977), 13: "There was no tradition of translating foreign books into Greek"; cf. Werner (1992), 14; Rochette (1995), 254; Most (2003); McElduff (2013), 11.

50. Whitmarsh (2013), 9.

51. As we shall see in Chapter 8.

52. Schironi (2009), 4 and 135.

53. Schironi (2009), 38; cf. 138: "This glossary is a collection of erudition and curiosities, not a treatise on languages or linguistic sensitivity." There is certainly evidence for sub-élite Egyptian/Greek bilingual glossaries, though in surprisingly small numbers: Kramer (2001), 4–5.

54. Momigliano (1975), esp. 7–8; cf. Asheri (1983), 18–19; Werner (1992), 12–14; Gruen (1998), xiii; Dillery (2014), xxxiv. Schironi (2009), 24–26 allows for the possibility of knowledge of Aramaic among Greeks living in Seleucid Asia, although seeing it as "very unlikely . . . that some of these erudites were able to read an original script"—certainly not cuneiform, though conceivably Aramaic script. Her approach assumes that the so-called " 'Graeco-Babyloniaca', clay tablets with Akkadian and Sumerian texts written in Greek letters" (4), are the work of Semitic scribes experimenting with Greek. A very judicious overview appears in Kramer (2001), 1–2.

55. Rochette (1997a), 81–83.

56. Miller (1997), 131–32 on Thuc. 1. 138. 1 and Plut. *Them.* 29. 3, with skepticism about the knowledge of Persian even of Ctesias of Cnidus, author of *Persica*, a skepticism shared by Almagor (2012), 21–22; Llewellyn-Jones (2010), 58–61 is more open to the possibility of Ctesias' bilingualism, though concluding with *non liquet.* The problem of Herodotus' "sources" is even more notorious. At the very least, he and Ctesias are somehow, presumably through interpreters, able to take part in a dialogue across language and script lines about the succession of empires, as attractively argued by Haubold (2013), chapter 2: "It remains true . . . that [Herodotus'] engagement with Mesopotamian literature was mediated and refracted—and yet it nevertheless informed some fundamental aspects of his work" (126). See too Moyer (2011), chapter 1 for Herodotus' encounter with contemporary Egyptian priestly culture's carefully crafted patternings of past time, a moment of "an important intersection of Greek and Egyptian historicities, and a reorientation of Greek historical awareness" (81).

57. See M. L. West (1997), 606–7, referring, in addition to Themistocles, to the case of Alcibiades (Ath. 535e), and to one Histiaeus of Miletus who, according to Herodotus, identified himself using the Persian language (6. 29. 2).

58. Most (2003), 387.

59. D. M. Lewis (1997), 351, summarizing his arguments in D. M. Lewis (1977), 12–15; cf. Rollinger (2009), 41–43.

60. On these individuals, see Hornblower (2008), 997, with reference to the important discussion in Robert (1950) of Herodotus' Carian Mys, who will have been trilingual in Carian, Persian, and Greek (38).

61. D. M. Lewis (1997), 351; note the view of Rollinger (2009), 42 that the Greeks in high secretarial positions may have been biliterate to some degree: "an elementary knowledge of cuneiform . . . appears to have been likely among these writers."

62. Sartre (2009), 380, quoted by Dillery (2014), 389, in the course of a valuable overview. It is worth stressing the word "author" in this quotation, since some

Greeks certainly did learn these languages in the early period of the Successor kingdoms; cf. Gruen (1998), xiii. If such was apparently in general the case with the Greek élite in the established cities, the situation in areas such as the Egyptian backcountry, where Greeks were significantly outnumbered, certainly appears to have been different: Kramer (2001), 2–3; cf. Moyer (2011), 31–32 (although Moyer ibid. does posit bilingual Greeks at the highest levels as well).

63. B. B. Powell (2002), 114.

64. See Haubold (2013), 141–42 for speculation on the identity of the individuals working with Antiochus I in his program of working with Babylonian ritual—although his Section heading of "Antiochus I writes Akkadian" (135) is not to be taken literally.

65. Bonfante (2011), 7.

66. Werner (1992), 13.

67. S. West (1969), 183.

68. Adams (2003), 437: "It is a myth that Greeks did not learn Latin"; cf. 15–16, with reference to the studies of Holford-Strevens (1993) and Rochette (1997a); cf. Dickey (2012), 4–6 on Greeks learning Latin. As we shall see, the individual remembered as the first to translate Greek literary texts into Latin, Livius Andronicus, was himself a Greek. Simon Hornblower reminds me of the study of a number of Greek epigrammatists from the time of Augustus by Williams (1978), 124–34, showing how they are working with Latin poetic models and even adapting Latinisms into their Greek, as with Parmenion's use of the Greek dative to represent the Latin ablative absolute (133–34 on *Ant. Pal.* 9. 304. 1). Rochette (1995), 248–49 stresses that the bilingualism of Greek and Latin in the Empire was not reciprocal; it was normative for the Roman élite, and not for the Greek.

69. Kramer (1983) and (2001) on the glossaries; Rochette (1997), 188–98, on the Virgil and Cicero translations. Rochette (1997), 320, stresses that Greek knowledge of Latin literature "est partielle et elle apparaît tardivement."

70. Brock (1994), 158. Kahane (1986) is an important study of "prestige" languages.

71. On this process in Late Antiquity in the West, see Woolf (2012a). As clearly demonstrated, however, by Millar (2006), 93–116, Greek remained the overwhelmingly dominant language of public affairs within the Eastern church well into the fifth century.

72. My thanks to Greg Woolf for the opportunity to read an unpublished paper on the comparative impermeability of ancient literate cultures, from which I quote these telling phrases.

73. See below, text accompanying note 134.

74. My thanks to Fiachra Mac Góráin in particular for discussion of this point. On the perils of the various metaphors for "translation," see Bellos (2011), 24–36.

75. Adams and Swain (2002), 20.

76. Pym (2000), 2, distinguishing between such "'intercultural' space" and the "cross-cultural" transfers "that go from one monocultural space to another" (2–3). Cf. Adams (2003), 1, and Meylaerts (2004), 290, on how historically multilingualism is the norm rather than the exception.

77. Jouanno (2002).

78. Meylearts (2004), 300; cf. 308: "les migrations textuelles et discursives rendent floues les distinctions entre les sources et les cibles."

79. De Crom (2011), 80 (original emphasis), referring to the studies of Pym (2000) and Meylaerts (2004).

80. Hermans (1999), 40.

81. B. B. Powell (2002), 46; Henkelman (2006), 810; Currie (2012), esp. 577–80.

82. Henkelman (2006), 810; see further below, text accompanying notes 131–32.

83. Schleiermacher (1813/1992), 37–38: he takes as read the difference of "oral/ written" encoded within *dolmetschen* (interpret) and *übersetzen* (translate) and proceeds to his own special application of the terms.

84. Wilss (1982) 17.

85. In general, on the importance of distinguishing between language and script in studies of bilingualism, see Adams and Swain (2002), 3–7. There are theoretical contexts in which it can be worthwhile to elide the difference between "interpreting" and "translating" (Gentzler [2001], 62, 67–69; Pöchhacker [2009], esp. 133–34), just as we shall regularly need to elide the rigidity of any "oral/textual" demarcation (Goody [1987]; Thomas [1992]; Lowrie [2009], 13–18), but I maintain the distinction provisionally as heuristically useful for the current argument, even if I shall qualify it when necessary.

86. Vermeer (1992), 1. 17.

87. Snellmann (1919); Hermann (1956); Balsdon (1979), 137–45; Montella (1982); Kurz (1986); Franke (1992); Vermeer (1992), 1. 175–77; Wiotte-Franz (2001); Mairs (2011); Bettini (2012), 88–121; McElduff (2013), 24–30.

88. Vermeer (1992), 1. 167; Mairs (2011), 66; McElduff (2013), 25, for the general reticence.

89. Hall (1989), 19–20.

90. Hall (1989), 19–20; M. L. West (1997), 618. Silius Italicus has a story about an interpreter (9. 77–99). Apollonius Rhodius tells us that Medea used Colchian to speak with her cousin Circe (4. 731), and Virgil alludes to the language

difference between Greeks and Trojans during the sack of Troy (*ora sono discordia*, 2. 423, with Horsfall (2008) *ad loc.*); see also A. Barchiesi (1992), 202–3, in connection with Ov. *Her.* 3. 2, *uix bene barbarica Graeca notata manu.*

91. See Vermeer (1992), 1. 168–69, for rarity of reference to interpreters in Xenophon; Adams (2003), 166–68, for rarity of such reference in ancient historians in general and Roman historians in particular; McElduff (2013), 25. For interpreters in Roman armies, see Hermann (1956), 44–45.

92. Pigres is a Carian name, and, for this period at any rate, one therefore infers that Pigres will have been trilingual (at least), like so many interpreters from Asia Minor: Asheri (1983), 21. Full tabulation of references to interpreters in Xenophon's *Anabasis*, with discussion, in Vermeer (1992), 1. 172–74.

93. See Pöchhacker (2009) for a theoretical discussion of "interpreting studies" in dialogue with translation theory, esp. 133–34 on the ways in which it is helpful to think of interpreting as "textual" in a larger sense. Further discussion of interpreting in Delisle and Woodsworth (1995), chapter 9 ("Interpreters and the Making of History"); Pöchhacker (2004).

94. Goody (1987), 261; B. B. Powell (2002), 59, (2009), 18. In a sense, as Derrida (1981) pointed out in "Plato's Pharmacy," this hierarchy goes back to Plato.

95. Gnanadesikan (2009), 65; 59–60 on the rebus (a reference I owe to Joshua Katz).

96. Gnanadesikan (2009), 67; cf. B. B. Powell (2009), 198; Goody (1987), 282.

97. Gnanadesikan (2009), 66–67.

98. Denecke (2013), 151; cf. 49: "Today, in the aftermath of the demise of the 'Sinographic sphere,' the people of East Asia ironically need to rely on English to understand each other."

99. B. B. Powell (2002), 113.

100. B. B. Powell (2009), 244; cf. Habinek (2009), 136, with reference to Kristeva (1989). If we consider the case of sign language, we see immediately that "language" does not necessarily have to be "speech" anyway: Sacks (2000), 13, 26; B. B. Powell (2009), 5. As Joshua Katz points out to me, the first reference in the West to sign language is in Plato's *Cratylus* (423e).

101. See above, text accompanying note 7.

102. Rajak (2009), 92.

103. Parkinson (1999), 68: "the hieroglyphic script . . . is expressive not only graphically but also visually"; cf. B. B. Powell (2002), 70–71.

104. See illustration and discussion in B. B. Powell (2002), 53–54.

105. See Schneider (2011), 184–85 on the fascinating case of Egyptian syllabic or "group writing," which, rather like *katakana*, one of the scripts in use in Japan,

was able to render foreign words pronounceable, and was used to transcribe magical texts from Aramaic or Canaanite without translating them.

106. Schneider (2011), 184.

107. Schneider (2011), 184; cf. Vermeer (1992), 1. 65 on rarity of translation in pre-Macedonian Egypt.

108. I am extremely grateful to Marwan Kilani (Oxford University) for permission to paraphrase here his main argument from a paper I heard him deliver at Stephanie Dalley's Workshop on Translation and Bilingualism in Ancient Near Eastern Texts (Wolfson College, Oxford, March 15, 2013). As he observed *per litteras,* we are at the mercy of the preservation of papyrus and of find-sites, and tombs are not an obvious depository for translations of poetry. For the latest account of the Astarte Papyrus, see Collombert and Coulon (2000), a reference I owe to Mr. Kilani.

109. My thanks to Marwan Kilani for this information. Schneider (2011), 183 cites, in addition to this treaty, a quadri-lingual inscription from Persian-occupied Egypt that dates to the reign of Darius I: we have here a case of the Persians reproducing locally the kind of multilingual/multiscripted display that they were familiar with from Mesopotamia, and this text therefore anticipates the multiscripted and bilingual inscriptions of the Ptolemaic period.

110. Survey of translation in cuneiform culture in Hallo (1996), 154–68.

111. Warburton (2007), 499.

112. Here I am much indebted to the ground-breaking comparative study of Denecke (2013), esp. 46–51, where she puts in dialogue the importance of the scripts involved at the beginnings of Japanese and of Latin literature.

113. Denecke (2013), 47.

114. Important discussion in Denecke (2013), 46–49.

115. As David Bellos points out to me, in practice readers of alphabetic script tend to scan for "grams," so that certain segments of texts, such as street names or advertizing slogans, can become "readable" to someone who does not know the language. The sign for "restaurant" in Russian, for example, will not be pronounced correctly by someone who does not know the Cyrillic script, but it will become familiar and "usable" to a tourist.

116. B. B. Powell (2009), 231. By "different" I mean "different," not "better": see Thomas (1992), 52–56 for important qualifications of the triumphalist claims that have sometimes been made for a supposed "superiority" of alphabetic writing and its impact.

117. B. B. Powell (2009), 231–32.

118. Cornell (1991), 17, well points out the experimental and decentralized way in which this process took place, remarking on how "the alphabet was and is a

universal instrument which can be used to represent the words of any language by anyone who wishes."

119. Ridgway (1996). Of course, this adaptation does not happen automatically; see Woolf (1994), 87 for "the groups in closest contact with Marseilles, some of whom did not adopt the Greek alphabet for more than three centuries after the arrival of the colonists, while others never developed writing"; cf. Prag (2013), 330–31 for further discussion. Note that I am using "alphabet" here in the strict sense of the unique "consonant plus vowel" writing system that resulted from the adaptation for the transcription of Greek of the Phoenician "alphabetic" script, which notated only consonants, not vowels: on these distinctions within the broad category of "alphabet" see Gnanadesikan (2009), 10.

120. Weiss (2009), 26–30; Wallace (2011); on the Roman adaptation of the Greek alphabet via the Etruscan version, see Ostler (2007), 43–45, 59–60.

121. See Luraghi (2010) for the strategies of the archaic Greek states in this regard.

122. Note that Latin V does duty for Greek Y at this period, since "y" was not introduced until the first century: Perl (1971).

123. Hoskin (2007), 1109: "it is within alphabetic culture that there emerge the practice and theorisation of translation as either 'word for word' or, as an apparently polar opposite, 'sense for sense.'"

124. Denecke (2013), 49; "biliterate" refers to the Japanese use of both Sino-Japanese and vernacular scripts.

125. Denecke (2013), 49.

126. Dionisotti (2005), 358, part of an extremely illuminating discussion.

127. George (2003), 1. 57–58. See the essays on the legacy of Mesopotamia in Dalley (1997), with the arresting observation of Dalley: "Babylonian and Assyrian culture did not die when cuneiform writing became obsolete. Scholarship persisted in central Mesopotamia, but was carried on in Greek. Babylonian cults with related literature (probably written in Aramaic) continued in Babylon [and other centers] . . ." (53).

128. Sumerian literary texts regularly had accompanying Akkadian translations in a bilingual layout, but it is important to note that the frequency of the translation of the Gilgamesh epic within cuneiform is often overstated. Only Tablet XII of the Standard Babylonian Gilgamesh epic is a scrupulous, practically word for word, translation of a Sumerian original (George [2003], 1. 47–48). The first eleven tablets form a composition that is informed in parts by Sumerian predecessors, but the Akkadian epic is in no sense a *translation* of that material, but rather a free composition (George [2003], 1. 18–24). For the later paraphrases in Hittite and Hurrian, see George (2003), 1. 24.

129. George (2003), 1. 70; cf. Tigay (1982), 251–55.

130. Illuminating discussions in the essays appear in Dalley (1997), demonstrating the persistence of Babylonian literary characters and motifs up to the period of early Islam (Dalley, chapter 8), and referring to, e.g., echoes of the Gilgamesh epic in one of the sacred writings of the Manichaeans, the *Book of Giants* (164) and in the *Alexander Romance* (170). See also in that volume S. Dalley and A. T. Rayes (113–14) and A. Salvesen (144–46) on the wide dissemination of dialogue or dispute poetry, originally in Sumerian and eventually making its influence felt in Aramaic, Hebrew, Middle Persian, and Syriac. Gilgamesh even surfaces as a demonic emblem in Second Temple Judaism (Jackson [2007]).

131. George (2007b), 457–58.

132. Henkelman (2006), 828–29; again, I stress the phrase "the epic itself." The quoted sentence continues: "except, perhaps, for a distant echo in the *Alexander Romance*"; Henkelman returns to this question in Henkelman (2010), concluding that a transmitted portion of the *Alexander Romance* shows unusual fidelity to a series of important aspects of the cuneiform epic, both in plot and in ethos, though he remains "inclined to postulate the existence of a particular oral tradition that was closely informed by the epic" (355). In any event, we are not dealing with a *translation* of the epic.

133. On Graeco-Arabic translation, see the survey of Daiber (2007) and esp. Gutas (1998), who opens his account: "from about the middle of the eighth century to the end of the tenth, almost *all* non-literary and non-historical secular Greek books that were available throughout the Eastern Byzantine Empire and the Near East were translated into Arabic" (1: original emphasis).

134. Gutas (1998), 194.

135. Southern (1953), 63–68.

136. Denecke (2013), 293; cf. 292: "But textual traditions, in particular the elite traditions that become the foundation of classical civilizations, do not travel like guns, germs, and steel; not even like coins, miniature paintings, or religious statuettes."

137. Pliny says Lenaeus was the first to write in Latin on the medicinal use of plants (*HN* 25. 5) and goes on to tell the story of Pompey's commission (25. 7), so this makes Lenaeus a likely candidate to be the first to translate Greek medical works into Latin (my thanks to David Langslow for discussion of this question of the "first translator"). Knowledge of Greek medicine, and of Latin terms for Greek medical language, is much earlier, for Plautus already makes fun of such talk (Adams [1995], 642, a reference I owe to Langslow [1999], 214). On knowledge of Greek medical terminology under the Republic, see Langslow (1999), and for a survey of the terminology and practice of the translation of

"technical" texts in general, concentrating on the Imperial period, see Fögen (2005).

138. *Pace* Montgomery (2000), 21–22, 37–38.

139. Possanza (2004); Gee (2013). Rawson (1985), 167, acutely points to the translated verses of Aratus as an exception to the general Roman exclusion of astronomy.

140. Rawson (1985), 28. There were reported translations of various Etruscan books on the *disciplina* into Latin by Tarquitius Priscus and Nigidius Figulus at the time of Cicero: see Macr. *Sat.* 3. 7. 2, 20. 2 on Tarquitius, and the testimony of John Lydus (*De Ost.* 27) that he is translating into Greek Nigidius' Latin translation from Etruscan of a brontoscopic calendar. The fascinating work of Turfa (2012) makes the best case that can be made for taking Lydus at his word; see in general on Roman adaptations/translations of this kind of material, Guittard (2009), with caveats on how little we know of the nature of Tarquitius' work (123).

141. Plin. *HN.* 18. 22; see Heurgon (1976); Fögen (2005), 96–97; McElduff (2013), 23–24. Considering the Etruscan examples, we need to qualify somewhat the description of Mago's work by Fögen (2005), 97, as "an isolated case in Rome of transforming non-Greek literature from the pen of a 'barbarian' into Latin."

142. Whether there was any "literature" in the first place for them to translate out of Carthaginian Punic or Etruscan is a question we address in Chapter 8.

Chapter 2 THE ROMAN TRANSLATION PROJECT

1. Leo (1913), 59–60; cf. Leo (1895/1912), 78; Mariotti (1952/1986), 52; Büchner (1979); Gentili (1979), 105; Gratwick (1982a), 90; Suerbaum (2002), 97; Boyle (2006), 27. Bibliography on translation from Greek to Latin in Traina (1989), 116–23; Rochette (1995), 245 n. 1; Suerbaum (2002), 6–7; Manuwald (2011), 282; McElduff and Sciarrino (2011), 8.

2. Leo (1913), 59; cf. Denecke (2013), 39 n. 40: "for Latin literature, Greek and Greeks were the only reference culture."

3. Leo (1913), 59: "Für die Übertragung eines Gedichtes aus einer Sprache in die andre gab es kein Vorbild und keinen Vorgang; den Griechen lag der Gedanke an eine solche Kunstübung fern."

4. McElduff (2013), 4.

5. Fundamental bibliography in Chapter 1, n. 87.

6. Snellmann (1919), 1. 154–55, on Val. Max. 2. 2. 2–3, who cites Apollonius Molo as the first Greek ambassador to speak to the senate without an interpreter as

intermediary, in 82/1; cf. Hermann (1956), 42; Kaimio (1979), 104; Montella (1982), 200–202; Rochette (2011), 550–52.

7. Snellmann (1919), 2. XII. 82, on Lyd. *Mag.* 3. 68 (foreigners having to use interpreters in Latin to Roman magistrates); 2. XII. 110, on Plut. *Cat. Mai.* 12 .4–5 (Cato speaking Latin to Athenians although he could speak Greek); 2. XII. 232, on Cic. *Fam.* 13. 54.5 (Cicero referring to his "friend and interpreter" in Cilicia, where he will have been able to speak Greek: on this last case, see Kaimio (1979), 114).

8. Horsfall (1979), 86. Cf. Momigliano (1975), 18–19 for an equally nuanced picture, stressing the advantage the Romans had over the Greeks in being able to choose whether to speak to them in Latin or Greek; important discussion in Adams (2003), 559 of the power accruing to a Roman who could make it clear to Greeks "that he could use their language even if they could not use his." See Rochette (2011), 550–51.

9. Dion. Hal. *Ant. Rom.* 19. 5 (urinated upon); App. *Sam.* 7. 2 (defecated upon): see Kaimio (1979), 96–97.

10. Gruen (1992), 64–65, 68–69, 237, 245; Adams (2003), 558–60, referring to Plut. *Cat. Mai.* 12. 4–5 (Cato in Athens); and Liv. 45. 29. 1–3 (Aemilius Paullus at Amphipolis).

11. Kurz (1986), 217; McElduff (2013), 29–30, esp. 30: "The interpreter was a tool like any other, used to maintain status, create distance, or create a political point."

12. E.g., Cic. *Phil.* 13. 12, *Div.* 2. 73; see *OLD* s.v. §§2 and 3b, and Fuhrmann (1970), 84–87.

13. This, at any rate, was the ideal; as David Bellos points out to me, oral interpretation in the modern world is observably never "word for word."

14. Jocelyn (1972), 1000, with n. 134 ad loc. referring to Cic. *Opt. Gen.* 14, *Ac.* 1. 10, Gell. *NA* 2. 23, 11.4.

15. Sherk (1969), 7: "the translators slavishly reproduced each word of the Latin, so that at times the Greek becomes intelligible only when the Latin idiom is uppermost in the mind"; cf. Brock (1979), 71; Adams (2003), 469–70.

16. On this much-discussed passage, see esp. Lennartz (1994), 44–67; and Glucker (2012), 52–56 for a discussion of all such phrases in Cicero.

17. On the force of *indiserti* here, see McElduff (2013), 115–16.

18. His language here is (characteristically and tellingly) ambiguous, since he could be taken to mean "If you're going to be a faithful interpreter, you won't render word for word." See Seele (1995), 94–99 for a diverting account of the various ways in which Horace's aphorism has been interpreted.

19. Bettini (2012), 110–11.

20. On the chronological significance of the fall of Troy in Hellenistic scholarship, see Feeney (2007a), 81–84, where this Horatian passage is unaccountably not cited. As Marco Fantuzzi points out to me, Horace is also taking up an interpretative position on the meaning of Homer's ἐπεί, for the scholia differ over whether the word here means "for all the time since" or just "after."

21. On Horace's career as a *scriba quaestorius,* attested in the Suetonian *Vita Horati,* see Taylor (1925); Armstrong (1986); on the office, Purcell (1983).

22. Sherk (1969), 19, while stressing that "there is no proof" that the *scribae* or their staff produced the official translations, argues that "such an assumption does satisfy the main requirements: a central office in Rome, a continuity of duty, and professional ability"; he concludes: "In my opinion the *scribae* in the *aerarium* or qualified persons on their staff made the translations." There is, then, a lot more at stake for Horace in distancing himself from this kind of translation than there is for Cicero.

23. Sherk (1969), 13.

24. Adams (2003), 469–70 on *Res Gestae* 9. 1 and 25. 2, with other examples; cf. Sherk (1969), 13–19, Rochette (1997a), 86.

25. Adams (2003), 504.

26. Bellos (2011), 169, 180, 211.

27. Adams (2003), 471; cf. in general 545–76 on "Latin as a language of power"; cf. Gruen (1992), 238; Larson (2011), 58; McElduff (2013), 32.

28. Interestingly, the Greek version of Augustus' *Res Gestae* is something of an outlier against this background, as the excellent discussion of Cooley (2009), 26–30 makes clear (see too Papaioannou [2011]). There are certainly examples of "Latinate Greek" in the Greek version, but in general it is "not simply a word for word rendering" (26), and according to Cooley it will have been produced locally, not in Rome, so that we find numerous accommodations to provincial perspectives in Galatia (30). This is actually closer to the norm that we observe in the ancient Near East, where the usual practice is to tailor parallel texts to the individual requirements and priorities of the separate audiences (Larson [2011]).

29. Brock (1979), 71; Dickey (2012), 15; McElduff (2013), 117.

30. Major discussion in Brock (1979); cf. Janse (2002), 343–46; Adams (2003), 470. Note the very important resistance in Rajak (2009), 142 to the inertial tendency to "explain Septuagint language as simply the natural way of translating a holy book."

31. Jocelyn (1969), 28; Kaimio (1979), 294; note the Section headings already in Blatt (1938): "1. Le libéralisme préchrétien" (217–20), "2. Le littéralisme chrétien" (220–26).

32. Bonner (1977), 212–13; Horsfall (1979), 89–90; Cribiore (2001), 194 on Homer's place in the Hellenistic curriculum.

33. Kaster (1995), 53.

34. Jocelyn (1969), 25, with further references; cf. Kaimio (1979), 292, with literature cited in n. 122.

35. Büchner (1979), 71 rightly argues that the translation was not a crib.

36. Kaimio (1979), 273.

37. Kaimio (1979), 284; see McElduff (2013), 24 for speculation.

38. On the gulf between Livius' classroom exposition and the text of his Homeric translation, see Bettini (2012), 116.

39. See Leo (1913), 52; Bonner (1977), 34–35 for speculation.

40. Swain (2002), 133; cf. E. G. Lewis (1976), 181–82. Important remarks on the Romans' selective adaptation of Greek *paideia* in Wallace-Hadrill (1985) and Corbeill (2001): we return to this topic in Chapter 5, in text accompanying notes 60–63.

41. Burkert (1992), 28–29.

42. Denecke (2013), 25.

43. Denecke (2013), 34.

44. McElduff (2013), 43 well stresses how "from Livius onwards, Roman literary translators *all translate in the same way*" (original emphasis); cf. Suerbaum (2002), 102.

45. Leo (1895/1912), 88–89, (1913), 59–60; Mariotti (1952/1986), 52; Traina (1970), 12, (1989), 97; Büchner (1979), 63; Kaimio (1979), 294; Rochette (1995), 251; Moatti (1997), 84–88; Possanza (2004), 29–39; McElduff (2004), 121, (2013), 43. See Rochette (1997a), 297–99, for the very different pragmatic and pedagogic motivations for translation of Latin works into Greek: "Dans le monde grec, la traduction n'a jamais formé un genre littéraire" (299).

46. Traina (1989), 97; Bettini (2012), 39.

47. Bellos (2011), 30; see Reynolds (2011) for a wide-ranging exploration of the various metaphors that have been used of poetic translation in English.

48. Kaimio (1979), 272: note Aulus Gellius referring to "the book of Livius entitled *Odyssey*" (18. 9. 5); cf. Hor. *Epist.* 2. 1. 69, referring to the *carmina Livi*. It is interesting that the practice of comedy is often different: see Lennartz (1994), 25–26 for cases where Plautus and Terence refer to their own comedies or to tragedies by the name of the Greek author: e.g., Plaut. *Rud.* 86 *(Alcumena*

Euripidi), Ter. *Eun.* 20 *(Menandri Eunuchum).* See Bellos (2011), 292 for the low status of the European or American translator in comparison with that of the translator in contemporary Japan, for example, where a prominent translator can get equal billing with the author on the dust jacket.

49. On the crucial importance of the imagery of warfare used to describe the Roman attitude to their rivalry with Greek literature, see Hutchinson (2013), 30–32.

50. On the patronizing of the Latin archaic, see Hinds (1998), 56–74.

51. Note the fine comment of Possanza (2004), 56 on Livius' sense of originality: "Unlike contemporary Hellenistic poets such as Apollonius and Callimachus, who labored under the oppressive influence of the great works of the past and, in a sense, wrote in the margins and between the lines of their classical pre-decessors, Livius had an open field for the rewriting of Greek literature in Latin. While Hellenistic poets had to discover ways to avoid being parrots of Homer, Livius could make the *Odyssey* new by translating it into Latin." Cf. Kerkhecker (2001), 65 on Ennius' analogous originality as a Homerizer in Latin. For Livius' "self-consciousness" about his translating, see Hinds (1998), 60–61.

52. It would not be too whimsical to see Livius as already aware that a translation is not working with "the assumption that the meaning of a source text is fixed and largely known (or at least knowable)" (Martindale [1993], 77).

53. As Marco Fantuzzi suggests to me.

54. Hinds (1998), 61; cf. McElduff (2013), 53, pointing out that "translated" as a translation of *uersutus* does not do justice to the powerful metaphor of shift in position.

55. Chaudhuri (1999), 41 (even if I would qualify his last clause in this case, given Homer's own interest in the mobility of his "turning" epithet).

56. Leo (1913), 74 makes the point clearly; on the calque as a mainstay of translation technique, see Bellos (2011), 175, 187–88; on the calque in Latin/Greek translation, see already Magie (1905) (who calls it *translatio*), summarized in Rochette (2010), 291. Sandy Hardie has kindly shared with me very suggestive work in progress in which he argues that the Camenae were already identified with the Muses in Rome before Livius.

57. Hinds (1998), 60–61; see Maltby (1991), s.v. *Camena* for the supposed etymology, and A. Hardie (2005) for further etymological discussion of *carmen*.

58. Dumézil (1970), 456; see Dunand and Lévêque (1975); Jocelyn (1990), 596; Feeney (1991), 115–16.

59. "Kühnheit und Selbstvertrauen," Leo (1913), 74, citing also *Morta* (fr. 23) for Homer's "Moira" and *Moneta* (fr. 21) for Homer's "Mnemosyne," where Livius

finds in a cult-title of Juno ("Reminder") an equivalent to "Memory," the mother of the Muses; cf. Fraenkel (1931), 603–4. See A. Hardie (2007), 556–59 for the inventiveness of Livius' choice, connecting Mnemosyne with the established advisory function of Juno Moneta on the Capitol, thereby "link[ing] central Rome with wider Greece" (559).

60. Martindale (1993), 85–86, on Borges (1970); as Cowan (2010), 42, well summarizes, in confronting the *Medea* of Euripides and the *Medea* of Ennius, Menard's "word-for-word reproduction of *Don Quixote* had an entirely different meaning from Cervantes's 'version,' purely by virtue of being written in the twentieth rather than the seventeenth century."

61. Suerbaum (1968), 9–10 acutely notices the issue, though he wishes to downplay its impact.

62. Esp. Schol. O, who canvasses essentially the options of S. West in Heubeck, West, and Hainsworth (1988), 73, quoted next in the text.

63. McElduff (2013), chapter 3.

64. Gowers (1993), 87–107: my thanks to one of the Press readers for this suggestion.

65. I agree with Kaimio (1979), 273 and Possanza (2004), 46 that Leo (1895/1912), 78 n. 2 is right in seeing the epic as coming after the first dramas.

66. Recently most associated with the important studies of Venuti (1995) and (1998); for debate, see Robinson (1997), 108–12; Chaudhuri (1999), 37–38; Boyden (2006); Bellos (2011), chapters 5 and 15.

67. Schleiermacher (1813/1992), 42.

68. Eco (2001), 22.

69. Rajak (2009), 128, 127.

70. Gentzler (2001), chapter 5, on the interest of contemporary polysystem translation theory in such cases; cf. Bellos (2011), 172: "Translating DOWN from a dominant language to a vernacular language is typically accompanied by substantial imports of vocabulary and syntactic constructions from the source."

71. Karlinsky (1985), 41, 44–45.

72. Dryden (1697/1992), 26.

73. As Leo (1913), 73, observed: "er übersetzte so, dass der Schein eines lateinischen Gedichtes entstand, nicht der eines griechischen Gedichts in lateinischer Sprache."

74. Possanza (2004), 48.

75. My thanks to Joshua Katz for this example.

76. Possanza (2004), 47, tracing the story back to Leo (1895/1912), 80 and (1913), 73–74, with bibliography in n. 55.

77. My thanks to Marco Fantuzzi, whose phrasing I have taken over here, for helping me see the force of the new Livian metaphors.

78. My thanks to one of the Press readers for these points of sameness and difference in fr. 30.

79. Possanza (2004), 49; cf. Knoche (1958), 322–23; Traina (1970), 19–21; Gentili (1979), 103.

80. Traina (1970), 13–18; Büchner (1979), 45; Kearns (1990), 48; Venuti (2008), 36.

81. Goldberg (1995), 72.

82. Traina (1970), 15–18.

83. Penetratingly observed by Possanza (2004), 48.

84. Hinds (1998), 56–58; Morgan (2010), 291–93.

85. Goldberg (2009a), 431.

86. McElduff (2013), 50: "the meter was an added layer of Romannness that presented this foreign text as already integrated into the culture and rhythm of Roman speech and song." Cf. Possanza (2004), 51–53; Goldberg (2009a), 431.

87. Mariotti (1952/1986), 25; Knoche (1958), 326–27; Possanza (2004), 51–52; Meyer (2004), 53–54; Farrell (2005), 425; Guittard (2007), 58–59; Goldberg (2009a), 431.

88. The important study of Mercado (2012) may have cracked the code, though I cannot help feeling that his approach covers the phenomena but does not yet take us into the mind of a composer: "a trochaic-amphibrachic tetrameter underlyingly" (2) may describe the data, but I find it hard to imagine that this is how Livius or Naevius conceived of their process.

89. So, attractively, Goldberg (2009b), 173–75; cf. the rather different approach of Kloss (1993), 96–97. Fortson (2011), 94, likewise canvasses the possibility that our surviving specimens of Saturnian are "different meters belonging to the same family and sharing certain structures"; it is also possible that shifts in Latin word-stress patterns led to successive generations redefining what could count as a Saturnian (Fortson [2011], 95).

90. Fortson (2011), 95.

91. Fraenkel (1957), 369 n. 1.

92. Such options continue to be alive for as long as Latin is interacting with Greek: for a model discussion of Cicero's options in talking of "atoms," see Reinhardt (2005).

93. See Heubeck in Heubeck, West, and Hainsworth (1988) on Hom. *Od.* 10. 135–39 for Circe and Circeii. For "Italy as a Homeric landscape," see Farrell (2004), 255–63; cf. Hutchinson (2013), 76.

94. Coleman (1999), 46, for such spellings and pronunciations as normal "before c. 150 BC"; cf. Biville (1987), 29; de Melo (2011), 322.

95. Rüpke (2012), 33.

96. Assmann (1996) and Ando (2005), chapter 3, offer very suggestive discussions.

97. See Chapter 7, text accompanying notes 33–40.

98. Feeney (1991), 116.

99. See Rüpke (2012), 55, and, in general on the theological challenges presented by the acts of translation and comparison involved in the *interpretatio Romana,* see Ando (2005): "the identity of the gods turns out to be distressingly and disconcertingly labile. It is not simply their names and forms, but the gods themselves who are πολυειδής and *multiplex*" (49). I am indebted to Marco Fantuzzi for discussion of this fragment.

100. Connors (2004), 202.

101. This is clear from Cic. *Brut.* 71, Aul. Gell. 3. 16. 11, 18. 9. 5; see Leo (1895/1912), 80; Mariotti (1952/1986), 23–24; Weiss (2004), xvii n. 22. It becomes something of an antiquarian cliché that the old shape of Greek letters is practically the same as that of current Latin letters: Plin *NH* 7. 210; Tac. *Ann.* 11. 14.3.

102. To a degree, such editorial decisions are faithful to Spenser's own cultivation of a self-conscious archaism, on which see Osselton (1990), a reference I owe to Russ Leo.

103. On the first-century introduction of Greek "y," see Perl (1971), and on "ph" for Greek φ, see Allen (1978), 26. Good remarks on false archaizing in Goldberg (2009c), 646. Yet it is always worthwhile checking on a hypothetical original spelling: restoring Plautus' orthography can restore a new dimension to his wit, as in Fontaine (2010).

104. On the continuity of the markedly Greek titles to many works of Latin literature, see Hutchinson (2013), 153. The problem of how to interpret the transmitted titles of Roman tragedy and comedy is very difficult, given how hard it is to assess the degree of change and "correction" introduced in the transmission over time; much depends on prior assumptions about how much Greek the audience might have understood. See Daly (1943); Henriksson (1956); Jocelyn (1969), 58–61. On the differences between Plautus (more Latinizing) and Terence (transliterating Greek, with the exception of *Phormio* for *Epidikazomenos*), see Lowe (2007), 120.

105. Above, text accompanying note 71. I thank Dawn Lavalle for the insights of a seminar paper on polysystem translation theory.

106. Goldberg (1995), 50–51; Malkin (1998), 178–91; Leigh (2010), 276–77; on the Homeric feel to the Sicilian locales, see Hutchinson (2013), 81.

107. Gruen (1990), 85 on the significance of the choice of the *Odyssey*; Cribiore (2001), 195–96 for the curricular preference.

Chapter 3 THE INTERFACE BETWEEN LATIN AND GREEK

1. Suerbaum (2002), 94–95, for the alternatives; cf. the skeptical discussion of Gruen (1990), 82–83: in favor of the entrepreneur scenario, Dumont and François-Gaillard (1998), 27; Carratello (1979), 21–22, with n. 67.
2. Feeney (1998), 52, referring to Jocelyn (1972), 991; Momigliano (1975), 17; Bakhtin (1981), 63; cf. Feeney (2005), 236–37. I should have referred to the major discussion of Toynbee (1965), 2. 430–31.
3. Feeney (2005), 237.
4. On Ennius' languages, see Toynbee (1965), 2. 431; Adams (2003), 117.
5. Adams and Swain (2002), 10, referring to Langslow (2002), 39, where he also cites the even more diverting example of "the emperor Charles V [who] is said to have spoken Castilian to God, German to his horses, French in council meetings, and Italian in salon conversation." Cf. Wallace-Hadrill (2008), 85. My thanks to Fiachra Mac Góráin for discussion of this point.
6. Bakhtin (1968), 470–72; cf. Bakhtin (1981), 61–63.
7. On the "cultural brokers" see Woolf (1998), 15.
8. See Affleck (2013) for (rather optimistic) speculation on the existence of collections of books in Rome before the conventional watershed moment of 168, when Aemilius Paullus captured the library of King Perseus of Macedon.
9. See Cole (1991), 381 on the previous importations of experts from Etruria and Atella: "Livius and Naevius were simply the latest in a long line of noncitizen professionals."
10. Chapter 1, text accompanying notes 76–79.
11. Well observed by Knoche (1958), 329.
12. As Ronnie Shi put it to me; cf. Wallace-Hadrill (2008), 19 on the origins of the writers of Latin literature as "a particularly striking aspect of the romanisation of Italy."
13. Wallace-Hadrill (2008), 19.
14. Bellos (2011), 60.
15. Clear taxonomy in Mayer (1999), whom I follow here. I owe much to Gitner (2012), whom I thank for permission to quote from his as-yet unpublished dissertation. The standard account is Löfstedt (1933), chapter 3; see also Coleman (1975) on syntax in particular; Adams (2003), 422–23.
16. Gitner (2012), 25; as he goes on to say, "[i]t is important . . . to keep in mind that the same word may be a striking *Fremdwort* in one context and an innocuous *Lehnwort* in another."
17. Gitner (2012), 26.

18. Mayer (1999), 158–59, citing, e.g., Catull. 51. 9, *lingua sed torpet.*
19. Verg. *G.* 4. 357; Catull. 64. 296: standard discussions of this "Greek accusative" in Fordyce (1977) on Verg. *Aen.* 7.503; Harrison (1991), 290–91; Courtney (2004).
20. Leo (1895/1912), 89. See Possanza (2004), 53 for Livius' *multa* (*Od.* fr. 20) translating Homer's ταρφέα (*Od.* 8. 379).
21. As remarked by Mayer (1999), 160, who observes that "grecism" continued to have to be shoehorned into the species of "rhetoric" by Latin grammarians because of this lack in the parent system.
22. Jocelyn (1972), 1019 n. 329; cf. Kaimio (1979), 303. *eglutro* in Liv. *Od.* fr. 6 comes from ἔκλουτρον, not a word of high poetic diction; it is attested only in the grammarian Pollux (10. 46), and was presumably part of the *koinē* that has gone under our radar. See M. Barchiesi (1962), 366 for the related *creterra* and *lepista* in Naev. *BP* fr. 31, and 290–91 for Naevius using domesticated Latin equivalents *(Runcus ac Purpureus)* for the Greek giants' names Ῥοῖτος or Ῥοῖκος and Πορφυρίων in *BP* fr. 8. Cf. Mariotti (1955/2001), 62–63.
23. Jocelyn (1999), 179–80 on Ennius' practice; cf. Housman (1972), 2. 825 on early dramatic poetry preferring the Latinizing accusative in—*em* to the later Classical Grecizing—*en* in Greek names such as *Anchisem.*
24. Courtney (1993), 65–66.
25. Watkins (1995a), 35, on *ILLRP* 1271a.
26. Kroll (1924), 249; Löfstedt (1933), 411–12; Jocelyn (1972), 1019 n. 331 and (1999), 180; Skutsch (1985), 66–67: these authorities note also Ennius' occasional choice of Greek morphology in the *Annales*, as with, e.g., the accusative form *aethera* (fr. 545).
27. On Ennius' modernizing agenda, see Hinds (1998), 56–63.
28. Jocelyn (1972), 1019 n. 331.
29. Degl'Innocenti Pierini (1977), 94.
30. Degl'Innocenti Pierini (1977), 108–9 (93–109 in general on Accius' grecisms).
31. Mayer (1999), 176, after fully documenting modern approaches.
32. Mayer (1999), 177–78, against the idea that such features are a natural result of a bilingual environment, noting that, e.g., "Grecisms are not to be found in the speeches of Cicero" (178).
33. Bellos (2011), 51–52; cf. Bettini (2012), 21–22.
34. Though niche areas can have their own specificity. In the field of Second World War history, which is regularly written by authors who could not order a cup of coffee in a German train station, a peculiar brand of foreignizing is observable. Anyone reading such books is exposed to *Reichsmarschall, General der*

Panzertruppen, Obergruppenführer, Gauleiter, and so on, as the author aims to impart a somewhat spurious air of authenticity to the narrative. This has become so much the norm that is disconcerting to read the history of the Third Reich by Evans (2003–2008), whose German is of a high standard, and to see actual translations instead of foreignizing transliteration ("Leader," for example, instead of "Führer," or "Regional Leader" for "Gauleiter").

35. Bellos (2011), 52.

36. Dickey (2012), 49–50 on the intimidatingly named *Colloquia of the Hermeneumata Pseudodositheana,* which are school textbooks.

37. See Glucker (2012), 48–52 for discussion of Ciceronian translations and etymologies that depend on the reader knowing the Greek terms at issue.

38. Bellos (2011), 195; cf. Mayer (1999), 178: "A Roman poet consciously departed from the norm, and knew that his practice would be scrutinized or even mocked if a reader failed to see any justification." I thank Anna Morpurgo Davies for discussion of the bilingual's urge for purism, in order to avoid the appearance of mere incompetence.

39. Adams (2003), 372; cf. Coleman (1999), 45–47.

40. Adams (2003), 372 with n. 142.

41. Feeney (1991), 111–12. On the knowledge of Roman religion in the first epics, see Feeney (1991), 109–12, 115–16, 119–20, 124, 128; on Roman religion in Plautus, see Dunsch (2009); in Ennius' tragedies, specifically as different from Greek belief, Jocelyn (1969), 214, 221–22, 225, 244–45, 251–52, 280; and in Accius, Rüpke (2012), chapter 4.

42. Jocelyn (1969), 248.

43. Jocelyn (1969), 308.

44. Jocelyn (1969), 351. For further acute examples of Ennian adaptation of Greek moral phraseology, see Cowan (2010), 43–45; Gildenhard (2010), 173–78.

45. See Chapter 5, text accompanying notes 93–96.

46. Adams and Mayer (1999), 2; cf. Watkins (1995b), 62: "the Latin literary language of the Republic and the Empire is not conservative but innovative and is in many respects an artificial construct." Even the apparently naturalistic language of Roman comedy is a highly "literary language": see Karakasis (2014), 566–68.

47. Already—as usual—remarked by Leo (1913), 34–38; cf. Jocelyn (1969), 38–39, with full references to detailed discussion in the commentary; Adams and Mayer (1999), 1–2; Halla-aho and Kruschwitz (2010), 134–35. There are many resources in the multi-authored section on "Prosa" in Suerbaum (2002), 57–83.

48. Adams (2005), 73–74, with the important observation in n. 10 that "there was no doubt much more writing or religious, military, legal, and financial kinds than extant sources would lead one to believe." Cf. Adams (2007), 37–38. On the valuable evidence for early elevated official language afforded us by Plautus, see also Fraenkel (1922/2007), 162–64, 414–15; Jocelyn (1969), 172.

49. Rich discussion in Fraenkel (1922/2007), 242–47; again, the various contributors on "gebundene Sprache" in Suerbaum (2002), 30–57 offer a range of views. How Hellenizing such hymns and *carmina* already were in the first place is an intensely controversial question, to which we return in Chapter 8.

50. Halla-aho and Kruschwitz (2010), esp. 139–53.

51. Halla-aho and Kruschwitz (2010), 132.

52. Jocelyn (1969), 39, with documentation; cf. Manuwald (2011) on the innovative language of Livius (193) and Naevius (195).

53. Boyle (2006), 93.

54. Fraenkel (1922/2007), 241.

55. Petersmann and Petersmann (2004), 245–46; Leo (1913), 3–4 already points decisively to the dialect of the head city, Rome, as the base of the new literary language.

56. Petersmann and Petersmann (2004), 242–44, referring to the arresting claim of Devoto (1967) that Latin underwent more rapid and deep change between 500 and 350 than it did between 350 and 1950 CE; see Adams (2007), 13–17, Ostler (2007), 27–29, and Leonhardt (2009), 58–59 on "standardization." I have learned much from the discussion of Gitner (2012), 189–90.

57. See Adams (2007), 112, 187 for discussion of whether it is appropriate to use the word "dialect" of varieties of Latin in Latium in the Republic, and 695 for how "[a]lready at the time of Plautus conditions were right for the inhabitants of rural Latium and elsewhere to be moved to accommodate their speech to that of Rome."

58. de Melo (2011), 338 on *Trin.* 609, *Truc.* 688–91; Dench (1995), 74–75; cf. Adams (2003), 153–54, (2007), 119–23, discussing also Lucilius' rebuke of a certain Vettius for using Praenestine words (as reported by Quint. *Inst.* 1. 5. 56). On the local pride of Praeneste down to the Social War, see Rawson (1991), 382–83, Wallace-Hadrill (2008), 106–16. Cf. Adams (2007), 692, on the "strong culture" of the Faliscans, the other main contender for a distinctive dialect of Latin (cf. 112 on their possible claim to the status of a local dialect, even if their language is normally regarded as a sister-language of Latin: Clackson [2004], 789).

59. Leo (1913), 3–4; Coleman (1999), 27 ("no trace of a Latin Robert Burns"); Petersmann and Petersmann (2004), 245. As Adams and Mayer (1999), 3, point

out, the differences are not very marked even within the various registers of literary Latin ("language of medicine," "legal Latin" and so on).

60. To quote again Adams and Mayer (1999), 2. The use of archaism in early poetry was first discussed in full by Fraenkel (1931), 604–6; again, excellent orienting account in Possanza (2004), 49–51.

61. Waszink (1960), 24; cf. Venuti (2008), 35.

62. Coleman (1999), 41; Livingston (2004), 23.

63. So Possanza (2004), 50; cf. Leo (1895/1912), 92; Fraenkel (1931), 606; Mariotti (1952/1986), 28.

64. M. Barchiesi (1962), 248, 291–92, 353, 403, 445, 462.

65. Whereas almost two centuries later Catullus could use precisely this strategy, going back to Ennius in order to create a "Homeric" patina for his mini-epic, Poem 64: Zetzel (1983).

66. Goldberg (2007a), 17–18; Goldschmidt (2013), 41–42.

67. Fraenkel (1931), 604–5 on Livius; Jocelyn (1972), 1018 n. 326; Goldschmidt (2013), 44–45.

68. Fraenkel (1931), 606.

69. Karlinsky (1985), 48.

70. See Henderson (1999), 42–43 on Terence's assertion of his distinctive success in the translatability of Greek culture.

71. Beard (1993), 63 (original emphasis).

72. Momigliano (1975), 36–37; cf. Rawson (1989), 423–24 on how Polybius exaggerates the fit between the Roman state and Greek constitutional theory. As Simon Hornblower points out to me, Polybius' insights into trends in Roman political norms receive a more positive press in recent scholarship (see, e.g., Millar [1998], 24); yet Rome remains not quite the match for Greek constitutional theory that it appeared to be.

73. Momigliano (1975), 11.

74. Wardy (2000), 87; cf. Eco (2001), 21. Bellos (2011), 182, marks out Luther's and the King James Bible as exceptional cases of individual impact, but remarks that "continuing waves of translated works in particular fields always leave the receiving language in a significantly different shape." For a wide-ranging discussion, including the examples of the translations by Chaucer and Tyndale into English, Amyot and Calvin into French, and Luther into German, see Delisle and Woodsworth (1995), chapter 2.

75. Dionisotti (2005), 372; see J. G. F. Powell (1995) for Cicero as a case in point.

76. Fruyt (2011).

77. Adams (2003), 762–64.

78. Wallace-Hadrill (2008), 65–69.

79. Dench (2005), 298–305: "The history of Roman linguistic self-consciousness is . . . intimately linked to the development of Greek linguistic self-consciousness and the reception of Greek language and literature in the Mediterranean world" (305); Wallace-Hadrill (2008), 57–58; Leonhardt (2009), 73–74. On "purism" as a concern in the second century in particular, see the varying accounts of Habinek (1998), 44–45; Dench (2005), 298–315; Gitner (2012), 183–84. On *Latinitas,* see Clackson (2011b).

80. See Momigliano (1975), 21, on "how formidable this nation was which could persuade men from Magna Graecia, Campania, Umbria and Africa to use their knowledge of Greek for the creation of a literature in Latin"; cf. Leo (1913), 76–77 on the degree to which Naevius, a Campanian, identifies with Rome and her historical mission in the *Bellum Punicum.*

81. Wallace-Hadrill (2008), 17; cf. 57 (of the Imperial period): "If Latin was the language normally associated of [*sic*] a Roman citizen, speaking Latin was neither a necessary nor a sufficient condition of being a Roman." This was already the case in the fourth century, as we see with the grant of citizenship to sixteen hundred non-Latin-speaking Capuans in 340 (Liv. 8.11.16), or to some Volscian towns in the aftermath of the war with the Latin league in 338 (Liv. 8.14. 5): see Eckstein (2006), 252–53, referring to Cornell (1995), 349, and 251–52 on the earlier case of the Etruscan town of Caere.

82. On this trading up on the part of especially upper-class Italians, see Adams (2003), 151–54; on the processes behind the spread of Latin in the peninsula, see Ostler (2007), 46–57.

83. Ostler (2007), 53–56; Leonhardt (2009), 49–52, 60–61.

84. Important discussion of these developments in Leonhardt (2009), 58–63: "Mit der Übernahme griechischer Literatur in Rom beginnt gleichzeitig auch der Prozess der sprachlichen Standardisierung" (58); "Die Fixierung der lateinischen Sprache ging aber von der Literatur aus, nicht von den Verwaltungsnotwendigkeiten" (63).

85. Such a suggestion has in fact been made by Sheets (1981), arguing that Livius Andronicus attempted to elevate the style of his epic by using glosses from other Italic languages; for criticism, see Kearns (1990); and Adams (2003), 122 n. 55. I have not been able to see Fisher (2014); if he is able to establish dynamic synchronic as well as diachronic interaction between the Latin literary language and contemporary Italic diction, I may have to reconsider.

86. Denecke (2013), 39 n. 40; cf. Dench (2005), 304; Adams (2003), 293, on the "abundant evidence" for the many languages whose primary speakers learned Latin, while there is "virtually none for Latin speakers learning any of these languages." We have here an analogy to the conditions in the Hellenistic world

that we discussed in Chapter 1: there too, speakers of other languages learned Greek, while the Greeks did not reciprocate.

87. de Melo (2011), 336; Adams (2003), 204–5 is more skeptical. On Etruscan and Punic as special cases, see Adams (2003), 165, 201, 204, 293, 755 (cautious on the extent of Roman knowledge of Etruscan and especially Punic).

88. Adams (2003), 151, 293–95, 755.

89. Chaudhuri (1999), 39, citing, e.g., "English *vis-à-vis* French after the Norman Conquest; several European languages *vis-à-vis* French after the eighteenth century"; see Gentzler (2001), 176–86. I thank Stephen Hinds for discussion, and for pointing out to me that such schemes can be too tidy, since the colonial situation can provoke all kinds of reactions, including "rescue" translations (as in the case of translation from Irish into English).

90. On "prestige" languages, see Kahane (1968), esp. 495–97 on the case of Greek as a prestige language for the Romans.

91. de Melo (2011), 337, referring to the fundamental study of Shipp (1953); major discussion in Jocelyn (1999), discussed with important qualifications by Adams (2003), 351–53, in the course of a full discussion of "code-switching," where a speaker switches from one language into another; cf. the terminological discussion of Mullen (2012), 18–20.

92. Adams (2003), 352; cf. A. Barchiesi (2009), 107.

93. Bellos (2011), 168.

94. Rafael (1993), 29.

95. Bellos (2011), 211, 205.

96. Kahane (1986), 497.

97. Bellos (2011), 169.

98. Chapter 2, text accompanying notes 26–28.

99. Dickey (2012), 5.

100. Dickey (2012), 41. Dickey is discussing evidence for language-learning by well-to-do people, and acknowledges (40) that our evidence for lower-rank Romans is much worse; it is easy to envisage even creoles and pidgins at this level of interaction: on pidgins, see Adams and Swain (2002), 16; Mullen (2012), 30 n. 104.

101. Fontaine (2010), 187. Important remarks on "una classe dirigente bilingue" in Canfora (1994), 19–25.

102. Horsfall (1979), 79; cf. Adams (2003), 3–8; Fewster (2002), 220–21. Fundamental are Adams (2003); and Adams, Janse, and Swain (2002); important survey in Mullen (2011). Extensive bibliography of bi- and multi-lingualism in Fögen (2003), 57–104 (covering Graeco-Roman antiquity).

103. *De or.* 2.61, cited by Rawson (1985), 46.

104. Horsfall (1979); Rawson (1989), 434.
105. Adams (2003), 322–23.
106. Wiseman (2004), 56; the etymology is attested in Plut. *Num.* 8.9–10, *Aem.* 2.2; Festus p. 22L. The first attested Aemilius to bear the *cognomen* Lepidus is the consul of 285: how many people got the joke at that time—or whether it *was* a joke at that time—is impossible to know. On such Greek-derived *cognomina*, see Solin (1971), 87–91, citing, e.g., Q. Publilius Philo (*cos.* 339, 327, 320, 315) and P. Sempronius Sophus (*cos.* 304); Bernstein (1998), 232.
107. Fontaine (2010), 200; cf. Manuwald (2011), 101–3, for a less far-reaching but still very positive assessment of the sophistication and Greek knowledge of Plautus' audience. First major study of Plautus' Greek in Middelmann (1938); cf. de Melo (2011), 336–38.
108. See Jocelyn (1969), 228–29, for comparable cases in Plautus, drawing attention to the Greek meaning of a character's name (*Capt.* 285–86; *Pseud.* 653–4; *Stich.* 174–75).
109. See Chapter 5, text accompanying notes 103–5.
110. Good observations in Suerbaum (2002), 26–27.
111. I thank Christopher Tuplin for this information given *per litteras*—and in general for his extremely generous responses to my enquiries, including the following reference to the Greek of Darius III.
112. As Christopher Tuplin points out to me; John Dillery refers me to the interesting case of the Thracian Seuthes in Xenophon's *Anabasis,* who has an interpreter but can understand most of the Greek he hears (7. 6. 8).
113. My thanks to David Bellos for this information.
114. Haubold (2007).
115. Fewster (2002), 229; Adams (2003), 757–58.
116. Veyne (1979), 8.
117. Eco (2001), 62 n. 2 (regularly, more than two cultures); cf. Conte (1994), 7; McElduff and Sciarrino (2011), 7–8. On the "cultural turn" in translation studies in the 1970s and 1980s, see Bassnett and Lefevere (1990), 1–13; Hermans (1999), 14–15; for a modern statement of the sociocultural aspects of translation see Pym, Shlesinger, and Jettmarová (2006).

Chapter 4 MIDDLE GROUNDS, ZONES OF CONTACT

1. Bernstein (1998), 58–78 (an extremely important book, from which I have learned much); Suerbaum (2002), 97; Manuwald (2011), 36–37.
2. This war is usually referred to as the "First Punic War," but the participants did not know it was their first war. I use "Great War" on analogy with the

Great War of 1914–1918, which did not become generally known as the "First World War" until the "Second" was well underway—though Pavlos Avlamis points out to me that the term "First World War" was already the title of a memoir of the war published in 1920, where the author refers to the coining of the phrase in a conversation with an American officer on September 10, 1918: Repington (1920), 2. 391.

3. As argued in the Introduction.

4. For the formulation of the go-between as the agent who creates differences between culture, as well as—or, even, rather than—dealing with them, I am indebted to Nicholas Purcell's Gray Lectures at Cambridge University in 2010, to which I refer with his permission.

5. A trait going back to the seventh century: Cornell (1995), 118.

6. Important discussion in Schiesaro (2005), 269 of the importance of "restoring some sense of geographical and chronological continuity between the emergence of tragedy at Rome and the world of postclassical Greek tragedy (and drama in general)."

7. Invaluable bibliographical orientation in J. R. Green (2008), 97–99, on "The spread of drama outside Athens"; see also the important collection edited by Bosher (2012), *in qua multum nuper amisimus.*

8. Willi (2008), chapter 5; Csapo (2010), 40. On the vigorous theater culture in Sicily, going back to the fifth century, see the stimulating overview in Hornblower (2008), 12–21.

9. Csapo (2010), 86 on the permanent theaters; Taplin (2007), 10; and Marconi (2012), 180 on the hypothesis, supported by vase-painting, of temporary structures.

10. On the theatrical culture of Magna Graecia, see La Penna (1979), 5–47; Gentili (1979), 16–17; Taplin (1993), (2007), esp. 5–21, (2012); Bernstein (1998), 235–36, 250 (on Tarentum); Willi (2008), chapter 5 (on Epicharmus); Csapo (2010), chapters 2 and 3, esp. 96–103; Manuwald (2011), 20–22, 26–29; Bosher (2012); Hutchinson (2013), 70–71; Le Guen (2014), 370–73.

11. Jocelyn (1969), 15, citing Dem. 19. 192 (Philip II), Plut. *Alex.* 4. 6, 29. 1–2 (Alexander), Diod. Sic. 20. 108. 1 (Antigonus); Revermann (1999–2000); Csapo (2010), 86, 173; Ceccarelli (2010), 100–101; Hanink (2014), 68–71; Le Guen (2014), 360–61 (on Alexander's dramatic celebrations of military victories).

12. On the Macedonian monarchy's attempt to appropriate Athenian tragedy, see Revermann (1999–2000) and Hanink (2014), 68–73, 89, who remarks that under Alexander "Macedon, like Athens, saw Greek tragedy as a critical part of its cultural life" (73); see below, text accompanying note 132, for the Roman

reaction. I thank Marco Fantuzzi for alerting me to the importance of the Macedonian connection.

13. See Dearden (2012), 281 for these, and other, cases, as evidence for the hypothesis of West Greek "local tragedians . . . writing for local audiences," with 285–86 for speculation on local production of locally written comedies; cf. Maffre (2000), 308.

14. Taplin (1993), (2007), (2012); E. G. D. Robinson (2004); Nervegna (2007), 16–17; Csapo (2010), chapter 2; Dearden (2012), 285–86 for speculation on local authorship of some of the plays depicted.

15. E. G. D. Robinson (2004), 200 n. 54.

16. Stephen Hinds suggests to me the attractive idea that some kind of prologue in the local language could have introduced a production in Greek: the prologues of Plautus and Terence, in which they discuss their adaptations of the Greek originals, could be a distant cousin of such a practice.

17. E. G. D. Robinson (2004), 206.

18. Wiseman (2000/2008), 123; a synthesis in Wiseman (2004), chapter 5. J. R. Green (2008), 267 is correct to say that "[t]he argument tends to be an associative one rather than readily demonstrable in concrete terms"; yet in association with the arguments of E. G. D. Robinson (2004) one feels confident in recognizing distinctive central Italian performance cultures; see further P. G. McC. Brown (2014), 406–7, on the strength of Wiseman's hypotheses.

19. Wiseman (2004), 114, 110; cf. Manuwald (2011), 27.

20. Dench (2005), 166 (original emphasis); cf. Morel (1989), 479; Cornell (1995), 163–64; Csapo (2010), 38, speaking generally of West Greece: "Drama became the primary vehicle of cultural Hellenization"; cf. Taplin (2007), 7; Revermann (2010), 93.

21. Burkert (2004), 12.

22. The conventional modern analogy involving Greece and America—genteel but effete high-status culture (Greece/Europe) vs. uncouth but preponderant military and political power (Rome/America)—applies to a much later period, as it has been generated to illustrate the situation under the high Roman Empire.

23. Morel (1989), 479.

24. Important discussion in E. G. D. Robinson (2004), esp. 207–11; cf. Curti, Dench, and Patterson (1996), 181–82; Wallace-Hadrill (2008), 23–25; and Ulf (2009), 89, on the dangers of casting the "natives" as passive recipients in many models of "Hellenization" or "acculturation."

25. Gigante (1971).

26. E. G. D. Robinson (2004), 209–11. On Blaesus of Capreae, a man with an Oscan name from a Greek part of Campania who wrote a play in Greek apparently on the god Saturn *(Satournos),* see Gigante (1971), 82; Rawson (1991), 475.

27. R. White (1991), 53–55, on such "mutual creative misunderstanding." On the "Greek genius for creative misunderstanding" in the Orientalizing period, see Lane Fox (2008), 72, 185, 187, 216, 255; and Malkin (2011), 137, 140, on the period of Greek colonization.

28. Malkin (2011), 46, has an excellent discussion for an ancient Mediterranean context; see the index sv. "middle ground"; cf. Wallace-Hadrill (2008), 23–25. Ulf (2009) is an extremely helpful account of "Rethinking cultural contacts," but I find his discussion of the power distribution in White's middle ground confused (98–99).

29. Cornell (1995), 322–24; cf. Wiseman (1994), 12–13; Curti (2000), 7, on the Roman Republic's "tremendous transformation" during the fourth century—"a quite incredible evolution."

30. Wiseman (1994), 13.

31. Cornell (1995), 338. His colleague Licinius did not have long to wait, as he became consul in either 364 or 361: see Oakley (1997–2005), 1. 692–93 for the possible dates.

32. Flower (2010), 50–51; cf. Cornell (1995), 340–44 and Forsythe (2005), 268–76, on this new nobility.

33. Gell. *NA* 5. 4. 3; Beck and Walter (2001), 1 F 23; *FRHist* 1 F31; see *FRHist* 3. 47 for discussion of the fragment, which is cited from a Latin text by our source, Aulus Gellius, so that it is "either the Latin version of Fabius Pictor or the work of another Fabius."

34. On Livy's need to distance his literary form of historiography from drama, see Feldherr (1998), chapter 5.

35. This is controversial, for some believe that the annual performances began only in 366, but I follow Bernstein (1998), 63–64 in seeing the settlement after the expulsion of the kings as the occasion for this innovation, linked to the dedication of the temple of Jupiter on the Ides of September.

36. The extra day was probably put on the twelfth, immediately before the Ides: Wissowa (1912), 454.

37. Rüpke (2005), 3. 1620.

38. It is tantalizingly difficult to know why this particular priestly college was the first to admit plebeians: for interesting speculation, see Satterfield (2008), 33–35.

39. Bernstein (1998), 62–78, esp. 73–74.

40. Festus p. 436L, our only source, is fragmentary at this point, and only the name of Laenas is recoverable. Bernstein (1998), 73, 119, refers to Laenas as the first attested curule aedile, but Livy gives us the names of the ones elected for 366 (7. 1. 2): see Broughton (1951–52), 1. 115.

41. On these opportunities, see Bernstein (1998), 74–75; Rüpke (2012), 23, 46. On Laenas' prominence, see Oakley (1997–2005), 2. 153.

42. My thanks to Dan-el Padilla Peralta and to one of the Press readers for suggesting this perspective of the creative use of crisis.

43. Colonna (1993), 343–47, on Caere, 343 on Castelsecco—I thank Alessandro Barchiesi and Elena Ducci for introducing me to this site on a beautiful day in June 2012.

44. Hanink (2014), 95–98, with reference to Csapo (2007), 103–4, who discusses similar arrangements for the first theaters at Delphi and Delos; see too Moretti (1999–2000) (a reference I owe to Peter Rhodes), who also discusses the sixth-century evidence for seating spectators on "rising rows of [wooden] seats" at Athens and Corinth (377).

45. Colonna (1993), 343; and Thuillier (2013), 831–82, on makeshift wooden theaters in "Classical" Etruria; Taplin (2007), 10, on Magna Graecia; Marconi (2012), 180, 189 on the shift from such wooden structures to permanent stone theaters in Sicily from the fourth to second centuries.

46. Rüpke (2012), 19. The international character of ancient spectacles was an important theme of the 2010 Gray Lectures given in Cambridge by Nicholas Purcell.

47. Oakley (1997–2005), 2. 51–52; Thuillier (2013), 832. Compare the regular summoning of experts in the *Etrusca disciplina* throughout the Republic in times of religious crisis, experts who were always marked as coming "from outside"; North (1989), 583–84; Beard, North, and Price (1998), 1. 20.

48. On such horizontal mobility, see Terrenato (2007), esp. 20; Rüpke (2012), 18.

49. As suggested by Bernstein (1998), 127; for Laenas as deriving from an originally Etruscan gentile name, see *RE* "Popillius Laenas" #20; Schulze (1904), 83, 186, 530; Kajanto (1965), 210.

50. Livy 7. 2 is the fundamental source, and the invaluable discussion of Oakley (1997–2005), 2. 51–53 is the place to start in appreciating the Etruscan dimension of the *ludi scaenici*.

51. Thuillier (1992).

52. Bernstein (1998), 23–51 ("Die Spiele der Könige"); Thuillier (2013), 832.

53. Szemerényi (1975), 307–16; Horsfall (1993a), 801; Bernstein (1998), 124–26; Dumont and François-Garelli (1998), 14–15; Adams (2003), 164; Manuwald (2011),

24–25. The word for "actor," *histrio,* is a much less certain case of such mediation from Greek via Etruscan: see Breyer (1993) 432–34 for arguments against Szemerényi (1975), 312–13.

54. Waszink (1960), 19–20; Szemerényi (1975), 316; Bernstein (1998), 126; Oakley (1997–2005), 2. 52; Moore (2012), 3: "In all probability . . . Roman theater started with music." For dancing to the music of the *tibia* as foundational to the Roman *ludus,* see Dupont (1993).

55. Vividly described by Fabius Pictor, Rome's first historian, as reported in Dion. Hal. *Ant.* 7. 71. 1–73. 5, *FRHist* 1 F15. We return in Chapter 8 to the larger question of what may be known about the general musical culture of Rome down to the third century.

56. Bernstein (1998), 127.

57. Extremely valuable overview in Manuwald (2011), 26–29.

58. Bernstein (1998), 127–28.

59. On the continuing popularity of the Oscan shows, attested in Cic. *Fam.* 7. 1. 3, Suet. *Iul.* 39. 1, *Aug.* 43. 1, see Jocelyn (1969), 14; Rawson (1991), 476; Horsfall (2003), 53; Manuwald (2011), 171 (with discussion of the Latin tradition that arose out of them, at an unknown date).

60. Rüpke (2012), 84. Contrast the more orthodox assumptions of Jocelyn (1969), 15: "It seems likely that the aediles would have presented this kind of [Oscan] drama before they tried the more sophisticated Athenian kind." A post-240 entry for the Oscan *atellana* would still allow time for Plautus to play with his audience's expectations about the nature of the comedies he was giving them: see the fascinating speculation in Traina (2013) on Plautus using the *atellana* name *Maccus* to refer to himself in *Asinaria* 11 in order to reassure his audience that there is a continuity between this new production of his and his old role in the Oscan farces. My thanks to Alessandro Barchiesi for this reference.

61. La Penna (1979), 22: "L'atellana campana era arte greca diversamente filtrata ed elaborata."

62. Fraenkel (1922/2007), 423 certainly thought this likely; cf. Rawson (1989), 428; Gruen (1990), 87.

63. Rawson (1991), 475; Horsfall (1993a), 803; Jocelyn (2000), 327; Sciarrino (2011), 47 n. 28. It looks as if L. Mummius first arranged for regular Artists of Dionysus to stage a drama for his triumph in 146 (Tac. *Ann.* 14. 21. 1), to be followed by Marius and Sulla: Leppin (1992), 169.

64. Attested in Liv. 39. 22. 1 and 10 (games of 186), Plb. 30. 22 (games of 167).

65. Important argument on this score in Le Guen (2014), 371–73, distinguishing between the professional associations of the *Dionysiaci technitae* "proper" and

other travelling troupes; I thank Professor Le Guen for her generous correspondence on this question.

66. Here I agree with Nervegna (2013), 70–71 and Le Guen (2014), 371–73.

67. Rawson (1991), 477–78, importantly stresses that Rome was part of a circuit for the Greek and Oscan troupes in the second and first centuries.

68. See Jory (1970), 230–31, for the Greek origins of most of the performers in Latin drama whom we can identify; cf. Gruen (1990), 87, on Livius' options in 240. P. G. McG. Brown (2002), 227, is correct to be cautious here, and Jory goes too far in identifying the personnel as coming from the "Artists of Dionysus" in Magna Graecia, for, as we have seen, there is no evidence that the *technitae* were in place in Italy at this early date. Still, the hypothesis that the first performers of the translated plays were Greek professionals remains attractive, and it may help explain some features of the Roman adaptations, as we shall see in the next section.

69. As pointed out to me by one of the Press readers. On the impact of the Roman wars on festival performances in Magna Graecia, see Leppin (1992), 169–76; Le Guen (2014), 373.

70. This hypothesis is associated in particular with the work of T. P. Wiseman, in a series of studies culminating especially in Wiseman (2004) and (2008), but the general view that the Romans formed their historical memory in part through such dramas goes back to German scholarship of the late nineteenth century: see Flower (1995), 170; cf. Manuwald (2001), 91–93, for more general criticisms of the approach that takes the "dramatic" quality of an historical account as evidence of its origins in a play.

71. For Naevius as the inventor of the form, see Leo (1913), 89–90; La Penna (1979), 55; Gruen (1990), 93–94.

72. Flower (1995), 184; Suerbaum (2002), 110. Accius' *Decius uel Aeneadae,* on the battle of Sentinum in 295, stands out as taking its subject matter from the middle period.

73. On the *fabula togata,* and its probable invention by one Titinius shortly before or after the year 200, see E. Stärk in Suerbaum (2002), 259–62; Manuwald (2011), 156–59. Manuwald (ibid.) and Wiseman (2008), 194–99 stress that the tidy divisions of *togata/praetexta* ("comic/serious" plays in Roman dress) are the work of late Republican scholars, and we must allow for the possibility of plays that crossed these lines in inventive ways.

74. Manuwald (2001), 101–2, 110, 158.

75. Rarity: Manuwald (2011), 141; controversial: Flower (1995), 187–90; cf. Gildenhard (2010), 157. For arguments against the hypothesis that dramas were staged

about such intensely polarizing events as the Bacchanalia crisis of 186 or the death of Gaius Gracchus in 121, see Flower (2000).

76. As argued by Flower (1995), 190; cf. Manuwald (2001), 110–12; (2011), 142.

77. Flower (1995), 188.

78. As Potter (1999) points out, if Bernstein (1998) is correct in his claim that only the *Ludi Romani* existed as a venue for staged drama before the introduction of the *Ludi Plebeii* in 220 or 216, then Wiseman's reconstruction faces difficulty.

79. La Penna (1979), 54; Jocelyn (2000), 342–49; Manuwald (2011), 143; Goldberg (2007b), 573–74, is more cautious about the possible similarities.

80. Conceivably in Latin, although the direct evidence for Atellan in Latin is much later than 240: Manuwald (2011), 170–71. Mime, too, is only attested late, in the second century: Manuwald (2011), 178.

81. As argued in the Introduction.

82. Feeney (2005), 233; cf. Wiseman (1994), 16; P .G. McC. Brown (2014), 407: "all the evidence suggests that what Livius Andronicus and his successors did was radically different from what had gone before at Rome." On the heightened generic awareness of the boundaries between Latin tragedy and comedy, as revealed by parody and paratragedy, see Manuwald (2014).

83. Well put by Chaudhuri (1999), 22: "Translation, the ground and medium of cultural exchange, is organically invested with destabilizing and distancing factors"; cf. Gildenhard (2010), 172. On the difference between Homer's and Livius' "me," see Chapter 2, text accompanying note 61.

84. Here I do no more than précis the admirable presentation of Gratwick (1982a), 84–86.

85. Gratwick (1982a), 86; cf. Moore (2012), 5–6: see Fraenkel (1922/2007), 230–31. Terence has much less non-trochaic or iambic sung verse than Plautus (less than 1 percent, as opposed to over 10 percent in Plautus): Duckworth (1952), 380; Moore (2012), 190, with 209 on Terence nonetheless maintaining highly sophisticated metrical variation. Moore (2012), 102–3, well cautions against taking "recitative" as a technical term, analogous to modern opera practices, though still allowing for the differences between polymetric and stichic passages.

86. So Fraenkel (1922/2007), 231; Oakley (1997–2005), 2. 53–54; Boyle (2006), 29.

87. W. J. Slater (1993), 195. The role of the chorus in new comedy remains very controversial, as Lucy Jackson and Marco Fantuzzi point out to me: see Marshall (2002) for an argument for the chorus as "an integrated dramatic character" (17) in Menander's *Dyscolus* at least, and Hunter (1983) 191 for an unusually prominent role for the chorus in Eubulus' *Garland-Sellers*. For choral dimen-

sions to two Plautine passages (*Poen.* 515–28 and *Rud.* 290–305), see Moore (2012), 129–30.

88. E. Stärk in Suerbaum (2002), 153.

89. Goldberg (1998), 16 on the implications of the performance space for the role of the chorus.

90. Jocelyn (1969), 19–20, 31 inclines to severe cutbacks on the chorus's songs: cf. Manuwald (2011), 138–39 for the view that tragedy is unlikely to have had "separating choral interludes." For a good statement of the other possibility, see Boyle (2006), 18–19.

91. Strzelecki (1952), 54–60; cf. Jocelyn (1969), 370–71; for the *coryphaeus*-hypothesis, see Hose (1999b), 124, with interesting remarks on the difference between the citizen chorus of Athenian drama and the professionals at Rome, who no longer mediate between actors and audience in the same manner (118–20).

92. Taplin (2012), 237–46.

93. W. J. Slater (1993), 194–96: "As far as I know, there is no good evidence that 'old tragedy'—in the sense of a tragedy of classical times reperformed at a Hellenistic festival—had a chorus" (196). Cf. Nervegna (2007), 40–41, taking in also the explicit evidence for reperformances of tragedies without their choruses in the late first century CE (Dio Chrys. *Or.* 19. 5).

94. Jocelyn (1969), 32.

95. From different perspectives, Fontaine (2014) and Petrides (2014) both stress that due attention to Italian performance traditions should nonetheless not distract from acknowledging that the new Latin comedies are profoundly Greek in more than a formal sense.

96. This second point is crucially made by Szemerényi (1975), 316–17, even if I would not concur with the implicit negative value judgment passed on the pre-240 period in Szemerény's description of the Roman shows from 364 to 241 as a "partly or grossly distorted refraction in the imperfect Etruscan mirror of the dazzling rays of Greek drama." See too Toynbee (1965), 2. 420. This long-existing Etruscan dimension complicates a more straightforward narrative whereby the entry to Campania is the entry way for Roman encounters with Hellenized drama, as in La Penna (2006), 4.

97. Terrenato (2007), 16, on the fourth to third centuries in Central Italy: "This was a unique period in which social structures that had been present in some form ever since the Middle Bronze Age were faced with the world of global empires."

98. Purcell (1994), 388, 401–2.

99. Note the cautions of Purcell (1994), 400 against taking at face value the extremely loaded testimony of Aristoxenus of Tarentum (around 320)

concerning the "barbarianization" of Poseidonia (reported in Ath. 632a.); cf. Bowersock (1995) on the closely related language of Strabo 6. 1. 253, which he convincingly sets in the same milieu; E. G. D. Robinson (2004), 209–10; J. R. Green (2012), 322, on the "sad nostalgia of [third century] ethnic Greeks" in the now Lucanian town of Paestum.

100. Curti, Dench, and Patterson (1996), 187, on a process going back to the third century; cf. Curti (2001), 21. I follow here the important arguments of Morel (1989), 479, 483–84, and Curti, Dench, and Patterson (1996), 185–87.

101. Lomas (2004), esp. 199–201.

102. Russo (2012); see Bispham (2007), chapter 1, esp. 67–68, for the acquisition of the first overseas provinces as important for the formation of a concept of Italy.

103. Cornell (1995), 362.

104. This is the main theme of the important chapter 3 of Dench (2005); n.b. 161–67 on our third-century period; cf. Dench (1995), 13; Curti, Dench, and Patterson (1996), esp. 187–88; Curti (2001), 19; Eckstein (2006), 252–57 on the continually evolving sense of Roman identity in the period after the dissolution of the Latin League in particular. In general, see now Bispham (2007), chapter 1, esp. 68–72. On the colonies as "staging posts of the Roman expansion in Italy, politically and militarily, of course, but also from an ideological and religious point of view," see De Cazanove (2000), 74; cf. Scheidel (2004), 22–24, on the role of colonization in diffusion of Roman culture. It is striking that the planting of Latin and Roman colonies, which had been so intense between the key year of 338 and the beginning of the Great War with Carthage, then virtually stopped for two generations, until 200 (Scheidel [2004], 12): the Romans are preoccupied with massive overseas wars at this time, but the pause reveals how closely tied to Italian conquest the program of colonization was (Scheidel [2004], 22).

105. Feeney (2005), 237–38, with references to Dench (1995), 74–76, on the various Roman strategies for "barbarianizing" the other Italians. Such strategies were also used by other Italian peoples, who were able to present themselves as the "Greeks" in the "Greek/barbarian" paradigm: see Dench (1995), 12; Curti, Dench, and Patterson (1996), 184–85.

106. J. Z. Smith (1990), 51.

107. See Feeney (2007a), 98 for another use of Smith's model, in connection with Roman synchronisms of their city's foundation-date with those of Greek cities.

108. Wallace-Hadrill (2008), 28 (original emphasis).

109. Wallace-Hadrill (2008), 19.

110. Purcell (1994), 403.

111. Purcell (1994), 403, speaking of the "epoch after Alexander," when Rome "attained true modernity, the latest in state management, going further even than Syracuse and Carthage in bringing to the west the new methods of the hellenistic age."

112. Weinstock (1957); Crawford (1993), 45; Burnett (1986), 73.

113. Burnett (1986), 73; see Toynbee (1965), 2. 438 n. 2 for interesting discussion of the phases of Roman shaving.

114. Burnett (1986), 70–71; cf. Dench (1995), 73–74, and (2005), 97, drawing out the implications for Athens "arguably [being] used as a model for an 'imperial' power."

115. Purcell (2003), 22, with convincing speculation on even longer-standing Roman receptiveness to Athenian ideology, going back to the expulsion of the kings and the establishment of the triad honored on the Capitoline (25–26, 30–32): the third century, in this respect as in others, sees a redirection and an intensification of an established phenomenon. On the related third-century Greek intellectual establishment of fifth- and fourth-century Athens as the benchmark for "Hellenism," see Connolly (2007), 21–26; the fixing of fifth-century Athens as a peak of literary history is already clear in the Parian Marble of the mid-third century (Rotstein [2014], 154–55).

116. Purcell (2003), 25.

117. For speculation on the significance of the statues, see Curti (2000), 81. Note Cornell (1995), 398, on how the Romans in this period were "trying to come to terms with the position in which they found themselves. The enthusiastic adoption of Hellenism was itself a part of this search for an identity."

118. Feeney (1998), 51–52, with reference to Garnsey and Saller (1987), 170, and, on the early part of the third century in particular, Weinstock (1957). Note how, once again, the proposed periodization of Flower (2010) dovetails very neatly with a vital watershed that I have identified on other grounds: this crucial phase of (especially religious) Hellenization coincides with her "Republic of the *nobiles* 1," whose onset she places in the year 300, although for quite different reasons (52).

119. Burkert (1985), 177–78, on Cybele; R. Parker (1996), 178, on Asclepius as "in general an 'imported god,' one brought in by states that had heard of his fame."

120. Burkert (1985), 179; my thanks to Marco Fantuzzi for advice on these cults.

121. Gallini (1973), 186.

122. See Bernstein (1998), 223–25, 227–29 for clear statements of the importance of seeing the development of the Roman games in general as a feature of the intense Hellenizing of the period; cf. Dumont and François-Garelli (1998), 16.

123. Wissowa (1912), 462–63.

124. Bernstein (1998), 234: "Natürlich hatten die 364 in Rom eingeführten *ludi scae-nici* von Anfang an unter griechischen Einflüssen gestanden."
125. Well stressed by La Penna (1979), 6; cf. Mayer (1995), 289–95 for the canonical frame of mind brought to bear by the first practitioners.
126. Easterling (1993), 562; cf. Easterling (1997), 212–13.
127. Jocelyn (1969), 8–9; Rawson (1989), 428; Manuwald (2011), 22.
128. Jocelyn (1969), 9; Cicero picks out the canonical three Attic tragedians as the models for Roman adaptation (*Acad.* 1. 10). Hose (1999b), 121–22 well shows how the marked concentration on the three tragedians in the first three Roman poets (Livius, Naevius, Ennius) loosens up with Pacuvius (five out of a dozen titles are from post-classical models) and Accius (eight out of forty-five, with seven unassignable); cf. Jocelyn (1969), 9. On the vigorous Sicilian drama available to them if they had wanted it as a model, see Dearden (2004), 126–29; Bosher (2013).
129. Potter (2012), 144; cf. Nervegna (2013), 59–60 on how "Roman dramatists drew from the repertoire of travelling Greek actors, evidently selecting the plays that had most appeal for audiences—the well-tested theatrical classics."
130. Jocelyn (1969), 9; cf. Csapo (2010), 39 on the evidence for the canonical three tragedians in tragedy-related vase-paintings, with Hanink (2014), 82 and n. 75 for further references; Potter (2012), 143–44 on new comedy. For the role of the theatrical companies in fixing the repertory's canon, see Easterling (1997) and Nervegna (2013), and in general on revivals of classic drama Nervegna (2007). On the canonization of Athenian drama in the third century, as part of a general canonization of "classical" Athenian culture, see Connolly (2007), 23–26; in fact, the tragic canon of the big three specifically is enshrined by the Athenians even earlier, in the third quarter of the fourth century, as argued by Hanink (2014).
131. On the "classics" as standard items in the repertory of the third-century Greek troupes, see Gratwick (1982a), 77, and the important discussion of Nervegna (2013), 58–60. See Cribiore (2001), 198–99 for the importance of tragedy, above all Euripides, in the standard Hellenistic education syllabus, and 199–200 for the popularity of Menander; see Dunsch (1999), 121, for this fundamental syllabus being in use at Rome before the end of the Hannibalic war, and 121–24 for a general case for the sophisticated knowledge of Hellenistic literary critical terminology from the same period onward (a point to which we return in Chapter 6).
132. Revermann (1999–2000); Hanink (2014), 68–71.
133. Leo (1913), 47; Feeney (2005), 229.
134. Whitmarsh (2004), 227.

135. Nervegna (2013), 6, well stresses that "Menander owed his canonization not to the scholarly activities pursued in the Library of Alexandria, but to actors and their repertoires"; but this initial phase had to be supplemented by scholarly activity in order for the transmission of entire works to carry on, as stressed by Easterling (1997), 223.

Chapter 5 A STAGE FOR AN IMPERIAL POWER

1. Crawford (1990), 94: "Sembra anche possibile sostenere che l'acquisizione della Sicilia Occidentale abbio generato a Roma in certa misura la consapevolezza di possedere un impero." See Leigh (2010), 269 on the "maritime moment" represented by Rome's crossing the straits of Messina in 264 and construction of her first major war fleet in 261, with "the perception that something very drastic had happened, that Rome had changed, had done so in a crucial way, and had done so very quickly." I am fully in agreement with Habinek (1998), 35–36 on the crucial links between the new literature and the imperial moment, though I date this moment at least a generation earlier.
2. Leo (1913), 47 ("kein zufälliges Anfangsjahr").
3. Frank (1928), 696–97, (1930), 70–71; Seaman (1954), 115; Toynbee (1965), 2. 421; Rawson (1989), 428; Gruen (1990), 79–92; Horsfall (1993a), 798; Bernstein (1998), 236; Blänsdorf (2000), 145–46 (skeptical); Suerbaum (2002), 27 (more guarded), 97 (more open); Dearden (2004), a particularly important argument; La Penna (2006), 15; Leigh (2010).
4. Horsfall (1993a), 798; Bernstein (1998), 235–36; Blänsdorf (2000), 145–46. On the continuing vibrancy of Greek theater culture in South Italy, see Rawson (1991), 468–74; Manuwald (2011), 21, 26–30.
5. Vassallo (2012), 225 on "the profound and refined cultural *koine*" in Sicily, where five of the twelve identified theaters from our period are in the Carthaginian sphere, including four cities (Segesta, Iato, Hippana, and Solunto), which were originally not Greek foundations (224); cf. Dearden (2004), 122–23 on the wide spread of theaters throughout Sicily from the fourth century; Spatafora (2013), 43 on the general artistic and architectural vocabulary shared among the diverse peoples of the island in the same period; Tribulato (2012a), 20 on the application of the theory of the "middle ground" to Sicilian interactions back into the Archaic and Classical period. Even linguistically, the Greek-speaking inhabitants of Sicily developed their distinctive "Sicilian Doric koina" during the late Classical and Hellenistic period: see Mimbrera (2012).
6. Especially well stressed by Dearden (2004).

7. Represented very pejoratively in a decline narrative by Livy, 25. 40. 1–2: see Rossi (2000); on the fights over the memory of this moment, see Flower (2003), Gowers (2010), 78–82. For general discussion of Sicily's crucial role in mediating "cultural exchange between the Roman and Hellenic cultures," see Cirucci (2013) (quotation from 142)—though even this paper gives little space to the period before Marcellus' capture of Syracuse.

8. Coarelli (1985), 12–21, dating the rebuilding to 263–252.

9. Coarelli (1985), 19–20.

10. Morel (1989), 482–83.

11. See Prag (2010a) on the "kinship diplomacy" prevalent in Sicily that Rome learned to participate in after entering the island.

12. See the nuanced discussion in Prag (2010b) of the formation of a stereotyped portrayal of a "barbarian" Carthage by some western Greeks in Sicily, together with an equally nuanced discussion of the considerably more messy ethnic and political situation masked by this discourse; on this model in Sicily, see Feeney (2007a), 44–52; on its adoption by the Romans, see Feeney (2007a), 52–57; Miles (2010), 117–21; Prag (2010b), 68–71.

13. Feeney (2007a), 56–57 for discussion of the implications of the Gigantomachic ecphrasis prominently on display in the early section of Naevius' *Bellum Punicum* (fr. 8).

14. Vian (1952), 285–86; Feeney (1998), 54 on the Gigantomachic statue set up by the brothers Ogulnii on the temple of Jupiter Optimus Maximus (Liv. 10. 23. 12).

15. Zonaras 8. 9.12; see Weinstock (1971), 16; Gruen (1992), 45; Prag (2010a), 186–89.

16. Feeney (2007a), 56; cf. Walbank (1957–1979), 1. 42 on the Greek historians of the Hannibalic War, "who wrote mainly from the Punic point of view"; Miles (2010), 16, 244. For suggestive remarks on the Great War in Sicily as formative for the Romans' historiographical self-consciousness, arising from debates with the Sicilian-based pro-Carthaginian histories, see Hanell (1958), 149: "Aus der Reaktion der sizilischen Griechen Rom gegenüber im ersten Punischen Krieg ist römische Geschichte als literarisches Phänomen hervorgegangen."

17. I do not know that this is susceptible of anything like proof, but it is attractive to posit that the Romans learned in general from the Sicilian Greeks how to practice a bold independence from the "mainland" in literature and culture: see the admirable arguments for this Sicilian capacity in Willi (2008) (Archaic and Classical periods) and (2012b) (Hellenistic period).

18. Such an interpretation of Naevius is by no means invalidated by the fact that he wrote the poem many years after the Great War, almost certainly during the Hannibalic war: see Fraenkel (1935), 632; Suerbaum (2002), 112 on Cic. *Sen.* 49–50.

19. Feeney (2007a), 57, with reference to the important arguments of Rawson (1989), 434, 438, 446.

20. Gruen (1990), 82; cf. 84, victory "would be marked by elevation of the *ludi* to a cultural event that announced Rome's participation in the intellectual world of the Greeks"; Bernstein (1998), 237–38; Leigh (2010), 278.

21. Probably: our sources (Varro, *Ling.* 5. 165; Liv. 1. 19. 3) date the occasion to the end of the Great War, but give the consul Manlius the *praenomen* Titus, and this man was consul not in 241 but in 235. For discussion, see Horsfall (2000), 355–56.

22. See Chapter 4, text accompanying note 11.

23. See Chapter 4, text accompanying note 132.

24. I thank one of the Press readers for suggesting the development of this point.

25. Hieron's mimetic rivalry is the main theme of the important study of Lehmler (2005), a theme adumbrated already (as pointed out by González [2006]) in Berve (1959), 74–75 and Finley (1968), 121; cf. De Sensi Sestito (1977) and R. J. A. Wilson (2013), 80–99 on the cultural achievements of Hieron. See Wolf and Lorber (2011) for compelling numismatic evidence for the tightness of the ties between Hieron and Ptolemy II (a reference I owe to Jonathan Prag).

26. Dearden (2004), 130.

27. Curti (2001), 20–21; cf. Lehmler (2005), 151 for Hieron's ambitious displays in fortification, which were to cause Marcellus so much trouble in the next war.

28. Well pointed out by Dumont and François-Garelli (1998), 15–16, remarking on the importance of Classical Athens and contemporary Syracuse as models (the fortification of Rome, however, had taken place much earlier, after the Gallic sack of 390). Comprehensive discussion of Hieron's ambitions in all these fields in Lehmler (2005), with condensed presentation in Veit (2013) (the same author).

29. Bernstein (1998), 237–38; Lehmler (2005), 206–7.

30. De Sensi Sestito (1977), 168–70; Lehmler (2005), 199–205.

31. Kowalzig (2008) 141.

32. For the start date of 238 see J. R. Green (2008), 69; Marconi (2012), 189; Veit (2013), 33; on the theater in general, Lehmler (2005), 122–35.

33. See Chapter 4, text accompanying notes 44–45.

34. Marconi (2012), 189 on the dates.

35. See esp. Bernstein (1998), 294–98; Boyle (2006), 22–23; Manuwald (2011), 57–62.

36. Bernstein (1998), 297–98; Goldberg (1998), 9–13; Manuwald (2011), 60–61.

37. Gruen (1992), 209; Rüpke (2012), 47.

38. On such associations with Greek and especially Sicilian theaters, see Champion (2004), 217–18; Kowalzig (2008), 143–44; Marconi (2012), 185–87. On the Roman reaction, see Dumont and François-Garelli (1998), 19; Blänsdorf (2000), 154.

39. Bernstein (1998), 267. In general, on how "a voluntary and selective Hellenization pushed [Rome] up to the international level," see Veyne (1979), 8.

40. As stressed by T. P. Wiseman in a lecture at Columbia University, 10 September, 2011.

41. My thanks to the Press reader who suggested this important perspective, of the Games as "a tool of imperial conquest."

42. Both elements highlighted as possible factors behind the innovation to the *Ludi* of 240 by Gildenhard (2010), 159–60.

43. To adapt the words of Curti (2001), 20, who is not referring specifically to the reform of 240 but speaking generally of the transformation of Italy under the impact of Rome in the third century.

44. Wissowa (1912), 462—a factor rightly stressed by Gruen (1990), 83 in connection with the reform of 240.

45. Flower (2010), 24–25: "It is . . . the *nobiles* who presided over the development of Latin literature (in both prose and poetry), of Roman art, and of the Latin language, which is often said to reach its 'classical' stage near the beginning of the first century." Note Manuwald (2011), 352 n. 10, pointing out how well the main rhythms of Republican drama fit with the periodizations suggested by Flower.

46. A key theme of Bayart (2005), as already quoted in the Introduction; see esp. 95: "we identify ourselves less with respect to membership in a community or a culture than with respect to the communities and cultures with which we have relations."

47. As discussed in the Introduction. Further discussion in Feeney (1998), 68–69; cf. Wallace-Hadrill (2008), 24; Ulf (2009), esp. 84; Bhabha (1994), 2: "It is in the emergence of the interstices—the overlap and displacement of domains of difference—that the intersubjective and collective experiences of nationness, community interest, or cultural value are negotiated."

48. Such a counterfactual is very seldom canvassed, so far as I discover: see, however, Mariotti (1965/2000), 7–8; Manuwald (2011), 19.

49. Assmann (1996), 33.
50. Toynbee (1965), 2. 421-22; Momigliano (1975), 7-8 ("The Mediterranean world had found a common language"). Bowersock (1990) remains a definitive treatment, concentrating on late antiquity.
51. I quote from the summary of Bowersock's overall argument in Assmann (1996), 33-34.
52. Toynbee (1965), 2. 432.
53. They always had been: see Feeney (1998), 26-27, 64-65 for how characteristic it is of the Romans from early times to maintain a sense of difference and distance in their adaptations from Greece. See Mariotti (1965/2000), 8-9 for their choices in 240.
54. Canfora (1994), 25-28.
55. Morel (1989), 515, using an analogy with modern Japan (quoted in Feeney [2005], 238). On the ultimately uncategorizable variety of Roman responses to Hellenism, see A. Barchiesi (2009).
56. This description of the model of Taussig (1993) comes from Feeney (1998), 67-68.
57. Gruen (1992), 52-83 on the Elder Cato; Wallace-Hadrill (2008), 23-25, 448-49.
58. Dench (2005), 314-15, on how "the use of Latin in literature" is "a deliberate choice that has to do with Roman imperial self-definition, a decisive non-Greek that may be used to emphasize the process of 'translating' the Greek cultural heritage: Rome is simultaneously a cultural heir of the Greek world and set at an angle, at a slight distance from that world, as befits a new ruling Mediterranean power."
59. Toynbee (1965), 2. 429 n. 4: "They wanted to be in the Hellenic world, but this on their own terms"; cf. Jocelyn (1990), 597; Canfora (1994), 34-36.
60. Chapter 1, text accompanying notes 137-42.
61. Rawson (1985), 267-68; Wallace-Hadrill (1988), 227, 232-33; cf. the brief but penetrating remarks of Jocelyn (1990), 621; and Horsfall (1993a), 807-9, with Henderson (1999), 65 on the Roman interaction with Greece involving processes of systematic exclusion.
62. Wallace-Hadrill (1988), 227, referring to Rawson (1985), 156. Cf. Corbeill (2001), 266-67; and Gildenhard (2007a), 136-40 on the key text of Cicero, *Tusc.* 1. 4-5, on the different Greek and Roman attitudes to music, geometry, and mathematics. Horace's *Epistle to Augustus* focuses hard on this issue: Feeney (2002), 187.
63. Chapter 1, text accompanying note 139. The later astronomical poem of Manilius is a remarkable intellectual achievement: see Volk (2009), who points

out that the Latin prose treatments of this subject are by contrast not "technically sophisticated" and do not enter "into the technical details of Hellenistic astronomy" (55).

64. For this whole perspective, I am indebted to Wallace-Hadrill (1988), 233–34.

65. On the apprenticeship-style education in place for other skills (medicine, architecture, e.g.), see Horsfall (1991), 61–64: these were not part of what an élite Roman thought it proper for his son to learn. Compare how important it is to Livy, in his account of the development of the *ludi scaenici,* to explain how young Roman men of status stopped taking part in the *ludi* once the singing and dancing became professionalized (*postquam ludus in artem paulatim uerterat,* Liv. 7. 2. 11): see P. G. McC. Brown (2014), 404.

66. On the expulsion of philosophers in 161 and 154 (or perhaps 173), see Gruen (1990), 177–78; Horsfall (1993a), 811–12; on the banning of the Latin *rhetores* by the censors in 92, see Suet. *Gramm.* 25. 2, with Kaster (1995), 273–74 for discussion of various speculations about their motives; Suerbaum (2002), 550–52.

67. Hutchinson (2013), 33 n. 12 comparing these Roman actions to the expulsion of all philosophers by one of the Antiochuses of Syria reported in Athen. 12. 547a–b.

68. Cf. Dench (1995), 74–76, 98, 105. Habinek (1998), chapter 4 has interesting remarks on the field of literature as a venue for "the jockeying for power between Rome and Italians" in the late Republic; this is a process that goes back to the third century.

69. On this process, see Henderson (1999), 42.

70. A major theme of Goldberg (2005).

71. Cf. Habinek (1998), 100: "Mechanisms for the consumption and distribution of literature that were appropriate for a Romanocentric enterprise were taxed by the expansion of the culture and of the reading community"; cf. Woolf (2009), 50.

72. Rawson (1991), 474, citing Cic. *De or.* 3. 43 and *Arch.* 5; cf. Wiseman (1983/1987).

73. Dench (2005), 351.

74. Corbeill (2001), 261; cf. Denecke (2013), 24–25 for the contrast with the tight organization of education by the Japanese state.

75. See Glucker and Burnett (2012), xi for this comparative case; cf. Momigliano (1975), 10–11 on how distinctive the Jews and Romans both were in their sense of superiority in their response to Hellenism; and Osterloh (2008), 171 on the way that "Judean elites were not passive recipients of foreign influences, but rather took an active role in the appropriation of Hellenistic and Roman sociopolitical and cultural attributes." My thanks to John Dillery, Tessa Rajak, and Tim Whitmarsh for making me think harder about the Jewish example.

76. Rajak (2009), 103.
77. On these authors, see conveniently Berthelot (2010), 183–84, with Dillery (2014), 357–85 for Demetrius; for the general background, Gruen (1998), chapter 4 ("Scriptural stories in new guise"); Rajak (2009), chapter 6, esp. 222–25.
78. On the novellas, see Wills (1995).
79. 2 Maccabees appears to be a Greek composition, not a translation from Hebrew or Aramaic. My thanks to John Dillery and Tessa Rajak for assistance on 1 and 2 Maccabees.
80. On the audience, see Millar (1993), 499–500.
81. Rajak (2002), 176.
82. Rajak (2009), 153.
83. Important remarks in Goldberg (2007b), 579–82.
84. Jocelyn (2000), 327.
85. Rüpke (2012), 48; he continues: "Nobles and gods seemed to have the same taste."
86. Gildenhard (2010), 160; see too the compelling speculation about the popular appeal of Roman drama (based on the actual evidence from the far better documented late Republic) in Horsfall (2003), 58–61.
87. Overview, and criticism, of such approaches in Gildenhard (2010), 161–64; Manuwald (2011), 134–35. I look forward to the publication of the Princeton dissertation by Brigitte Libby on the topic of the Trojan myth in Latin literature.
88. "[T]ragedies . . . discussed the legitimacy of rulers, conflicts between conquerors and conquered, the question of the significance of gods and seers or philosophical issues; and they included situations such as the aftermath of a war, confrontation with foreigners or struggles within families," Manuwald (2011), 135; cf. La Penna (1979), 56; Boyle (2006), 61–63, 86–87; Gildenhard (2010), 161–64 for criticism of overly precise identification. Leigh (2004), esp. 20–23 convincingly makes analogous claims for the nature of the points of reference we should be aiming to establish between the Roman experience and translated comedy.
89. Gildenhard (2010), 164–67 (quotation from 161); note the comparison between Rome and the Hellenistic cities "where tragedy played an important role in the entertainment culture, but only possessed a marginal political relevance" (166); cf. the criticisms of this schematism in the review of Cowan (2011) and the remarks of Henderson (1999), 43 against reading Terence as "just entertainment." Gildenhard (2010), 165 n. 41 himself expresses reservations about the "political dimension of the [Athenian] plays."

90. Cf. Revermann (1999–2000), 466 on how important studies of reception and reperformance will be for "an evolution of our field beyond the Athenocentric civic-ideology approach."

91. Hanink (2014), 219; she builds there on the important arguments of Heath (2009), 472–74 on the way that international tragic performance will have been one factor predisposing Aristotle to seeing tragedy as having a "universal" character.

92. See Chapter 7, section entitled "New Horizons."

93. McElduff (2013), 78; she continues: "The conquest of Greek forms of drama via translation, which made those forms and their authors more known to the Roman people, paralleled Roman conquest of Greece itself, which resulted in greater knowledge of and control over Greece."

94. McElduff (2013), 78; cf. Gruen (1990), chapter 4 for the crucial role of Plautus in mediating Greek culture to Rome.

95. Gildenhard (2010), 172.

96. A test case for the aphorism of Chaudhuri (1999), 22: "Translation, the ground and medium of cultural exchange, is organically invested with destabilizing and distancing factors."

97. In general, on the theme of "Greece or Rome?" see Moore (1998), chapter 3.

98. See Vogt-Spira (1996), 23–25, Moore (1998), 56–58 on the power of these lines.

99. On the power of Plautus' regular ironic use of "barbarian" to allude to Latin and Roman (e.g., *Asin.* 11; *Trin.* 19), see Moore (1998), 54–55.

100. Henderson (1999), chapter 2; Leigh (2004), chapter 5.

101. Stressed in this connection by Cowan (2010), 41.

102. If Traina (2013) is correct, then Plautus' use of *Maccus* to refer to himself will have a connotation of a third language, since Oscan is the language of the Atellan farces for which, on this hypothesis, Plautus will already have been famous.

103. As Stephen Hinds suggests to me. Such acknowledgments of language-difference are extremely rare in Greek epic or tragedy: see Chapter 1, text accompanying notes 88–90.

104. N. W. Slater (2000), 317.

105. See N. W. Slater (2000), 321–22.

106. Vogt-Spira (2000), esp. 273; Cowan (2010).

107. Cowan (2010), 49.

108. Revermann (1999–2000), 465–66.

109. As suggested by Revermann (1999–2000), 462 in the case of a Macedonian staging of Euripides' *Bacchae*.

110. Ennius is upping the ante with his introduction of the word *barbarica*, for the word βαρβαρικός "does not occur in Attic tragedy" (Jocelyn [1969], 249).

111. So D. Fowler (2000), 52–53, likewise against attempts to downplay the frisson of Ennius' language.

112. Toynbee (1965), 2. 429 n. 4; Jocelyn (1990), 597; Gruen (1992), 6–51; Canfora (1994), 34–35.

113. Feeney (2007a), 37, 55.

114. Chapter 2, text accompanying note 99.

115. We see a parallel with the histories of Manetho and Berossus in this regard.

116. Feeney (1998), 75.

117. On the "mobile sensibility" of Greenblatt (1980), chapter 6, generated in the contact zones between Western Europe and the New World, see Feeney (1998), 69–70, with reference to N. W. Slater (1993), 120.

118. Gruen (1990), 79–123; Gruen (1992), esp. chapter 5 on the theater.

119. J. Z. Smith (1982), xii, quoted in Feeney (1998), 8.

120. Gratwick (1982a), 81; Bernstein (1998), 245–51; Blänsdorf in Suerbaum (2002), 146–49; Manuwald (2011), 43–45; P. G. McC. Brown (2014), 406; Franko (2014), 410–14.

121. Bernstein (1998), 250–51.

122. Rawson (1991), 477–79; Franko (2014), 414.

123. Reitzenstein (1918), 248–49; cf. Waszink (1960), 19–20.

124. Franko (2013), 345.

125. Translation of Olson (2011).

126. Gruen (1992), 215–18, to whom Franko (2013) is reasonably close, with his suggestion that we have here a Plautine aesthetic at work, as "Anicius crowds the stage with a boisterous conflation of Greek and Roman elements" (343) in a spirit of "farce or parody" (347); Günther (2002); cf. MacMullen (1980), 5, suggesting that Anicius' idea was to get his Greek artists "to perform like two armies on the stage, to illustrate his victorious campaigns in Thrace" [*sic:* actually, Illyria].

127. Reitzenstein (1918), 248–49; cf. Bernstein (1998), 25–27, 126 on performances of this kind in Etruria and Rome. Such performances may be glimpsed much further south: see E. G. D. Robinson (2004), 206, referring to the evidence published by Pontrandolfo (1992) "for figures wearing half-masks in Paestan wall-paintings as early as the mid-4th century BC, where pugilists appear to be miming their fight in the context of funeral games, accompanied by a double flute."

128. This would then be an example of what Edmondson (1999), 88 calls "the adaptation of indigenous spectacles through contact with exogenous cultural

forms"; cf. Goldberg (1995), 39 on how it was "a Roman show fashioned from Greek elements." But, after all, as Marco Fantuzzi points out to me, "Many experiments are failures; but not all failures are experimental."

129. See Chapter 4, text accompanying note 11. Edmondson (1999), 79 compares Aemilius' games to the Nikephoria at Pergamum, which had recently been "reorganized into a major *stephanites agon* by Eumenes II in 182–181 to commemorate his victory over Prusias I of Bithynia and the Galatians"; cf. 79 with n. 27 for how Aemilius' victory games in Greece became a template for later Roman victors, including L. Lucullus and M. Antonius.

130. Flower (2004a), 328–29.

131. Edmondson (1999), 80–81 on the burgeoning scale and competitiveness of spectacles at Rome in this period, and in general on the international scale of the competition.

132. Edmondson (1999), 87; cf. Gibson (2012), 265 on the international dialogue in play here.

Chapter 6 A LITERATURE IN THE LATIN LANGUAGE

1. Rüpke (2012), 208 ("[b]y the second century").

2. Gratwick (1982a), 81.

3. On the importance of keeping "prose" in the category of "literature," see Sci-arrino (2011), 17.

4. To reprise the insights of Hinds (1998), 63–74.

5. Compagnon (2004), 27; cf. Laird (2006), 25: "The problem of defining literature has perhaps been exaggerated: it can be regarded as a synthetic, evaluative category, the development of which is historically contingent." Compagnon (2004), 28 cuts the Gordian knot: "literature is an inevitable tautology. *Literature* is *literature*, whatever the authorities (professors, publishers) include in literature."

6. E.g., Goldhill (1999); Whitmarsh (2004), 1–5.

7. Ford (1991), 127. The very important recent study of Roman (2014) argues for "autonomy" of a certain kind as a valuable perspective for the study of Latin literature from the first century BCE on. See the "brisk note on the inescapable word 'literature'" in Hutchinson (2013), 6 n. 2.

8. Hermans (1999), 139 provides a lucid introduction to the theory of Luhmann (1995) of literature as a "differentiated social system," with "a degree of autonomy with regard to other systems such as religion, politics, or education."

9. Feeney (2005), referring to the studies of Bonner (1977) and Kaster (1988) for accounts of these developed institutions; cf. Goldberg (2005), 41–43, and esp. 41

for the work performed on Ennius' *Annales* in the first century as constitutive of the category of "literature." My working definition is very close to that of Habinek (2009), 116, for whom "Rome did not develop a literary culture in the sense of professional authors, a preserved and transmitted canon, and intertextual reference and critique until the late third century B.C."

10. Parker (2009), 214 n. 120, referring to finds of the *Aeneid* at Vindolanda (9. 473), and on Masada (4. 9); cf. Millar (2002–2006), 1. 31 on these *Aeneid* finds as evidence of the imperial reach of Latin literature, even while stressing the lack of impact of such literature on the inhabitants of the Greek-speaking East.

11. A desperately tangled tale: see Gruen (1990), 87–91, and the more skeptical Horsfall (1976), who allows for at least a *collegium poetarum* associated with the *aedes Herculis Musarum* from around 179 (86). Rüpke (2012), 86–87 crucially links this development to a new kind of systematic differentiation in response to the new scenic tradition.

12. Citroni (2003), 175–76; Goldberg (2005), chapter 2.

13. Cf. Lowrie (2007), 414 on the many factors already in place by "the beginning of the second century" that qualify for "a goodly portion of . . . [the] criteria" stipulated by Goldberg (2005), as necessary for a "literature." The critique of Rüpke (2000) by Gildenhard (2001) makes telling points, but Rüpke is correct to stress a degree of differentiation in Roman society in response to the new initiatives; further, only by overemphasizing a certain kind of aesthetic autonomy as part of a definition of "literary system" can Gildenhard argue that Rüpke's stress on the political dimension to Roman literary activities rules the literary out of consideration as a system. In general, I find much to agree with in the nuanced discussion of Lowrie (2009), 52–54.

14. Compagnon (2004), 16. There is much of value in Miner (1978), who distinguishes similarly between the "literary system" and the "critical system."

15. Important general remarks in Conte (1994), 7.

16. Such is the major argument of Goldberg (2005).

17. See Chapter 4, text accompanying notes 131–33.

18. Possanza (2004), 47; cf. Leo (1913), 59 on Andronicus: "es war nur eine Literatur"; Kerkhecker (2001), 39: "Literatur heißt für sie: Auseinandersetzung mit den Griechen."

19. Russell (1981), 44; cf. Kerkhecker (2001), esp. 39–40; Citroni (2003), 171–80; Farrell (2005), 427.

20. Barthes (1971), 170, in the translation of C. Cosman (Compagnon [2004] 16).

21. R. F. Thomas (1993), 204.

22. Important argument in Citroni (2003), 171–80.

23. It is likely that the versatile Ion wrote a comedy in addition to his more prominent tragedies (Schol. Ar. *Pax* 835–7 refers to "comedies")—not to mention "satyr dramas, dithyrambs, elegies, lyric poems (paeans, encomia, hymns), and works in prose" (Fantuzzi and Hunter (2004), 17: see their discussion in the same context of Ion's paradigmatic role as the master of many genres in Callimachus' thirteenth *Iambus*). My thanks to Marco Fantuzzi for help with Ion.

24. Gratwick (1982a), 82; Taplin (1993), 92.

25. Denecke (2013), 28.

26. I quote this sentence from Stephen Hinds, *per litteras*. On the twinned libraries of the Augustan age, and their far-reaching implications, see Horsfall (1993b); on the twinned libraries as indicative of an underlying conception of two separate literary histories, see Hutchinson (2013), 12–13.

27. Fraenkel (1931), 605.

28. Russell (1981), 44; cf. Kenney (1982), 5; Fantham (1990), 220; Jocelyn (1990), 620. Even more radically, as I shall argue in Chapter 8, there was at Rome no phase of preliterary "oral" composition and transmission of literature: the Roman project is born embedded in the procedures of the literary.

29. Zenodotus of Ephesus, the first librarian at Alexandria from *c.* 284, and Aristophanes of Byzantium, head of the Library from *c.* 194, both produced editions of Homer with some exegetical dimension; yet it was the work of Aristarchus of Samothrace, head of the Library from *c.* 153, that began the main current flowing into our surviving exegetical scholia.

30. Fränkel (1932), 306 has convinced most scholars that Livius Andronicus was using pre-Aristarchan exegetical notes when he incorporated into his translation of *Od.* 8. 378–79 a gloss that now survives as a scholion on that passage: on Livius fr. 20, see Lennartz (1994), 155–56; Possanza (2004), 53–54. In general, on the translator-poets' use of such explanatory material in their writings, see Mariotti (1965/2000), chapter 1; Feeney (1991), 100–101, with earlier references; Lennartz (1994), esp. 144–51; Possanza (2004), 53–56.

31. Gildenhard (2007b), 76 n. 16, reprising a theme first sounded by Clausen (1964); cf. R. F. Thomas (1993), 198. See Goldberg (1995), 91–92 for a discriminating discussion.

32. Important discussions of this point in Mariotti (1965/2000), 9–10; cf. Possanza (2004), 73 n. 74, 74 n. 81.

33. On the implications of *dicti studiosus*, see Skutsch (1968), 5–7; Suerbaum (1968), 271–75; Kerkhecker (2001), 76–77; cf. the important overviews of Ennius' quasi-Callimachean intellectual and generic range in Kerkhecker (2001), 48–50;

Acosta-Hughes and Stephens (2012), 207–10. For particularly striking examples of bold philological play in Ennius' *Annales,* inspired by Alexandrian scholarship, see Zetzel (1974); cf. Skutsch (1968), 6–7 and (1985), 8–9.

34. Important discussion in Acosta-Hughes and Stephens (2012), 208–10.

35. Acosta-Hughes and Stephens (2012), 171, 202–3.

36. Harder (2012), 1. 41, 64. Fantuzzi and Hunter (2004), 462–63 rightly stress that Callimachus is not for Ennius the pervasive model for a certain kind of aesthetic that he later became in the Roman tradition.

37. Important discussion in Kerkhecker (2001), 63–66, with full references; cf. Lowrie (2007), 414 on how "Ennius' allusions to Callimachus mean not only that the Alexandrian poets belonged to the category of literature in the alluding poet's conception, but that he also conceived of his own work as literary."

38. Important discussion of this development in Schwindt (2000); on the "archival sensibility" as described by Whitmarsh (2004), see above Chapter 4, note 134.

39. Degl'Innocenti Pierini (1977), 55–73; Rawson (1985), 268–71; Courtney (1993), 56–64; Dangel (1995), 47–54; Schwindt (2000), 52–58; E. Stärk in Suerbaum (2002), 163–65.

40. Degli'Innocenti Pierini (1977), 58–67; Dangel (1995), 48, 382–86. For the *Didascalica* as a prose work, see Courtney (1993), 60. All the other works of Accius are in verse of one kind or another, as are the literary-critical works of Volcacius Sedigitus, Porcius Licinus, and Valerius Soranus, discussed below, so it would make sense for Accius' *Didascalica* also to be a verse work: but Courtney raises many doubts.

41. Degli'Innocenti Pierini (1977), 68–73; Dangel (1995), 51, 386–89.

42. Prisc. *GL* 2. 30. 12 K = fr. 3 Funaioli; cf. Lucilius 351–55 Marx. See Dangel (1995), 51–54.

43. For the issues, see Chapter 3, text accompanying note 29.

44. Leo (1913), 390–91: "schon im Plan dieses Buches tat sich das erwähnte Bewußtsein der neugewonnen Kulturstellung Kund" (391).

45. Gell. 15. 24 (fr. 1 Courtney); Schwindt (2000), 59–64; Suerbaum (2002), 291–94.

46. Schwindt (2000), 58.

47. Courtney (1993), 82–92; Schwindt (2000), 64–70; Suerbaum (2002), 288–91; Welsh (2011).

48. Gell. 17. 21.44 (fr. 1 Courtney), on the arrival of the Muse; Courtney (1993), 87–91 on the reconstructions from the Suetonian Life of Terence.

49. Leo (1913), 362–68; Zetzel (1981), 10–26; Rawson (1985), 269–70, 273, 277; Kaster (1995), 68–70; Suerbaum (2002), 552–57; Goldberg (2005), 60–62.

50. Zetzel (1981), 25; cf. Goldberg (2005), 62.

51. The history of these developments given by Suetonius in his *De Grammaticis et Rhetoribus* establishes a crucial turning point with the visit to Rome of Crates of Mallos in 168 (2. 1). Yet this glamorized "first contact," when a representative of one of the prestigious Hellenistic schools of learning first set foot in Rome, distracts attention from the long-standing familiarity with the practices of Hellenistic learning in Rome: Leo (1913), 351–68; Zetzel (1981), 10–11; Kaster (1995), 62.

52. Leo (1913), 356–57: "Aber es war doch wieder etwas vollkommen Neues, daß die griechischen Forschungsmethoden auf eine andre Sprache und in einer andren Sprache geschriebene Werke angewendet werden sollten."

53. Goldberg (2005) is crucial on the role of the curriculum; Rawson (1985), 98: "Only in one subject, but that the most basic of all, *grammatica,* does it become hard to distinguish Greeks and Greek scholarship clearly from Roman."

54. Waszink (1960), 33, 26; cf. Manuwald (2011), 137, 196: "from the second Roman dramatist onwards a Roman dramatic tradition was added to the Greek one, and later poets were confronted with both"; Hutchinson (2013), 13.

55. Hutchinson (2013), 14; see Baraz (2012), 114 for this perspective in Cicero.

56. Standard discussion in McKeown (1987), 37–45.

57. On this supplementation of the cult epithet, see Feeney (1991), 128.

58. Cf. the attractive arguments of Leigh (2010), 276 for the view that "the works of Livius and Naevius have a great deal in common, and . . . their poetic reimagination of what it means to sail the seas between Carthage, Sicily, and Rome leaves its mark on the opening books of the *Aeneid.*"

59. Goldberg (1995), 89–90 on *Annales* frr. 2–11 Sk.

60. Kerkhecker (2001), 66; Goldschmidt (2013), 55–56; Hutchinson (2013), 36. On the significance of the metrical choice as a move against the Saturnian, the previous meter of Latin epic, see, on the first line of the new epic, *Musae quae pedibus magnum pulsatis Olympum,* Hinds (1998), 56–57; Morgan (2010), 291–92. A. Barchiesi (cited by Hinds [1998] 56 n. 6) observes that the pun picked out by Hinds on metrical "feet" in *pedibus* calls attention to the fact that the Saturnian was not made up of metrical feet: if we knew confidently how to scan the Saturnian, then it could be that the word *pedibus* is the moment in the line when the reader realizes that this line is not a Saturnian.

61. Krostenko (2013) on fr. 73 Blänsdorf. The one line we have quoted from the so-called *Carmen Priami* looks like the product of a similarly nostalgic individual: see Timpanaro (1978), 99; Courtney (1993), 44. On these two pieces, see Morgan (2010), 296–98, and in general, on the way that "the Saturnian, as a metre perceived to be untainted by Greek cultural influence, could operate

as the vehicle for anxieties about the Hellenization of Rome," see Morgan (2010), 286–310 (quotation from 287).

62. Gell. 17. 21. 44 (fr. 1 Courtney): *Poenico bello secundo Musa pinnato gradu/ intulit se bellicosam Romuli in gentem feram;* discussion in Courtney (1993), 83–86 (for whom Naevius is at issue); Schwindt (2000), 68–69 (Ennius); Welsh (2011) (Livius Andronicus).

63. On the interesting literary-historical work being performed in this and other poets' "epitaphs" of the second century, see Schwindt (2001), 11–13.

64. See Sharrock (2009), 68–95 for a rich account of Terence's strategies in his prologues; cf. Manuwald (2011), 290–92, together with Rüpke (2012), 210 on the "connoisseurship" presupposed by the discussion of models in the comic prologues. On the importance of Naevius as a major model for Plautus, see de Melo (2014), 455.

65. For Terence's insistent presentation of his work as that of "writing," see Sharrock (2009), 79, referring to *An.* 1, 5; *Haut.* 43; *Eun.* 7, 36; *Phorm.* 3; *Hec.* 27, 56; *Ad.* 16, 25.

66. Pecere (2010), 9, on the evidence of Suet. *Vita Ter.* 5.

67. As argued by Goldberg (2005), 62–75.

68. Here I agree with the points made by Farrell (2007) against the attempts of Goldberg (2005) to deny the value of applying the category of "literary" to comic scripts before their incorporation into the curriculum.

69. On the sophistication required of a Plautine audience, especially as regards jokes about comic prototypes and tragic parody, see Leigh (2000), 5–8; on comic engagement with tragedy in particular, see Fraenkel (1922/2007), 49–51, 65, 140–41, 234–42; Boyle (2006), 56–57; Manuwald (2011), 312–17; Manuwald (2014). As Stephen Hinds points out to me, a lot of this no doubt went over the head of many in the audience, who still could have picked up on the atmosphere, finding such "competitive fun and cross-talk inherent to comic performance."

70. McCarthy (2000), 7–8; as "comic" in the last phrase quoted shows, she is there discussing Plautus, but she explicitly identifies "stylization, secondariness, and dialogism" as characteristic of "early Latin literature as a whole and Plautus in particular" (8).

71. See Chapter 5, text accompanying notes 93–95.

72. Well stressed by Cowan (2013), 330.

73. Such language is radical to the Latin tradition, and it "anticipates" the metapoetic language of repetition in the Augustan poets and their successors, so finely analyzed by Conte (1986), 60–63 in his discussion of the overt language of "again, again" in Ov. *Fast.* 3. 71–72.

74. Or perhaps (as Ingo Gildenhard suggests to me) she says that she will "bring back to life by means of commemoration the obliterated enmities," with *memoria* going with *renouare*, rather than with *oblitteratas*, as appears to be the universal interpretation of editors. Or perhaps both interpretations are felt (as suggested to me by Seth Schein): this reperformance will renew the memory of the previous performance *(memoria renouare)*, and it will do so by rescuing it from its momentary oblivion *(oblitteratas memoria)*.

75. Manuwald (2011), 190–91.

76. Similarly, as suggested by Dangel (1995), 325, Electra's language in Accius' *Agamemnonidae* seems to allude to the language used by Atreus in the earlier play to describe the grandparents' generation: *"renouare* [fr. 44] rapelle *iterum* [frr. 198–99] et *extinctas* [fr. 43], *quietum* [fr. 199]."

77. Fantham (2003), 102, pointing to Pacuvius' *"Atalanta, Chryses, Iliona,* and *Medus,* all named for their protagonists, and all dealing with continuations of better-known myths." Cf. Manuwald (2003), 38; and Schierl (2006), 29, on reworkings of prior Latin models by Pacuvius.

78. Cowan (2010), 45; cf. Cowan (2013), 332–33.

79. Cowan (2010), 49.

80. Jocelyn (1969), 4; E. Stärk in Suerbaum (2002), 152 (the burden of proof is on those who argue for model-free independent composition); Schierl (2006), 12, 28–29; Boyle (2006), 88–90 (great independence in the "second wave," within a system still keyed in to Greek templates, increasingly post-Classical ones). Important arguments for the other case, especially for the possibility of direct work from epic or mythographic models, not existing tragedies, in Manuwald (2011), 134, 213, 289.

81. Major discussion in Nervegna (2013), 76–99 of the Greek practices and of their significance for Roman *contaminatio;* cf. Schiesaro (2005), 274.

82. Nervegna (2013), 99.

83. See Chapter 4, text accompanying notes 71–74. If Pacuvius' *Antiopa* dates to shortly before 191 (Manuwald [2011], 214), then it will be at least ten years after the death of Naevius, which fell in 200 at the latest (Suerbaum [2002] 106).

84. Manuwald (2011), 158, 196.

85. Shi (2011), 100, with reference to Momigliano (1990), 90–91.

86. M. Barchiesi (1962), 224–54; Shi (2011), 126–31.

87. Elliott (2013), 234: her important arguments make a strong case for this view (see esp. chapter 5, *"Imperium sine fine:* the *Annales* and universal history"). On the sense of imperial mission in Livius' *Odyssey,* Naevius' *Bellum Punicum,* and Ennius' *Annales,* see Dench (2005), 57–58.

88. Elliot (2013), 210–32 ("The *Annales* and Roman prose historiography").

89. Overview in Suerbaum (2002), 129–33.

90. See Sciarrino (2011), 17–19 for arguments against excluding Roman prose from the category of literature as a result of misguided assumptions about the "aesthetic" and the "poetic."

91. The massive topic of the Roman adoption of Greek historiography would be the subject of another book, or two. For orientation, see Suerbaum (2002), 345–437.

92. See Chapter 1, text accompanying notes 30–33.

93. Gruen (1990), 10; Dillery (2002), 2–3; *FRHist* 1. 161 (with interesting speculation on "a family tradition of diplomacy in the Greek East").

94. Acilius: Gell. 6. 14. 9; Plut. *Cato* 22. 4; Postumius Albinus: Cic. *Acad.* 2. 137, *FRHist* 4 T7 (with Carneades); *FRHist* 4 T1 (inscriptional evidence for his honorific statues).

95. See Dench (2005), 314 on the Greek of Postumius Albinus.

96. On the audiences captured by the Greek histories, see Dillery (2002), 8–9; *FRHist* 1. 168.

97. Important arguments in Dillery (2002); cf. Cornell (2010), 103 on how Fabius was not "correcting" Greek views about his people, as had Berossus and Manetho, but rather accepting the Greek perspective on Roman origins.

98. Dillery (1999); see Dillery (2014) for the subtle accommodations in Berossus and Manetho between the forms of Greek ethnographic history and the various inherited patterns of their own traditions; cf. De Breucker (2011) and Haubold (2013), 142–77 on this feature of Berossus.

99. Stressed by Gildenhard (2003a), whose list I abbreviate and paraphrase here, against an overemphasis on oral tradition: I second his recommendation of Eigler, Gotter, and Luraghi (2003) as the best introduction to the range of commemorative practices in mid-Republican culture, and their importance for the new historiography. See *FRHist* 1. 169 on "what passed for a historical tradition in Rome before Fabius"; cf. Oakley (1997–2005), 1. 21–38; Purcell (2003) in general on historical consciousness in Rome before formal historiography.

100. As it is described by Gildenhard (2003a); for this crucial point, see Cornell (2010), 104–5 and *FRHist* 1. 169, acknowledging Momigliano (1966), 61 for his recognition that "this was a truly revolutionary step"; cf. Timpe (2011), 165–66 on the "unforeseen and revolutionary consequences" of the new historiographical literary format; Rüpke (2012), 215 for the "explosive import" of the application of new techniques of explanation, argumentation, and systematization to the writing of history in Rome. Of course, it was "a truly revolutionary step" in the first place for Herodotus to use the narrative modes of

Homer in order to impose structure and significance upon the morass of material at *his* disposal: see R. Rutherford (2012), esp. 16–17.

101. On the indispensable importance of Greek historiographical models and templates for Fabius' structure, see esp. Timpe (1972); Beck (2003); as Timpe (2011), 163 puts it, Fabius' history "was absolutely unthinkable without Greek political and literary impulses."

102. Timpe (1988), 275–81 is fundamental here, arguing that Fabius is not transcribing an oral tradition but working with the structures of a Greek source in his reworking of the foundation story; cf. Feeney (2007a), 249 n. 126 on how Fabius is "not somehow writing down what was already 'there' in an oral tradition." Andrew Gallia is currently working on the topic of the revolutionary impact of the forms of historiography in Rome; I thank him for dialogue on this question.

103. von Holzinger (1912); cf. Frier (1999), 261–62, Hillen (2003), 113, and other sources cited in Feeney (2007a), 249 n. 126.

104. Momigliano (1966), 63: "Ma la formulazione, la presentazione era greca." Bispham and Cornell in *FRHist* 3. 20–21 argue for the role also of an actual drama on the subject staged in Rome (so Wiseman [1998] Chapter 1).

105. Dion. Hal. *Ant. Rom.* 1. 74. 1, *FRHist* 1 F5a.

106. Originally suggested by F. Jacoby, *FGrH* 566, Komm., 538: see Möller (2004). Timaeus' own date for the foundation of Rome fell before the first Olympiad, in "814/13," the thirty-eighth year before the first Olympiad" (Dion. Hal. *Ant. Rom.* 1. 74 . 1, *FGrH* 566 F60).

107. Momigliano (1966), 60–61 on the *pompa circensis* (Dion. Hal. 7. 71.1–73.5, *FRHist* 1 F15) and the causes of the Hannibalic War (Polyb. 3. 8. 1–8, *FRHist* 1 F22).

108. For Greeks on Roman origins, see Gruen (1992), chapter 1; Wiseman (1995), chapter 4; for the general background of Greek inserting outsiders into the plots of their own mythic and historiographical frameworks, Bickerman (1952) remains a classic; cf. Momigliano (1966), 61–62 on this as the key background for Fabius' initiative, together with Cornell (2010). On Fabius' history as a response to the anti-Roman Greek historians of the Punic Wars, see Rawson (1989), 425; note that the uncertainty over the time of Fabius' composition of his history makes it impossible to know for sure whether he was reacting to these historians: see *FRHist* 1. 167.

109. Erskine (2001) makes this point clearly for the Trojan myth in the early Roman historiographical tradition: "the myth is very much a collaboration between Greeks and Romans" (40); cf. Cornell (2010), 104–6.

110. Attractively suggested by M. Barchiesi (1962), 233–34; see Gruen (1992), 35 for the impossibility of deciding on the priority of Naevius' *Bellum Punicum* or Fabius Pictor's history.

111. Gabba (2001), 591: "La <creazione storiografica> a Roma alla fine del III secolo rispondeva ad esigenze politiche di fronte al mondo magnogreco e greco, che prima non esistevano. Questo non è un preconcetto, è un dato di fatto."

112. Feeney (2007a), 96, 98, referring to Beck and Walter (2001), 92, 59; Dillery (2002), 8.

113. Purcell (2003), 34.

114. This tidy version would be complicated if, as mooted by Bispham and Cornell in *FRHist* 1. 169, the translation of Fabius Pictor's history into Latin took place before Cato's work was published.

115. Sciarrino (2011), chapter 4.

116. Here I follow Bispham and Cornell in *FRHist* 1. 205–13 on the importance of Italy as the leading concept in the organization of the *Origines*.

117. Note Cato's wonderful riposte to the apologies of Postumius Albinus for errors in his Greek: "Well, no one forced you to write in Greek" (Polyb. 39. 12, *FRHist* 4 T3, F1); cf. Plut. *Cat. Mai.* 12. 4–5, on Cato speaking Latin to Athenians although he could speak Greek.

118. For nuanced accounts of Cato's life-long relationship with Hellenism, see Gruen (1992), 52–83; Bispham and Cornell in *FRHist* 1. 194–95. Cf. Rawson (1991), 249–50 on the enthusiasm for things Greek in the Latin annalist Cassius Hemina: "If our general picture of Cassius is right, it is plain that the production of histories in Latin was not necessarily part of an anti-Greek reaction, even in the subtle and modified sense in which alone it is true of Cato."

119. Feeney (2007a), 99–101.

120. See *FRHist* 1. 193—not to mention a mysterious *carmen de moribus*, "probably in prose," either "a didactic work on personal conduct" or "a work of antiquarian character on the customs *(mores)* of the ancient Romans" (ibid.).

Chapter 7 THE IMPACT AND REACH OF THE NEW LITERATURE

1. Goldberg (2005).

2. Manuwald (2011), 98, citing Plaut. *Poen.* 5–35; Ter. *Hec.* 28–48.

3. Goldberg (1998), 13–16; cf. MacMullen (1991), esp. 420–21 arguing for the socially exclusive nature of the small audiences.

4. The main source is Liv. 34. 44. 5, 54. 3–8; see Rawson (1991), 536–37; Goldberg (1998), 14–15; Manuwald (2011), 107.

5. Manuwald (2011), 104–5; Franko (2014), 418–21; on travelling re-performances, see Rawson (1991), 477–79; Franko (2014), 414.

6. Horsfall (2003), 64–68.

7. Levine (1988), 21 (original emphasis): see chapter 1 for the full picture, including the big shift that made Shakespeare a "classic" (30–34).

8. Levine (1988), 23.

9. Despite such heroic experiments as the London Globe, appositely cited as a parallel by Goldberg (1998), 20.

10. See Chapter 5, "Acting Greek."

11. I could have taken Henderson (1999), chapter 2, focusing on education and father-son relationships, or Leigh (2004), with a range of examples, including the same themes of education (chapter 5).

12. See Chapter 4, text accompanying note 73.

13. Rawson (1991), 477–79; see her whole picture of the popularity of theatrical culture in Italy (Chapter 26).

14. See above Chapter 5, text accompanying notes 71–73, for discussion of the important insights of Wiseman (1983/1987) and Rawson (1991), 474. For a vivid picture of "Rome and the Italian background" for the period after ours, roughly in the time of Cicero, see Rawson (1985), chapter 2.

15. *SEG* 26. 1123 fr. III, col. A (*FRHist* 1 T7): see *FRHist* 1. 168 for the Sicilian interest in Fabius Pictor.

16. See Chapter 1, text accompanying notes 38–39.

17. See Skutsch (1985), 168 for a favorable report of the emendation of L. Havet.

18. Moatti (1997), 61–63; Scheidel (2004).

19. Scheidel (2004), 26. Seneca gives a particularly vivid expression of this Roman characteristic in *Ad Helviam* 7. 7.

20. I am indebted here to the excellent arguments of Moatti (1997), esp. 97–141, and of Rüpke (2012), esp. chapters 4, 5, and 6.

21. Waszink (1960), 25–26 (an overlooked paper, with much of enduring value); Rüpke (2012), 89 on Livius Andronicus "placing the gods involved in genealogical relation to each other, using a dense net of data on their descent and ancestry," as when "Zeus is not simply *Iuppiter,* but *Saturni filie* [fr. 2]."

22. Stressed already by Fraenkel (1922/2007), 66 (with 310–11 and 396), making clear the long-standing familiarity with "the colourful world of Greek fable . . . even if it was never represented as a coherent whole" before Livius Andronicus. Cf. on the domestication of and familiarity with Greek mythic and religious figures before 240, Jocelyn (1969), 11, 14; Kaimio (1979), 186–87; Jocelyn (1990), 596–97; Horsfall (1993a), 799–800.

23. Rüpke (2012), 33; cf. 89, on Livius' *Odyssey*: "the Greek narratives, having been translated into Latin, could be accommodated as an extension of the Romans' own world and narrative horizon."

24. See Dangel (1995), 376 for intriguing speculation on how this genealogy could set up a context for the *devotio* of Decius, showing it to have been a very late expiation for original Trojan transgressions.

25. The wonderful chapter 3 ("Mythological material") of Fraenkel (1922/2007) is still indispensible: cf. Horsfall (1993a), 800–801, reinforcing the correctness of Fraenkel's insights even seventy years after first publication; Middelmann (1938), 48–69; Suerbaum (2002), 27–28. On mythography in the basic Hellenistic curriculum, see the material collected by Dillery (2002), 2 n. 6.

26. Ennius' description of this ritual in his *Annales* shuffles the pack, putting all the female divinities first (240–41) in a "bravura performance" that smuggles the adulterous Mars into the female verse, beside Venus (Gildenhard (2003b), 101): see Skutsch (1985), 324–25, and Suerbaum (2002), 28 on the importance of seeing the state and the epicist engaged in their own distinctive, yet related, brands of Hellenism.

27. Rüpke (2012), 52 summarizing the findings of his chapter 4.

28. Boyle (2006), 91; Manuwald (2011), 295–96.

29. Schierl (2006), 535–36, referring to Arist. *Phys.* 195b 31–33.

30. Boyle (2006), 91: see Schierl (2006), 233–34 for the philosophical background.

31. Feeney (1991), 121–22.

32. Feeney (1991), 122.

33. Important discussion in Rüpke (2012), chapter 6, to which I am here indebted.

34. See Chapter 2, text accompanying notes 92–97.

35. Feeney (1991), 113–15, 128.

36. Feeney (2007b), 131; Gildenhard (2003b), 82–84.

37. Rüpke (2012), 33.

38. Hutchinson (2013), 181.

39. Elliott (2013), chapter 5; cf. Gildenhard (2003b), 102 (after describing the stylistic and intellectual range of the *Annales*): "While the title and the subject matter firmly anchor the *Annales* in Roman cultural practice, the actual poetry follows its own criteria of distinction."

40. Elliott (2013), 234 n. 3.

41. On C. Julius Caesar Strabo (aedile 90), the first member of the nobility to write drama, see E. Stärk in Suerbaum (2002), 167–68; see P. White (1993), 8 and Goldberg (1995), 132–34 for the shift in conventional status among writers of poetry portended by Strabo and Lucilius.

42. On the relocation of the fragment to the opening sequence, I agree with Gildenhard (2007b), 78 that Kissel (1990), 776–87 is correct.

43. See above, text accompanying note 17.

44. Gildenhard (2007b), 79; I follow here Gildenhard's excellent arguments about Ennius' authority-claims (75–79).

45. In addition to Gildenhard (2007b), 75–79, see Gildenhard (2003b), 102: "Ennius himself, in the poem, emphasized his *literary,* rather than his social authority vis à vis his audience" (original emphasis; cf. 113); cf. P. Hardie (2010), 422 on Ennius' claims to knowledge and authority even via the title of his *Annales,* despite being "an outsider and of low social status in Rome"; Shi (2011), 158–59 on how "the once invisible epic poet was demanding to be recognized as an essential figure in Roman society."

46. My thanks to Leon Grek for the phrase "epistemological crisis," and for discussion of this point.

47. Gildenhard (2003b), 113, summarizing a compelling case for Ennius' new strategies of self-positioning (109–13); cf. Shi (2011), 150–62. For arguments against the older *poeta/cliens* model, see Gruen (1990), 106–22 and esp. Goldberg (1995), 113–34. Helpful overviews of the terms of debate in the case of Ennius in Rossi and Breed (2006), 402–8; P. Hardie (2007), 130–31.

48. Rawson (1985), 38–9.

49. On this very controversial subject, see Chapter 6, text accompanying note 11; on the rituals of 207, see Chapter 8, "Elaboration of Cultic Song: A *Carmen* for Juno."

50. On this scenario for Livius Andronicus, e.g., instead of the usual version by which he is brought to Rome as a slave, see above Chapter 3, text accompanying note 1. Badian (1972) was an important reorientation, demolishing the accepted view of Cato bringing Ennius to Rome as his client (154–63).

51. Full discussions of our surviving evidence in Gruen (1990), chapter 3; Goldberg (1995), chapter 5. Manuwald (2011), 93–95 has a very judicious overview, stressing the mobility of the first poets and their lack of dependent links to particular individuals or families.

52. Habinek (1998), 37; Manuwald (2011), 96: "Granting the Temple of Minerva as a meeting place to writers and actors was a religious and political decision of the nobility. . . . The decision indicates an increasing recognition of writers and actors as an important group within society." On the difficult question of the later downward turn in the status of actors, see P. G. McC. Brown (2002), 225.

53. Sciarrino (2011), 47–51.

54. Testimonia, references and discussion in Suerbaum (2002), 104–7.

55. See E. Stärk in Suerbaum (2002), 159, with the nice remark: "Er [Accius] war ein echter Sproß des *genus irritabile uatum.*"

56. Sciarrino (2011), 86; see the valuable discussions of the personal and social relations of Naevius (85–7) and Ennius (87–99).

57. Habinek (1998), 37; see Woolf (2009) on the setting for "the documentary explosion of official texts in Rome during the last two centuries B.C.E." (64), and, in general on the acceleration in writing systems in the second century, Moatti (1997), 105–6.

58. Rüpke (2012), 86; cf. Moatti (1997), 102–7.

59. Valuable discussion of the issues in Lowrie (2009), esp. 1–23, 52. We look forward to the posthumous publication of Don Fowler's *Unrolling the Text,* in preparation by Tom Phillips.

60. I find virtually nothing to disagree with in the powerful arguments of Lowrie (2009), 13–18; and H. N. Parker (2009). Habinek (2009), 114–15 rightly stresses the way that a text such as Virgil's *Aeneid* is deeply aural in its structures and rhythms, referring to the study of B. G. Campbell (2001): it remains that case that sensitivity to such patterns can be for the Romans also inextricably part of silent and solitary reading, as shown by the studies of punctuation in Townend (1969) and (1969–70), who reveals how solitary readers are relying on their rhetorical training to follow the run of the language.

61. Rüpke (2001), summarized in Rüpke (2012), 84–86. Rüpke's approach is partly motivated by a supposed continuity between the occasions for song in the aristocratic *convivia* of the second century and the ones of the lost past mentioned by Cato in his *Origines:* see below Chapter 8, note 8, for discussion of this possibility. For now, I note my agreement with Goldberg (2006), 434: "No link between archaic musical practice and later literary development is ever explicit in the sources."

62. H. N. Parker (2009), 204–5, and 208 on the function of *recitationes;* cf. 206: "nowhere in Catullus, Horace, Propertius, Tibullus or Ovid do we find a single suggestion that these poets ever 'performed' at their own or anyone else's *convivia.*" At the *recitatio* the poet distanced himself from a professional's or an actor's status by being "seated" with "a text open before him . . . not us[ing] his hands . . . and avoid[ing] facial expressions" (H. N. Parker [2009], 203).

63. See Skutsch (1985) *ad loc.* and the comprehensive discussion of Ennius' vocabulary of textuality and song in Lowrie (2009), 28–32. Cf. Kerkhecker (2001), 76: "Er singt nicht, er schreibt"; P. Hardie (2010), 422, differing from the argument of Rüpke (2001) for oral performance: "Ennius draws attention to the writtenness of his poem" referring to frr. 164 and 404–6.

64. Pecere (2010), 3.

65. Habinek (2005), 275 n. 29.
66. See Lowrie (2009), 31–32 for discussion of the intriguing *Scipio* 1–2 Vahlen and *Epigrams* 15–16 Vahlen.
67. Classen (1992), 133–34.
68. Jocelyn (1972), 1010; cf. Hutchinson (2008), 26; Pecere (2010), 3–4.
69. Mariotti (1952/1986), 75–77.
70. Cribiore (2001), 196–97.
71. Suet. *Gram.* et Rhet. 2. 2; see Gratwick (1982a), 60; Goldberg (2005), 25 n. 14; and Kaster (1995), 65 for the *Annales* as Lampadio's template. For Naevius as following the example of Livius, see Fraenkel (1935), 637–38.
72. Suerbaum (1992) remains an important discussion of how much Livius and Naevius could have fitted on a single roll (a maximum of c. 1850 Saturnians, according to his calculations), but given our ignorance of the possibilities of the book before the standardization of the second century, I share the reservations of A. Barchiesi (2002) about how firm these conclusions are.
73. This is a long shot: the first Greek historian to divide his history into books, Ephorus, had died at least a century before Fabius Pictor began his history. But note Bispham and Cornell in *FRHist* 1. 169: "Only three fragments [of Fabius Pictor] are preserved with book numbers. Two of these (F4e, F31) are from the Latin version, while the third (F4c), from the *OGR*, could be from either . . . we cannot be sure that the same book structure was reproduced in the Greek version." In fact, on this evidence, we cannot be sure that the Greek version had a book structure as such, and it could have been introduced in translation. As for Cincius Alimentus, the only two fragments that mention book numbers (F6, *OGR* 18.1 and F7, *OGR* 17. 1–3) are listed in *FRHist* as "Possible fragments," since they could be from another Cincius, an antiquarian, not an annalist (*FRHist* 1. 182). Classen (1992), 133 somewhat overstates the case when he says that there is no evidence for the division of the first Roman histories into books.
74. Jocelyn (1972), 1010; Classen (1992), 133–34; Shi (2011), 147–48; Elliott (2013), 213–14; Goldschmidt (2013), 23–24.
75. Jocelyn (1972), 1010; Skutsch (1985), 5. The most exciting example we have of the book being presented as an artistic unit in the *Annales* is the Herculaneum find that appears to show that the name of King Pyrrhus was the very last word in "his" book, Book 6: see Kleve (1990), 6 for the suggestion that the "very name of Pyrrhus may have ended the book (Burrus, *pezzo* VI, fr. 2, line 3)"; cf. Suerbaum (1995) on the artistic unity of the "Pyrrhus-book."
76. Goldberg (2006), 437.

77. Rüpke (2012), 88–91.

78. P. Hardie (2010), 422; cf. Sciarrino (2011), 201 for the stimulating suggestion that Cato also envisaged his impact continuing through his texts after his death. I keep to a footnote the strange account of Suetonius concerning Q. Vargunteius (*Rhet. et gram.* 2. 2). According to Suetonius, C. Octavius Lampadio and Vargunteius "carefully reviewed poems that has as yet not been widely circulated *(parum adhuc diuulgata)* . . . and by reading and commenting upon them made them known to the rest of the population as well" (tr. Kaster [1995]). Suetonius then mentions the work of Lampadio on Naevius' *Bellum Punicum,* discussed above, and continues: "so Quintus Vargunteius later did in the case of Ennius' *Annales,* which he used to recite before a large audience on specific days." I agree with Goldberg (2006), 428 that this is "occasionally dubious history": there is every reason to think that Ennius was in fact popular in his day and after his death, as Goldberg shows, although I am more skeptical about granting even that there was a falling-off at all, given Suetonius' procrustean parallels with what he thought the great figure of Crates had been doing. Whatever we decide on these questions, Suetonius here is no kind of evidence that recitation was the primary medium for the first reception of Ennius. Indeed, the logic of his narrative implies the opposite; he is saying (again, almost certainly erroneously) that the written text of Ennius was not well known until the later recitations of Vargunteius made the poem popular. I thank Bob Kaster for discussion of this passage.

79. Lowrie (2009), 60; cf. Breed (2006), 158 on how the "temporal scope" of writing "potentially makes the sense of community for [Virgilian] pastoral and for poetry expandable, expandable to include readers in many circumstances and in many time periods."

80. See Habinek (1998), 7 for the utility of the model of Anderson (1991) for the student of the Roman Republic. On the impact of Ennius on the Roman imagination via the school curriculum during the Republic and down into the Augustan period, see Goldschmidt (2013), 18–33.

81. Anderson (1991), 188 (original emphasis).

82. Here I owe much to discussion with Jo Quinn, who kindly let me read and quote from some advance text for her forthcoming Balmuth Lectures at Tufts University, where she adduces the Jews as well as the Greeks as *comparandi:* "our perception of the importance of collective identity at a supra-political level in the ancient Mediterranean has in fact been distorted by the traditional focus on a small number of rather unusual and unusually literate ancient societies, such as those that arose among Greek and Hebrew speakers." The

role of the Jewish body of writings in connecting far-flung members of the same language-group is, as implied here, an important parallel for the Greek and Roman cases.

83. See above, text accompanying notes 57–58.
84. Woolf (2009).
85. Woolf (2009), 46–48.
86. Woolf (2009), 61.
87. Woolf (2009), 64.
88. See above, "The New Professionals."
89. See Chapter 2, text accompanying notes 41–43.
90. See Introduction, note 8.
91. Woolf (2012b), 297.
92. D. M. Lewis (1994), 18; cf. 28: "My inclination is to doubt that there was all that much literacy about, whether for the noble or for the common man."
93. D. M. Lewis (1994), 18; Tuplin (2011), 157–58.
94. Langslow (2002), 45.
95. Tuplin (2011), 158.
96. Robson (2013), 43, picking out the Assyrian king Assurbanipal (ruled 668–627) as "especially literate and cultured," because "[a]s a boy he had trained for the priesthood as he was not (yet) a direct heir to the throne."
97. Wide-ranging discussion in Charpin (2010), 53–67.
98. Woolf (2009), 48.

Chapter 8 ACTS OF COMPARISON

1. See Chapter 4, text accompanying notes 105–8.
2. Watkins (1995a), 45–50 on a Faliscan and a Picene text, both from around 600; cf. Crawford (2011), 1. 14–15 on two Paelignian inscriptions and a Marrucine one that "display stress-accent metre, alliteration, and formulaic language"; he concludes "we suppose . . . that [the metrical features in question] were widespread in early Italy." Such short compositions will have been the norm, according to Fortson (2011), 95.
3. Jocelyn (1972), 991; cf. Adams and Mayer (1999), 1: "of the Italic peoples only [the Romans] in the course of time embarked upon the enterprise of committing newly composed poems to writing as texts." See Feeney (2005), 230 with n. 22 on the improbability of a transmitted Oscan dramatic literature.
4. Harris (1989), 154.

5. Fascinating introduction to this material in Turfa (2012); cf. North (2000) on the large mass of underground religious and prophetic texts in Etruscan (and in Latin) that must have been circulating in the middle Republic.

6. Harris (1971), 9; cf. already Toynbee (1965), 2. 433: "The Etruscans had taken the further step of producing a literature in their own language, but the Etruscan literature may have been limited to the single province of disquisitions on matters of religious ritual."

7. We consider Etruscan knowledge of Greek myth in Chapter 9.

8. Farrell (2007), 285 on the mime scripts; Jory (2009) on the libretti for pantomime, making an excellent analogy with modern scripts for cinema and television (169): "These cinema and television scripts, like the libretti of pantomime, have no independent existence outside of the cinema or the television screen, but they require a special expertise and technique in writing and are recognized as works of art in their own right. Despite this, they are unlikely to survive for even the 500 years of Lucan's libretti, although the plays and novels they are based on will."

9. Horsfall (2003), 53: "'In Etruscan'? 'On Etruscan topics'? When? For whom? We have really no idea"; cf. Dench (2005), 314 n. 49.

10. Cornell (2011).

11. Cornell (2011), 182.

12. Not an option canvassed by Cornell (2011); not endorsed by Harris (1971), 10: "There is no corroboration of the view that there were histories by Etruscans written in Greek."

13. Summary of the possibilities in Cornell (2011), 203.

14. Baines (2011), 54—and this despite the fact that, as he goes on to say, "from the beginning of the Dynastic period onward (c. 3000) the past was curated intensively in writing." Again, there is no necessary value judgment involved in remarking on these different ways of curating the past. Jo Quinn prods me to consider denaturalizing the assumption that there are such things as "societies" in the first place: I look forward to her forthcoming work on Punic identities for an opening. If an Etruscan had wanted to write an "Etruscan history" in 300 or 250, of whom would he have written? Of "the Etruscans"? Or of the people of Volsinii, or Volterra?

15. Huss (1985), 504–6; sources cited by Baurain (1992), 159. My thanks to Jo Quinn for her generous help on these issues.

16. Millar (2002–2006), 2. 263; for similar positions, see Krings (1991), esp. 667; Baurain (1992); Miles (2010), 13. Jo Quinn refers me to Kerr (2010), 177 for a refutation of the claims that have been made for a Punic inscription from

Libya *(Bir ed-Dreder LP 6)* as the "sole surviving specimen of Phoenician lyric poetry."

17. J. C. Quinn (forthcoming publication of Balmuth Lectures at Tufts University; quoted with permission): cf. ibid.: "the romantic idea that there is a lost world of Phoenician prose and poetry written on papyrus does not come from the ancient sources."

18. Baurain (1992), 164.

19. On the rich intercultural work evident in royal Numidian architecture in exactly this period, see Quinn (2013a), 210: "The builders bolstered their prestige by co-opting global references, and their legitimacy by co-opting local ones."

20. Krings (1991), 659–60; Baurain (1992), 165–71. There is much controversy over Sallust's reference in his *Jugurtha* to *libri Punici* of King Hiempsal (written by him or belonging to him?); here he says that in an excursus on the geography and peoples of Africa he is giving ethnographic information *uti ex libris Punicis, qui regis Hiempsalis dicebantur, interpretatum nobis est* ("as it was interpreted to me from Punic books that were said to be King Hiempsal's," 17.7). Krings and Baurain both believe the work was actually in Greek, while Paul (1984), 74, stressing that "a Greek source or sources can be detected" in the excursus," follows the suggestion of Trüdinger (1918), 217–19 that Sallust "found the reference to *libri Punici* in a [Greek or Latin] source." If Sallust is referring to books written in Punic, and if we take his language at face value, the scenario that presents itself is that someone who could read the original was interpreting/translating the text orally to Sallust: this might explain the otherwise rather puzzling imperfect in *dicebantur,* which would be a focalized reference to the *viva voce* context ("books in Punic which the person interpreting them to me said belonged to Hiempsal").

21. Collected by Gsell (1928–1929), 212–15; Rochette (1997b).

22. Gsell (1928–1929), 193. My thanks to John Henderson for discussion of Carthaginian Greek.

23. For up-to-date discussion, see the papers in Prag and Quinn (2013), many of which touch upon Carthaginian participation in the cultural exchanges of the western Mediterranean. Accordingly, I retract the ignorant remarks advanced in Feeney (2009), 9.

24. Van Dommelen and López-Bertran (2013), 274–75, with bibliographical orientation.

25. On the adoption of the Roman cult of Ceres/Demeter (Dion. Hal. *Ant. Rom.* 6. 17. 2–4 and 94. 3), taking in also Italic features of the cult, see Spaeth (1996), 7–9.

26. I gladly thank Brigitte Le Guen for her generous replies to my enquiries, and for her encouragement of the idea that Greek troupes (though not the *technitae* of Dionysus) may well have included Carthage on their circuit.

27. Brouillet (1994), 63, #58.

28. Alter (1992).

29. Jo Quinn refers me to Sparks (2005), 269 for this shared characteristic: "Regarding the large civilizations in Israel's ancient context, only in Greece do we find that ethnicity played an important role in its notions of identity."

30. Young (2007), 180–83 on the comparatively high level of instability and linguistic variation even in the transmission of the text of Gilgamesh.

31. Young (2002), 383; cf. Young (2007), 183.

32. Parkinson (2009), 62; cf. Parkinson (1999), 127. My thanks to Tom Hare for help with these issues, and to Stephen Hinds for clarifying what is at stake in the comparison.

33. Parkinson (2009), 12, 13: see 12–16 for speculation on oral readings of the literature for larger numbers.

34. Parkinson (2009), 176; cf. 187, 210–11. As pointed out by Ryholt (2012), 159, in the Greco-Roman period literary texts were, by contrast, hardly ever used as part of scribal training.

35. I. Rutherford (2013), 24; I thank Tom Hare for cautioning me to acknowledge our ignorance about numbers and reach of a possible readership.

36. Overview in I. Rutherford (2013), 24–27; cf. Quack (2005), 4.

37. George (2007a), 41–2; cf. (2003), 7 for speculation on the original oral performance contexts.

38. George (2007a), 41; cf. Charpin (2010), 39, 186, 205, 215; Tinney (2011), 584, 589.

39. Charpin (2010), 193, 196, 208.

40. George (2007b), 455.

41. George (2003), 1. 59.

42. See Chapter 1, text accompanying notes 130–31.

43. Charpin (2010), 67.

44. Robson (2013), 40 on cuneiform culture in the first millennium: "So far as we know, all of those engaged in such literary and scholarly activities made their livelihoods from this knowledge, whether through royal patronage, priestly employment, or solicitation of private clients for performance of ritual."

45. Baurain (1992), 175–76 on the Carthaginians.

46. See too Jocelyn (1990), 595–604.

47. Norden (1898), 1. 160–61; Conte (1994), 20–22; Scheid (2008), 17–18. See Norden (1898), 1. 157–58; Courtney (1995), 201–2; and Watkins (1995b), 199–200 for arresting "song"-layouts of Cato *De Agr.*, 141. 2–3. The core of Cato's *carmen*

appears to be much older than the *Carmen Arvale,* for Watkins (1995b), 202 sees the language as predating Cato's "fixation" of the prayer by "half a millennium."

48. On the antiquity of the *pompa,* see Bernstein (1998), 41–48.
49. See Chapter 5, text accompanying note 123.
50. See Chapter 3, text accompanying notes 47–48.
51. Horsfall (1994), 62–63.
52. See Chapter 4, text accompanying notes 111–23.
53. I am grateful to Sandy Hardie for sharing his work in progress on the Camenae; I am indebted here to his arguments about the importance of this Pythagorean moment in fixing the significance of King Numa in the tradition. For the likelihood that this is the period in which the tradition of the kings in general received some kind of crystallization, see C. Smith (2011), 40–41.
54. Humm (2005), 564–72 on these developments.
55. Humm (2005), with the review of Bispham (2008).
56. Although, e.g., Gratwick (1982b), 139 has it that it is "at best doubtful whether any of them were authentic."
57. Cic. *Brut.* 55, 61; *Sen.* 16 (the speech); *Tusc* 4. 4 (the *carmen*—"the word does not necessarily imply a verse-form," Gratwick [1982b], 138); scattered references to the maxims collected by Suerbaum (2002), 80. Discussion in Suerbaum (2002), 80–83, and extremely interesting, though ultimately rather inconclusive, wide-ranging speculation in Humm (2005), 521–39. In discussing the *carmen* that Cicero says was praised by Panaetius (*Tusc.* 4. 4), scholars tend to assume that Panaetius could read Latin, which is possible, or even likely, given the circles he moved in, but it is not something we should take for granted; the *carmen* could have been in Greek.
58. Rüpke (2012), 26; cf. 86: "Whatever the historicity of this text, it remains an isolated datum."
59. Fortson (2011), 99, with reference to Williams (1968), 361–65, 693; cf. Mariotti (1952/1986), 25, 34 and (1965/2000), 14–15 on the contribution to the new literature of the sacral language of *carmina* and the general stylistic resources of the language.
60. Fortson (2011), 93; see above Chapter 2, text accompanying note 39.
61. van Sickle (1987) and (1988), building on the original insight of Leo (1913), 45.
62. Courtney (1995), 229: see Morgan (2010), 304–5.
63. Fortson (2011), 98.
64. E.g., Blänsdorf (2000), 145–46, 148–49; Oakley (1997–2005), 2. 53: "It passes belief that [Livius] created out of nothing the metres of Latin tragedy and comedy: he must have built on the work of his predecessors."

65. Gratwick (1982a), 92–93; cf. P. G. McC. Brown (2014), 401–2.

66. Gratwick (1982a), 86.

67. As observed by Gildenhard (2003a), this is "one of the most striking deficiencies of Zorzetti's model: it floats in an ahistorical limbo, covering, without further distinction, a period of over half a millennium (ca. 750 to 240). The changes that Roman society underwent in this period were immense."

68. Esp. Zorzetti (1991), with references to earlier work at 311 n. 2; accepted broadly by e.g. Habinek (1998) and (2005), and by Suerbaum (2002), 49–51 ("§107.1. Die Konzeption einer lyrischen Kultur [Cic. *Tusc.* 4,3f.]"). According to Zorzetti (1991), 313, "[t]he various forms of poetic expression mentioned [by Cic. *Tusc.* 4. 3] together add up to a complete morphology of the archaic genres of *mousikê—gnome, psogos* and *epainos*—as practiced by the Greeks in their *symposia* and *komoi*."

69. Momigliano (1957) is still well worth consulting for a history of the controversy; for the latest overview of the possible interpretations of Cato's reported words, see Bispham and Cornell in *FRHist* 3. 141–43.

70. It is extremely strained to interpret *multis saeculis ante suam aetatem* (Cic. *Brut.* 75) as meaning anything other than that Cato says the custom belonged to a long time before his own: Horsfall (1994), 70; H. and A. Petersmann in Suerbaum (2002), 41; Farrell (2005), 423. In general, then, I share the skepticism about the existence of these *carmina* expressed by many scholars, e.g., Dahlmann (1950); Horsfall (1994), 72–73; Goldberg (1995), 43–46; Gildenhard, (2001); Lowrie (2009), 48–52.

71. Overview in Rathje (1990); synthesis in Zaccaria Ruggiu (2003), with a thesis of a major rupture in continuity between the fifth and second centuries. We must always bear in mind that there were substantial differences between Greek and Roman dining practices at various times, especially as regards whether participants reclined or sat, or whether respectable women were present or not: Rathje (1990), 279–88; C. Smith (1996), 109–10.

72. So, convincingly, Cole (1991), 379; cf. Horsfall (1994), 71; Farrell (2005), 423.

73. Fortson (2011), 95.

74. See, rather, Farrell (2005), 427 on Livius' *Odyssey*: "As an epic poem in Latin, . . . as a written text rather than a song, and possibly as a composition by a professional man of letters rather than a member of the political or social elite, it seems to represent, even if it did not literally start, a revolution in Roman cultural life"; Beard and Crawford (1985), 15: "It is striking that the literary tradition of the late Republic did not emerge from a native primitive strand of Latin literature. While there are a few scanty traces of a crude native dramatic tradition, there was no early development of, for example, epic or ballad. The

Romans had nothing comparable with the *Iliad, Odyssey,* or *Beowulf.* Essentially Roman literature started from cold in the second half of the third century BC."

75. See, e.g., Freudenburg (2013) on Varro's calquing of the origins of Roman drama and satire on putative Greek models, or Gabba (1984), 84 on the comparative technique used by Plutarch's sources to "recover" the social structure of Numa's Rome by analogy with Solon's Athens: "Whoever interpreted the Rome of Numa as a Rome organized according to its crafts clearly did so by following the model of the Athens of Solon, ignoring the vast difference in social and economic conditions." What Cato's motivation was is irrecoverable; he may have been distancing his own practice as an historian from these different modes of commemoration, or he may have been creating an idealizing model of early Rome, in keeping with the models of austerity in the song-culture of Arcadia, for example (as reported by Polybius, 4. 20. 8).

76. Horsfall (1994), 72–73.

77. Excellent methodological remarks in Cole (1991), 377–78; and in Goldberg (2006), 429, on Cic. *Tusc.,* 1. 3, who picks out the "three quite distinct levels of witness" that Cicero's argument "conflates and distorts." Cf. in general C. Smith (2011), 22–23 on the related methodological issues in studying the testimonia that make up the traditions about the Roman kings.

78. See Citroni (2003) on Cicero's constructions of Roman literary history in the *Tusculans* as seen from this point of view; cf. Schnurbusch (2011), 170–71 on Cicero's need to present early Rome as already embodying high culture.

79. See the penetrating analysis of Cicero's procedure at *Tusc.* 4. 3 in Cole (1991), 378.

80. Gildenhard (2003a), referring esp. to Suerbaum (2002), 5.

81. I am agnostic about the antiquity or the venue of the "hymns" that Dionysius of Halicarnassus reports as commemorating in the Augustan period the divine origins of Romulus and Remus (*Ant. Rom.* 1. 79. 10–11) and the piety and justice of Coriolanus (8. 62. 3): see Wiseman (2008), 45 on our ignorance of Dionysius' sources. If forced to guess as to venue, I would suggest songs in the *pompa circensis,* although the only songs attested explicitly for the *pompa* are scurrilous and ribald material (Dion. Hal. *Ant. Rom.* 7. 72. 10–12).

82. Suerbaum (2002), 51 performs this conflation, as noted by Gildenhard (2003a). In general, I share the reservations of Lowrie (2006) concerning the attempts by Habinek (2005) to trace continuities from the literary record back into prehistory, as in seeing, e.g., "comedic parody" as "preserv[ing] for the literary and cultural historian evidence of the 'preliterary' song types of archaic Rome" (Habinek [2005], 53).

83. On the general methodological problem of the indispensability of comparison with Greece for the student of early Rome, see Raaflaub (2005).

84. Zorzetti (1991), 322: "But even in the experience of the diverse Greek *poleis,* the levels of development in the literary sphere differed widely in quality, quantity, and time." So Phillips (1991), 386, in responding to the project of comparison with "the cultural traditions of the archaic Greek city," well asks "But which city?"

85. See Goody (1987) for a discussion of the various forms that this interaction can take.

86. R. L. Fowler (2012). Cf. R. L. Fowler (2004b), 225 on how, with the transcriptions of the poems of Homer and Hesiod by the late eighth century, "clearly a critical point on the scale of literacy, and preservation, had been passed. The lyric poets were the same. The sudden preservation of so many literary texts soon after writing re-enters the Greek world is not accidental, and a 'hard' oralist view cannot explain why there are no texts from any earlier period." Cf. B. B. Powell (2002), 12–13.

87. Neither in bulk, nor in quality, for, as Zorzetti (1991), 322 puts it, the "Roman tradition claimed the existence, not of a great poetry, but of the poetry associated with the rites of a civilized and mature city."

88. Norden (1939): see Scheid (1990) for a magisterial account of the priesthood. I thank John Scheid and Mark Vessey for their stimulating comments on a paper (presented to the Triennial Conference in Cambridge in July 2011) that is the germ for this section.

89. As with so many archaic texts, the process of transcription has introduced modernisms, and Scheid (forthcoming) makes a convincing case that the text as we have it is the work of Augustan-era antiquarianism, produced to go with the reconstruction of the College around 32–31, and not at all necessarily part of the *ritus* of the *Fratres Arvales* before that time: it is, after all, addressed to the "wrong" deity, Mars, not Dea Dia. The *Fratres Arvales,* then, were not singing these exact words in 350. But someone was singing something very like them. My thanks to John Scheid for making it possible for me to read this forthcoming paper.

90. Courtney (1995), 201. For *sta berber* = "stay put," see Katz (1998), 214–16.

91. Even this rebarbative text is considerably more user-friendly than the corrupt and confused original text, as in the diplomatic text of Scheid (1990), 619.

92. Rüpke (1993), 27: "Die vermutlich durch Eduard FRAENKEL vermittelte Erkenntnis, daß das 'urlateinische Arvallied' formal aus dem Griechischen herzuleiten sei, ließ NORDEN die Arbeit an dem fast fertigen Manuskript abbrechen und sie erst neun Jahre später aufnehmen."

93. Norden (1939), 242; see his general discussion, 187–203 and 245–78.

94. J. U. Powell (1925), #160, lines 47–48, 57–60: originally dating probably to the fourth century (Bremer [1981] 205).

95. Courtney (1995), 203. For other examples, and discussion, see Horsfall (1994), 61.

96. Norden (1939), 246–48.

97. Norden (1939), 245: "Diese traditionelle Klassifikation: vorliterarisch = national, literarisch = hellenisierend lässt sich nicht mehr aufrechthalten."

98. I. Rutherford (2001), 59 discussing the question of who performed paeans in Greece, remarks that "in one case singers are represented as a group of priests. These are the Cretan παιήονες of the *Homeric Hymn to Apollo*. It is uncertain whether groups of priests ever performed παιᾶνες in real life. Certainly, it is much more common for the performers to be, not priests or people with a special sacred function, but citizens."

99. On this crucial feature of Roman priesthood, see Rüpke (2005), 1419–39; Rives (2007), 83.

100. Rüpke (2012), 30–31.

101. Furley and Bremer (2001), 1. 5; cf. von Wilamowitz-Moellendorf (1921), 242: "Die gottesdienstliche Poesie der alten Zeit ist verloren."

102. Bremer (1981), 203.

103. Bremer (1981), 204.

104. *PMG* 871; tr. Furley and Bremer (2001), #12. 1. This cult song is quoted in Pulleyn (1997), 149 along with other similarly unelaborate offerings, such as the Athenian prayer for rain quoted by Marcus Aurelius (5. 7 = *PMG* 854): ὗσον, ὗσον, ὦ φίλε Ζεῦ, κατὰ τῆς ἀρούρας τῆς Ἀθηναίων καὶ τῶν πεδίων ("Rain, rain, O dear Zeus, on the ploughland of the Athenians and on their plains," tr. Pulleyn).

105. J. U. Powell (1925), #160, lines 1–6; tr. Furley and Bremer (2001).

106. Cole (1991), 380, including also the Spartan verses quoted by Plutarch (*Mor.* 238ab = *PMG* 870), in which three choruses consisting of "old men, mature warriors, and youths proclaim to all present that they were/are/will be valorous fighters."

107. See Watkins (1995b), chapter 18, on the Tables of Iguvium, for a discussion of "the poetic form of Umbrian liturgical language" (214), and for an account of how certain sacrificial and liturgical formulae were shared by diffusion across central Italy's "linguistic area (German *Sprachbund*")" (218–19). Maddeningly, there is one single reference to singing in the Tables, saying no more than "Have the cult-hymn sung," *ařkani kanetu,* as translated by Weiss (2010), 223. So we know there was a hymn, but its text was not inscribed.

108. Norden (1939), 274–75: "erst in einer literarisch interessierten Zeit kommen gelegentlich Namen zum Vorschein, aber Anonymität blieb für kultische Gemeindepoesie doch die Regel."

109. Wiseman (2008), 45 makes the very important point that the poem of someone like Naevius always has his name attached to it, unlike the anonymous priestly hymns and other *carmina*: his inference, that "these *carmina* were first composed in an oral culture and only later preserved in writing," may be true for some cases, though not, I think, in the cases of the hymns under consideration.

110. Zorzetti (1991), 322.

111. Griffith (2009), 78.

112. Feeney (1998), 39, referring to Page (1955), 254 n. 5. In general, see the references collected there for the independence of surviving Lesbian hymns from cult contexts.

113. Scheid (2003), 178; cf. 99, and Scheid (2007), esp. 444–46; Scheid (2008), esp. 22–23. See Furley and Bremer (2001), 1. 112 on the distinction "between cult hymns composed for religious service only—they tend to be simple and without literary embellishment—and literary hymns which draw on the former for their structure but ultimately serve a different goal: the entertainment and edification of their human audience." This distinction is serviceable, but very distorting if either term is pressed too hard (as Furely and Bremer immediately go on to say *ad loc.*): see C. G. Brown (1990), 174–75 (a reference I owe to Ewen Bowie).

114. See n. 107 above for the Iguvine Tables, and *CIL* 6. 32323. 147–49 for the singing of the *Carmen Saeculare* and its composition by Q. Horatius Flaccus. As Hutchinson (2013), 50 n. 10 points out, it is more regular in Greek inscriptions to find the words of the hymn recorded (as in *CA* pp. 132–73), and this Grecizing tendency is followed up in the *Acta* for the *Ludi Saeculares* of 204 CE, where the words of the hymn are transcribed (Pighi (1965), 224–25).

115. A. Barchiesi (2000), 182.

116. Furley and Bremer (2001), 1. 112.

117. Zorzetti (1991), 322.

118. Levene (1993), 65–66.

119. Gagé (1955), 349–70; MacBain (1982), 65–71; Gruen (1990), 85–87; A. Hardie (2007), 552–53; Welsh (2011); Forsythe (2012), 64–67.

120. Wissowa (1912), 426: "griechisch . . . von Anfang bis zu Ende."

121. MacBain (1982), 65–71.

122. Palmer (1997), 110–12 (Greek knowledge); 108 (Livius Salinator, the son of the previous owner of Livius Andronicus on the freedman hypothesis, or else the man who gave him citizenship).

123. MacBain (1982), 70.
124. A. Hardie (2007), 552–53, with references.
125. MacBain (1982), 70 on the Etruscan connection: see Feeney (1984), 193 for discussion and references.
126. As one of the Press readers suggests to me.
127. On the Metaurus as the immediate result of Juno's final reconciliation following Livius Andronicus' *carmen*, see E. L. Harrison (1984), 114–15; Feeney (1984), with earlier literature (adding Badian [1972], 160 n. 2).
128. Wiseman (2008), 25, well stressing Livy's choice of *conditum*, "composed," therefore "written down" to describe the act of composition (27. 37. 7).
129. So, still, Suerbaum (2002), 99, though Fraenkel (1957), 379 n. 4 already makes the case against.
130. Carratello (1979), 51; Jocelyn (1990), 612.
131. Of course it is impossible to know whether Livius' *carmen* was the first such commissioned in Rome, though I share the skepticism of Gruen (1990), 83 n. 17 and Suerbaum (2002), 96 on the only other possibly attested case we have, the *carmen* at the *Ludi Saeculares* of 249 mentioned, uniquely, by the scholion to Hor. *CS* 8.
132. Zorzetti (1991), 318.
133. Zorzetti (1991), 322; above, text accompanying note 110.
134. I do not think that I accept all of the very interesting argument of Welsh (2011) concerning the significance of the rites of 207 in the scholarly reconstructions of Accius and Porcius Licinus, but I certainly agree with him that the rite appears to have been flagged as one of the "first moments" in Roman literary history. We know from his discussion of the origins of the Roman scenic tradition in 7. 2 that Livy regarded Livius Andronicus as the *protos heuretes* in that department, and he may be giving him primary status in this other development in Book 27 as well.
135. Cole (1991), 381.
136. Horsfall (1976), 79; Gruen (1990), 87–91; Welsh (2011), 4–6.
137. Gagé (1955), 356: "le *sicut patrum memoria* n'est sans doute qu'une impropriété d'expression de Tite-Live"; for a supposed reference to the *Ludi Saeculares* see Mattingly (1957), 161; Bernstein (1998), 129. Rather, as seen by Leo (1913), 58 n. 2, *patrum* here must mean the senators of 200, remembering the events of 207.
138. Here I report the fascinating article of Dubourdieu and Moreau (1986), to which I was referred by Ted Champlin.
139. Solin (1990), 62; cf. Dubourdieu and Moreau (1986), 724–25 for the link with the Pontifex Maximus.
140. Gell. 15. 24 (fr. 1 Courtney); see Dubourdieu and Moreau (1986), 718.

141. Dubourdieu and Moreau (1986), 720–24.
142. On this and the following passages in Obsequens, see Gagé (1955), 363–64; MacBain (1982), 127–35; Forsythe (2012), 66–67.
143. Flower (2010), 81 on "the complete collapse of the last traditional republic of the *nobiles* by the early 80s. . . . That republic . . . was finally destroyed when Sulla marched on Rome in 88."
144. Forsythe (2012), 64–67.
145. Scheid (2003), 99.
146. For yet broader comparative perspectives, I recommend once more the remarkable study of Denecke (2013), comparing the Chinese-Japanese and Greek-Roman cases.
147. Here I follow Catto (2003), a reference I owe to Mark Whittow.
148. Butterfield (2009) stresses the dialogic nature of the formation of an English vernacular, which emerged from a Francophone environment that embraced England along with France: again, there are thought-provoking parallels with the Hellenophone environment from which a vernacular Latin literature emerged.
149. Catto (2003), 25.
150. Catto (2003), 38.
151. Catto (2003), 37.
152. See Chapter 2, text accompanying note 71, and Chapter 3, text accompanying note 69. My thanks to Michael Wachtel for discussion of the Russian case.
153. McLean (1963), 201.
154. Figes (2002), 49. Note how McLean continues shortly after the passage referred to in the previous footnote: "Perhaps few major artistic masterpieces had as yet appeared; but there was already a substantial body of both verse and prose of high quality, and even more important, the indispensible ground work had been carried out which made possible the magnificent achievements that were to follow."
155. See above, note 152.
156. See Chapter 3, text accompanying notes 35–39.

CONCLUSION

1. Rüpke (2012), 89.
2. Wiseman (1974/1987), 207–8 on the antiquity of the Nautii and Geganii; 209 on the claims of the Caecilii (Festus p. 38 L) and Mamilii (Festus p. 116 L).
3. Cornell (2010), 104–5.
4. Purcell (2003).

5. Purcell (2003), 25–26.
6. Purcell (2003), 30–31; cf. Wiseman (2000/2008), 138 arguing for Roman construction of their "liberation" moment as analogous with that of Athens. In general, on the "mnemotecnica istituzionalizzata" in the indigenous world of early Italy, "outside" conventional history, see Curti (2002).
7. Rüpke (2012), chapter 6; cf. the important observations of Curti (2001), esp. 21.
8. See the first two chapters of Feeney (2007a), where I should have cited Moatti (1997), 74–81; cf. Quinn (2013b) for a wide-ranging account of Polybius' "interweaving" (συμπλοκή) of history in response to the dominance of Rome, revisiting the classic account of Walbank (1975) and showing how his "Mediterranean community maps onto Roman hegemony, but it does not simply reproduce that hegemony; instead, the text reinterprets, and at points subverts it" (352).
9. Feeney (2007a), 24–25. On Manetho's lack of impact, see above Chapter 1, text accompanying notes 38–39. As Dillery (2014), xxv compellingly puts it, Manetho and Berossus had their own rather similar strategies: "Babylon and Egypt had to be shown to be both unique, indeed the originating centers of civilization, and yet also relevant to, even intimately connected to the history of all humanity, especially the Greco-Macedonian world, extending down to the period contemporary with the historians themselves." Yet the pre-Christian Greeks could, and on the whole did, hold back from engaging with these visions.
10. See Chapter 6, text accompanying note 109.
11. Cornell (2010), 104.
12. Cornell (2010), 104.
13. Bickerman (1952) is still the place to start; see Erskine (2005) for invaluable modern orientation. Malkin (2011) now puts this approach within a convincing overall picture of the network systems of the Greeks.
14. I. Rutherford (2013), 25.
15. S. West (2013), 88.
16. Erskine (2005), 131–32.
17. Malkin (2011), 5.
18. The best overview is now Erskine (2005).
19. Scheer (2011).
20. Erskine (2005), 125.
21. See Chapter 5, text accompanying notes 112–13.
22. Erskine (2005), 128.
23. Erskine (2005), 132.

24. Erskine (2005), 122–24 takes the peoples of Daunia in southeast Italy as a test case.
25. The bibliography is massive, and I make no pretense to proper acquaintance with it. For orientation, see de Grummond (2006) and Simon (2013).
26. Osborne (1998), 176–84.
27. See Quinn (2013b), 347–48 for the fascinating case of the ideological program behind the Attalid dedication on the acropolis (Paus. 1. 25. 2), that depicted the mythical battle of the Giants, the battles of the Athenians against the Amazons and then the Persians at Marathon, and finally the Pergamene defeat of the Gauls in Mysia, around 237.
28. Coarelli (1996), esp. 177; cf. Farrell (2004), 257–58.
29. See above Chapter 4, text accompanying notes 18–19, for the compelling reconstructions summarized in Wiseman (2004), chapter 5.
30. Wiseman (2004), 114.
31. Cristofani (1990), 61 (#3. 2. 13).
32. C. Smith (1996), 174, who is against the identification with *"the"* Minotaur; cf. Wiseman (2008), 2: "What we see is quite mysterious. . . . The image must have a meaning, but it was probably never written down."
33. See Chapter 7, text accompanying note 22.
34. Fraenkel (1922/2007), 66. Nonetheless, I am sure that A. Barchiesi (2009), 107 is right to remark that the Romans' "appropriation of Greek culture is from the very start much more systematic and respectful than the more imaginative and nonchalant approach of the Etruscans."
35. See Chapter 7, text accompanying notes 23–24.
36. See the judicious discussion of R. L. Fowler (2000), xxvii–xxix, discriminating between the "early Greek mythographers" and the specialized Hellenistic forms of "mythography," beginning in the late fourth century with the *Tragodumena* of Asclepiades (*FGrHist* 12).
37. Fraenkel (1922/2007), 310 n. 77.
38. Rüpke (2012), 210; his chapter 14, from which this quotation comes, is an important account of this process.
39. Rüpke (2012), 210.
40. Narrative of these events in Polyb. 21. 13; Liv. 37. 33.
41. Wissowa (1912), 555–59, esp. 557–58 on their stopping places, marked by Dionysius of Halicarnassus as "the Forum, Capitol, and many other places both private and public" (*Ant. Rom.* 2. 70. 2).
42. For speculation that he may have been stalling to allow time for diplomacy to work on the panicked Antiochus III, see Scullard (1970), 205.

43. Errington (1989), 284.
44. See Boedeker (1988) and Dewald (1997) on Hdt. 9. 114–21.
45. See Chapter 3, text accompanying note 114.
46. Plb. 38. 21–22 = Diod. Sic. 32. 24: see Feeney (2007a), 54–55 for discussion and references.
47. For discussion of this controversial section of the monument, see Morgan (2010), 305.
48. Elliott (2013), 278.
49. Skutsch (1985), 535–36.
50. Shi (2011), 147.
51. See Chapter 7, text accompanying notes 80–82, for the parallel with the Greeks and the Jews in this regard.

References

Acosta-Hughes, B., and S. A. Stephens. 2012. *Callimachus in Context: From Plato to the Augustan Poets.* Cambridge.

Adams, J. N. 1995. *Pelagonius and Latin Veterinary Terminology in the Roman Empire.* Leiden.

———. 2003. *Bilingualism and the Latin Language.* Cambridge.

———. 2005. "The *Bellum Africum*," in Reinhardt, Lapidge, and Adams. 73–96.

———. 2007. *The Regional Diversification of Latin 200 BC–AD 600.* Cambridge.

Adams, J. N., M. Janse, and S. Swain. 2002. *Bilingualism in Ancient Society: Language Contact and the Written Text.* Oxford.

Adams, J. N., and R. G. Mayer. 1999. *Aspects of the Language of Latin Poetry.* Proceedings of the British Academy 93. Oxford.

Adams, J. N., and S. Swain. 2002. "Introduction," in Adams, Janse, and Swain. 1–20.

Affleck, M. 2013. "Priests, patrons, and playwrights: Libraries in Rome before 168 BC," in König, Oikonomopoulou, and Woolf. 124–36.

Allen, W. S. 1978. *Vox Latina: The Pronunciation of Classical Latin*². Cambridge.

Almagor, E. 2012. "Ctesias and the importance of his writings revisited." *Electrum* 19, 9–40.

Alter, R. 1992. *The World of Biblical Literature.* New York.

Anderson, B. R. O'G. 1991. *Imagined Communities: Reflections on the Origin and Spread of Nationalism.* London.

Ando, C. 2005. "Interpretatio Romana." *Classical Philology* 100, 41–51.

Armstrong, D. 1986. "Horatius eques et scriba: Satires 1.6 and 2.7." *Transactions of the American Philological Association* 116, 255–88.

Asheri, D. 1983. *Fra ellenismo e iranismo: Studi sulla società e cultura di Xanthos nella età Achemenide.* Bologna.

Asper, M. 2001. "Gruppen und Dichter: Zu Programmatik und Adressatenbezug bei Kallimachos." *Antike und Abendland* 47, 84–116.

Assmann, J. 1996. "Translating gods: Religion as a factor of cultural (un)translatability," in S. Budick and W. Iser (eds.), *The Translatability of Cultures: Figurations of the Space Between.* Stanford. 25–36.

———. 2002. *The Mind of Egypt: History and Meaning in the Time of the Pharaohs,* tr. A. Jenkins. New York.

———. 2005. "*Periergia:* Egyptian reactions to Greek curiosity," in Gruen (2005). 37–49.

Avlamis, P. 2013. "Does triviality translate? The *Life of Aesop* travels East," in Whitmarsh and Thomson. 261–84.

Azize, J., and N. Weeks (eds.). 2007. *Gilgameš and the World of Assyria.* Leuven.

Badian, E. 1972. "Ennius and his friends," in O. Skutsch (ed.), *Ennius.* Fondation Hardt Entretiens 17. Vandoeuvres-Geneva. 149–208.

Bagnall, R. S. 2002. "Alexandria: Library of dreams." *Proceedings of the American Philosophical Society* 146, 348–62.

Baines, J. 2011. "Ancient Egypt," in A. Feldherr and G. Hardy (eds.), *The Oxford History of Historical Writing.* Vol. 1, *Beginnings to AD 600.* Oxford. 53–75.

Bakhtin, M. M. 1968. *Rabelais and His World,* tr. H. Iswolsky. Cambridge, MA.

———. 1981. *The Dialogic Imagination: Four Essays,* ed. M. Holquist, tr. C. Emerson and M. Holquist. Austin, TX.

Balsdon, J. P. V. D. 1979. *Romans and Aliens.* London.

Baraz, Y. 2012. *A Written Republic: Cicero's Philosophical Politics.* Princeton.

Barchiesi, A. 1992. *P. Ovidii Nasonis Epistulae Heroidum 1–3.* Florence.

———. 2000. "Rituals in ink: Horace on the Greek lyric tradition," in M. Depew and D. Obbink (eds.), *Matrices of Genre: Authors, Canons, and Society.* Cambridge, MA. 166–82.

———. 2002. Review of Rüpke (2001). *Bryn Mawr Classical Review* 06. 26.

———. 2009. "Roman perspectives on the Greeks," in Boys-Stones, Graziosi, and Vasunia. 98–113.

Barchiesi, M. 1962. *Nevio epico: Storia, interpretazione, edizione critica dei frammenti del primo epos latino.* Padua.

Barthes, R. 1971. "Réflexions sur un manuel," in S. Doubrovsky and T. Todorov (eds.), *L'Enseignement de la littérature.* Paris. 170–77.

Bassnett, S., and A. Lefevere (eds.) 1990. *Translation, History, and Culture.* London.

Baurain, C. 1992. "La place des littératures grecque et punique dans les bibliothèques de Carthage." *L'Antiquité Classique* 61, 158–77.

Bayart, J. F. 2005. *The Illusion of Cultural Identity,* tr. S. Rendall, J. Roitman, C. Schoch, and J. Derrick. Chicago.

Beard, M. 1993. "Looking (harder) for Roman myth: Dumézil, declamation and the problems of definition," in F. Graf (ed.), *Mythos in mythenloser Gesellschaft: Das Paradigma Roms.* Stuttgart. 44–64.

Beard, M., and M. Crawford, 1985. *Rome in the Late Republic: Problems and Interpretations.* London.

Beard, M., J. North, and S. Price. 1998. *Religions of Rome.* Cambridge.

Beck, H. 2003. "'Den Ruhm nicht teilen wollen': Fabius Pictor und die Anfänge des römischen Nobilitätsdiskurses," in Eigler, Gotter, Luraghi, and Walter. 73–92.

Beck, H., and U. Walter. 2001. *Die frühen Römischen Historiker.* Vol. 1, *Von Fabius Pictor bis Cn. Gellius.* Stuttgart.

Bellos, D. 2011. *Is That a Fish in Your Ear? Translation and the Meaning of Everything.* New York.

Bernstein, F. 1998. Ludi Publici: *Untersuchungen zur Entstehung und Entwicklung der öffentlichen Spiele im republikanischen Rom.* Stuttgart.

Berthelot, K. 2010. "Early Jewish literature written in Greek," in J. J. Collins and D. C. Harlow (eds.), *The Eerdmans Dictionary of Early Judaism.* Grand Rapids, MI. 181–99.

Berve, H. 1959. *König Hieron II.* Munich.

Bettini, M. 2012. *Vertere: Un' antropologia della traduzione nella cultura antica.* Turin.

Bhabha, H. 1994. *The Location of Culture.* London.

Bickerman, E. 1952. "Origines Gentium." *Classical Philology* 47, 65–81.

Bispham, E. 2007. *From Asculum to Actium: The Municipalization of Italy from the Social War to Augustus.* Oxford.

———. 2008. Review of Humm (2005). *Journal of Roman Studies* 98, 188–89.

Bispham, E., and C. Smith (eds.). 2000. *Religion in Archaic and Republican Rome and Italy: Evidence and Experience.* Edinburgh.

Biville, F. 1987. *Graphie et prononciation des mots grecs en latin.* Louvain.

Blänsdorf, J. 2000. "Livius Andronicus und die Anverwandlung des hellenistischen Dramas in Rom," in Manuwald. 145–56.

———. 2011. *Fragmenta Poetarum Latinorum Epicorum et Lyricorum praeter Ennium et Lucilium*[4]. Berlin.

Blatt, F. 1938. "Remarques sur l'histoire des traductions latines." *Classica et Medievalia* 1, 217–42.

Boedeker, D. 1988. "Protesilaos and the end of Herodotus." *Classical Antiquity* 7, 30–48.

Bonfante, L. (ed.). 2011. *The Barbarians of Ancient Europe: Realities and Interactions.* Cambridge.

Bonner, S. F. 1977. *Education in Ancient Rome.* Berkeley.

Borges, J. L. 1970. "Pierre Menard, author of the *Quixote*," in *Labyrinths,* tr. D. A. Yates and J. E. Irby. Harmondsworth. 62–71.

Bosher, K. (ed.). 2012. *Theater Outside Athens: Drama in Greek Sicily and South Italy.* Cambridge.

———. 2013. "Infinite variety: Ancient Greek drama in Sicily," in Lyons, Bennett, and Marconi. 111–21.

Bowersock, G. W. 1990. *Hellenism in Late Antiquity.* Cambridge.

———. 1995. "The barbarism of the Greeks." *Harvard Studies in Classical Philology* 97, 3–14.

Bowman, A. K., and G. Woolf (eds.). 1994. *Literacy and Power in the Ancient World.* Cambridge.

Boyden, M. 2006. "Language politics, translation, and American literary history." *Target* 18, 121–37.

Boyle, A. J. 2006. *An Introduction to Roman Tragedy.* London.

Boys-Stones, G. R., B. Graziosi, and P. Vasunia (eds.). 2009. *The Oxford Handbook of Hellenic Studies.* Oxford.

Braun, M., A. Haltenhoff, and F.-H. Mutschler (eds.). 2000. *Moribus antiquis res stat Romana: Römische Werte und römische Literatur im dritten und zweiten Jahrhundert vor Christus.* Munich.

Braund, D., and C. Gill (eds.). 2003. *Myth, History and Culture in Republican Rome: Studies in Honour of T. P. Wiseman.* Exeter.

Breed, B. W. 2006. *Pastoral Inscriptions: Reading and Writing Virgil's Eclogues.* London.

Bremer, J. M. 1981. "Greek hymns," in H. S. Versnel (ed.), *Faith, Hope and Worship: Aspects of Religious Mentality in the Ancient World.* Leiden. 193–215.

Breyer, G. 1993. *Etruskiches Sprachgut im Lateinischen unter Ausschluss des spezifisch onomastischen Bereiches.* Leiden.

Brock, S. 1979. "Aspects of translation technique in antiquity." *Greek, Roman, and Byzantine Studies* 20, 69–87.

———. 1994. "Greek and Syriac in Late Antique Syria," in Bowman and Woolf. 149–60.

Broughton, T. R. S. 1951–1952. *The Magistrates of the Roman Republic.* 2 vols. New York.

Brouillet, M. S. (ed.). 1994. *From Hannibal to Saint Augustine: Ancient Art of North Africa from the Musée du Louvre.* Michael C. Carlos Museum, Emory University, Atlanta.

Brown, C. G. 1990. "Honouring the goddess: Philicus' Hymn to Demeter." *Aegyptus* 70, 173–89.

Brown, P. G. McC. 2002. "Actors and actor-managers at Rome in the time of Plautus and Terence," in Easterling and Hall. 225–37.

———. 2014. "The beginnings of Roman comedy," in Fontaine and Scafuro. 401–8.

Büchner, K. 1979. "Livius Andronicus und die erste künstleriche Übersetzung der europäischen Kultur." *Symbolae Osloenses* 54, 37–70.

Buffagni, C., B. Garzelli, and S. Zanotti (eds.). 2011. *The Translator as Author: Perspectives on Literary Translation.* Berlin.

Burkert, W. 1985. *Greek Religion: Archaic and Classical,* tr. J. Raffan. Oxford.

———. 1992. *The Orientalizing Revolution: Near Eastern Influence on Greek Culture in the Early Archaic Age,* tr. M. E. Pinder and W. Burkert. Cambridge, MA.

———. 2004. *Babylon, Memphis, Persepolis: Eastern Contexts of Greek Culture.* Cambridge, MA.

Burnett, A. M. 1986. "The iconography of Roman coin types in the third century BC." *Numismatic Chronicle* 146, 67–75.

Butterfield, A. 2009. *The Familiar Enemy: Chaucer, Language, and Nation in the Hundred Years War.* Oxford.

Caldelli, M. L. 2012. "Associazioni di artisti a Roma: Una messa a punto," in K. Coleman and J. Nelis-Clément (eds.), *L'Organisation des spectacles dans le monde romain: Entretiens sur l'antiquité classique,* vol. 58. Vandoeuvres-Geneva. 131–71.

Campbell, B. G. 2001. *Performing and Processing the* Aeneid. New York.

Campbell, D. R. M. 2011. "Translation among the Hittites," in McElduff and Sciarrino. 161–75.

Canfora, L. 1994. "Roma 'città greca.'" *Quaderni di storia* 39, 3–41.

Carratello, U. 1979. *Livio Andronico.* Rome.

Catto, M. 2003. "Written English: The making of the language 1370–1400." *Past & Present* 179, 24–59.

Ceccarelli, P. 2010. "Tragedy in the civic and cultural life of Hellenistic city-states," in Gildenhard and Revermann. 99–150.

Champion, C. B. 2004. *Cultural Politics in Polybius's Histories.* Berkeley.

Charpin, D. 2010. *Reading and Writing in Babylon,* tr. J. M. Todd. Cambridge, MA.

Chaudhuri, S. 1999. *Translation and Understanding.* New Delhi.

Cirucci, G. 2013. "The Roman conquest of Sicily and its consequences," in Lyons, Bennett, and Marconi. 134–43.

Citroni, M. 2003. "I proemi delle Tusculanae e la costruzione di un'immagine della tradizione letteraria romana," in M. Citroni (ed.), *Memoria e identità: La cultura romana costruisce la sua immagine.* Florence. 149–84.

——. 2013. "Horace's *Epistle* 2. 1, Cicero, Varro, and the ancient debate about the origins and the development of Latin poetry," in J. Farrell and D. Nelis (eds.), *Augustan Poetry and the Roman Republic.* Oxford. 180–204.

Clackson, J. 2004. "Latin," in R. D. Woodard (ed.), *The Cambridge Encyclopedia of the World's Ancient Languages.* Cambridge. 789–811.

—— (ed.). 2011a. *A Companion to the Latin Language.* Oxford.

——. 2011b. "Classical Latin," in Clackson (2011a). 236–56.

Classen, C. J. 1992. "Ennius: Ein Fremder in Rom." *Gymnasium* 99, 121–45.

Clausen, W. V. 1964. "Callimachus and Latin poetry." *Greek, Roman, and Byzantine Studies* 5, 181–96.

Clifford, J. 1988. *The Predicament of Culture: Twentieth-Century Ethnography, Literature, and Art.* Cambridge, MA.

Coarelli, F. 1985. *Il Foro Romano.* Vol. 2, *Periodo reppublicano e augusteo.* Rome.

——. 1996. *Revixit Ars: Arte e ideologia a Roma: Dai modelli ellenistici alla tradizione repubblicana.* Rome.

Cole, T. 1991. Response to Zorzetti. *Classical Journal* 86, 377–82.

Coleman, R. G. G. 1975. "Greek influence on Latin syntax." *Transactions and Proceedings of the Philological Society* 74, 101–56.

——. 1999. "Poetic diction and the poetic register," in Adams and Mayer. 21–93.

Collombert, P., and L. Coulon. 2000. "Les dieux contre la mer: Le début du 'papyrus d'Astarté' (pBN 202)." *Bulletin de l'Institut français d'archéologie orientale* 100, 193–242.

Colonna, G. 1993. "Stutture teatriformi in Etruria," in *Spectacles sportifs et scéniques dans le monde Étrusco-italique.* Rome. 321–47.

Compagnon, A. 2004. *Literature, Theory, and Common Sense,* tr. C. Cosman. Princeton.

Connolly, J. 2007. "Being Greek/being Roman: Hellenism and assimilation in the Roman empire." *Millennium Jahrbuch zu Kultur und Geschichte* 101, 93–119.

Connors, C. 2004. "Monkey business: Imitation, authenticity, and identity from Pithekoussai to Plautus." *Classical Antiquity* 23, 179–207.

Conte, G. B. 1986. *The Rhetoric of Imitation: Genre and Poetic Memory in Virgil and Other Latin Poets,* ed. C. Segal. Ithaca, NY.

——. 1994. *Latin Literature: A History,* tr. J. B. Solow, rev. D. Fowler and G. W. Most. Baltimore.

Cooley, A. E. 2009. *Res Gestae Divi Augusti: Text, Translation, and Commentary.* Cambridge.

Corbeill, A. 2001. "Education in the Roman Republic: Creating traditions," in Y. L. Too (ed.), *Education in Greek and Roman Antiquity*. Leiden. 261–87.

Cornell, T. J. 1978. Review of Wardman (1976). *Classical Review* 28, 110–12.

——. 1991. "The tyranny of the evidence: A discussion of the possible uses of literacy in Etruria and Latium in the archaic age," in *Literacy in the Roman World, JRS Suppl. Series* 3. Ann Arbor, MI. 7–33.

——. 1995. *The Beginnings of Rome: Italy and Rome from the Bronze Age to the Punic Wars (c. 1000–264 BC)*. London.

——. 2010. "Universal history and the early Roman historians," in P. Liddel and A. Fear (eds.), *Historiae Mundi: Studies in Universal History*. London. 102–15.

——. 2011. "Etruscan historiography," in Marincola (2011). 175–204.

——. 2013. *The Fragments of the Roman Historians*. 3 vols. Oxford.

Courtney, E. 1993. *The Fragmentary Latin Poets*. Oxford.

——. 1995. *Musa Lapidaria: A Selection of Latin Verse Inscriptions*. Atlanta, GA.

——. 2004. "The 'Greek' accusative." *Classical Journal* 99, 425–31.

Cowan, R. 2010. "Medea in Roman Republican tragedy," in H. Bartel and A. Simon (eds.), *Unbinding Medea: Interdisciplinary Approaches to a Classical Myth from Antiquity to the 21st Century*. London. 39–52.

——. 2011. Review of Gildenhard and Revermann (2010). *Bryn Mawr Classical Review* 11.49.

——. 2013. "Haven't I seen you somewhere before? Optical allusions in Republican tragedy," in Harrison and Liapis. 311–42.

Crawford, M. 1990. "Origini e sviluppi del sistema provinciale romano," in G. Clemente, F. Coarelli, and E. Gabba (eds.), *Storia di Roma*. Vol. 2, *L'impero mediterraneo I*. Turin. 91–121.

——. 1993. *The Roman Republic²*. Cambridge, MA.

Crawford, M., W. M. Broadhead, J. P. T. Clackson, F. Santangelo, S. Thompson, and M. Watmough. 2011. *Imagines Italicae: A Corpus of Italian Inscriptions*. 3 vols. London.

Crespo, E. 2007. "The linguistic policy of the Ptolemaic kingdom," in M. B. Hatzopoulos (ed.), ΦΩΝΗΣ ΧΑΡΑΚΤΗΡ ΕΘΝΙΚΟΣ: *Actes du Ve Congrès international de dialectologie grecque*. Athens. 35–49.

Cribiore, R. 2001. *Gymnastics of the Mind: Greek Education in Hellenistic and Roman Egypt*. Princeton.

Cristofani, M. (ed.). 1990. *La grande Roma dei Tarquini: Catalogo della mostra*. Rome.

Csapo, E. 2007. "The men who built the theatres: *Theatropolai, theatronai, arkhitektones*," in P. J. Wilson (ed.), *The Greek Theatre and Festivals: Documentary Studies*. Oxford. 87–115.

——. 2010. *Actors and Icons of the Ancient Theater*. Oxford.

Currie, B. 2012. "The *Iliad*, Gilgamesh, and Neoanalysis," in F. Montanari and A. Rengakos (eds.), *Homeric Contexts: Neoanalysis and the Interpretation of Oral Poetry*. Berlin. 535–72.

Curti, E. 2000. "From Concordia to the Quirinal: Notes on religion and politics in mid-republican/hellenistic Rome," in Bispham and Smith. 77–91.

——. 2001. "Toynbee's Legacy: Discussing aspects of the Romanization of Italy," in S. Keay and N. Terrenato (eds.), *Italy and the West: Comparative Issues in Romanization*. Exeter. 17–26.

——. 2002. "Fra mito e storia: Gli indigeni e la percezione del passato," in M. L. Nava and M. Osanna (eds.), *Immagine e mito nella Basilicata Antica*. Venosa. 47–62.

Curti, E., E. Dench, and J. R. Patterson. 1996. "The archaeology of central and southern Roman Italy: Recent trends and approaches." *Journal of Roman Studies* 86, 170–89.

Dahlmann, H. 1950. "Zur Überlieferung über die 'altrömischen Tafellieder'." *Abhandlungen der Akademie der Wissenschaften und der Literatur, Geistes- und Sozialwissenschaftlichen Klasse* 17, 1193–1202.

Daiber, H. 2007. "Die griechisch-arabische Wissenschaftsüberlieferung in der arabisch-islamischen Kultur in Übersetzungen des 8.–10. Jahrhunderts," in Kittel, House, and Schultze. 1206–17.

Dalley, S. (ed.). 1997. *The Legacy of Mesopotamia*. Oxford.

Dalley, S. and A. T. Rayes. 1997. "Mesopotamian contact and influence in the Greek World 2. Persia, Alexander, and Rome," in Dalley. 107–24.

Daly, L. 1943. "The entitulature of pre-Ciceronian writings," in *Classical Studies in Honor of William Abbott Oldfather*. Urbana, IL. 20–38.

Dangel, J. 1995. *Accius: Oeuvres (fragments)*. Paris.

Dearden, C. 2004. "Sicily and Rome: The Greek context for Roman drama." *Mediterranean Archaeology* 17, 121–30.

——. 2012. "Whose line is it anyway? West Greek comedy in its context," in Bosher (2012). 272–88.

De Breucker, G. 2011. "Berossos between tradition and innovation," in Radner and Robson. 637–61.

De Cazanove, O. 2000. "Some thoughts on the 'religious romanization' of Italy before the Social War," in Bispham and Smith. 71–76.

De Crom, D. 2011. "Translation and directionality in the Hebrew-Greek tradition," in McElduff and Sciarrino. 77–87.

de Grummond, N. T. 2006. *Etruscan Myth, Sacred History, and Legend*. Philadelphia.

de Melo, W. 2011. "The language of Roman comedy," in Clackson (2011a). 321–43.

———. 2014. "Plautus' dramatic predecessors and contemporaries in Rome," in Fontaine and Scafuro. 447–61.

De Sensi Sestito, G. 1977. *Gerone II: Un monarco ellenistico in Sicilia*. Palermo.

Degl'Innocenti Pierini, R. 1977. *Studi su Accio*. Florence.

Delisle, J., and J. Woodsworth (eds.). 1995. *Translators through History*. Amsterdam.

Dench, E. 1995. *From Barbarians to New Men: Greek, Roman, and Modern Perceptions of Peoples from the Central Apennines*. Oxford.

———. 2005. *Romulus' Asylum: Roman Identities from the Age of Alexander to the Age of Hadrian*. Oxford.

Denecke, W. 2013. *Classical World Literatures: Sino-Japanese and Greco-Roman Comparisons*. Oxford.

Derrida, J. 1981. *Dissemination*, tr. B. Johnson. Chicago.

Devoto, G. 1967. "La crisi del latino nel V secolo a.C.," in *Scritti minori*. Vol. 2. Florence. 362–68.

Devy, G. N. 1993. *In Another Tongue: Essays on Indian English Literature*. Frankfurt am Main.

Dewald, C. 1997. "Wanton kings, pickled heroes, and gnomic founding fathers: Strategies of meaning at the end of Herodotus' *Histories*," in D. H. Roberts, F. M. Dunn, and D. Fowler (eds.), *Classical Closure: Reading the End in Greek and Latin Literature*. Princeton. 62–82.

Dickey, E. 2012. *The Colloquia of the Hermeneumata Pseudodositheana*. Vol. 1, *Colloquia Monacensia-Einsidlensia, Leidense-Stephani, and Stephani*. Cambridge.

Dillery, J. 1999. "The first Egyptian narrative history: Manetho and Greek historiography." *Zeitschrift für Papyrologie und Epigraphik* 127, 93–116.

———. 2002. "Quintus Fabius Pictor and Greco-Roman historiography at Rome," in J. F. Miller, C. Damon, and K. S. Myers (eds.), *Vertis in Usum: Studies in Honor of Edward Courtney*. Munich. 1–23.

———. 2007. "Greek historians of the Near East: Clio's 'other' sons," in Marincola (2007). 1.221–30.

———. 2014. *Clio's "Other" Sons: Berossus and Manetho: With an Afterword on Demetrius*. Ann Arbor, MI.

Dionisotti, A. C. 2005. "Translator's Latin," in Reinhardt, Lapidge, and Adams. 357–75.

Droysen, J. G. 1836. *Geschichte des Hellenismus*. 2 vols. Hamburg.

Dryden, J. 1697/1992. "On translation," in Schulte and Biguenet. 17–31.

Dubourdieu, A., and Ph. Moreau (1986). "*Imbrex* et *Tegula*: La technique des applaudissements à Rome." *Latomus* 45, 718–30.

Duckworth, G. E. 1952. *The Nature of Roman Comedy: A Study in Popular Entertainment*. Princeton.

Dumézil, G. 1970. *Archaic Roman Religion*, tr. P. Krapp. Chicago.

Dumont, J. C., and M.-H. François-Garelli. 1998. *Le Théâtre à Rome*. Paris.

Dunand, F., and P. Lévêque (eds.). 1975. *Les Syncrétismes dans les religions de l'antiquité*. Colloque de Besançon (22–23 octobre 1973). Leiden.

Dunsch, B. 1999. "Some Notes on the Understanding of Terence, *Heauton Timorumenos* 6: *Comoedia duplex, argumentum simplex*, and Hellenistic scholarship." *Classica et Mediaevalia* 50, 97–131.

———. 2009. "Religion in der römischen Komödie: Einige programmatische Überlegungen," in A. Bendlin and J. Rüpke (eds.), *Römische Religion im historischen Wandel: Diskursentwicklung von Plautus bis Ovid*. Stuttgart. 17–56.

Dupont, F. 1993. "Ludions, *lydioi*: Les danseurs de la *pompa circensis*: Exégèse et discours sur l'origine des jeux à Rome," in *Spectacles sportifs et scéniques dans le monde étrusco-italique*. Rome. 189–210.

Easterling, P. E. 1993. "The end of an era? Tragedy in the early fourth century," in A. H. Sommerstein, S. Halliwell, J. Henderson, and B. Zimmermann (eds.), *Tragedy, Comedy and the Polis*. Bari, Italy. 559–69.

———. 1997. "From repertoire to canon," in P. Easterling (ed.), *The Cambridge Companion to Greek Tragedy*. Cambridge. 211–27.

Easterling, P., and E. Hall (eds.). 2002. *Greek and Roman Actors: Aspects of an Ancient Profession*. Cambridge.

Eckstein, A. M. 2006. *Mediterranean Anarchy, Interstate War, and the Rise of Rome*. Berkeley.

Eco, U. 2001. *Experiences in Translation*, tr. A. McEwen. Toronto.

Edmondson, J. 1999. "The cultural politics of public spectacle in Rome and the Greek East, 167–166 BCE," in B. Bergmann and C. Kondoleon (eds.), *The Art of Ancient Spectacle*. Studies in the History of Art Symposium Papers 34. Washington, DC. 77–95.

Eigler, E., U. Gotter, N. Luraghi, and U. Walter (eds.). 2003. *Formen römischer Geschichtsschreibung von den Anfängen bis Livius: Gattungen, Autoren, Contexte*. Darmstadt.

Elliott, J. 2013. *Ennius and the Architecture of the* Annales. Cambridge.

Errington, R. M. 1989. "Rome against Philip and Antiochus." *Cambridge Ancient History*² 8. 244–89.

Erskine, A. 2001. *Troy between Greece and Rome: Local Tradition and Imperial Power*. Oxford.

———. 2005. "Unity and identity: Shaping the past in the Greek Mediterranean," in Gruen (2005). 121–36.

Evans, R. J. 2003–2008. *The Third Reich Trilogy*. London.

Fantham, E. 1989. "The growth of literature and criticism at Rome," in G. A. Kennedy (ed.), *The Cambridge History of Literary Criticism*. Vol. 1, *Classical Criticism*. 220–44.

———. 2003. "Pacuvius: Melodrama, reversals and recognitions," in Braund and Gill. 98–118.

Fantuzzi, M., and R. Hunter. 2004. *Tradition and Innovation in Hellenistic Poetry*. Cambridge.

Farrell, J. 2001. *Latin Language and Latin Culture: From Ancient to Modern Times*. Cambridge.

———. 2004. "Roman Homer," in Fowler (2004a). 254–71.

———. 2005. "The origins and essence of Roman epic," in Foley. 417–28.

———. 2007. Review of Goldberg (2005), *American Journal of Philology* 128, 283–86.

Feeney, D. 1984. "The reconciliations of Juno." *Classical Quarterly* 34, 179–94.

———. 1991. *The Gods in Epic: Poets and Critics of the Classical Tradition*. Oxford.

———. 1998. *Literature and Religion at Rome: Cultures, Contexts, and Beliefs*. Cambridge.

———. 2002. "*Una cum scriptore mea*: Poetry, principate, and the traditions of literary history in the *Epistle to Augustus*," in T. Woodman and D. Feeney (eds.), *Traditions and Contexts in the Poetry of Horace*. Cambridge. 172–87.

———. 2005. "The beginnings of a literature in Latin." *Journal of Roman Studies* 95, 226–40.

———. 2007a. *Caesar's Calendar: Ancient Time and the Beginnings of History*. Berkeley.

———. 2007b. "The history of Roman religion in Roman historiography and epic," in J. Rüpke (ed.), *A Companion to Roman Religion*. Malden. 129–42.

———. 2009. "Virgil's tale of four cities: Troy, Carthage, Alexandria and Rome." The Ninth Syme Memorial Lecture. Victoria University of Wellington.

Feldherr, A. 1998. *Spectacle and Society in Livy's History*. Berkeley.

Fewster, P. 2002. "Bilingualism in Roman Egypt," in Adams, Janse, and Swain. 220–45.

Figes, O. 2002. *Natasha's Dance: A Cultural History of Russia*. New York.

Finley, M. 1968. *A History of Sicily*. Vol. 1, *Ancient Sicily to the Arab Conquest*. London.

Fisher, J. 2014. *The Annals of Quintus Ennius and the Italic Tradition*. Baltimore.

Flaig, E. 1999. "Über die Grenzen der Akkulturation: Wider die Verdinglichung des Kulturbegriffs," in Vogt-Spira and Rommel. 81–112.

Fletcher, K. 2008. "Systematic genealogies in Apollodorus' *Bibliotheca* and the exclusion of Rome from Greek myth." *Classical Antiquity* 27, 59–91.

——. forthcoming. "Hyginus' *Fabulae*: Toward a Roman mythography," in R. S. Smith and S. Trzaskoma (eds.), *Writing Greek and Roman Myth: Mythography in the Ancient World*. Peeters.

Flores, E. 2000–2006. *Quinto Ennio: Annali*. Naples.

——. 2011. *Liui Andronici* Odusia. *Introduzione, edizione critica e versione italiana*. Naples.

Flower, H. I. 1995. "*Fabulae praetextae* in context: When were plays on contemporary subjects performed in Republican Rome?" *Classical Quarterly* 45, 170–90.

——. 2000. "*Fabula de Bacchanalibus*: The Bacchanalian cult of the second century BC and Roman drama," in Manuwald (2000). 23–35.

——. 2003. "Memories of Marcellus: History and memory in Roman Republican culture," in Eigler, Gotter, Luraghi, and Walter. 39–52.

——. 2004a. "Spectacle and political culture in the Roman Republic," in Flower (2004b). 322–44.

——. (ed.). 2004b. *The Cambridge Companion to the Roman Republic*. Cambridge.

——. 2010. *Roman Republics*. Princeton.

Fögen, T. 2003. "*Utraque Lingua*": *A Bibliography on Bi- and Multilingualism in Graeco-Roman Antiquity and in Modern Times*. Essen.

——. 2005. "The transformation of Greek scientific knowledge by Roman technical writers: On the translating of technical texts in antiquity." *Antike Naturwissenschaft und ihre Rezeption* 15, 91–114.

Foley, J. M. (ed.). 2009. *A Companion to Ancient Epic*. Malden, MA.

Fontaine, M. 2010. *Funny Words in Plautine Comedy*. Oxford.

——. 2014. "Between the two paradigms: Plautus," in Fontaine and Scafuro. 516–37.

Fontaine, M., and A. C. Scafuro (eds.). 2014. *The Oxford Handbook of Greek and Roman Comedy*. Oxford.

Ford, A. 1991. "Unity in Greek criticism and poetry," review of Heath (1989). *Arion*, Third Series, 1: 125–54.

Fordyce, C. J. 1977. *P. Vergili Maronis Aeneidos: Libri VII–VIII*. Oxford.

Forsythe, G. 2005. *A Critical History of Early Rome: From Prehistory to the First Punic War*. Berkeley.

——. 2012. *Time in Roman Religion: One Thousand Years of Religious History*. New York.

Fortson, B. W. 2011. "Latin prosody and metrics," in Clackson (2011a). 92–104.

Fowler, D. 2000. "Deviant focalization in Vergil's *Aeneid*," in *Roman Constructions: Readings in Postmodern Latin*. Oxford. 40–63.

Fowler, R. L. 2000. *Early Greek Mythography*. Vol. 1, *Texts*. Oxford.

—— (ed.). 2004a. *The Cambridge Companion to Homer*. Cambridge.

——. 2004b. "The Homeric question," in R. L. Fowler (2004a). 220–32.

——. 2012. "Written work." *Times Literary Supplement* March 16, 28.

Fraenkel, E. 1922/2007. *Plautine Elements in Plautus (Plautinisches im Plautus)*, tr. T. Drevikovsky and F. Muecke. Oxford.

——. 1931. "Livius Andronicus." *Real-Encyclopädie der klassischen Altertumswissenschaft* Suppl. V. 598–607.

——. 1935. "Naevius." *Real-Encyclopädie der klassischen Altertumswissenschaft* Suppl. VI. 622–40.

——. 1957. *Horace*. Oxford.

Frank, T. 1928. "Rome and Carthage: The first Punic War," *Cambridge Ancient History*[1] 7. 665–98.

——. 1930. *Life and Literature in the Roman Republic*. Berkeley.

Franke, P. R. 1992. "Dolmetschen in hellenistischer Zeit," in Müller, Sier, and Werner. 85–96.

Fränkel, H. 1932. "Griechische Bildung in altrömischen Epen." *Hermes* 67, 303–11.

Franko, G. F. 2013. "*Anicius vortit barbare:* The scenic games of L. Anicius Gallus and the aesthetics of Greek and Roman performance," in Harrison and Liapis. 343–60.

——. 2014. "Festivals, producers, theatrical spaces, and records," in Fontaine and Scafuro. 409–23.

Fraser, P. M. 1972. *Ptolemaic Alexandria*. Oxford.

Freudenburg, K. 2013. "The afterlife of Varro in Horace's *Sermones:* Generic issues in Roman satire," in T. D. Papanghelis, S. J. Harrison, and S. Frangoulidis (eds.), *Generic Interfaces in Latin Literature: Encounters, Interactions, and Transformations*. Berlin. 297–336.

Frier, B. W. 1999. *Libri Annales Pontificum Maximorum: The Origins of the Annalistic Tradition.*[2] Ann Arbor, MI.

Fruyt, M. 2011. "Latin vocabulary," in Clackson (2011a). 144–56.

Fuhrmann, M. 1970. "*Interpretatio:* Notizien zur Wortgeschichte," in *Sympotica Franz Wieacker: Sexagenario Sasbachwaldeni a Suis Libata*. Göttingen. 80–110.

Furley, W. D., and J. M. Bremer. 2001. *Greek Hymns: Selected Cult Songs from the Archaic to the Hellenistic Period*. 2 vols. Tubingen.

Gabba, E. 1984. "The *collegia* of Numa: Problems of method and political ideas." *Journal of Roman Studies* 74, 81–86.

———. 2001. "Ancora sulle origin di Roma." *Athenaeum* 89, 589–91.

Gagé, J. 1955. *Apollon romain: Essai sur le culte d'Apollon et le développement du "ritus Graecus" à Rome des origines à Auguste.* Paris.

Gallini, C. 1973. "Che cosa intendere per ellenizzazione: Problemi di metodo." *Dialoghi di Archaeologia* 7, 175–91.

Gardner, A. 2013. "Thinking about Roman imperialism: Postcolonialism, globalisation and beyond?" *Britannia* 44, 1–25.

Garnsey, P., and R. Saller. 1987. *The Roman Empire: Economy, Society and Culture.* Berkeley.

Gee, E. 2013. *Aratus and the Astronomical Tradition.* Oxford.

Gentili, B. 1979. *Theatrical Performances in the Ancient World: Hellenistic and Early Roman Theatre.* Amsterdam.

Gentzler, E. 2001. *Contemporary Translation Theories*². Clevedon, UK.

George, A. R. 2003. *The Babylonian Gilgamesh Epic: Introduction, Critical Edition, and Cuneiform Texts.* 2 vols. Oxford.

———. 2007a. "The epic of Gilgamesh: Thoughts on genre and meaning," in Azize and Weeks. 37–65.

———. 2007b. "Gilgamesh and the literature of Mesopotamia," in Leick. 447–59.

Gibson, B. 2012. "Festivals and games in Polybius," in Smith and Yarrow. 263–77.

Gigante, M. 1971. *Rintone e il teatro in Magna Graecia.* Naples.

Gildenhard, I. 2001. Review of Linker and Stemmler (2000) and of Braun, Haltenhoff, and Mutschler (2000). *Bryn Mawr Classical Review* 07.04.

———. 2003a. Review of Suerbaum (2002). *Bryn Mawr Classical Review* 09.39.

———. 2003b. "The 'Annalist' before the Annalists: Ennius and his *Annales*," in Eigler, Gotter, Luraghi, and Walter. 93–114.

———. 2007a. Paideia Romana: *Cicero's* Tusculan Disputations. Cambridge.

———. 2007b. "Virgil vs. Ennius, or: The undoing of the annalist," in W. Fitzgerald and E. Gowers (eds.), Ennius Perennis: *The* Annals *and Beyond.* Cambridge. 73–102.

———. 2010. "Buskins & SPQR: Roman receptions of Greek tragedy," in Gildenhard and Revermann. 153–85.

Gildenhard, I., and M. Revermann (eds.). 2010. *Beyond the Fifth Century: Interactions with Greek Tragedy from the Fourth Century BCE to the Middle Ages.* Berlin.

Girard, R. 1961/1965. *Deceit, Desire, and the Novel: Self and Other in Literary Structure (Mensonge romantique et vérité romanesque),* tr. Y. Freccero. Baltimore.

Gitner, A. 2012. *Horace and the Greek Language: Aspects of Literary Bilingualism.* PhD diss., Princeton.

Glucker, J. 2012. "Cicero's remarks on translating philosophical terms—some general problems," in Glucker and Burnett. 37–96.

Glucker, J., and C. Burnett. 2012. *Greek into Latin from Antiquity until the Nineteenth Century.* London.

Gnanadesikan, A. 2009. *The Writing Revolution: Cuneiform to the Internet.* Chichester, UK.

Goldberg, S. M. 1986. *Understanding Terence.* Princeton.

———. 1995. *Epic in Republican Rome.* Oxford.

———. 1998. "Plautus on the Palatine." *Journal of Roman Studies* 88, 1–20.

———. 2005. *Constructing Literature in the Roman Republic.* Cambridge.

———. 2006. "Ennius after the banquet." *Arethusa* 39, 427–47.

———. 2007a. "Antiquity's antiquity," in W. Verbaal, Y. Maes, and J. Papy (eds.), *Latinitas Perennis.* Vol. 1, *The Continuity of Latin Literature.* Leiden. 17–20.

———. 2007b. "Research report: Reading Roman tragedy." *International Journal of the Classical Tradition* 13, 571–84.

———. 2009a. "Early Republican epic," in Foley. 429–39.

———. 2009b. "Fact, fiction, and form in early Roman epic," in D. Konstan and K. A. Raaflaub (eds.), *Epic and History.* Malden, MA. 167–84.

———. 2009c. Review of Flores (2000–2006). *Paideia* 64, 637–55.

Goldhill, S. 1999. "Literary history without literature: Reading practices in the ancient world." *SubStance* 88, 57–89.

———. 2005. Review of S. Stephens (2003). *Gnomon* 77, 99–104.

Goldschmidt, N. 2013. *Shaggy Crowns: Ennius'* Annales *and Virgil's* Aeneid. Oxford.

González, J. M. 2006. Review of Lehmler (2005). *Bryn Mawr Classical Review* 08.40.

Goody, J. 1987. *The Interface between the Written and the Oral.* Cambridge.

Gordon, A. E. 1969. "On the origins of the Latin alphabet: Modern views." *California Studies in Classical Antiquity* 2, 157–70.

Gowers, E. 1993. *The Loaded Table: Representations of Food in Roman Literature.* Oxford.

———. 2010. "Augustus and 'Syracuse.'" *Journal of Roman Studies* 100, 69–87.

Gratwick, A. S. 1982a. "Drama," in Kenney and Clausen. 77–137.

———. 1982b. "Prose literature," in Kenney and Clausen. 138–55.

———. 1993. *Plautus:* Menaechmi. Cambridge.

Green, J. R. 2008. "Theatre production: 1996–2006." *Lustrum* 50, 7–302, 367–91.

———. 2012. "Comic vases in South Italy: Continuity and innovation in the development of a figurative language," in Bosher. 289–342.

Green, P. 1982. *Ovid: The Erotic Poems.* London.

Greenblatt, S. 1980. *Renaissance Self-Fashioning: From More to Shakespeare.* Chicago.

Griffith, M. 2009. "Greek lyric and the place of humans in the world," in F. Budelmann (ed.), *The Cambridge Companion to Greek Lyric.* Cambridge. 72–94.

Gruen, E. S. 1990. *Studies in Greek Culture and Roman Policy.* Berkeley.

———. 1992. *Culture and National Identity in Republican Rome.* Ithaca, NY.

———. 1998. *Heritage and Hellenism: The Reinvention of Jewish Tradition.* Berkeley.

——— (ed.). 2005. *Cultural Borrowings and Ethnic Appropriations in Antiquity.* Stuttgart.

——— (ed.). 2011. *Cultural Identity in the Ancient Mediterranean.* Los Angeles.

Gsell, St. 1928–1929. *Histoire ancienne de l'Afrique du Nord,* Vol. 4³. Paris.

Guittard, C. 2007. Carmen *et prophéties à Rome.* Turnhout, Belgium.

———. 2009. "Traduire l'Étrusque: De l'Étrusque au Latin et du Latin à l'Étrusque," in B. Bortolussi, M. Keller, S. Minon, and L. Sznajder (eds.), *Traduire, transposer, transmettre dans l'antiquité gréco-romaine.* Nanterre. 113–25.

Günther, L.-M. 2002. "Griechische Bühnenkunst bei den römischen Siegesspielen des L. Anicius," in N. Ehrhardt and L.-M. Günther (eds.), *Widerstand— Anpassung—Integration: Die griechische Staatenwelt und Rom: Festschrift für Jürgen Deininger zum 65 Geburtstag.* Hamburg. 121–33.

Gutas, D. 1998. *Greek Thought, Arabic Culture: The Graeco-Arabic Translation Movement in Baghdad and Early 'Abbasid Society (2nd–4th/8th–10th centuries).* London.

Habinek, T. N. 1998. *The Politics of Latin Literature: Writing, Identity and Empire in Ancient Rome.* Princeton.

———. 2005. *The World of Roman Song: From Ritualized Speech to Social Order.* Baltimore.

———. 2009. "Situating literacy at Rome," in Johnson and Parker. 114–40.

Hall, E. 1989. *Inventing the Barbarian: Greek Self-definition through Tragedy.* Oxford.

Halla-aho, H., and P. Kruschwitz. 2010. "Colloquial and literary language in early Roman tragedy," in E. Dickey and A. Chahoud (eds.), *Colloquial and Literary Latin.* Cambridge. 127–53.

Hallo, W. W. 1996. *Origins: The Ancient Near Eastern Background of Some Modern Western Institutions.* Leiden.

Hanell, K. 1958. "Zur Problematik der älteren römischen Geschichtsschreibung." *Histoire et historiens dans l'antiquité: Entretiens Fondation Hardt.* Vol. 4. Vandoeuvres-Geneva. 149–84.

Hanink, J. 2014. *Lycurgan Athens and the Making of Classical Tragedy.* Cambridge.

Harder, A. 2012. *Callimachus* Aetia: *Introduction, Text, Translation, and Commentary.* 2 vols. Oxford.

Hardie, A. 2005. "The ancient etymology of 'carmen.'" *Papers of the Langford Latin Seminar* 12, 71–94.

———. 2007. "Juno, Hercules, and the Muses." *American Journal of Philology* 128, 551–92.

Hardie, P. 2007. "Poets, patrons, rulers: The Ennian traditions," in Eigler, Gotter, Luraghi, and Walter. 129–44.

———. 2010. "Epic," in A. Barchiesi and W. Scheidel (eds.), *The Oxford Handbook of Roman Studies*. Oxford. 420–34.

Harris, W. V. 1971. *Rome in Etruria and Umbria*. Oxford.

———. 1989. *Ancient Literacy*. Cambridge, MA.

Harrison, E. L. 1984. "The *Aeneid* and Carthage," in T. Woodman and D. West (eds.), *Poetry and Politics in the Age of Augustus*. Cambridge. 95–115.

Harrison, G. W. M., and V. Liapis (eds.). 2013. *Performance in Greek and Roman Theatre*. Leiden.

Harrison, S. J. 1991. *Vergil:* Aeneid *10*. Oxford.

Haubold, J. 2007. "Xerxes' Homer," in E. Bridges, E. Hall, and P. J. Rhodes (eds.), *Cultural Responses to the Persian Wars*. Oxford. 47–64.

———. 2013. *Greece and Mesopotamia: Dialogues in Literature*. Cambridge.

Haubold, J., G. B. Lanfranchi, R. Rollinger, and J. M. Steele (eds.). 2013. *The World of Berossos: Classica et Orientalia*, vol. 5. Wiesbaden.

Heath, M. 1989. *Unity in Greek Poetics*. Oxford.

———. 2009. "Should there have been a *polis* in Aristotle's *Poetics?*" *Classical Quarterly* 59, 468–85.

Heller, A. 2014. Review of Haubold, Lanfranchi, Rollinger, and Steele (2013), *Bryn Mawr Classical Review* 05. 50.

Henderson, J. 1999. *Writing Down Rome: Satire, Comedy, and other Offences in Latin Poetry*. Oxford.

Henkelman, W. F. M. 2006. "The birth of Gilgameš (Ael. *NA* XII. 21). A case-study in literary receptivity," in R. Rollinger and B. Truschnegg (eds.), *Altertum und Mittelmeerraum: Die antike Welt diesseits und jenseits der Levante*. Stuttgart. 807–56.

———. 2010. "Beware of dim cooks and cunning snakes: Gilgameš, Alexander, and the loss of immortality," in Rollinger, Gufler, Lang, and Madreiter. 323–59.

Henriksson, K. E. 1956. *Griechische Büchertitel in der römischen Literatur*. Helsinki.

Hermann, A. 1956. "Dolmetschen im Altertum: Ein Beitrag zur antiken Kulturgeschichte," in K. Thieme, A. Hermann, and E. Glässer (eds.), *Beiträge zur Geschichte des Dolmetschens*. Munich. 25–59.

Hermans, T. 1999. *Translation in Systems: Descriptive and Systemic Approaches Explained*. Manchester.

Heubeck, A., S. West, and J. B. Hainsworth. 1988. *A Commentary on Homer's Od-yssey*. Vol. 1, *Introduction and Books i–viii*. Oxford.

Heurgon, J. 1976. "L'agronome carthaginois Magon et ses traducteurs en latin et en grec." *Comptes rendus de l'Académie des Inscriptions et Belles-Lettres.* 441–56.

Hillen, H. J. 2003. *Von Aeneas zu Romulus: Die Legenden von der Gründung Roms.* Dusseldorf.

Hinds, S. 1998. *Allusion and Intertext: Dynamics of Appropriation in Roman Po-etry.* Cambridge.

Hoffmann, F. 2012. "Hieratic and demotic literature," in C. Riggs (ed.), *The Oxford Handbook of Roman Egypt.* Oxford. 543–62.

Holford-Strevens, L. A. 1993. "*Vtraque lingua doctus:* Some notes on bilingualism in the Roman Empire," in *Tria Lustra: Essays and Notes Presented to John Pinsent.* Liverpool Classical Papers No. 3. Liverpool. 203–13.

Hölkeskamp, K.-J. 1995. "*Oratoris maxima scaena.* Reden vor dem Volk in der poli-tischen Kultur der Republik," in M. Jehne (ed.), *Demokratie in Rom? Die Rolle des Volkes in der Politik der römischen Republik.* Stuttgart. 11–49.

Holmes, J. S. 1988. *Translated! Papers on Literary Translation and Translation Studies.* Amsterdam.

Hornblower, S. 2008. *A Commentary on Thucydides.* Vol. 3, *Books 5.25–8.109.* Oxford.

Horsfall, N. 1976. "The *collegium poetarum*." *Bulletin of the Institute of Classical Studies of the University of London* 23, 79–95.

——. 1979."*Doctus sermones utriusque linguae?*" *Échos du monde classique* 22, 79–95.

——. 1991. "Statistics or states of mind?," in J. H. Humphrey (ed.), *Literacy in the Roman World.* JRA Suppl. Vol. 3. Ann Arbor, MI. 59–76.

——. 1993a. "Roma," in G. Cambiano, L. Canfora, and D. Lanza (eds.), *Lo spazio letterario della Grecia antica.* Vol. 1.2, *L'Ellenismo.* Rome. 791–822.

——. 1993b. "Empty shelves on the Palatine." *Greece and Rome* 40, 58–67.

——. 1994. "The prehistory of Latin poetry: Some problems of method." *Rivista di Filologia e di Istruzione Classica* 122, 50–75.

——. 2000. *Virgil, Aeneid 7: A Commentary.* Leiden.

——. 2003. *The Culture of the Roman Plebs.* London.

——. 2008. *Virgil, Aeneid 2: A Commentary.* Leiden.

Hose, M. 1999a. "Post-colonial theory and Greek literature in Rome." *Greek, Roman, and Byzantine Studies* 40, 303–32.

——. 1999b. "Anmerkungen zur Verwendung des Chores in der römischen Tragödie der Republik," in P. Riemer and B. Zimmermann (eds.), *Drama 7: Der Chor in antiken und modernen Drama.* Stuttgart. 113–38.

Hoskin, K. 2007. "Translation and the linguistic codification of ancient Greek," in Kittel, House, and Schultze. 1109–17.

Housman, A. E. 1972. *The Collected Papers of A. E. Housman*, ed. J. Diggle and F. R. D. Goodyear. Cambridge.

Humm, M. 2005. *Appius Claudius Caecus: La république accomplie*. Paris.

Hunter, R. 1983. *Eubulus: The Fragments*. Cambridge.

——— (ed.). 2003. *Theocritus: Encomium of Ptolemy Philadelphus*. Berkeley.

———. 2011. "The letter of Aristeas," in A. Erskine and L. Llewellyn-Jones (eds.), *Creating a Hellenistic World*. Swansea. 47–60.

Huss, W. 1985. *Geschichte der Karthager*. Munich.

Hutchinson, G. O. 2008. *Talking Books: Readings in Hellenistic and Roman Books of Poetry*. Oxford.

———. 2013. *Greek to Latin: Frameworks and Contexts for Intertextuality*. Oxford.

Jackson, D. R. 2007. "Demonising Gilgameš," in Azize and Weeks. 107–14.

Janse, M. 2002. "Aspects of bilingualism in the history of the Greek language," in Adams, Janse, and Swain. 332–90.

Jocelyn, H. D. 1969. *The Tragedies of Ennius²*. Cambridge.

———. 1972. "The poems of Quintus Ennius." *Aufstieg und Niedergang der römischen Welt* 1. 2, 987–1026.

———. 1990. "Forme letterarie e vita sociale," in A. Momigliano and A. Schiavone (eds.), *Storia di Roma*. Turin. 2. 1. 595–629.

———. 1999. "Code-switching in the Comoedia Palliata," in Vogt-Spira and Rommel. 169–95.

———. 2000. "Accius' *Aeneadae aut Decius*: Romans and the Gallic Other," in Manuwald (2000). 325–61.

Johnson, W. A., and H. N. Parker. 2009. *Ancient Literacies: The Culture of Reading in Greece and Rome*. Oxford.

Jory, J. 1970. "Associations of actors in Rome." *Hermes* 98, 224–53.

———. 2009. "The pantomime dancer and his libretto," in E. Hall and R. Wyles (eds.), *New Directions in Ancient Pantomime*. Oxford. 157–68.

Jouanno, C. 2002. *Naissance et métamorphoses du Roman d'Alexandre: Domaine Grec*. Paris.

Kade, O. 1968. *Zufall und Gesetzmässigkeit in der Übersetzung*. Leipzig.

Kahane, H. 1986. "A typology of the prestige language." *Language* 62, 495–508.

Kaimio, J. 1979. *The Romans and the Greek Language*. Helsinki.

Kajanto, I. 1965. *The Latin Cognomina*. Helsinki.

Karakidis, E. 2014. "The language of the *palliata*," in Fontaine and Scafuro. 555–79.

Karlinksy, S. 1985. *Russian Drama from its Beginnings to the Age of Pushkin*. Berkeley.

Kaster, R. A. 1988. *Guardians of Language: The Grammarian and Society in Late Antiquity*. Berkeley.

———. 1995. *Suetonius* De Grammaticis et Rhetoribus. Oxford.

Katz, J. T. 1998. "*Testimonia Ritus Italic:* Male genitalia, solemn declarations, and a new Latin sound law." *Harvard Studies in Classical Philology* 98. 183–217.

Kearns, J. M. 1990. "ΣΕΜΝΟΤΗΣ and dialect gloss in the *Odussia* of Livius Andronicus." *American Journal of Philology* 111, 40–52.

Keay, S. 2013. "Were the Iberians hellenised?" in Prag and Quinn. 300–319.

Kenney, E. J. 1982. "Books and readers in the Roman world," in Kenney and Clausen. 3–32.

Kenney, E. J., and W. V. Clausen (eds.). 1982. *The Cambridge History of Classical Literature*. Vol. 2, *Latin Literature*. Cambridge.

Kerkhecker, A. 2001. "Zur internen Gattungsgeschichte der römischen Epik: Das Beispiel Ennius," in Schmidt. 39–95.

Kerr, R. M. 2010. *Latino-Punic Epigraphy: A Descriptive Study of the Inscriptions*. Tübingen.

Kim, L. 2013. "Orality, folktales and the cross-cultural transmission of narrative," in Whitmarsh and Thomson. 300–21.

Kissel, W. 1990. *Aules Persius Flaccus: Satiren, herausgegeben, übersetzt und kommentiert*. Heidelberg.

Kittel, H., J. House, and B. Schultze (eds.). 2007. *Übersetzung: Ein internationales Handbuch zur Übersetzungsforschung*. Vol. 2. Berlin.

Kleve, K. 1990. "Ennius in Herculaneum." *Cronache ercolanesi* 20, 5–15.

Kloss, G. 1993. "Zum Problem des römischen Saturniers." *Glotta* 71, 81–107.

Knoche, U. 1958. "Über die Aneignung griechischer Poesie im älteren Rom." *Gymnasium* 65, 321–341.

Koenen, L. 1993. "The Ptolemaic King as a religious figure," in A. W. Bulloch, E. S. Gruen, A. A. Long, and A. Stewart (eds.), *Images and Ideologies: Self-Definition in the Hellenistic World*. Berkeley. 25–115.

König, J., K. Oikonomopoulou, and G. Woolf (eds.). 2013. *Ancient Libraries*. Cambridge.

Kowalzig, B. 2008. "Nothing to do with Demeter?" in M. Revermann and P. Wilson (eds.), *Performance, Iconography, Reception: Studies in Honour of Oliver Taplin*. Oxford. 128–57.

Kramer, J. 1983. *Glossaria Bilinguia in Papyris et Membranis Reperta*. Bonn.

———. 2001. *Glossaria Bilinguia Altera*. Munich.

Krings, V. 1991. "Les lettres grecques à Carthage," in C. Baurain, C. Bonnet, and V. Krings (eds.), *Phoinikeia Grammata: Lire et écrire en Méditerranée*. Namur, Belgium. 649–68.

Kristeva, J. 1989. *Language—the Unknown: An Initiation into Linguistics*, tr. A. M. Menke. New York.

Kroll, W. 1924. *Studien zum Verständnis der römischen Literatur*. Stuttgart.

Krostenko, B. A. 2013. "The poetics of Naevius' 'epitaph' and the history of Latin poetry." *Journal of Roman Studies* 103, 46–64.

Kurz, I. 1986. "Dolmetscher im alten Rom." *Babel* 32, 215–20.

Laird, A. 2006. "The value of ancient literary criticism," in A. Laird (ed.), *Oxford Readings in Ancient Literary Criticism*. Oxford. 1–36.

Lamberton, R. 1986. *Homer The Theologian: Neoplatonist Allegorical Reading and the Growth of the Epic Tradition*. Berkeley.

Lane Fox, R. 2008. *Travelling Heroes: Greeks and Their Myths in the Epic Age of Homer*. London.

Langslow, D. R. 1999. "The language of poetry and the language of science: The Latin poets and 'Medical Latin,'" in Adams and Mayer. 183–225.

———. 2002. "Approaching bilingualism in corpus languages," in Adams, Janse, and Swain. 23–51.

La Penna, A. 1979. *Fra teatro, poesia e politica romana*. Turin.

———. 2006. *La cultura letteraria a Roma*². Bari, Italy.

Larson, J. 2011. "Bilingual inscriptions and translation in the ancient Mediterranean world," in McElduff and Sciarrino. 50–61.

Le Guen, B. 2014. "The diffusion of comedy in the Hellenistic world," in Fontaine and Scafuro. 361–77.

Lehmler, C. 2005. *Syrakus unter Agathokles und Hieron II: Die Verbindung von Kultur und Macht in einer hellenistischen Metropole*. Frankfurt am Main.

Leick, G. (ed.). 2007. *The Babylonian World*. New York.

Leigh, M. 2000. "Primitivism and power: The beginnings of Latin literature," in O. Taplin (ed.), *Literature in the Roman World*. Oxford. 4–26.

———. 2004. *Comedy and the Rise of Rome*. Oxford.

———. 2010. "Early Roman epic and the maritime moment." *Classical Philology* 105, 265–80.

Lennartz, K. 1994. *Non verba sed vim: Kritisch-exegetische Untersuchungen zu den Fragmenten archaischer römischer Tragiker*. Stuttgart.

Leo, F. 1895/1912. *Plautinische Forschungen zur Kritik und Geschichte der Komödie*². Berlin.

———. 1913. *Geschichte der römischen Literatur*. Vol. 1, *Die archaische Literatur*. Berlin.

Leonhardt, J. 2009. *Latein: Geschichte einer Weltsprache*. Munich.

Leppin, H. 1992. *Histrionen: Untersuchungen zur sozialen Stellung von Bühnenkun-*

stlern im Westen des römischen Reiches zur Zeit der Republik und des Principats. Bonn.

Levene, D. S. 1993. *Religion in Livy.* Leiden.

Levine, L. W. 1988. *Highbrow/Lowbrow: The Emergence of Cultural Hierarchy in America.* Cambridge, MA.

Lewis, D. M. 1977. *Sparta and Persia.* Leiden.

———. 1994. "The Persepolis tablets: Speech, seal and script," in Bowman and Woolf. 17–32.

———. 1997. *Selected Papers in Greek and Near Eastern History,* ed. P. J. Rhodes. Cambridge.

Lewis, E. G. 1976. "Bilingualism and bilingual education: The ancient world to the Renaissance," in J. A. Fishman, *Bilingual Education: An International Sociological Perspective,* Rowley, MA. 150–200.

Linker, B., and M. Stemmler (eds.). 2000. *Mos Maiorum: Untersuchungen zu den Formen der Identitätsstiftung und Stabilisierung in der römischen Republik.* Stuttgart.

Livingston, I. 2004. *A Linguistic Commentary on Livius Andronicus.* New York.

Llewellyn-Jones, L., and J. Robson (trans.). 2010. *Ctesias' History of Persia: Tale of the Orient.* London.

Löfstedt, E. 1933. *Syntactica: Studien und Beiträge zur historischen Syntax des Lateins.* Vol. 2. Lund, Sweden.

Lomas, K. 2004. "Italy during the Roman Republic, 338–31 B.C.," in Flower (2004b). 199–224

Lowe, N. J. 2007. *Comedy: Greece and Rome New Surveys in the Classics* No. 37. Cambridge.

Lowrie, M. 2006. Review of Habinek (2005). *Bryn Mawr Classical Review* 04. 34.

———. 2007. Review of Goldberg (2005). *Classical Philology* 102, 412–16.

———. 2009. *Writing, Performance, and Authority in Augustan Rome.* Oxford.

Luhmann, N. 1995. *Social Systems,* tr. J. Bednarz. Stanford.

Luraghi, N. 2010. "The local scripts from nature to culture." *Classical Antiquity* 29, 68–91.

Lyons, C. L, M. Bennett, and C. Marconi. (eds.). 2013. *Sicily: Art and Invention between Greece and Rome.* Los Angeles.

MacBain, B. 1982. *Prodigy and Expiation: A Study in Religion and Politics in Republican Rome.* Brussels.

MacMullen, R. 1980. "Roman elite motivation: Three questions." *Past and Present* 88, 3–16.

———. 1991. "Hellenizing the Romans (2nd century B.C.)." *Historia* 40, 419–38.

Maffre, J.-J. 2000. "Comédie et iconographie: Les grands problèmes," in J. Leclant and J. Jouanna (eds.), *Le théâtre antique: La comédie.* Paris. 269–315.

Magie, D. 1905. *De Romanorum iuris publici sacrique uocabulis in Graecum sermonem conuersis*. Leipzig.

Mairs, R. 2011. "*Translator, traditor*: The interpreter as traitor in Classical tradition." *Greece and Rome* 58, 64–81.

Malkin, I. 1998. *The Returns of Odysseus: Colonization and Ethnicity*. Berkeley.

———. 2000. "A colonial middle ground: Greek, Etruscan, and local elites in the Bay of Naples," in C. L. Lyons and J. K. Papadopoulos (eds.), *The Archaeology of Colonialism*. Los Angeles. 151–81.

———. 2011. *A Small Greek World: Networks in the Ancient Mediterranean*. Oxford.

Maltby, R. 1991. *A Lexicon of Ancient Latin Etymologies*. Leeds.

Manuwald, G. (ed.). 2000. *Identität und Alterität in der frührömischer Tragödie*. Wurzburg.

———. 2001. *Fabulae Praetextae: Spuren einer literarischen Gattung der Römer*. Munich.

———. 2003. *Pacuvius, summus tragicus poeta: Zum dramatischen Profil seiner Tragödien*. Munich.

———. 2011. *Roman Republican Theatre*. Cambridge.

———. 2014. "Tragedy, paratragedy, and Roman comedy," in Fontaine and Scafuro. 580–98.

Marconi, C. 2012. "Between performance and identity: The social context of stone theaters in late Classical and Hellenistic Sicily," in Bosher. 175–207.

Marincola, J. (ed.). 2007. *A Companion to Greek and Roman Historiography*. 2 vols. Malden, MA.

——— (ed.). 2011. *Greek and Roman Historiography*. Oxford.

Mariotti, S. 1952/1986. *Livio Andronico e la traduzione artistica: Saggio critico ed edizione dei frammenti dell'Odyssea*.[1]Milan, [2]Urbino.

———. 1955/2001. *Il Bellum Poenicum e l'arte di Nevio: Saggio con edizione dei frammenti del* Bellum Poenicum, ed. P. Parroni[3]. Bologna.

———. 1965/2000. "Letteratura latina arcaica e alessandrinismo." *Belfragor* 20, 34–48 = *Scritti di filologia classica*. Rome. 5–20.

Marshall, C. W. 2002. "Chorus, metatheatre, and Menander, *Dyskolos* 427–41." *Scholia* 11. 3–17.

Martindale, C. 1993. *Redeeming the Text: Latin Poetry and the Hermeneutics of Reception*. Cambridge.

Mattingly, H. B. 1957. "The date of Livius Andronicus." *Classical Quarterly* 7. 159–63.

Mayer, R. G. 1995. "*Graecia capta*: The Roman reception of Greek literature." *Papers of the Leeds International Latin Seminar* 8, 289–307.

———. 1999. "Grecism," in Adams and Mayer. 157–82.

McCarthy, K. 2000. *Slaves, Masters, and the Art of Authority in Plautine Comedy*. Princeton.

McElduff, S. 2004. "More than Menander's acolyte: Terence on translation." *Arethusa* 33, 120–9.

———. 2013. *Roman Theories of Translation: Surpassing the Source*. New York.

McElduff, S., and E. Sciarrino. 2011. *Complicating the History of Western Translation: The Ancient Mediterranean in Perspective*. Manchester.

McKeown, J. C. 1989. *Ovid:* Amores. Vol. 2, *A Commentary on Book One*. Liverpool.

McLean, H. 1963. "The adventures of an English comedy in eighteenth-century Russia: Dodsley's *Toy Shop* and Lukin's *Scepetil'nik*," in *American Contributions to the Fifth International Congress of Slavists*. 2 vols. The Hague. 2. 201–12.

Mercado, A. 2012. *Italic Verse: A Study of the Poetic Remains of Old Latin, Faliscan, and Sabellic*. Innsbruck.

Meyer, E. A. 2004. *Legitimacy and Law in the Roman World*: Tabulae *in Roman Belief and Practice*. Cambridge.

Meylaerts, R. 2004. "La traduction dans la culture multilingue: À la recherche des sources, des cibles et des territoires." *Target* 16, 289–317.

Middelmann, F. 1938. *Griechische Welt und Sprache in Plautus' Komödien*. Bochum.

Miles, R. 2010. *Carthage Must Be Destroyed: The Rise and Fall of an Ancient Civilization*. London.

Millar, F. 1993. *The Roman Near East: 31 BC–AD 337*. Cambridge, MA.

———. 1998. *The Crowd in Rome in the Late Republic*. Ann Arbor, MI.

———. 2002–2006. *Rome, the Greek World, and the East*. 3 vols. eds. H. M. Cotton and G. M. Rogers. Chapel Hill, NC.

———. 2006. *A Greek Roman Empire: Power and Belief under Theodosius II (408–450)*. Berkeley.

Miller, M. C. 1997. *Athens and Persia in the fifth century BC: A Study in Cultural Receptivity*. Cambridge.

Millett, M. 1990. *The Romanization of Britain: An Essay in Archaeological Interpretation*. Cambridge.

Mimbrera, S. 2012. "The Sicilian Doric koina," in Tribulato. 223–50.

Miner, E. 1978. "On the genesis and development of literary systems: Part I." *Critical Inquiry* 5, 339–53.

Moatti, C. 1997. *La Raison de Rome: Naissance de l'esprit critique à la fin de la République (IIer-Ier siècle avant Jésus-Christ)*. Paris.

Möller, A. 2004. "Greek chronographic traditions about the first Olympic games," in R. Rosen (ed.), *Time and Temporality in the Ancient World*. Philadelphia. 169–84.

Momigliano, A. 1957. "Perizonius, Niebuhr and the character of early Roman tradition." *Journal of Roman Studies* 47, 104–14.

———. 1966. "Linie per una valutazione di Fabio Pittore," in *Terzo contributo alla storia degli studi classici e del mondo antico*. Vol. 1. Rome. 55–68.

———. 1975. *Alien Wisdom: The Limits of Hellenization*. Cambridge.

———. 1977. *Essays in Ancient and Modern Historiography*. Oxford.

———. 1990. *The Classical Foundations of Modern Historiography*. Berkeley.

Montella, C. 1982. "Il *fidus interpres* nella prassi della traduzione orale." *Annali dell' Istituto universitario orientale di Napoli, sezione linguistica* 4, 197–212.

Montgomery, S. L. 2000. *Science in Translation: Movements of Knowledge through Cultures and Time*. Chicago.

Moore, T. J. 1998. *The Theater of Plautus: Playing to the Audience*. Austin, TX.

———. 2012. *Music in Roman Comedy*. Cambridge.

Morel, J.-P. 1989. "The transformation of Italy, 300–133 B.C. The evidence of archaeology." *Cambridge Ancient History*[2] 8. 477–516.

Moretti, J.-C. 1999–2000. "The theater of the sanctuary of Dionysus Eleuthereus in late fifth-century Athens." *Illinois Classical Studies* 24/25, 377–98.

Morgan, L. 2010. Musa Pedestris. *Metre and Meaning in Roman Verse*. Oxford.

Most, G. W. 2003. "Violets in crucibles: Translating, traducing, transmuting." *Transactions of the American Philological Association* 133, 381–90.

Moyer, I. S. 2011. *Egypt and the Limits of Hellenism*. Cambridge.

Mullen, A. 2011. "Latin and other languages: Societal and individual bilingualism," in Clackson (2011a). 527–48.

———. 2012. "Introduction: Multiple languages, multiple identities," in A. Mullen and P. James (eds.), *Multilingualism in the Graeco-Roman Worlds*. Cambridge. 1–35.

Müller, C. W., K. Sier, and J. Werner (eds.). 1992. *Zum Umgang mit fremden Sprachen in der griechisch-römischen Antike*. Stuttgart.

Nervegna, S. 2007. "Staging scenes or plays? Theatrial revivals of 'old' Greek drama in Antiquity." *Zeitschrift für Papyrologie und Epigraphik* 162. 14–42.

———. 2013. *Menander in Antiquity: The Contexts of Reception*. Cambridge.

Norden, E. 1898. *Die antike Kunstprosa: Vom VI. Jahrhundert v. Chr. bis in die Zeit der Renaissance*. 2 vols. Leipzig.

———. 1939. *Aus altrömischen Priesterbüchern*. Lund.

North, J. A. 1989. "Religion in Republican Rome," *Cambridge Ancient History*[2] 7.2. 573–624.

———. 2000. "Prophet and text in the third century BC," in Bispham and Smith. 92–107.

Oakley, S. P. 1997–2005. *A Commentary on Livy Books VI-X*. 4 vols. Oxford.

Olson, S. D. 2011. *Athenaeus: The Learned Banqueters, Volume VII: Books 13.594b–14*. Cambridge, Mass.

Osborne, R. 1998. *Archaic and Classical Greek Art*. Oxford.

Osselton, N. 1990. "Archaism," in A. C. Hamilton (ed.), *The Spenser Encyclopedia*. Toronto. 52–53.

Osterloh, K. L. 2008. "Judea, Rome and the Hellenistic *Oikoumenê;* Emulation and the Reinvention of Communal Identity," in E. Irinisci and H. M. Zellentin (eds.), *Heresy and Identity in Late Antiquity*. Stuttgart. 168–206.

Ostler, N. 2007. Ad Infinitum. *A Biography of Latin*. London.

Palmer, R. E. A. 1997. *Rome and Carthage at Peace*. Stuttgart.

Papaioannou, S. 2011. "The translation politics of a political translation: The case of Augustus' *Res Gestae*," in McElduff and Sciarrino. 62–74.

Parker, H. N. 2009. "Books and reading Latin poetry," in Johnson and Parker. 186–229.

Parker, R. 1996. *Athenian Religion: A History*. Oxford.

Parkinson, R. B. 1999. *Cracking Codes: The Rosetta Stone and Decipherment*. London.

——. 2009. *Reading Ancient Egyptian Poetry: Among Other Histories*. Chichester, UK.

Parsons, P. 2007. *City of the Sharp-Nosed Fish: Greek Lives in Roman Egypt*. London.

Pavese, C. 1961. *This Business of Living: Diary: 1935–1950*, tr. A. E. Murch. London.

Pecere, O. 2010. *Roma antica e il testo: Scritture d'autore e composizione letteraria*. Rome.

Pelling, C. B. R. 1988. *Plutarch: Life of Antony*. Cambridge.

Perl, G. 1971. "Die Einführung der griechischen Buchstaben Y und Z in das lateinische Alphabet." *Philologus* 115. 196–233.

Petersmann, H., and A. Petersmann. 2004. "Standardisierung und Destandardisierung der lateinischen Sprache in diachroner Sicht," in A. Hornung, C. Jäkel, and W. Schubert (eds.), *Studia Humanitatis ac Litterarum Trifolio Heidelbergensi Dedicata*. Frankfurt am Main. 235–54.

Petrides, A. K. 2014. "Plautus between Greek comedy and Atellan farce: Assessments and reassessments," in Fontaine and Scafuro. 424–43.

Phillips, C. R., III. 1991. Response to Zorzetti. *Classical Journal* 86, 382–89.

Pighi, G. B. 1965. *De Ludis Saecularibus Populi Romani Quiritium Libri Sex*². Amsterdam.

Pöchhacker, F. 2004. *Introducing Interpretation Studies*. London.

——. 2009. "Issues in interpreting studies," in J. Munday (ed.), *The Routledge Companion to Translation Studies*. London. 128–40.

Pontrandolfo, A. 1992. "Personaggi mascherati nella tradizione figurativa dell'Italia meridionale." *Atti e Memorie della Società Magna Graecia* 3a, ser.1, 263–71.

Possanza, D. M. 2004. *Translating the Heavens: Aratus, Germanicus, and the Poetics of Latin Translation.* New York.

Potter, D. 1999. Review of Bernstein (1998). *Bryn Mawr Classical Review* 04.07.

———. 2012. "Old and new in Roman foreign affairs," in Smith and Yarrow. 134–51.

Powell, B. B. 2002. *Writing and the Origins of Greek Literature.* Cambridge.

———. 2009. *Writing: Theory and History of the Technology of Civilization.* Chichester, UK.

Powell, J. G. F. 1995. "Cicero's translations from Greek," in J. G. F. Powell (ed.), *Cicero the Philosopher.* Oxford. 273–300.

Powell, J. U. 1925. *Collectanea Alexandrina.* Oxford.

Prag, J. R. W. 2010a. "Kinship diplomacy between Sicily and Rome," in D. Bonanno, C. Bonnet, N. Cusumano, and S. Péré-Noguès (eds.), *Alleanze e parentele: Le "affinità elettive" nella storiografia sulla Sicilia antica.* Rome. 179–206.

———. 2010b. "Tyrannizing Sicily: The Despots Who Cried 'Carthage!'" in A. Turner, K. O. Chong-Gossard, and F. Vervaet (eds.), *Private and Public Lies: The Discourse of Despotism and Deceit in the Graeco-Roman World.* Leiden: 51–71.

———. 2013. "Epigraphy in the western Mediterranean: a Hellenistic phenomenon?," in Prag and Quinn. 320–47.

Prag, J. R. W., and J. C. Quinn (eds.). 2013. *The Hellenistic West: Rethinking the Ancient Mediterranean.* Cambridge.

Pulleyn, S. 1991. *Prayer in Greek Religion.* Oxford.

Purcell, N. 1983. "The *apparitores:* A study in social mobility." *Papers of the British School at Rome* 51, 125–73.

———. 1994. "South Italy in the fourth century B.C." *Cambridge Ancient History*[2] 6. 381–403.

———. 2003. "Becoming historical: The Roman case," in Braund and Gill. 12–40.

Pym, A. 2000. *Negotiating the Frontier: Translators and Intercultures in Hispanic History.* Manchester.

———. 2010. *Exploring Translation Theories.* London.

Pym, A., M. Shlesinger, and Z. Jettmarová (eds.). 2006. *Sociocultural Aspects of Translating and Interpreting.* Amsterdam and Philadelphia.

Quack, J. F. 2005. *Einführung in die altägyptische Literaturgeschichte.* Vol. 3, *Die demotische and gräko-ägyptische Literatur.* Munster.

Quinn, J. C. 2013a. "Monumental power: 'Numidian Royal Architecture,'" in Prag and Quinn. 179–215.

———. 2013b. "Imagining the Imperial Mediterranean," in B. Gibson and T. Harrison (eds.), *Polybius and his World: Essays in Memory of F. W. Walbank*. Oxford. 337–52.

Raaflaub, K. A. 2005. "The conflict of the orders in archaic Rome: A comprehensive and comparative approach," in Raaflaub (ed.), *Social Struggles in Archaic Rome: New Perspectives on the Conflict of the Orders*[2]. Malden, MA. 1–46.

Radner, K., and E. Robson (eds.). 2011. *The Oxford Handbook of Cuneiform Culture*. Oxford.

Rafael, V. L. 1993. *Contracting Colonialism: Translation and Christian Conversion in Tagalog Society under Early Spanish Rule*[2]. Durham, NC.

Rajak, T. 2002. *Josephus: The Historian and his Society*[2]. London.

———. 2009. *Translation and Survival: The Greek Bible of the Ancient Jewish Diaspora*. Oxford.

Rathje, A. 1990. "The Homeric banquet in central Italy," in O. Murray (ed.), *Sympotica: A Symposium on the* Symposion. Oxford. 279–88.

Rawson, E. 1985. *Intellectual Life in the Late Roman Republic*. Baltimore.

———. 1989. "Roman tradition and the Greek world." *Cambridge Ancient History*[2] 8. 422–76.

———. 1991. *Roman Culture and Society: Collected Papers*. Oxford.

Reinhardt, T. 2005. "The language of Epicureanism in Cicero: The case of atomism," in Reinhardt, Lapidge, and Adams. 151–77.

Reinhardt, T., M. Lapidge, and J. N. Adams (eds.). 2005. *Aspects of the Language of Latin Prose*. Proceedings of the British Academy 129. Oxford.

Reitzenstein, R. 1918. "Livius und Horaz über die Entwicklung des römischen Schauspiels." *Nachrichten der Gesellschaft der Wissenschaft Göttingen, philologische-historische Klasse*. 233–58.

Repington, C. à C. 1920. *The First World War, 1914–1918: Personal Experiences of Lieut.-Col. C. À Court Repington*. London.

Revermann, M. 1999–2000. "Euripides, tragedy and Macedon: Some conditions of reception." *Illinois Classical Studies* 24/25, 451–67.

———. 2010. "Situating the gaze of the recipient(s): Theatre-related vase paintings and their contexts of reception," in Gildenhard and Revermann. 69–97.

Rewi, P. 2010. *Whaikorero: The World of Maori Oratory*. Auckland, NZ.

Reynolds, M. 2011. *The Poetry of Translation: From Chaucer & Petrarch to Homer & Logue*. Oxford.

Ribbeck, O. 1897. *Scaenicae Romanorum Poesis Fragmenta*. Vol. 1, *Tragicorum Romanorum Fragmenta*[3]. Leipzig.

Richardson, J. H. 2012. *The Fabii and the Gauls: Studies in Historical Thought and Historiography in Republican Rome*. Stuttgart.

Richter, H. E. 1938. *Übersetzen und Übersetzungen in der römischen Literatur.* Coburg.

Ridgway, D. 1996. "Greek letters at Osteria dell'Osa." *Opuscula Romana* 20, 87–97.

Rives, J. B. 2007. *Religion in the Roman Empire.* Malden, MA.

Robert, L. 1950. *Hellenica: Receuil d'épigraphie de numismatique et d'antiquités grecques.* Vol. 8. Paris.

Robinson, D. 1997. *Translation and Empire: Postcolonial Theories Explained.* Manchester.

Robinson, E. G. D. 2004. "Reception of comic theatre amongst the indigenous South Italians." *Mediterranean Archaeology* 17, 193–212.

Robson, E. 2013. "Reading the libraries of Assyria and Babylonia," in König, Oikonomopoulou, and Woolf. 38–56.

Rochette, B. 1994. "Traducteurs et traductions dans l'Égypte gréco-romaine." *Chronique d'Égypte* 69, 313–22.

———. 1995. "Du grec au latin et du latin au grec: Les problèmes de la traduction dans l'antiquité gréco-latine." *Latomus* 54, 245–61.

———. 1997a. *Le Latin dans le monde grec: Recherches sur la diffusion de la langue et des lettres latines dans les provinces hellénophones de l'empire romain.* Brussels.

———. 1997b. "Sur le bilinguisme dans les armées d'Hannibal." *Les Études Classiques* 65, 153–59.

———. 2010. "Greek and Latin bilingualism," in E. J. Bakker (ed.), *A Companion to the Ancient Greek Language.* Malden, MA. 549–63.

———. 2011. "Language policies in the Roman Republic and Empire," in Clackson (2011a). 549–63.

Rodríguez-Noriega Guillén, L. 2012. "On Epicharmus' literary and philosophical background," in Bosher. 76–96.

Rollinger, R. 2009. "Near Eastern perspectives on the Greeks," in Boys-Stones, Graziosi, and Vasunia. 32–47.

Rollinger, R., B. Gufler, M. Lang, and I. Madreiter (eds.). 2010. *Interkulturalität in der Alten Welt: Vorderasien, Hellas, Ägypten und die vielfältigen Ebenen des Kontakts.* Wiesbaden.

Roman, L. 2014. *Poetic Autonomy in Ancient Rome.* Oxford.

Roselaar, S. T. (ed.). 2012. *Processes of Integration and Identity Formation in the Roman Republic.* Leiden.

Rosén, H. 2012. "Greek in Latin, Greek into Latin—reflections on the passage of patterns," in Glucker and Burnett. 1–18.

Rossi, A. 2000. "The tears of Marcellus: History of a literary motif in Livy." *Greece and Rome* 47, 56–66.

Rossi, A., and B. W. Breed. 2006. "Introduction: Ennius and the traditions of epic." *Arethusa* 39, 397–425.

Rotstein, A. 2014. *Literary History in the Parian Marble.* Cambridge, MA.

Rüpke, J. 1993. *Römische Religion bei Eduard Norden: Die "Altrömischen Priesterbücher" im wissenschaftlichen Kontext der dreißiger Jahre.* Marburg.

———. 2000. "Räume literarischer Kommunikation in der Formierungsphase römischer Literatur," in Braun, Haltenhoff, Mutschler. 31–52.

——— (ed.). 2001. *Von Menschen und Göttern erzählen: Formkonstanzen und Funktionswandel vormoderner Epik.* Stuttgart.

———. 2005. *Fasti Sacerdotum.* 3 vols. Stuttgart.

———. 2012. *Religion in Republican Rome: Rationalization and Ritual Change.* Philadelphia.

Russell, D. A. 1981. *Criticism in Antiquity.* London.

Russo, F. 2012. "The beginning of the First Punic War and the concept of Italy," in Roselaar. 35–50.

Rutherford, I. 2001. *Pindar's Paeans: A Reading of the Fragments with a Survey of the Genre.* Oxford.

———. 2013. "Greek fiction and Egyptian fiction: Are they related, and, if so, how?" in Whitmarsh and Thomson. 23–37.

Rutherford, R. 2012. "Structure and meaning in epic and historiography," in E. Foster and D. Lateiner (eds.), *Thucydides and Herodotus.* Oxford. 13–38.

Ryholt, K. 2012. *The Carlsberg Papyri 10: Narrative Literature from the Tebtunis Temple Library.* Copenhagen.

Sacks, O. 2000. *Seeing Voices: A Journey into the World of the Deaf.* New York.

Salvesen, A. 1997. "The legacy of Babylon and Nineveh in Aramaic sources," in Dalley. 139–62.

Sartre, M. 2009. *Histoires grecques: Snapshots from Antiquity,* tr. C. Porter. Cambridge, MA.

Satterfield, S. 2008. *Rome's Own Sibyl: The Sibylline Books in the Roman Republic and Early Empire.* PhD dissertation, Princeton.

Scheer, T. S. 2011. "Ways of becoming Arcadian: Arcadian foundation myths," in Gruen (2011). 11–25.

Scheid, J. 1990. *Romulus et ses frères: Le collège des frères arvales, modèle du culte publique dans la Rome des empereurs.* Rome.

———. 1995. "*Graeco ritu*: A typically Roman way of honoring the gods." *Harvard Studies in Classical Philology* 97, 15–31.

———. 2003. *An Introduction to Roman Religion,* tr. J. Lloyd, Bloomington, IN.

———. 2007. "*Carmen* et prière: Les hymnes dans le culte public de Rome," in Y. Lehmann (ed.), *L'Hymne antique et son public.* Turnhout, Belgium. 439–50.

——. 2008. "Le *carmen* dans la religion romaine." *Mythos*, n.s., 2, 17–24.

——. forthcoming. "I sacerdozi 'arcaici' restaurati da Augusto: L'esempio degli arvali," in *Sacerdos: Figure del sacro nella società romana.* 177–89.

Scheidel, W. 2004. "Human mobility in Roman Italy, I: The free population." *Journal of Roman Studies* 94, 1–26.

Scheuble, S. 2010. "Griechen und Ägypter im ptolemäischen Heer—Bemerkungen zum Phänomen der Doppelnamen im ptolemäischen Ägypten," in Rollinger, Gufler, Lang, and Madreiter. 551–60.

Schierl, P. 2006. *Die Tragödien des Pacuvius: Ein Kommentar zu den Fragmenten mit Einleitung, Text, und Übersetzung.* Berlin.

Schiesaro, A. 2005. "Republican tragedy," in R. Bushnell (ed.), *A Companion to Tragedy*. Malden, MA. 269–86.

Schironi, F. 2009. *From Alexandria to Babylon: Near Eastern Languages and Hellenistic Erudition in the Oxyrhynchus Glossary (P.Oxy. 1802 + 4812)*, Sozomena 4. Berlin.

——. 2013. "The early reception of Berossos," in Haubold, Lanfranchi, Rollinger, and Steele. 235–54.

Schleiermacher, F. 1813/1992. "*From* 'On the different methods of translating,'" tr. W. Bartscht, in Schulte and Biguinet. 36–54.

Schmidt, E. A. (ed.). 2001. *L'Histoire littéraire immanente dans la poésie latine*. Fondation Hardt Entretiens 47. Vandoeuvres-Geneva.

Schneider, T. 2011. "Three histories of translation: Translating in Egypt, translating Egypt, translating Egyptian," in McElduff and Sciarrino. 176–88.

Schnurbusch, D. 2011. *Convivium: Form und Bedeutung aristokratischer Geselligkeit in der römischen Antike*. Stuttgart.

Schulte, R., and J. Biguenet (eds.). 1992. *Theories of Translation: An Anthology of Essays from Dryden to Derrida*. Chicago.

Schulze, W. 1904. *Zur Geschichte lateinischer Eigennamen*. Berlin.

Schwindt, J. P. 2000. *Prolegomena zu einer "Phänomenologie" der römischen Literaturgeschichtsschreibung: Von den Anfängen bis Quintilian*. Göttingen.

——. 2001. "Literaturgeschichtsschreibung und immanente Literaturgeschichte: Bausteine literarhistorischen Bewusstseins in Rom," in Schmidt. 1–38.

Sciarrino, E. 2011. *Cato the Censor and the Beginnings of Latin Prose: From Poetic Translation to Elite Transcription*. Columbus, OH.

Scullard, H. H. 1970. *Scipio Africanus: Soldier and Politician*. Ithaca, NY.

Seaman, W. M. 1954. "The understanding of Greek by Plautus' audience." *Classical Journal* 50, 115–19.

Seele, A. 1995. *Römische Übersetzer: Nöte, Freiheiten, Absichten: Verfahren des literarischen Übersetzens in der griechisch-römischen Antike*. Darmstadt.

Selden, D. 1998. "Alibis." *Classical Antiquity* 17, 299–412.

Sharrock, A. 2009. *Reading Roman Comedy: Poetics and Playfulness in Plautus and Terence*. Cambridge.

Sheets, G. A. 1981. "The dialect gloss, Hellenistic poetics and Livius Andronicus." *American Journal of Philology* 102, 58–78.

Sherk, R. K. 1969. *Roman Documents from the Greek East:* Senatus Consulta *and* Epistulae *to the Age of Augustus*. Baltimore.

Shi, V. S. 2011. *The Genealogy of Epic*. Senior Thesis, Princeton University.

Shipp, G. P. 1953. "Greek in Plautus." *Wiener Studien* 66, 105–12.

Simon, E. 2013. "Greek myth in Etruscan culture," in Turfa (2013). 495–512.

Skutsch, O. 1968. *Studia Enniana*. London.

———. 1985. *The* Annals *of Q. Ennius*. Oxford.

Slater, N. W. 1993. "Improvisation in Plautus," in G. Vogt-Spira (ed.), *Beiträge zur mündlichen Kultur der Römer*. Tübingen. 113–24.

———. 2000. "Religion and identity in Pacuvius' *Chryses*," in Manuwald (2000). 315–23.

Slater, W. J. 1993. "Three problems in the history of drama." *Phoenix* 47, 189–212.

Smith, C. 1996. *Early Rome and Latium: Economy and Society c. 1000 to 500 BC*. Oxford.

———. 2011. "Thinking about kings." *Bulletin of the Institute of Classical Studies of the University of London* 54, 21–42.

Smith, C., and L. M. Yarrow (eds.). 2012. *Imperialism, Cultural Politics, and Polybius*. Oxford.

Smith, J. Z. 1982. *Imagining Religion: From Babylon to Jamestown*. Chicago.

———. 1990. *Drudgery Divine: On the Comparison of Early Christianities and the Religions of Late Antiquity*. London.

Snellmann, W. I. 1919. *De Interpretibus Romanorum Deque Linguae Latinae cum aliis Nationibus Commercio*. Leipzig.

Solin, H. 1971. *Beiträge zur Kenntnis der griechischen Personennamen in Rom*. Helsinki.

———. 1990. *Namenpaare: Eine Studie zur römischen Namengebung*. Helsinki.

Southern, R. W. 1953. *The Making of the Middle Ages*. London.

Spaeth, B. S. 1996. *The Roman Goddess Ceres*. Austin, TX.

Sparks, K. L. 2005. "Ethnicity," in B. T. Arnold and H. G. M. Williamson (eds.), *Dictionary of the Old Testament: Historical Books*. Leicester. 268–72.

Spatafora, F. 2013. "Ethnic identity in Sicily: Greeks and non-Greeks," in Lyons, Bennett, and Marconi. 37–47.

Stephens, S. A. 2003. *Seeing Double: Intercultural Poetics in Ptolemaic Alexandria*. Berkeley.

Sterling, G. E. 2007. "The Jewish appropriation of Hellenistic historiography," in Marincola (2007). 1. 231–43.

Strzelecki, L. 1952. "De re metrica tragicorum Romanorum quaestiones." *Tragica*. Vol. 1. Warsaw. 41–66.

Suerbaum, W. 1968. *Untersuchungen zur Selbstdarstellung älterer römischer Dichter*. Hildesheim.

———. 1992. "Zum Anfang der Bücher in der archaischen lateinischen Dichtung: Naevius, Ennius, Lukrez und Livius Andronicus auf Papyrus-Rollen." *Zeitschrift für Papyrologie und Epigraphik* 92, 153–73.

———. 1995. "Der Pyrrhos-Krieg in Ennius' *Annales* VI im Lichte der ersten Ennius-Papyri aus Herculaneum." *Zeitschrift für Papyrologie und Epigraphik* 106, 31–52.

——— (ed.). 2002. *Handbuch der lateinischen Literatur der Antike*. Vol. 1, *Die archaische Literatur: Von den Anfängen bis zu Sullas Tod: Die vorliterarische Periode und die Zeit von 240 bis 78 v. Chr.* Handbuch der Altertumswissenschaft 8.1. Munich.

Swain, S. 2002. "Bilingualism in Cicero? The evidence of code-switching," in Adams, Janse, and Swain. 128–67.

Szemerényi, O. 1975. "The origins of Roman drama and Greek tragedy." *Hermes* 103, 300–332.

Taplin, O. 1993. *Comic Angels and Other Approaches to Greek Drama through Vase-Paintings*. Oxford.

———. 2007. *Pots & Plays: Interactions between Tragedy and Greek Vase-Painting of the Fourth Century B.C.* Los Angeles.

———. 2012. "How was Athenian tragedy played in the Greek West?" in Bosher. 226–50.

Taussig, M. 1993. *Mimesis and Alterity: A Particular History of the Senses*. New York.

Taylor, L. R. 1925. "Horace's equestrian career." *American Journal of Philology* 46, 161–70.

Terrenato, N. 2007. "The clans and the peasants: Reflections on social structures and change in Hellenistic central Italy," in van Dommelen and Terrenato. 13–22.

Thomas, R. 1992. *Literacy and Orality in Ancient Greece*. Cambridge.

Thomas, R. F. 1993. "Callimachus back in Rome," in M. A. Harder, R. F. Regtuit, and G. C. Wakker (eds.), *Callimachus: Hellenistica Groningana I*. Groningen. 197–215.

Thompson, D. J. 1994. "Literacy and power in Ptolemaic Egypt," in Bowman and Woolf. 67–83.

Thuillier, J.-P. 1992. "Sur les origines étrusques du théâtre romain," in C. Landes and V. Kramérovskis (eds.), *Spectacula*. Vol. 2, *Le théâtre antique et ses spectacles*. Lattes. 201–8.

———. 2013. "Etruscan spectacles: Theater and sport," in Turfa (2013). 831–40.

Tigay, J. H. 1982. *The Evolution of the Gilgamesh Epic.* Philadelphia.

Timpanaro, S. 1978. *Contributi di filologia e di storia della lingua latina.* Rome.

Timpe, D. 1978. "Fabius Pictor und die Anfänge der römischen Historiographie." *Aufstieg und Niedergang der römischen Welt* 1.2, 928–69.

———. 1988. "Mündlichkeit und Schriftlichkeit als Basis der frührömische Überlieferung," in J. von Ungern-Sternberg and J. Reinau (eds.), *Vergangenheit in mündlicher Überlieferung: Colloquium Rauricum* Band 1. Stuttgart. 266–86.

———. 2011. "*Memoria* and historiography in Rome," in Marincola (2011). 150–74.

Tinney, S. 2011. "Tablets of schools and scholars: A portrait of the Old Babylonian corpus," in Radner and Robson. 577–96.

Torallas Tovar, S. 2010. "Linguistic identity in Graeco-Roman Egypt," in A. Papaconstantinou (ed.), *The Multilingual Experience in Egypt, from the Ptolemies to the 'Abbāsids.* Burlington, VT. 17–43.

Townend, G. B. 1969. "Some problems of punctuation in the Latin hexameter." *Classical Quarterly* 19, 330–44.

———. 1969–1970. "Virgil unpunctuated." *Proceedings of the Virgil Society* 9, 76–86.

Toynbee, A. 1965. *Hannibal's Legacy: The Hannibalic War's Effects on Roman Life.* 2 vols. Oxford.

Traina, A. 1970. *Vortit barbare: Le traduzione poetiche da Livio Andronico a Cicerone.* Rome.

———. 1989. "Le traduzioni," in G. Cavallo, P. Fedeli, and A. Giardina (eds.), *Lo Spazio letterario di Roma antica.* Vol. 2, *La circolazione del testo.* Rome. 93–123.

———. 2013. "Da *Maccus* a *Plautus* (Sul v. 11 dell'*Asinaria*)." *Eikasmos* 24, 157–58.

Tribulato, O. 2012a. "'So many Sicilies': Introducing language and linguistic contact in ancient Sicily," in Tribulato (2012b). 1–46.

———. (ed.). 2012b. *Language and Linguistic Contact in Ancient Sicily.* Cambridge.

Trüdinger, K. 1918. *Studien zur Geschichte der griechisch-römischen Ethnographie.* Basel.

Tuplin, C. 2011. "The limits of Persianization: Some reflections on cultural bias," in Gruen (2011). 150–82.

Turfa, J. M. 2012. *Divining the Etruscan World: The Brontoscopic Calendar and Religious Practice.* Cambridge.

———. (ed.). 2013. *The Etruscan World.* London.

Ulf, C. 2009. "Rethinking cultural contacts." *Ancient West and East* 8, 81–132.

van Dommelen, P., and M. López-Bertran. 2013. "Hellenism as subaltern practice: Punic rural cults," in Prag and Quinn. 273–99.

van Dommelen, P., and N. Terrenato (eds.). 2007a. *Articulating Local Cultures: Power and Identity under the Expanding Roman Republic. JRS* Suppl. 63, Portsmouth, RI.

van Dommelen, P., and N. Terrenato. 2007b. "Introduction: Local cultures and the expanding Roman Republic," in van Dommelen and Terrenato (2007a). 7–12.

van Sickle, J. 1987. "The elogia of the Cornelii Scipiones and the origin of epigram at Rome." *American Journal of Philology* 108, 41–55.

———. 1988. "The first Hellenistic epigrams at Rome." *Bulletin of the Institute of Classical Studies of the University of London* 35, 143–56.

Vassallo, S. 2012. "The theater of Montagna dei Cavalli-Hippana," in Bosher. 208–25.

Veit, C. 2013. "Hellenistic kingship in Sicily: Patronage and politics under Agathokles and Hieron II," in Lyons, Bennett, and Marconi. 27–36.

Venuti, L. 1995. *The Translator's Invisibility: A History of Translation.* London.

———. 1998. *The Scandals of Translation: Towards an Ethics of Difference.* London.

———. 2008. "Translation: Between the universal and the local." *PN Review* 35.2, 34–37.

———. 2012. (ed.). *The Translation Studies Reader*[3]. London.

Verbrugghe, G. P., and J. M. Wickersham. 2001. *Berossos and Manetho Introduced and Translated: Native Traditions in Ancient Mesopotamia and Egypt.* Ann Arbor, MI.

Vermeer, H. J. 1992. *Skizzen zu einer Geschichte der Translation.* 2 vols. Frankfurt.

Veyne, P. 1979. "The hellenization of Rome and the question of acculturations." *Diogenes* 106, 1–27.

Vian, F. 1952. *La Guerre des géants: Le mythe avant l'époque hellénistique.* Paris.

Vogt-Spira, G. 1996. "Die Kulturbegegnung Roms mit den Griechen," in M. Schuster (ed.), *Die Begegnung mit den Fremden: Wertungen und Wirkungen in Hochkulturen vom Altertum bis zur Gegenwart.* Stuttgart. 11–33.

———. 2000. "Ennius, Medea: Eine Fremde in Rom," in Manuwald (2000). 265–75.

Vogt-Spira, G., and B. Rommel (eds.). 1999. *Rezeption und Identität: Die kulturelle Auseinandersetzung Roms mit Griechenland als europäisches Paradigma.* Stuttgart.

Volk, K. 2009. *Manilius and His Intellectual Background.* Oxford.

von Holzinger, K. 1912. "Diokles von Peparethos als Quelle des Fabius Pictor." *Wiener Studien* 34, 175–202.

von Wilamowitz-Moellendorf, U. 1921. *Griechische Verskunst.* Berlin.

Walbank, F. W. 1957–1979. *A Historical Commentary on Polybius.* 3 vols. Oxford.

———. 1975. "*Symploke*: Its role in Polybius' Histories." *Yale Classical Studies* 24, 197–212.

Wallace, R. 2011. "The Latin alphabet and orthography," in Clackson (2011a). 9–28.

Wallace-Hadrill, A. 1988. "Greek knowledge, Roman power." *Classical Philology* 83, 224–33. Review of Rawson (1985).

———. 2008. *Rome's Cultural Revolution.* Cambridge.

Warburton, D. A. 2007. "Egypt and Mesopotamia," in Leick. 487–502.

Wardman, A. E. 1976. *Rome's Debt to Greece.* London.

Wardy, R. 2000. *Aristotle in China: Language, Categories and Translation.* Cambridge.

Waszink, J. H. 1960. "Tradition and personal achievement in early Latin literature." *Mnemosyne* ser. 4. 13, 16–33.

Watkins, C. 1995a. "Greece in Italy outside Rome." *Harvard Studies in Classical Philology* 99, 35–50.

———. 1995b. *How to Kill a Dragon: Aspects of Indo-European Poetics.* New York.

Weinstock, S. 1957. "Victor and Invictus." *Harvard Theological Review* 50, 211–47.

———. 1971. *Divus Julius.* Oxford.

Weiss, M. 2004. "Preface" to Livingston. xi–xix.

———. 2009. *Outline of the Historical and Comparative Grammar of Latin.* Ann Arbor, MI.

———. 2010. *Language and Ritual in Sabellic Italy: The Ritual Complex of the Third and Fourth* Tabulae Iguvinae. Leiden.

Welsh, J. 2011. "Accius, Porcius Licinus, and the beginning of Latin literature." *Journal of Roman Studies* 101, 1–20.

Werner, J. 1992. "Zur Fremdsprachenproblematik in der griechische-römischen Antike," in Müller, Sier, and Werner. 1–20.

West, M. L. 1969. "Near Eastern material in Hellenistic and Roman literature." *Harvard Studies in Classical Philology* 73, 113–34.

———. 1997. *The East Face of Helicon: West Asiatic Elements in Greek Poetry and Myth.* Oxford.

West, S. 1969. "The Greek version of the legend of Tefnut." *Journal of Egyptian Archaeology* 55, 161–83.

———. 2013. "Divine anger management: The Greek version of the Myth of the Sun's Eye (*P.Lond.Lit.* 192)," in Whitmarsh and Thomson. 79–90.

White, P. 1993. *Promised Verse: Poets in the Society of Augustan Rome.* Cambridge, MA.

White, R. 1991. *The Middle Ground: Indians, Empires, and Republics in the Great Lakes Region, 1650–1815.* Cambridge.

Whitmarsh, T. 2004. *Ancient Greek Literature.* Oxford.

———. 2013. "The romance between Greece and the East," in Whitmarsh and Thomson. 1–19.

Whitmarsh, T., and S. Thomson (eds.) 2013. *The Romance between Greece and the East*. Cambridge.

Willi, A. 2008. *Sikelismos: Sprache, Literatur und Gesellschaft im griechischen Sizilien (8.-5. Jh. v. Chr.)*. Basel.

———. 2012a. "Challenging authority: Epicharmus between epic and rhetoric," in Bosher. 56–75.

———. 2012b. "We speak Peloponnesian: Tradition and linguistic identity in post-classical Sicilian literature," in Tribulato. 265–88.

Williams, G. W. 1968. *Tradition and Originality in Roman Poetry*. Oxford.

———. 1978. *Change and Decline: Roman Literature in the Early Empire*. Berkeley.

Wills, L. M. 1995. *The Jewish Novel in the Ancient World*. Ithaca, NY.

Wilson, P. 2002. "The musicians among the actors," in Easterling and Hall. 39–68.

Wilson, R. J. A. 2013. "Hellenistic Sicily, c. 270–100 BC," in Prag and Quinn. 79–119.

Wilss, W. 1982. *The Science of Translation: Problems and Methods*. Tübingen.

Wiotte-Franz, C. 2001. *Hermeneus und Interpres: Zum Dolmetscherwesen in der Antike*. Saarbrucken.

Wiseman, T. P. 1974/1987. "Legendary genealogies in late-Republican Rome," in Wiseman (1987). 207–18.

———. 1983/1987. "*Domi nobiles* and the Roman cultural élite," in Wiseman (1987). 297–305.

———. 1987. *Roman Studies: Literary and Historical*. Liverpool.

———. 1989. "Roman legend and oral tradition." *Journal of Roman Studies* 79, 129–37.

———. 1994. *Historiography and Imagination: Eight Essays on Roman Culture*. Exeter.

———. 1995. *Remus: A Roman Myth*. Cambridge.

———. 1998. *Roman Drama and Roman History*. Exeter.

———. 2000/2008. "Liber: Myth, drama and ideology in Republican Rome," in Wiseman (2008). 84–139.

———. 2004. *The Myths of Rome*. Exeter.

———. 2008. *Unwritten Rome*. Exeter.

Wissowa, G. 1912. *Religion und Kultus der Römer*[2]. Munich.

Wolf, D., and C. Lorber. 2011. "The 'Galatian Shield without Σ' series of Ptolemaic bronze coins." *Numismatic Chronicle* 171, 7–53.

Woolf, G. 1994. "Power and the spread of writing in the West," in Bowman and Woolf. 84–98.

———. 1998. *Becoming Roman: The Origins of Provincial Society in Gaul*. Cambridge.

———. 2009. "Literacy or literacies in Rome?," in Johnson and Parker. 46–68.

———. 2012a. "Reading and religion in Rome," in J. Rüpke and W. Spickerman (eds.), *Reflections on Religious Individuality: Greco-Roman and Judaeo-Christian Texts and Practices*. Berlin. 193–208.

———. 2012b. *Rome: An Empire's Story*. Oxford.

Young, J. M. 2002. "The stabilization of the Biblical Text in the light of Qumran and Masada: A challenge for conventional Qumran chronology?" *Dead Sea Discoveries* 9, 364–90.

———. 2007. "Textual stability in Gilgamesh and the Dead Sea Scrolls," in Azize and Weeks. 173–84.

Zaccaria Ruggiu, A. 2003. *More regio vivere: Il banchetto artistocratico e la casa romana di età arcaica*. Rome.

Zagagi, N. 2012. "What do Greek words do in Plautus?" in Glucker and Burnett. 19–36.

Zetzel, J. E. G. 1974. "Ennian experiments." *American Journal of Philology* 95, 137–40.

———. 1981. *Latin Textual Criticism in Antiquity*. Salem, NH.

———. 1983. "Catullus, Ennius, and the Poetics of Allusion." *Illinois Classical Studies* 8, 251–66.

Zorzetti, N. 1991. "Poetry and ancient city: The case of Rome." *Classical Journal* 86, 311–29.

Index